10/04

All the **News** That's **FIT TO SELL**

All the **News** That's **FIT TO SELL**

HOW THE MARKET TRANSFORMS INFORMATION INTO NEWS

James T. Hamilton

PRINCETON UNIVERSITY PRESS   PRINCETON, NEW JERSEY

ISBN: 0-691-11680-6
Library of Congress Cataloging-in-Publication Data
Hamilton, James, 1961–
All the news that's fit to sell: how the market transforms information into news / James
T. Hamilton.
p.   cm.
Includes bibliographical references and index.
ISBN 0-691-11680-6 (alk. paper)
1. Television broadcasting of news—United States.   2. Television broadcasting of news—
Economic aspects—United States.   3. Press—United States.   4. Press—Economic aspects—
United States.   I. Title.
PN4888.T4H355 2004
070.1′95—dc21   2003042894

British Library Cataloging-in-Publication Data is available
This book has been composed in Minion Typeface with American Typewriter display
Printed on acid-free paper.∞
www.pupress.princeton.edu

Printed in the United States of America

10   9   8   7   6   5   4   3   2   1

For Matthew

WHO ALWAYS BRINGS GOOD NEWS

Contents

Acknowledgments

Like the journalists I study, I have benefitted greatly from helpful sources, assistants, editors, and readers. Joe Kalt first sparked my interest in media economics and introduced me to the study of rational ignorance. I learned a great deal from conversations about the media with colleagues at Duke, including Sara Beale, Joel Fleishman, Bruce Jentleson, Fritz Mayer, Ellen Mickiewicz, David Paletz, and Chris Schroeder. As a visitor at the Kennedy School's Joan Shorenstein Center on the Press, Politics, and Public Policy I received many helpful suggestions from Alex Jones, Tom Patterson, and the students in my media economics class. I especially appreciate the time and insights of people who read drafts of the book: Larry Bartels, Matthew Baum, Phil Cook, Tyler Cowen, Jack Hamilton, and Markus Prior. Komal Bazaz and Chi Leng provided expert research assistance. The book also benefitted greatly from the efforts and insights of Lucinda Fickel, who worked as a research assistant for four years on the project. Tim Sullivan and Peter Dougherty at Princeton University Press provided very helpful advice on how to revise (and rename) the book. I owe a continuing debt to my parents, who weekly sent me clippings from press articles about the media. My wife Nancy gave me the freedom to claim all forms of media consumption, even channel surfing, as "research." This book is dedicated to my son Matthew, who taught me to see the media (and many other aspects of life) in a new light.

Introduction _____

"WHO KILLED HARD NEWS?" If *Dateline* or the *Daily News* were covering the demise of serious reporting about public affairs, this might be the headline. The question evokes many elements of a good story—an air of mystery, a tinge of violence, a hunt for a perpetrator. Reporters writing about problems with the news media like to focus on such human interest angles. Tales of greed, stupidity, and conspiracy make good copy. Yet as intriguing as profiles of media moguls and network anchors may be, they ultimately miss defining the main determinants of news. This book shows that the news is principally produced by market forces and shaped by the particular economics of information goods.

The idea that a special set of economic circumstances governs media markets is not universally accepted. As chairman of the Federal Communications Commission (FCC) in the 1980s, Mark Fowler declared that television was simply a "toaster with pictures" and held that the same market mechanisms that worked for appliances worked for television broadcasting. Rejecting concerns about the dearth of public affairs or educational programming, Fowler emphasized that media content flows from the types of preferences people express in the marketplace. As he put it, "The public's interest, then, defines the public interest."[1] When asked in 2001 about the digital divide, the gap in Internet access and use across demographic groups in the United States, FCC Chairman Michael Powell noted, "I think there's a Mercedes divide. I'd like one, but I can't afford it." In other words, markets are markets; the same principles that govern the sale of cars and toasters also work well in newspaper, television, and Internet markets. I disagree with this assessment. My goal in writing this book is to demonstrate how the specific economic characteristics of information goods affect both the supply and demand of news products.

A brief look at a daily newspaper reveals many of the incentives that affect news markets. My consumption of the newspaper does not prevent you from consuming the same account of events. Once a paper publishes, the knowledge generated by its reporters circulates widely, even to those who have not paid to read the paper. There are many ways the product could be assembled—just take a look at the same edition of any number of papers—with a focus on particular types of stories, formats, or political viewpoints. You cannot really know what is in an edition until you consume part of it, since events change daily.

This means a paper will try to establish a brand name for a particular style and approach to the news. The cost of putting together the first copy is high, since the efforts of numerous reporters and editors are required to produce the news. But additional copies are relatively low in cost, because they involve only the cost of paper and distribution; these distribution costs approach zero for editions posted on the Internet. The stories readers choose to look at in a day's edition will depend on what they personally find interesting, what information may help them in their jobs, or what products they are thinking about buying. While society as a whole might benefit if readers followed news of politics and government, stories about public affairs may often go unread or even unwritten. The small chance that an individual reader's political action can influence events makes it unlikely he or she will search out the information helpful in making a voting decision.

The logic of these incentives explains many outcomes in media and politics. People remain rationally ignorant about the details of public policy because they have such a low probability of influencing the course of events. Reporters and editors do not invest in learning about public affairs since the labor market provides little reward for these skills. News about government will be underprovided and underconsumed, even as these trends are noted and bemoaned. The high fixed costs of putting together the news (the cost of that first newspaper copy) limits the variety offered, which means consumers will be dissatisfied with media products since their exact, ideal combinations of style and substance will not necessarily be met. The chase for additional consumers means that content will often reflect the preferences of those least interested in hard news, rather than the interests of loyal readers and viewers more interested in public affairs. The need to establish consistent expectations about content pushes news outlets to cover stories in predictable ways and to use personalities as a way to build brand recognition. Competitors' ability to confirm and appropriate a story once an idea is circulated reduces the incentives for journalists to spend large amounts of time on original, investigative reporting. The difficulties of translating the public benefits from excellent news coverage into private incentives for owners or reporters can leave stories about government undone.

Hence, the death of hard news. But popular explanations for problems with the media focus on more human, and more entertaining, dilemmas. According to current accounts, the media are biased because of the left-wing or right-wing designs of journalists. Hard news loses out because of the dumbing down of reader and viewer interests. Broadcast journalists are more frequently celebrities than reporters and more likely to offer product spinoffs (such as their books or speeches) than true political insights. These stories of media bias, soft news, and celebrity culture often point to misplaced values as the culprit in media markets. The analysis offered in this book shows these phenomena are better explained as arising from economic choices rather than from human foibles or failings.

Consider first the case of media bias. In chapter 2, I show that nonpartisan reporting emerged as a commercial product in American newspaper markets in the 1870s. Before that time, many papers openly proclaimed association with a particular political party. Two economic changes, however, led to the rapid decline of the partisan press. The development of expensive high-speed presses made it possible for a newspaper to serve many more readers within a given city. To reach more readers, and therefore spread the high fixed costs across many consumers, newspapers stopped talking about politics in an explicitly partisan manner. Independent papers could draw readers from across the political spectrum. At the same time, advertising became an important way for companies with nationally and locally distributed brands to raise awareness of their products. Papers with larger audiences attracted more attention from advertisers, another incentive to increase readership. As a result, papers began to drop overt political bias and proclaim their independence in covering news of government and politics.

Though nonpartisan newspaper coverage emerged from technological change, elements of partisanship reemerged in television because of changes in channel competition. In the 1990s the three major network evening news programs faced increasing competition for viewers from cable programs. In chapter 3, I show that producers attempting to halt the slide in ratings focused in particular on the marginal viewers, those who sometimes tuned into the network evening news and sometimes chose other fare. The programs focused on retaining young female viewers, who carry a greater premium in the advertising market because they often make family purchasing decisions. Covering political issues of interest to younger females meant more coverage of gun control, and the problems of families with children. Since younger females were more likely to be Democrats, talking about political issues that interested them meant that on the margin the network news programs devoted more time and stories to liberal issues. But the motives of network producers were not ideological. The commercial pressure to retain the interest of younger viewers translated into coverage that focused on topics traditionally associated with the Democratic party.

The Fox News Channel offers a similar example of conscious product positioning. As the number of channels received in cable households grew, the expected audience size a new channel could garner declined. In the late 1960s, U.S. television households received an average of only seven channels. In that broadcast environment, each major network had the incentive to offer unbiased news coverage to attract audiences in the tens of millions. By 2000, households received an average of sixty-three channels. In that universe, a cable programmer would be happy to capture the attention of a million viewers. A conservative cable channel program might not attract ten million viewers, but it might draw two million viewers. This logic of niche programming gave rise to the Fox News Channel, which chapter 3 shows has the most conservative audience among major media outlets.

Laments that the rise of soft news reflects a general decline in tastes also miss the economic factors driving news content. Consumers today can choose from a wide spectrum of news products that vary in their emphasis of news about government and politics (hard news) or human interest and entertainment figures (soft news). A number of factors may lead editors and producers to favor soft news. In broadcast markets, viewers aged 18–34 command higher advertising rates. News outlets may cater to the preferences of these younger viewers, who are much less likely to express interest in traditional hard news stories. Hard news topics will lose out if they involve greater expense, such as the travel costs involved in international coverage. Media companies once covered public affairs in part because this brought prestige to the firms' owners and regulatory protection in the case of licensed broadcasters. Now that newspapers and television channels are part of large publicly traded firms, the focus on profits demanded by shareholders means less attention to public affairs reporting. Hard news may have positive spillovers for society in terms of increased scrutiny on government or corporate officials. But if media outlets cannot earn a return from this scrutiny, they will be less likely to exercise it and more likely to seek returns in serving advertisers or entertaining consumers. With chapters on local newspapers and television stations and on reviewing thirty years of network news programming, I show how these economic conditions have affected the amount of hard news provided across different cities and over time.

Some critics also decry journalists as celebrities. But they miss how fame can help consumers overcome a particular type of ignorance, namely, uncertainty about the content of a news product. Though the events of the world change daily, if reporters become part of the news product, a consumer can develop some expectation about the content of a given news program. The development of brand reputations is even more important as the number of news outlets expands, because reputations based on past consumption allow a paper or program to stand out among competitors. Chapter 8 shows that even as the average audience for a network evening news program has declined, the salaries for network anchors have increased. Anchors are increasingly valuable in the struggle to attract audiences for advertisers to sell to. Political pundits are another example of journalists who become part of the news product. Pundits strategically adopt their language to satisfy audience demands. For a set of journalists who appear in print and on television, I demonstrate that they are much more likely to focus on entertainment values and much less likely to use abstract terms or analyze group actions when they are on television. Predictable product positioning is also evident in the use of ideological language. Pundits with liberal reputations are more likely to use positive words and focus on group concepts, while conservative pundits use terms that stress individualism and language that conveys ambivalence or negative tones.

Many popular commentators view the Internet as a cure-all for media problems, since they believe it will allow voters to find the information needed to

judge politicians and policies. In chapter 7, I show instead that rational ignorance still holds sway on the Internet. While hard news terms appear on more
websites than soft news topics, this in part arises from the posting of information by government and nonprofit organizations, who are less concerned with
profit. Yet, in terms of the demand expressed for information, individuals are
much more likely to search on the Internet for soft news or information about
product purchases than for details about government policies. Advertisers are
willing to pay much more for association with search results about products or
entertainment topics than about public affairs information. A person interested in product information is a valuable target for advertisers. The attention
of a voter searching for information about global warming or tax policy is
worth less on the Internet, however, since his or her influence on these topics is
so small. I do find that the Internet expands the overall audience for high quality news. In hard copy sales, the top 5 among America's largest 100 newspapers
account for 21.5 percent of the total circulation. In terms of linking activity, the
top 5 websites of these newspapers garner 41.4 percent of the total traffic. The
Internet provides a way for consumers around the country (and internation-
ally) to gain access to papers such as the *New York Times* and *Washington Post.*

Journalists' memoirs often end on a downbeat note, with both print and
broadcast reporters expressing a yearning for the days when the news carried
more information about government and politics. Yet it is hard to quantify the
exact evils that may arise from lack of news coverage or consumption. If voters
can use short cuts such as party labels and endorsements to judge among candidates, then their rational ignorance about the details of policies represents a
net savings to society. Democracy involves delegating many decisions to elected
officials and frees voters from learning the intricacies of many issues. Time not
spent worrying about politics can be time spent in leisure, with family, or
among friends. If too many voters lack information on too many topics, however, politicians can enjoy too much freedom to pursue policies that con-
stituents would reject if they were the actual decision makers. The social sci-
ences currently do not provide good answers on how much news is enough to
make democracy's delegated decision making work well. In the analysis of media markets, economics lives up to its reputation as the "dismal science" in part
because it does a dismal job of assessing the impact of information on politics.

But economics does offer guidance on how to achieve specific goals in media
markets. If you are willing to assume a need to increase hard news provision
and consumption, then thinking about market incentives will increase the likelihood that policy recommendations will meet their targets. In chapter 9, I
demonstrate the difficulty of conducting a true benefit-cost analysis of government actions to "improve" news markets. The temptation for public officials to
turn media policies into incumbent protection acts also suggests caution in using government power to change outcomes in news coverage. I believe there
are at least four sets of policies that could be adopted to increase the circulation

of hard news. Efforts to make the actions of government more transparent could reduce the costs of reporters covering politics. Laws that strengthen the Freedom of Information Act and favor the distribution of government data on the Internet, for example, can stimulate hard news production by reducing the resources journalists need to devote to gathering information. Nonprofits can subsidize the creation of news through multiple avenues: direct ownership of news outlets, support for journalist training, creation of research on policy issues, or provision of additional resources to commercial companies to cover specific topics. The development of professional norms among journalists that encourage hard news reporting offers some scope to widen coverage. Defining digital and Internet property rights provides another avenue to increase the distribution of news about politics and government. By expanding the type of information that enters the public domain and encouraging Internet policies that favor the free flow of data, government decisions about infrastructure and copyright can increase the circulation of news.

The road map for this book follows the familiar path of theory, evidence, and policy prescriptions. Chapter 1 lays out the main economic ideas that explain media content, while chapter 9 details how policies to improve media markets might work. The chapters in between offer examples of how economics predicts the type of news offered in the marketplace. Chapter 2 offers a historical analysis of the rise of nonpartisan reporting as a commercial product. Chapters 3 and 4 take a snapshot of news products in 1999 and 2000 and analyze the impact of reader interests on media content. Chapter 5 looks across local newspapers and local television news programs to see how public affairs content truly does vary with the local public's interests in news. Chapter 6 explores how the mix of hard and soft news on the network evening news programs changed from 1969 to1998 with the advent of cable competition, deregulation, and changes in company ownership. Chapter 7 shows how rational ignorance and the high returns for entertaining or personally useful information strongly influence news on the Internet. Chapter 8 reveals how the person becomes part of the product for media goods, a point that explains the increasing returns for network anchors and the tendency of political pundits to shape their arguments depending on whether they are expressed in print or on television.

Adding another volume to the shelves of books about journalism requires a bit of hubris, a belief that there is something new to be said about the media. I hope this book demonstrates how economic factors influence news content and how economic incentives offer a way to improve media policies. Too often problems with reporting are couched in personal, entertaining stories about media titans or network anchors. I believe the more fundamental truth is that our problems lie not in our media stars but in ourselves. Those making efforts to improve media markets need to recognize that news emerges not from individuals seeking to improve the functioning of democracy but from readers seeking diversion, reporters forging careers, and owners searching for profits.

Chapter **1**

Economic Theories of News

NEWS IS A COMMODITY, not a mirror image of reality. To say that the news is a product shaped by forces of supply and demand is hardly surprising today. Discussions of journalists as celebrities or of the role of entertainment in news coverage all end up pointing to the market as a likely explanation for media outcomes. Debates about a marketplace of ideas reinforce the notion that exchange drives expression. Yet most people simply use the market as a metaphor for self-interest. This book explores the degree that market models can actually be used to predict the content of news and evaluate its impact on society. Focusing on media economics shows how consumers' desires drive news coverage and how this conflicts with ideals of what the news ought to be.

News stories traditionally answer five questions, the "five Ws": who, what, where, when, and why. On the other hand, economic models have their own essential building blocks: tastes, endowments, technologies, and institutions. The bits of information packaged together to form a news story ultimately depend on how these building blocks of economic models interact. What information becomes news depends on a different set of five Ws, those asked in the market:

1. Who cares about a particular piece of information?
2. What are they willing to pay to find it, or what are others willing to pay to reach them?
3. Where can media outlets or advertisers reach these people?
4. When is it profitable to provide the information?
5. Why is this profitable?

A journalist will not explicitly consider each of these economic questions in crafting a story. The stories, reporters, firms, and media that survive in the marketplace, however, will depend on the answers to these questions, which means media content can be modeled as if the "five economic Ws" are driving news decisions. If the five economic Ws dictate the content of the news, then we should be able to use our understanding of markets to analyze and even predict media content in the United States across time, media, and geography. The chapters that follow explore the power of market imperatives through three centuries of reporting, within different media such as newspapers, radio, broadcast and cable television, and the Internet, and across local and national media markets.[1]

The results range from the predictable to the counterintuitive to the speculative. News content is clearly a product. Its creation and distribution depends on the market value attached to the attention and tastes of different individuals, the technologies affecting the cost of information generation and transmission, and the values pursued by journalists and media owners. Though news is often defined as what is new and surprising, expectations of the familiar often drive consumption. While the expansion of news sources may open up alternative voices in the market, it can also create a tradeoff of breadth versus depth as the number of outlets increases. Economics does well in explaining the types of coverage that arise. Yet it faces limitations as a tool in evaluating the outcomes of media markets. Valuing the impact of news content involves valuing the outcomes of political decisions, decisions in which dollars are only one of the measures that help define social welfare. Despite these limitations in assessing the desirability of media and political outcomes, economics has a great deal to offer in explaining how the media operate. Chapter 1 develops the set of economic ideas and models that explain how the market generates news coverage and briefly discusses the policy levers available to influence media markets.

News as an Information Good

This book's title, *All the News That's Fit to Sell: How the Market Transforms Information into News*, raises questions about what is information and what is news. There are many ways to describe an event and many ways to convey these descriptions using words, images, and sound. I view information as any description that can be stored in a binary (i.e., 0,1) format.[2] Text, photographs, audio soundtracks, films, and data streams are all forms of information. I define news as the subset of information offered as news in the marketplace.[3] As a guide to what information products can be labeled as news, I use the market categories employed to devise Nielsen ratings, define advertising rates, and organize Internet sites. Much of my analysis will focus on news specifically relating to politics, government, and public affairs.

The news lends itself to economic analysis because it has the general characteristics of information goods, characteristics economists describe using terms such as public goods, experience goods, multiple product dimensions, and high fixed costs/low variable costs. Each of these features has implications for how information is transformed into a good through the marketplace.

Public goods are defined by a lack of both rivalry and exclusion in consumption. One person's consumption of a public good—for instance, an idea—does not diminish the ability of another to consume the good. A person can consume a public good without paying for it, since it may be difficult or impossible to exclude any person from consumption. In contrast, one person's consumption of a private good prevents another's consumption, and one cannot consume without paying for it. To see that news is more like a public good than a private good, consider the contrast between two products—an apple and a news story about apple contamination. If I consume an apple, it is not available for consumption by another. If I do not pay for the apple at a store, I cannot consume it. The apple is clearly a private good. A news story about contaminated apples is more like a public good. If I read the story about apples, my consumption does not prevent others from reading the same story. I may be able to read the story, view it on television, or hear about it from a friend without paying any money or directly contributing to its cost of creation. In this sense, news goods are public goods.

You can divine a great deal about some products by conducting a search before you consume, since you can observe their characteristics. Furniture and clothes are examples of these search goods because you can learn about a product's quality by observation and handling prior to a purchase.[4] To assess the quality of other goods such as food or vacation spots, you need to experience or consume them. A news story about a particular event is an experience good, since to judge its quality you need to consume it by reading or watching the story. The notion that news stories vary in quality underscores that news products have multiple dimensions. Stories can vary in length, accuracy, style of presentation, and focus. For a given day's events, widely divergent news products are offered to answer the questions who, what, where, when, and why. News stories are thus highly differentiated products that can vary along many dimensions.[5]

The structure of high fixed costs/low variable costs that characterizes the production of information goods readily applies to news stories. Imagine that you set out to produce a day's edition of a newspaper.[6] There are tremendous fixed costs, that is, costs that do not vary with the number of units produced once you decide to make the first unit. You need to pay for reporters to research topics, editors to make sense of the offerings, a production staff to lay out and compose the paper, and a business staff to solicit ads. The variable costs, which by definition will depend on the number of units produced, include the paper, ink, and distribution trucks used to deliver the finished products. The first copy costs—the cost of producing the first unit of a newspaper—are extremely high relative to the variable costs. Once you have made the first copy of the paper, however, the additional costs of making another are the relatively moderate costs of copying and distribution.

These basic features of information goods—public goods, experience goods, product dimension differentiation, and high fixed costs/low variable costs—go a long way toward explaining which types of information ultimately end up being offered by the market as news. The difficulties of excluding people who have not paid for information from consuming it may discourage the creation of some types of news. We often define news as that which is new. The uncertainty surrounding the content of a story prior to its consumption, however, leads news outlets to create expectations about the way they will organize and present information. Firms may stress the personalities of reporters since these can remain constant even as story topics change, so that readers and viewers can know what to expect from a media product even though they may not know the facts they are about to consume. The role that journalists play in attracting viewers to programs creates a set of economic "superstars" who earn high salaries for their ability to command viewer attention.[7] This use of celebrity to create brand positions in the news also relates to product differentiation. The many different aspects of an event, such as which of the 5Ws to stress or how to present a topic, allows companies to choose particular brands to offer. Yet the high fixed costs of creating an individual news product may limit the number of news versions actually offered in a market.

Four Types of Information Demands

At a newsstand, the *New York Times, People, Fortune,* and *Car and Driver* are all within arm's reach. These publications compete for shelf space in displays and attention in readers' minds. One way to make sense of the many different types of news offered in the market is to categorize demands for information by the types of decisions that give rise to the demands. Anthony Downs (1957) noted that people desire information for four functions: consumption, production, entertainment, and voting. An individual will search out and consume information depending on the marginal cost and benefits. The cost of acquiring information can include subscription to a newspaper, payment for cable television, or the time spent watching a television broadcast or surfing the Internet. Even information that appears free because its acquisition does not involve a monetary exchange will involve an opportunity cost; reading or viewing the information means one is forgoing the chance to pursue another activity. Since a person's attention is a scarce good, an individual must make a trade-off between making a given decision based on current knowledge or searching for more information.[8] The benefits of the information sought depend on the likelihood that a person's decision would be affected by the data and the value attached to the decision that is influenced. A person deciding how much information to consume will weigh the additional costs associated with gaining another unit of information with the additional benefits of making a better informed decision.[9]

To benefit fully from most types of information, a person needs to consume it. Consider how a person demands information for consumption, production, or entertainment. Information that aids consumption includes price, quality, and location data. Consumers searching for a good movie on Friday evening might buy a newspaper to get film reviews, viewing times, and theater locations. If they do not search out the information, they will not easily find a movie screening that matches their interests. People also search out data in their role as producers or workers. A computer network administrator might subscribe to *PC World* to get reviews for hardware purchases. If the administrator does not consume the data, the benefits from possibly making a better computer purchase for the office network are not realized. Entertainment information, information desired simply for itself and not as an aid in making another type of decision, is another clear example in which a person needs to consume the data to realize the benefits. A fan may follow the career of a celebrity for fifteen years or fifteen minutes. If the fan misses an interview of the favorite celebrity in the *People* edition or *Entertainment Tonight* episode the chance for enjoyment is missed, too. Because the people who benefit from the information express a demand for it, the markets for consumer, producer, and entertainment information work relatively well.[10]

A different calculus dominates the fourth type of information demand identified by Downs, information that helps a person participate as a citizen. A voter thinking about casting a ballot for Candidate A versus Candidate B might consider how information will aid this decision.[11] The costs of gathering information about the candidates include reading and viewing time and subscription costs. For a given voter there may be a large difference in value between the policies of Candidate *A* versus Candidate *B*. Additional information about the details of the candidates' policies may help a voter choose the correct candidate from the voter's perspective. The probability that a given voter will change the final election outcome, however, is extremely small. The net expected benefits to a voter of becoming more informed about political policies are defined as (Benefit of Candidate *A* versus Candidate *B*) × (Increase in probability that voter makes the correct decision) × (Probability vote is decisive in election) − (Costs of becoming informed). This value would be negative for nearly all individuals in an election, since their odds of influencing the outcome are infinitesimal. Downs established that voters do not demand information on policy details and choose to remain "rationally ignorant."[12]

The logic of free riding in politics predicts that an individual will not vote, since the likelihood of making a difference is so small. The theory of rational ignorance says that a person will not learn the details of policy since the returns for casting an informed ballot versus an uninformed ballot are negligible. These theories are born out in part by the levels of political participation in American politics. In 2000, only 51.2% of eligible voters cast ballots.[13] Survey evidence in 2000 confirmed a state of affairs evident since the origin of national opinion surveys—most Americans cannot answer questions about the details of government or the specifics of policy proposals. Although rational ignorance and free riding may describe the lack of demand for political information among the majority of Americans, there is a sizable minority that votes and stays informed. For the producers of news, this translates into a large absolute number of potential viewers and readers interested in public affairs coverage.[14]

Why would individuals demand information about politics in a world in which a person's vote is unlikely to have an impact? At least three explanations may hold true, each of which involves a demand for knowledge for its own sake. Some people feel a duty to vote and derive ideological satisfaction from participating in politics. For these individuals, learning about candidates and policies is part of performing the duties of democracy. The people participate and learn not because they believe they will make a difference, but because they believe this is the proper way to live in a democracy. A second explanation for learning about policy details is that for some individuals knowledge about politics is inherently interesting. Interest in statistics, strategies, and arcane details about basketball gave rise to ESPN's *SportsCenter*. The intricacies of design and execution fuel interest in the *Food Channel*. In a similar way, C-SPAN and *The NewsHour with Jim Lehrer* become destinations for those entranced by life inside the Washington Beltway. A third demand for political coverage lies in the human elements of drama embedded in political races. The human interest stories involved in elections will attract a segment of viewers in search of entertaining stories. But satisfying this demand will lead news outlets to substitute horse race coverage of who is ahead and who is behind for policy discussions, and will shift the focus to candidates' personal lives rather than their policy pronouncements.

If a voter approaches learning about politics as an investment decision, the result will be rational ignorance.[15] Why spend the time divining the proper policies for world trade, global warming, or missile defense systems, since your likelihood of affecting these policies is minuscule?[16] The low demand for public affairs information as voter information translates into fewer incentives for outlets to offer the coverage and sparse rewards for journalists interested in providing this type of news. Rational ignorance among consumers generates rational omissions among reporters. The result may be less than optimal amounts and types of public affairs coverage.

Duty, diversion, and drama will generate some expressed demand for news about government and politics. The viewers who believe in the duty to become informed, the readers who follow policies with the interest of sports fans, and the consumers who like the drama of elections and the foibles of potential candidates all express interest in some form of political coverage. By consuming this information these consumers may become more informed voters. The improved precision of their decisions may benefit others, too, who have not taken the time to follow news about politics. Since readers and viewers who learn about government do not calculate the full benefits to society the demand for news content about public affairs gives rise to what economists term positive externalities. The broader benefits to society are really external to the consumers' decisions about how much time and energy to devote to reading and viewing news. A consumer may watch political talk shows to learn who is ahead in the polls or who has fallen into scandal. As a by-product, the viewer learns about the details of policies and makes a more informed voting decision. The aggregation of this effect across readers and viewers means that more informed decisions are made in elections. The ultimate impact of information will depend on how the markets for political information work, a topic discussed later in the chapter. The point here is that since individuals do not calculate the full benefit to society of their learning about politics, they will express less than optimal levels of interest in public affairs coverage and generate less than desirable demands for news about government.

A Spatial Model of News Product Locations

Each day editors and producers assembling news products choose stories that answer the five Ws of reporting. Reporters covering the same event for separate news outlets will answer these five questions differently. Versions of the news will vary because assessments of what transpires, judgments about the relative importance of actions, or decisions about the likelihoods of causes and effects may differ. Consumer interests also vary widely. Some readers want the latest from Hollywood, others follow events in Washington, and some want to know what happens in their hometown. If news products were readily transparent and fully understood before consumption, then readers or viewers could consume only the mix of stories they were interested in. If developing and transmitting a story were costless, the market would offer as many versions of a story as there are demands among consumers. Yet the nature of news stories means they need to be consumed to be fully understood, and the costs of assembling these stories mean that only so many versions will be told. The varieties of interests, uncertainties about product content, and costs of constructing descriptions of events all combine in the marketplace to generate "brands" in news. Brands economize on uncertainty and search costs by presenting consumers with a readily understood approach to the news. In this sense, brands allow the familiar to guide consumer choices about what is new(s).[17]

Economists model the decisions about what product brands will be offered in a market similarly to decisions producers make about what physical spaces to locate their offerings. Models of product variety are thus often called "spatial models" of product location. An early forerunner of these location models is the theory developed by Harold Hotelling (1929), whose model of firm location answered the following question: If two ice cream vendors could choose to locate on a beach filled with hungry consumers, where would each locate? Customers prefer not to walk on the sand in the sun, so they patronize the nearest vendor. Knowing this, each vendor chooses to locate at the exact middle of the beach, so each gets half the market. This result laid the groundwork for the application of spatial models to politics, where Anthony Downs (1957) showed that two parties in search of votes would similarly converge on the middle of the road in their selection of policy positions. Predicting the locations of products in these models is much more difficult if the number of products is greater than two, if the products are defined along more than one dimension (e.g., if the ice creams can vary in quality in addition to vendor location), or if the number of consumers with tastes for different locations varies greatly depending on the type of good offered.[18]

The assumptions and operations of a spatial location model fit the branding of news in the marketplace well. News directors making decisions about what stories will fill the twenty-two minutes of content on a half-hour broadcast, or editors running story conferences about front-page layouts, all seek to carve out a niche through their content selections. Their decisions about what information to offer as news will depend on audience interests, costs of assembling stories, readers'/viewers' expectations about their treatment of the news, and the likely actions of their competitors. Traditional definitions of what is newsworthy rely on the formula of who, what, where, when, and why. I believe that the news goods offered in the market are actually shaped by another set of five Ws. The information that is produced will depend on how editors and producers answer these five questions: Who cares about a particular piece of information? What are they willing to pay to find it, or what are others willing to pay to reach them? Where can media outlets or advertisers reach these people? When is it profitable to provide the information? Why is this profitable? A spatial model of location captures well how these influences determine the types of news offered in a marketplace. In a previous work called *Channeling Violence: The Economic Market for Violent Television Programming* (1998), I developed a simple spatial model of the profit-maximizing decisions made by entertainment programming strategists to offer shows with varying levels of violent content. Because decisions about news content are similarly driven by profit calculations, a comparable model described below helps explain the level of public affairs content in news products. Though the model applies to print, broadcast, and Internet outlets, I will for simplicity develop the description of news goods offered by television programmers.[19]

Viewers vary in the degree that they want to know about the details of politics and government. Some news programs focus mainly on entertainment, health, or life-style information and carry very little public affairs information. These programs, which include *Entertainment Tonight* and *Inside Edition*, are often labeled as "soft news."[20] At the other end of the spectrum, programs such as *The NewsHour with Jim Lehrer* are called "hard news" because of their focus on the details of government and politics. In between there are programs that offer a mix of soft and hard news topics.

Assume that there are three types of television news viewers: those who prefer soft news programs, those who like a mix of hard and soft news topics, and those who want programs with high levels of public affairs content. The returns for capturing these viewers will depend on how much advertisers are willing to pay, which is based on the demographics of those watching. A programmer deciding on the level of public affairs coverage to offer in a news program will consider the number of viewers attracted to that type of information, the value advertisers place on these viewers, and the number of channels contending for viewers' attention. Profits for a given news program will also depend on the costs of assembling the information and producing the stories, which may vary by type of news product. There are a finite number of channels contending for viewer attention, a limit derived from the combination of technology and regulation involving spectrum signals and cable channel capacity. A news producer will decide on whether to offer a program with low, medium, or high levels of public affairs content depending on the profits offered in each of these "genres." Channels will eventually be distributed across the news programming spectrum so that the profits of a firm are equal across the three types of programming. If profits are not equal, then a channel has an incentive to switch programming into the news genre with the higher profits. This simplified model yields the following predictions about news programming.[21] In describing these hypotheses I will use the term "soft news" to refer to programs with low levels of public affairs information and "hard news" to refer to shows with high levels of public affairs information.[22]

Soft news programs will be more prevalent if advertisers value those viewers more highly. In the terms of the model, the number of programs with low public affairs content will increase as the value of soft news consumers rises. An increase in advertising rates makes the soft news programming market more profitable, which draws programmers to this genre until profits are equalized across the three types of programming (low, medium, and high levels of public affairs news). If viewer satisfaction is related to the number of channels offering particular types of programming, this implies that consumers of soft news programming should be more satisfied with television news since they will have more viewing options as the number of channels offering this type of information product increases.

If programmers pay less for soft news, then they will be more likely to program this type of information. In equilibrium, the profits of firms in each of the three markets of low, medium, and high public affairs content will be equal. Consider what happens, however, if soft news programming becomes less costly. Profits in this genre increase. More firms will leave the high and moderate public affairs programming options and start to offer soft news programming, until profits are once again equalized. Relative to a world where all programs cost the same, if low public affairs content is cheaper, then it will be more likely to be offered by channels. Thus as the cost of soft news programming decreases, the number of soft news programs increases and the number of shows with moderate or high levels of public affairs coverage decreases. Similarly, if hard news programming were to decrease in cost, then the number of channels offering this genre would increase and soft news offerings would decline. Costs here refer to the fee that channels pay for the program, which may be the cost of producing the program if it is produced internally or the price paid to outside production companies if the show is produced by another company.

As the number of channels increases, the number of soft news programs will increase. Technology often sets constraints on the number of channels contending for viewers in a given area. The Federal Communications Commission's (FCC) allocation of the broadcast spectrum limits the number of over-the-air signals broadcast in a market. The physical capacity of cable technology limits the number of cable networks offered in a given franchise area. Over time these constraints have relaxed, so that viewers can choose from an increasing number of channels. Reception of television programming through satellite dishes has also expanded the number of channels. The model demonstrates that as channels are added, the number of soft news programs will increase. New entrants distribute themselves across programming genres so that equilibrium profits remain equal across the low, medium, and high public affairs content market niches. As the number of programs offered increases, the number of competitors in each of these market niches will increase. Markets across the United States currently differ in the number of channels offered within a viewing area. The model predicts that the number of soft news programs offered should be higher in areas with a higher number of stations or channels overall.

The number of soft news shows grows as the number of viewers attracted to this genre increases. Broadcasters sell audiences to advertisers. As the number of viewers attracted to programs with low public affairs content increases, profits from offering this type of programming will attract more channels into this market. The demographic audience for television changes by the hour each day. As the number of viewers of soft news programming increases, holding other factors constant, programmers will find it more profitable to offer shows with low public affairs content to attract these viewers. Thus one would predict that soft news offerings will vary in part as the television audience changes during the day. Cities also vary in their demographic makeup, so that cities with higher numbers of consumers of soft news should have more programs aimed at these viewers.

The average rating for soft news programs goes down as the number of soft news programs increases. By assumption the number of viewers attracted to programming with low public affairs content is fixed. Consider what happens as the number of overall channels expands or the value that advertisers place on consumers of soft news programming increases. The model predicts in both cases that the number of competitors offering soft news programs will increase. This means that the number of viewers of a soft news program will decline. This is a reminder that if programming in a particular niche becomes more attractive to broadcasters—for example, because of an increase in advertising rates—this does not mean that the rating for a show in that niche will increase.[23]

If broadcasters were led to internalize the benefits to society of hard news programming, more programs with high public affairs content would be offered. If news about politics and government contributes to better voting decisions by readers and viewers, these effects are not generally reflected in the decisions of broadcasters since they are not led to consider the full benefits to society of their shows. If broadcasters did consider these benefits, their decision-making calculus would change. Assume that channels offering high public affairs content programming did consider the positive externalities generated by their shows.[24] As the benefits of the externalities generated by a program increase, programs with high public affairs content become more profitable. This causes programmers to shift into this program niche and away from the provision of shows with low or moderate levels of public affairs information. Hence, as the beneficial externalities generated by hard news programs increase, more of these programs would be offered if channels were led to consider the total benefits to society of these shows.

An additional implication of the model rests on how one interprets programming costs. The costs of assembling and producing a story are a function of technology and the level of story quality chosen. Variations in quality within a genre of programming are not represented in this model, since all outlets providing a given type of news are assumed to have the same cost structure. Yet the model does imply that there may be a trade-off between breadth and depth in the news marketplace. A drop in cost within one genre of coverage will stimulate entry into that area as competitors seek the (temporary) lure of greater profits. If hard news costs were to decrease, for example, the model indicates that the number of outlets offering news with high public affairs content will increase. Costs might decline because of a new technology that made news production or transmission cheaper. Costs might also decline if there were changes in professional norms about story quality, corporate ownership preferences about journalism standards, or regulatory expectations about news content. This would reflect a change in the definition of what constitutes quality news within a given programming genre, for example, what constitutes quality hard news programming. In this sense lower costs would translate into less depth in providing the details of public affairs coverage. For viewers of programs with high public affairs content, the trade-off implied means that changes in costs will yield more outlets offering hard news and fewer details offered within a hard news story. Overall, the limited resources provided by advertising or subscription revenues create here a tradeoff between the number of outlets in a genre and the depth of coverage offered.

Economics is often defined as the study of individual decision making under conditions of scarcity. The spatial model of news outlet location presented here shows how the individual decisions that generate news content can be explained by the basic building blocks of an economic model: tastes, endowments, technology, and institutions. These factors interact in the spatial model so that the news coverage that emerges can be predicted as if news outlet managers were answering the 5Ws of the information marketplace. The tastes and endowments of readers and viewers enter the model through two questions: 1) Who cares about a particular piece of information? and 2) What are they willing to pay to find it, or what are others willing to pay to reach them? These questions stress that preferences of readers and viewers will matter in the marketplace depending on what demographic group holds them. For example, since individuals vary in terms of their endowments of wealth, advertisers will care more about reaching certain demographic groups depending on the products they hope to sell to these individuals. News products sold through subscription will also vary content depending on the willingness of individuals to pay for certain types of coverage. Technology enters the picture in the third and fourth questions: 3) Where can media outlets or advertisers reach people? and 4) When is it profitable to provide the information. Technology of production and distribution of information affects how audiences can be assembled to be sold to advertisers, how easily information can be gathered, and how many outlets can ultimately survive in the marketplace given the interests of consumers and the revenues derived from subscriptions or advertising. The influence of institutions can be found in the fifth W: 5) Why it is profitable to provide a given amount or type of news good? Institutions such as copyright laws, privacy statutes, and the First Amendment form the set of property rights that define how news goods are marketed.

Shared Preferences

If information products were costless to produce, each person would be able to choose a unique version of the day's events corresponding to tastes for style and content. If news producers offered content based on a motive other than profit, such as a desire to inform readers or viewers about decisions likely to affect their civic lives, then interests would not drive content. The fixed costs of assembling a story limit the number of versions that will be offered in the marketplace, since there may not be enough individuals interested in a story to cover its initial costs of assembly and distribution.[25] The profit motive also dictates that the type of news stories delivered will depend in part on consumer tastes. This means that whether a story is covered or the way that it is described will depend ultimately on shared preferences, the degree that people express a taste for a particular type of news. The spatial model reflects this by dividing consumers into three separate groups depending on their preferences for low, medium, or high levels of public affairs content. Shared preferences are also important in explaining at least three effects in information markets: externalities generated by consumption of news coverage; the bundling of different types of information within the same news product; and the epidemic-like spread of interests, called "information cascades," among readers or viewers.

Whether a particular type of news is offered in a marketplace will depend on the number of people who share an interest in the topic and their value, as measured by their willingness to pay for the information good or the willingness of advertisers to spend dollars to reach these consumers. In stark terms, this means that the degree that my desire to learn about a news topic will be fulfilled depends on who else cares about the topic. Newsworthiness will be a function of numbers of consumers and their value in the marketplace. If hard news information is desired by an educated group of consumers, a local news print or broadcast outlet may provide it if the number of these consumers is sufficiently large and the advertising or subscription fees are lucrative enough. Once the public affairs information is produced, it is a public good available to all. In this sense the presence of a core group of consumers large enough to generate coverage can be thought of as generating a positive externality, since other consumers may benefit from the coverage even if they were not the targets of advertisers and did not pay for the creation of the information. Hard news generates an additional positive externality, since its consumption may lead to more informed voting decisions that yield better public policies for a community. How many educated consumers it takes to generate hard news coverage in a local print or broadcast market is an open question. The Internet offers a way to aggregate like-minded consumers across a broader area, so news versions might be more likely to be offered through this aggregation. The survival of Internet news sites will still depend, however, on the ability to gain revenues through advertising or subscription fees.

Shared preferences also affect the combination or bundling of information in news goods. The nature of broadcast television means that stories proceed one at a time, with the same number and type of stories provided to each consumer of a broadcast. This means that story editors will choose news topics by considering the effects on the likelihood that target consumers will stay with the news program and not switch channels. This is a general aspect of television markets, where programmers must consider the ability to retain consumers to sell to advertisers rather than the intensity of preferences for viewers for particular types of programs. Newspapers do not face the same constraint, since the physical layout of the news allows readers to skip entire stories or sections while heading for their favorite types of news.

In an Internet world, where stories could be consumed and priced individually, there are still incentives to bundle stories together as a single good rather than to price them individually. Shapiro and Varian (1999) stress how bundling goods together can narrow the dispersion of prices consumers are willing to pay for a good, which can lead to higher revenues for producers since prices are often set in relation to the lower willingness to pay for goods in an information market. Though they make this point in reference to the bundling of software components, the same argument can be modified (as it is below in table 1.1) to apply to news products.[26] Consider two consumers, Matthew and Jamie, who vary in their willingness to pay for two types of information, domestic news and foreign news. If the day's domestic news and foreign news were each sold separately for $1.20, then Matthew would buy the domestic news and Jamie would buy the foreign news and the online service would earn $2.40. If each product were priced at $1.00, Matthew and Jamie would buy both products and the news provider would earn $4.00. If the domestic and foreign news were combined into a single product and priced at $2.20, however, Matthew and Jamie would each buy the bundle and the news outlet would earn $4.40. Shapiro and Varian point out that bundling allows producers to charge higher prices in some cases, since the willingness to pay for the combination of goods is less dispersed than the willingness to pay for the individual goods. They note that this explains outcomes in media markets, such as the combination of articles in a magazine and the combination of issues of a periodical into a unit offered as a subscription.

The nature of news as an experience good also gives rise to shared preferences. Because it is at times difficult to assess the quality of an information product without consuming it, readers or viewers will use the consumption of others as information about the desirability of a given good. This phenomenon can give rise to information cascades, in which the actions of a small initial group of consumers can multiply or cascade through a market as later consumers base their decisions on the actions of earlier readers or viewers.[27] When a story initially is offered in the marketplace, readers or viewers may decide to consume or ignore it. Their reactions can be visible to others, since individuals often learn through conversation what programs, publications, or stories others are following. To the extent that consumers base their decisions in part on

TABLE 1.1
Incentives for Bundling News Goods

	Willingness to Pay For	
	Domestic News	Foreign News
Matthew	$1.20	$1.00
Jamie	$1.00	$1.20

evidence of prior consumption by others, demand for particular news products may multiply in a cascading fashion. The social desirability of these cascades is an open empirical question. If the early readers or viewers choose wisely, then later consumers can save on search costs by taking into account the fact that others have followed a given news program or account. If the early choosers go down the wrong path, such as choosing a given version of a story that neglects facts available at the time, then others may follow suit and express a demand for a particular story or news version. These effects are variously referred to as cascades, epidemics, buzz, or bandwagons, and will be explored below in the section on the marketplace of ideas. The key point here is that the nature of news as an experience good can lead individuals to use the consumption of others as a factor in deciding what types of news to demand.[28]

Number of Competitors

"More news is better news" appears to be an axiom favored in discussions about the news marketplace. A corollary is that more competitors will yield better outcomes, as is often the case in the market for other goods. Yet the impact of the number of competitors on the quantity and quality of reporting is actually a question left open by economic theory. Models that explore how the number of competitors can change the content of news focus on the trade-off of breadth versus depth, the herding instincts in coverage among journalists, the impact of ownership on program duplication, and the race to the bottom in quality selections. The likely impact of each of these effects on a given media market is an empirical question.

The spatial model of news location reveals how an increase in the number of competitors can set up a trade-off between depth and breadth in coverage. Consider the increase in the number of competitors allowed in a marketplace that arises if the FCC were to expand the number of spectrum allocations in an area. This increase in N could lead to an increase in the outlets offering news in each of the news categories of low, moderate, and high public affairs content. Consumers might be more likely to find a program closer to their ideal show, since there will be more programs in each of the genres of news programming. Suppose, however, that the costs of news programming with moderate amounts of public affairs programming were to drop. This might occur if firms were able to buy news from a wire or video service rather than make their own stories, or if the firms simply reduced the hard news portion of their mix of stories because they no longer felt regulatory pressure or professional scrutiny of their "public service" function. In this case more outlets would be attracted by the temporary profits in moderate news programming, which would increase the total number of options offered to viewers in this genre. The drop in cost here can be viewed as a decrease in product quality, as it could result in less information being offered in the news product. Yet this decrease in depth is accompanied by an increase in breadth, if one sees more viewing options in a given category as representing more choices for some consumers. This shows that under some circumstances, the market for news locations can yield more breadth of outlets at the same time that quality of coverage or depth is declining.

A race to the bottom in news coverage is another way to model how competitor numbers can influence news content. Suppose that there were only a small number of viewing options in a broadcast market, a situation enjoyed by the three major networks in the early decades of television. With a small number of firms, collusion about product quality or composition can be easily facilitated. One could view news directors from the broadcast networks in the 1960s as fairly confident that their competitors would provide nightly news programming with high public affairs content. The FCC at the time required local broadcast stations to report on their public affairs coverage, so regulatory pressures reinforced the focus on hard news. The networks were owned by, or identified with, individuals willing to trade-off some profits for the psychic rewards of being identified as good corporate citizens. The industry trade association, the National Association of Broadcasters, helped facilitate quality restrictions through broadcaster codes. As cable technology and changes in spectrum allocation generated more competitors in the television marketplace, however, it became harder to maintain informal restrictions on the type of information products offered. Collusion about quality, even if it has positive externalities for society, is harder to maintain as the number of potential stations that might defect and offer a more popular programming genre increases. This yields a version of a race to the bottom. As the number of competitors increases, it becomes more likely a station will offer soft news as a programming alternative. This will lead eventually to a model where competitors compete to locate in all three programming genres rather than only two. The diversity of viewing options has increased, which can translate into greater consumer happiness. The decline in the number of outlets offering hard news programming, however, can lead some to prefer the outcomes where competition was less likely to yield soft news programming since this type of programming carries fewer civic benefits (i.e., positive externalities).

These examples from the spatial model show how an increase in the number of competitors may increase diversity but may decrease quality, as measured by depth of coverage or type of news programming offered. Models also exist that show how an increase in the number of competitors can actually decrease diversity, as measured by the number of unique perspectives or story selections offered in a marketplace. If an increase in competitors increases the number of journalists covering a given story, this can ultimately lead to a herding phenomenon that reduces the number of original takes on a story. As the number of journalists covering a story grows, an individual reporter may be more likely to simply go with the angle and events developed by previous reporters. The individual journalist faces the decision of whether to incur the costs of creating a story from scratch or taking the path pursued by other reporters. In this situation an increase in the number of journalists who have covered a story in a particular way increases the signal to a subsequent reporter that this is the best way to pursue a story. In addition, journalists may face greater penalties within their news organizations for going against a perceived wisdom in coverage the greater the consensus is among journalists covering a story. This herding reduces the likelihood that each journalist will investigate and write a unique story. In one sense this is efficient, since fewer resources overall are devoted to the fixed costs of building the details of a story. Herding can also lead to errors of fact and interpretation, however. If the early reporters investigating a story get it wrong, herding by later reporters can magnify the problem.[29]

Competition can also decrease diversity in situations where separate ownership of outlets leads to the duplication of news offerings. This result was first developed in a model of television programming developed by Steiner (1952), who contrasted programming outcomes when channels were owned by a monopoly versus separate competitors. To see how a monopoly might lead to more diverse news products, consider a market with the following characteristics.[30] There are three types of news programming (soft news, mixed news, and hard news) and three television channels. Consumers only view their most preferred type of programming; if it is not offered, they do not view news programming. Assume there are 5,000 viewers who prefer a moderate amount of public affairs coverage, 2,500 who prefer soft news, and 1,250 who prefer hard news. If the three channels are controlled by a single entity, then this monopolist will choose to broadcast each type of news. This strategy will garner 8,750 viewers that the monopolist can sell to advertisers, since each type of viewer will prefer watching their favorite type of news over nonviewing. Consider what happens, however, if each channel is owned independently so that there are three competitors in the marketplace. In this situation two channels would show programs with moderate amounts of public affairs programming and split the market for these viewers, so that each channel got 2,500 viewers. The third channel would offer soft news programming and gain 2,500 viewers. Overall, 7,500 consumers would choose to view television and 1,250 would not view news programming. With each of the outlets owned separately, no channel has an incentive to provide hard news programming. The monopolist cares about total audiences for the three channels and thus ends up offering programming that may only appeal to a small segment of the audience. Each outlet in the competitive market cares not about the total audience viewing but about the number of viewers attracted to its show. This logic leads to program duplication, since it is more profitable for two channels to show the same genre of moderate public affairs and split the audience for this type of information than for one of the channels to offer moderate and another offer hard news. Under these assumptions, increased competition leads to decreased diversity in news offerings.[31]

Ownership

Owners vary in the degree that they seek profits, public goods, or partisan ends. The spatial model assumes that profit-maximizing news media outlets value audiences based on consumers' willingness to pay for information or marketability to advertisers. Since many print, broadcast, and online news organizations are owned by publicly traded stock companies, taking profit maximization as the prime motive for news firm managers has credence. The spatial model makes clear that the pursuit of profits does not mean that all outlets will choose soft news or that none will offer hard news. The variations in consumer tastes and differences in production costs will generate an array of news offerings. Some companies or programs will develop brand positions that signal a low amount of public affairs coverage while others will develop a reputation for high public affairs content. In both cases the pursuit of profit drives the brand location and decision about a day's news content and style.

When ownership control resides in a family or individual, additional motives may come into play with the operation of a news outlet. The theory of rational ignorance clearly demonstrates that there is a divergence between what people want to know and what they should know. If a newspaper or television station covered topics only with an eye toward revenues and ratings, then information important to civic decisions might not reach readers and viewers. When ownership is concentrated in an individual or family, then these people may take pleasure in sacrificing some profits for the sake of the public good (as they perceive it). These owners may identify with the communities their outlets are published in and try to encourage civic participation through information provision. This is one of the ideas behind public policies that encourage local control of media outlets. The owners may also enjoy the recognition that goes with public service actions. Here the provision of news about public affairs may earn an owner a reputation for altruism. The very fact that ownership of media outlets provides the chance for public recognition means that these companies, like sports franchises, may be more likely than other firms to have control concentrated in families or individual investors.[32] Ownership by publicly traded stock companies, however, is increasingly the dominant form of control in media industries.[33]

While it may not always be profitable to supply public affairs information, the impact of news about government and politics creates a third motive for news outlet owners—a desire to influence the outcome of elections. This is most evident in the early evolution of the popular press in the United States. In the eighteenth and nineteenth centuries, political parties provided newspapers in the United States with direct and indirect support. Some outlets were published by the parties. Other newspapers were supported through the awarding of public printing contracts. Parties also provided sympathetic papers with payments in election years. Newspapers were clearly identified with particular parties in the same way that news outlets today have brand reputations for their mix of hard and soft news. In the late nineteenth century the rise of advertising, innovations in printing technology that increased the importance of scale economies, and demographic changes in the size of the reading public made it more profitable for newspapers to adopt "objective" or nonpartisan approaches to public affairs. Chapter 2 explores how objectivity evolved in the market as a commercial product, as publishers frequently found it more profitable to remove partisan coverage in order to attract more readers.

Charges that press outlets are biased toward a particular party continue to this day.[34] Ownership theory offers three explanations that would be consistent with charges of partisan bias. The spatial model indicates that news outlets will choose brand locations in part with an eye toward audience tastes and the location of competitors. To the extent that it is profitable to cover public affairs from a Democratic or Republican perspective, news outlets may stake out niches with these brand identifications. This may be particularly true in arenas where there are multiple news outlets contending for attention, such as cable news channels or Internet websites. A second explanation would be that in firms controlled by a family or individual, the owners are willing to trade off profits for political ideology. In these situations a family might pursue a partisan agenda in the press even if this came at the expense of some advertising or subscription revenues. The final explanation for partisan bias lies in the difficulties of owner control in large companies. Publicly traded stock companies are often large entities that involve the delegation of decision-making authority among hundreds if not thousands of workers. Even if a firm's board of directors is out to maximize profits and its managers adopt this goal, the difficulties of monitoring employee performance because of hidden information or action means that journalists may have some freedom to inject bias. The degree to which partisan ends are still consciously pursued in media industries is pursued further in chapters 3 and 6.

As ownership of news outlets passes to companies in multiple business lines, a separate set of ownership influences may affect media content. If high public affairs content is chosen as a profit-maximizing brand location, then transfer of ultimate ownership to a nonmedia company may not affect the mix of news stories offered. If hard news is offered by a firm because of ideological or personal satisfaction by workers or owners, however, the transfer of a news outlet to a nonmedia company could bring a change in news coverage. Self-coverage, self-promotion, and self-dealing are three additional worries associated with ownership of media properties by conglomerates. News workers may be reluctant to provide unfavorable news coverage of the parent company. Allegations of this nature have been made about ABC's treatment of stories about Disney World and NBC's handling of information about the nuclear power industry, a sector important to its parent company General Electric. Companies that provide entertainment programming as well as news may be tempted toward self-promotion. As soft news becomes prevalent in many news venues, companies may prefer to promote their own entertainment products during news program coverage of television, music, and movies. Self-dealing may also arise from the increasing trend toward vertical integration in information industries. When a company controls both information conduits and content providers, there are circumstances under which the firm may favor internally produced news programming over news content offered by a third party. The conflict between Time Warner—which owned cable systems and CNN—and Fox over the inclusion of the Fox News Channel in New York City cable packages highlights the potential for these problems.

Technology

If costs can drive content in media markets, the prime determinant of costs is the technology of information production and distribution. The creation of a news story involves large first copy costs and often negligible additional costs for more copies of the story. Producing a story entails the costs involved in assembling the facts of an event, paying for the expertise of a reporter with valuable experience and contacts, and hiring editors who can help make sense of what information belongs in the news product. Once the version of the story is produced to be sold to the first viewer or consumer, the marginal cost of producing another copy is relatively small in newspaper markets and near zero in television, radio, and Internet markets. When news outlets are deciding whether to make their own versions of a story or buy a version in the market, the large fixed costs involved in creating a story mean that news organizations will often simply buy information on the market rather than make their own version. This pattern has held from the time of printed inserts in nineteenth-century papers, to the use of wire service stories by local newspapers and use of news service footage in local television broadcasts, to the use of wire service stories on Internet sites today. Local outlets can carry national and international stories without developing their own expertise in this coverage.[35] Since news service stories will end up being offered in local markets across the country, the news services design the content to fit across markets. The technologies, such as the telegraph or Internet, that make buying stories easier can also lead to more homogeneous coverage. News services may be less likely to inject partisan coverage, for example, since their products are designed to sell in markets where partisan allegiances may vary greatly.

The large fixed costs of assembling a story mean that within a given news organization managers will face incentives to repeat stories rather than create new ones. A broadcast television station will recycle stories across dinner hour and late night news broadcasts.[36] A media company will face incentives to own outlets in print, broadcast, and Internet markets, since the creation of stories to be sold in one medium generates information that can be resold through other distribution channels. The development of knowledge among reporters also influences content and style decisions. A print journalist who writes about a given area may be able to resell the information by appearing on television talk shows. The journalist's parent publication may even pay the reporter to make broadcast appearances, since this promotes the brand name of the publication. Print and broadcast news outlets may seek out alliances so that reporters in one media can convey their information in another media. Print reporters may appear regularly on a broadcast partner network, which lowers the costs to the network of developing expertise. The fixed cost of learning also tips the balance in story selection toward continuing coverage of a given event rather than undertaking new investigations. This prolongs the life of stories, since journalists may find it cheaper to write a "reaction" story that follows up on a topic they understand from prior reporting.

The technology of information distribution also influences content through the structure of costs. Economies of scale in newspaper distribution help explain why most cities have only one local daily newspaper. To realize the cost savings associated with scale, newspapers can face incentives to use content to add particular groups of readers. In the late nineteenth century, papers adopted "objective" coverage of politics since this allowed them to attract both Democratic and Republican readers to sell to advertisers. The savings associated with attracting additional readers to spread costs meant that there were strong incentives to leave out partisan material that would alienate a particular set of readers. The logic of information bundling also explains why papers may add some story topics to gain marginal groups of readers.

The costs involved in setting up a cable transmission system in a city point toward a single provider, since from a technical standpoint duplicating two cable systems in an area would be wasteful. The awarding of a local monopoly in cable transmission, however, can create separate setup problems with the pricing of cable content. The integration of ownership of the cable conduit with ownership of cable content, for example, cable channels, also can affect news content. If cable subscription prices are set "too high," then marginal cable viewers may choose not to pay for cable packages or channels that carry news that they would purchase in the absence of cable market power. If vertical integration leads a cable operator to favor channels in which it owns an interest, this means that some news channels may not be offered because the cable system favors its own productions.

At first glance the Internet might seem to offer relief from distribution cost worries. Once a news site is up and running with stories the marginal cost of another web surfer logging onto the site is effectively zero. The spatial model emphasizes that costs in a particular news segment limit the number of providers that can earn profits there. If the Internet drops these fixed costs, then one would think that many more news outlets can survive in a genre such as hard news provision. The limits on human attention and information processing, however, mean that in a world of many Internet sites there will still be advantages to size. Sites may have to engage in significant advertising, often in print or broadcast media, in order to raise awareness of their existence and brand location. This reintroduces the problem of fixed costs and gives established media outlets advantages in the operation of Internet news markets.

Speed of information transmission also affects content through supply and demand side pressures.[37] Satellite and Internet technologies give news outlets the ability to provide immediate coverage of events. This raises consumers' utility to the extent that they prefer current knowledge to future knowledge, an assumption often made about consumption patterns. The speed of transmission and existence of quickly retrieved electronic data, however, may reduce the time for reasoned analysis by some journalists. In a world where reporters face demand for news now, they may be more likely to engage in herding. Rather than investigate and develop a story, a reporter may look at the efforts of others and use a similar take on a news event. The quick transmission technology also makes it more likely a consumer has heard about popular stories from friends or coworkers. This can create the expectation that a story will be covered by a favored news outlet in a particular way. The cascading of information can lead to demands for quick story coverage. Not all outlets will react in the same way to these pressures, since the spatial model predicts that it will still be profitable for some outlets to develop brand names for high public affairs content combined with extensive analysis.

Revenues and Values

For information products there is always a disconnect between the revenues companies earn and the values society members place on the information. The failure of readers and viewers to incorporate the civic benefits of learning about politics in their decision making makes this disconnect greater for news with high public affairs content. News outlets such as cable television channels, newspapers, and some Internet sites gain part of their revenues through subscription charges. The cost of adding another reader or viewer is near zero for a cable channel and Internet site and relatively low for a newspaper. The news provider charges a price P to recover the fixed costs that went into assembling the stories. This price deters some consumers from buying the product, since their willingness to pay for the stories is less than P. From society's perspective this is inefficient. Once the stories are created, the marginal cost of providing a version of the cable news program for an additional consumer is zero. The viewer is willing to pay a price P^* greater than zero, so the value to society of the viewing is greater than the cost to society ($P^* > 0$). Since P^* is less than P, however, some consumers will not buy the channel and society will forgo the opportunity of viewing where benefits exceed costs.

The news provider needs to charge a nonzero price to cover the fixed costs of story assembly. This problem of pricing the news is an inherent tension built into the pricing of information goods. In the long run nonzero prices for information goods create incentives for companies to enter the field, for reporters to develop expertise, and for news outlets to spend the resources to develop brand names for particular types of coverage. This is the logic behind the granting of patents and copyrights, which are legal protections that create incentives for individuals to develop ideas. Once the information is created, in the short run any price above marginal cost (which is normally zero for information products) is inefficient since it discourages information consumption by readers and viewers who value the product more than its marginal cost of production. The problem is exacerbated for news with high public affairs content because individuals do not fully factor in the benefits to society of their civic knowledge when they decide how much they are willing to pay for news goods. The failure of news outlets to earn revenues from the value of better voting decisions means that news programs or products that focus on hard news will be underproduced.

Newspapers, television channels, radio stations, and Internet sites derive their other revenues from advertising sales. When news outlets sell "eyeballs" to advertisers the question becomes, What content can attract readers or viewers rather than what value will consumers place on content? This sets up at least two biases when outlets rely on advertising revenues.[38] Programs that appeal to smaller groups of readers or viewers may be less likely to be produced, since other factors being equal a media firm will be interested in selling larger audiences to advertisers. Even if a minority of potential readers or viewers values coverage of a given issue very strongly, this does not translate into higher revenues for a firm since the company gains money by attracting viewer attention rather than from extracting payments based on intensity of preferences. Once people are watching a program or reading a news entry, advertisers care about the chance to divert their attention to a commercial product. The advertisers do not care directly about the value readers or viewers place on the content surrounding the commercial or advertisement. A second bias in advertiser supported media is against expensive programming. If a programmer can attract X viewers with a low-cost program or a high-cost program, the programmer will choose the low-cost program even if the high-cost program is more highly valued by consumers. These two biases could hurt the production of hard news programming, since it may appeal to a relative minority of readers and viewers and may entail higher costs of production than other news genres.

Evaluating the Marketplace of Ideas

The metaphor of news coverage as a marketplace of ideas generates more questions than answers. Why would a marketplace of ideas generate truth? Whose truths matter? What is the impact of ideas on social outcomes? Does ignorance generate efficiency? Does lack of coverage translate into mistaken beliefs? What cues do people use to get by in economic and political marketplaces? Economic models do well in predicting how information is transformed into news in the media marketplace.[39] Notions such as public goods, rational ignorance, fixed costs, and spatial competition help explain which varieties of news products emerge. Economics does less well in assessing the outcomes of news markets, primarily for two reasons. Determining the impact of news coverage on individuals' political decisions is an empirical field still open to much debate.[40] Evaluating the outcomes of government decisions is even more controversial, since economics is only one of many possible ways to measure social welfare.

Consider how economics might be used to determine the value of news coverage that affects a particular government decision between options A and B. News about the pending decision may affect the information that citizens possess, the amount of political participation by individuals, the number of views expressed in debates, the number of speakers involved in policy discussions, and the quality of views expressed. These factors can affect the probability that option A or B is chosen, so they have an instrumental value that depends on their relative influence on the final decision. Each factor also has an intrinsic value, since individuals may value diversity of opinion or freedom of expression as goods in and of themselves. If one were able to assess how political information affects political opinions, the next step would be to determine how opinions translate into electoral effects and policy outcomes. Nearly all political decisions involve delegated decision making, so one needs a model of how the information possessed by voters affects the choices made by their agents in the legislative and executive branches.[41]

The consumption of political information by an individual gives rise to at least three possible types of value. The individual can gain satisfaction from the news simply as an information product consumed for the pleasure of knowledge. There are the intrinsic values the person may place on being informed about politics, that arise from a sense of duty and the value that others place on this from the notion that informed citizens are valuable. The third value arises from the impact of this information on government decision making between

options *A* and *B*. The theory of rational ignorance stresses that any one individual has a small probability of affecting a government action. If we set this
aside, the problem still remains of how to value the contribution of information in making the choice between two government policies. Economics offers
the standard of efficiency to judge outcomes, which in some sense translates
into the question of which option will lead to a greater social pie to divide. The
problem with using this standard to derive a monetary value of *A* versus *B*,
however, is that all judgments about efficiency begin with a presumption about
what distribution of income one starts with. Since many political questions involve choices about the best distribution of income, they invoke questions that
cannot be answered using a standard of efficiency. While there are many standards one could use to supplement efficiency, there is no one best way to aggregate how individuals value social outcomes using a fair decision rule.

This means that economics yields partial, not final, answers in questions
about news coverage. Models of media content can point to the direction of
likely market failures. The spatial model and other concepts from information
economics can predict which types of news coverage are likely to be underproduced. The magnitudes of these failures are more difficult to predict, and placing a dollar value on them is even more problematic. If one is willing to make
assumptions about media effects and stipulate particular ends for media policy, however, then economics can provide more help in the design of policies
chosen to achieve a given set of outcomes.

Policy Levers

The theory of rational ignorance suggests that news about government will be
underprovided and underconsumed relative to a world where people considered the full benefits to society of being informed voters. Economics offers a series of policy tools to deal with situations of positive externalities, that is, situations where people do not fully incorporate the benefits to society of their
actions as producers or consumers.[42] Each of the following tools can be applied
to the market failures associated with news about politics, with the ultimate
goal of increasing the creation and consumption of political information.

Lower the cost of information production and access. When reporters or media
outlets are trying to decide on their mix of stories, costs play a role in determining what types of information get developed into news programming. The
government influences the costs of many stories about public policy, since the
government determines the access to data and personnel involved in the policies. One way to tilt production of news goods more toward hard news coverage is to lower the costs to reporters of researching stories. The Freedom of
Information Act provides journalists with a way to gain access to government

data. Updated legislation instructs agencies to provide information in electronic form, so that people outside the government can more readily study its actions. Most agencies do not make their data readily accessible online, since data generate scrutiny and the potential for unwanted publicity. Government policies that make data more accessible to the public online will make it easier for reporters to write about policy actions.

Change the property rights of broadcasters/cable operators. Broadcasters currently receive licenses from the Federal Communications Commission for free, in exchange for the promise to broadcast in the "public interest, convenience, and necessity." Expectations about what this promise entails have varied with presidential administrations. FCC Chairman Mark Fowler declared in the 1980s that "the public's interest ... defines the public interest."[43] In the 1990s Chairman Reed Hundt led debates over whether broadcasters had responsibilities beyond market dictates in deciding on program content. Proposals for broadcasters to provide free time to political candidates or provide public affairs programming related to local community interests arise from the notion that the zero monetary price for a license carries an implicit price in programming content. Cable operators enjoy a similar grant to use public right of ways in laying cable networks. As part of franchise agreements cable operators often promise to provide access channels for public use and to cover local government events. Once these agreements are in place, however, cable systems have few incentives to make these access channels entertaining or enlightening, since audiences who view these channels are not watching channels that generate revenues through subscriptions or advertising revenues.

Tax and subsidy provisions for information. Starting with early postal regulations that allowed newspapers to be sent for free or at reduced rates, the government has often used tax revenues to subsidize information markets. Government grants to the private sector for environmental, medical, and social science research can be seen as subsidies meant to correct market failures arising from rational ignorance. Government subsidizing of the Internet's forerunner has paid large social dividends, especially when one considers how the Internet increases the potential for citizen access to political data. Funding by the government for public broadcasting also helps subsidize the provision of hard news.

Public provision of information. The government devotes significant resources to the creation of statistics that track social outcomes, information that helps facilitate coverage of particular types of government action. The time devoted by agency officials to speaking with the press, energy expanded in creating government websites, and money spent on publications by the Government Printing Office all involve the use of government funds for the creation or distribution of political information. Election concerns in the legislative and executive branches will generate incentives for politicians to lower the costs to reporters of covering particular issues.

Regulation of ownership structures. Current communications policy in broadcast and newspaper markets places limits on the nature of media company ownership. Broadcast networks cannot be wholly owned by foreign corporations, the same company cannot own a newspaper and broadcast station in a local market, and a firm cannot own stations covering more than 35% of the national television audience. These measures are meant to encourage decentralized, local control of media outlets, with the hope in part that local owners may have goals other than the maximization of profits. Such policies are meant to have an impact on the content of news coverage. The impacts are designed to be indirect in part because of fear that more direct attempts to regulate content would violate the First Amendment's stricture that Congress shall make no law abridging the freedom of the press.

Antitrust enforcement. Traditional antitrust enforcement focuses on markets where consumers are damaged by business actions that raise price above the marginal cost of the provision of a good. This is a hallmark of the functioning of information markets, however, since the elevation of price above marginal cost is what allows a firm to earn revenues to cover the substantial fixed costs of producing the first copy of a news product. Most current proposals to use antitrust actions against media firms focus on the size of media firms and the consolidation of ownership of media properties. An assumption is often made that a reduction in the number of owners in a media market leads to a reduction in the variety of opinions offered. The theories recounted here demonstrate that this is an empirical question. The dispersion of consumer demands for different types of news may still generate a diversity of news products. Under some conditions more consolidated ownership can generate more program diversity, since a consolidated owner is less likely to duplicate a program that already serves a particular audience and therefore more likely to offer a niche program.

Copyright. The availability of information on the Internet raises new questions about who owns data about current events. Courts recognize that some proprietary interest in the creation of data needs to be recognized to give reporters incentives to expend resources to develop information. Once the data have been created, however, the tension remains that allowing someone to charge more than zero for the information will exclude some consumers who value the information more than its marginal cost of distribution. The degree that the government favors creation or copying in Internet disputes will affect incentives for outlets to develop extensive data or distribute information.

Stimulation of demand for information through education/advertising. Though acquisition of political information rarely makes sense as a personal investment, there are citizens who enjoy the consumption of this information. They may feel a duty to be informed, or follow politics for the sheer joy of consuming knowledge, or be fascinated by the human drama elements of elections. Some of these demands are correlated with education. To the extent that classroom instruction stimulates interest in politics, attempts to improve schooling may translate into increased demand for news about government. Just as private interest advertising may increase demand for particular types of goods, government advertising about public information sources will also facilitate the consumption and dispersion of political data.

Creation of norms to encourage the production of political information. Professions often emerge as solutions to market failure problems, so that individuals are led to consider goals aside from simple profit maximization in their decision making. Efforts that discuss journalism as a profession may help encourage reporters and owners to consider the broader public benefits to their work. While the returns for soft news may be attractive for some media outlets, the spatial model predicts that some reporters and firms will try to cover public affairs from a hard news perspective. Psychic rewards that focus on personal integrity and duty may help compensate reporters that try to provide more political information than might be demanded through the profit motive.

Nonprofit provision of political information. Nonprofits face a dilemma in the provision of information, since their nonpartisan status in the tax code often prevents them from direct participation in electoral politics. Nonprofits can, however, play a role in the development and distribution of the information about government actions. Surveys among the general public, studies of the impact of policies, and support for experiments in different policy areas are all ways that nonprofits can create and spread data about politics. Nonprofit support for broadcast and print outlets can also be a way to subsidize the discussion of public affairs.

Conclusions

Individual ignorance about politics may be rational, but is it efficient? That is a question that is rarely raised in discussion of media policies. From an individual's standpoint, investing the time and effort to cast an informed vote rarely makes sense because of the small probability that a single vote will change a social outcome. Despite this logic, some voters do follow politics and many voters do cast ballots. Imagine a world where information were free, voting was costless, and people cast ballots knowing and understanding their interests and the positions of politicians. How would electoral outcomes and government decisions differ from those made in today's world of rational ignorance? If the social decisions reached would be identical, then today's ignorance represents a bargain. Elections are determined and policies decided upon without each citizen becoming fully informed about the details of policies. Freeing the voter from developing personal positions on foreign and domestic policies is one of the great savings involved in a representative democracy, where voters economize on information gathering by delegating decisions to others. Formulating media policy in a world of rational ignorance and delegated decision making comes down to the question of how many informed voters it takes to run a democracy. The rhetorical answer is based on the ideal of every voter gathering information and going to the polls. This rhetorical answer may even be necessary to sustain the ideology that prompts some voters to learn about politics and cast their votes. From the perspective of social costs and benefits, however, the question remains—How much information is "enough" for a democratic society?

Delegated decision making and rational ignorance are not limited to the operation of the political marketplace. In the economic marketplace, shareholders delegate the decision to maximize profits to managers, who in turn delegate choices to workers, who produce goods that are purchased by consumers. Consumers may not fully investigate the product dimensions of each good they buy. Instead they rely on brand reputations and the purchases of others. In the market some consumers will take the time to learn about prices and qualities, and their efforts can lead firms to make decisions that benefit consumers who have not taken the time to read up or shop around. The search for information in politics is similar, though individual voters face even smaller incentives to learn about politicians than they do about products. If one were to analyze the impact of a particular media policy on political decisions, the process would involve investigating the current costs and benefits of the creation and spread of political information and the impact on public policy decisions.

Would the First Amendment pass a cost-benefit test? Assessing the impact of the First Amendment on political decisions would involve quantifying a number of reactions to media content. How satisfied are consumers with the media products they consume? In many markets the price of a good is used to proxy the value that consumers derive from its consumption. This is difficult for media products for several reasons. The monetary price of the media product is often zero, since broadcast programs and Internet sites are consumed for free. Advertising revenues provide support for media content, which means that prices do not capture the value to individuals of their consumption. For some products with subscription prices economists could glean some information about the value that people derive from their consumption. Yet the broader value to society of informed political decisions would again not be reflected in these values of personal enjoyment from consumption of political information.

Economists use surveys to get at individuals' willingness to pay for goods not actively traded on markets, goods such as the preservation of the Grand Canyon or the protection of the spotted owl. Individuals are asked questions about placing a dollar value on protecting or shifting priorities. Survey instruments could help measure the willingness of voters to pay for policies that generate more informed decisions overall. This could in part measure the ex post facto regret that voters might feel if they went into the ballot booth rationally ignorant, cast their votes, and then after the fact regretted the policy decisions made by their elected officials. Comparing the states of world generated by media policies could also involve placing a value on the difference between social outcomes that arise with different levels of political information. This would explicitly involve using efficiency, a measure of the size of the social pie, to determine the value of political outcomes.

Since political information is costly to produce, decisions to create or distribute it will inevitably involve personal incentives, including money, fame, ideology, and reelection. The theories in this chapter demonstrate how the five Ws of the economic marketplace currently determine what information is transformed into news. Using economics to evaluate the outcomes of electoral and government decisions is more problematic, because of the difficulties of predicting media effects and of judging all government decisions with the single standard of efficiency. Economics does offer suggestions to reach particular goals of media policies, once they are selected. If one wished to increase the consumption and distribution of hard news, for example, then lowering the costs of accessing government information, increasing the amounts spent on generation of outcome statistics by the government, and encouraging the generation of data by nonprofit foundations are all possible policy recommendations. These measures would be consistent with the view that the best media policies lie in encouraging private actors to pursue public ends. They would also be consistent with the view that while the media market may appear to offer what people want rather than what they need, in a world of delegated decision making this may turn out to be all that people need to monitor and influence government. Reaching these conclusions involves judgment decisions about how well economics predicts the generation and transmission of news, the focus of the chapters that follow.

Chapter **2** _____

A Market for Press Independence:
The Evolution of Nonpartisan Newspapers
in the Nineteenth Century

IMAGINE a world where patronage drives news coverage. Editors seeking favors from political parties slant the discussion of government policies. Newspapers trying to sell space to advertisers tailor the way they cover politics in order to gain more readers to market. News coverage is sold to the highest bidders—including readers, advertisers, and politicians. To the media's harshest critics, this imaginary world exists today in the biased way that politics is covered in the United States. Most readers and viewers would reject this as a current description of journalism in America, where objectivity is seen as a guiding principle in reporting. Yet for nearly half of the history of the American press, newspapers acknowledged and proclaimed that their judgments about news were influenced by partisan considerations. Understanding why newspapers abandoned strong party affiliations and embraced editorial independence requires going back in time to see how the notion of independent news coverage evolved. This chapter traces the path to objective news judgment by studying newspaper markets in the top fifty cities in America from 1870 to 1900.

Though we often talk about covering the news objectively as an ethical or professional norm, objective news coverage is a commercial product that emerges from market forces.[1] The decision by a newspaper to offer a partisan versus an independent interpretation of events depends on a number of factors: the political preferences of potential readers in a city; the size of the potential audiences for news coverage; the technology and costs of information generation and transmission; the varieties of products offered by competitors; the demand by advertisers for readers as potential consumers; and the size of partisan subsidies or favors. In 1870 most daily newspapers covering current events in the top fifty cities in America chose a partisan affiliation. Republican papers accounted for 54% of all metropolitan dailies and gathered 43% of the total circulation in these cities. Democratic papers comprised 33% of daily newspapers and 31% of circulation. Newspapers that chose to identify themselves as "independent" of party accounted for 13% of dailies and 26% of circulation.[2] In 1880 the percentage of daily newspapers choosing to identify as independent jumped to 34% of all dailies; these independent newspapers generated 55% of the aggregate circulation of dailies. The appeal of nonpartisan coverage continued to grow, so that by 1900 independent newspapers accounted for 47% of metropolitan dailies.

What drove the switch to independent coverage? There were a number of changes in newspaper markets during this time period: an increase in the number of potential readers; a decline in the cost of paper; changes in printing technology that increased the number of papers a press could print per hour and that increased the cost of presses; and the rise of advertising as a way to market goods. Many of these changes increased the economies of scale involved in newspaper production. New presses involved high capital costs, which could be spread across the sale of more papers as circulation increased. The speed of the new presses made it possible for an individual paper to reach a larger audience with a given edition of the news. A higher circulation paper might be more attractive to an advertiser, who could reach more readers with a single ad and who could avoid the fixed costs of negotiating ads with multiple news outlets. From a paper's perspective, these market changes meant that higher circulation could bring lower average and marginal costs and higher ad revenues, so some lowered subscription prices to attract more readers. With increasing advantages for increased circulation, papers faced the challenge of how to grow. Within a given city, strongly partisan ones faced natural bounds on their circulations. Democratic newspapers had greater appeals for Democrats, and Republican ones catered to the views of their party loyalists. If a paper chose to be independent in coverage, however, the owner might draw readers from all parties and allegiances. As circulation became paramount, papers chose independence as the easiest way to attain large-scale circulation.

The evidence in this chapter demonstrates that independent news coverage grew as scale economies became more important. The analysis here—of the newspaper markets in the fifty largest cities in America in 1870, 1880, 1890, and 1900—underscores how papers chose affiliations based on the relative returns generated by local party allegiances and production technology. Democratic papers circulated widely where Democrats earned a higher percentage of the vote; Republican newspapers did well where Republican candidates fared well. This could be because election outcomes in an area were influenced by a paper's political orientation, so that Democratic coverage generated Democratic votes. To take account of this, the chapter also demonstrates that Republican and Democratic papers garnered different circulations based on local demographic characteristics—such as the percentage of the population that was foreign-born or black—that were associated with party preferences but not caused by paper coverage. Papers with independent affiliations had higher circulations in larger cities, consistent with the idea that owners chose independent affiliation where advertising was more prevalent and where scale economies could be achieved. The growth in independent affiliation was most pronounced from 1870 to 1880 for the largest newspapers. Among papers whose circulations ranked in the top 10% of those analyzed, independents accounted for 25% in 1870 and 75% in 1880. For a given city population, a paper was more likely to achieve a scale economy size (e.g., a circulation in the top 20% or top 10% nationwide) if it chose an independent affiliation.

The benefits to large-scale circulation were significant and increasing over time in these local newspaper markets. Papers with the largest circulations had lower prices per square inch for consumers, generated higher subscription revenues per square inch for newspaper owners, and earned higher total subscription revenues. These differences between smaller newspapers and those with the largest circulations increased dramatically from 1870 to 1900. Larger circulations brought higher ad prices, as did location in larger cities (which had more potential advertisers and consumers). Even with these higher ad prices, larger newspapers offered advertisers a more desirable price in terms of the cost per thousand readers, since they reached so many subscribers. The lower subscription costs made possible by economies of scale and advertiser support greatly increased the number of readers. In 1870, .25 daily papers per person circulated in the fifty largest cities, while this increased to .55 by 1900. In terms of political news coverage, papers with larger circulations and in larger towns were more likely to have their own correspondents covering Congress in Washington, D.C. In terms of overall editorial resources, independent newspapers had larger staffs than their partisan counterparts.

The decisions by some newspaper owners to cover politics without a partisan bias came at predictable times and at predictable places. Understanding why these papers chose to abandon party affiliation in favor of independent reporting requires a review of how economics influences content decisions.[3]

Why Choose to Be Independent?

For a reader, a daily metropolitan newspaper in the 1870s offered a mix of local, national, and international news. For an economist, the same newspaper offers evidence on how experience goods with high fixed costs and multiple varieties come to market. The generation of news through reporting, editing, and layout involves costs that are fixed regardless of the number of issues printed. Though each individual in a city might prefer a different assortment of stories reported, the size of fixed costs will limit the variety of newspapers offered in the marketplace. The larger the city, the greater the number of papers that could be supported by readers. The types of papers offered will correspond to the interests of readers. Since a reader needs to consume it to determine its full content, newspapers are called "experience goods." In order to signal to potential readers the type of good offered, newspapers will develop reputations or brand names. The easiest way to indicate the paper's brand position is to include it in the name, for example, *The Republican* or *The Democrat*. The mix of brand locations chosen across cities and over time in the late nineteenth century can be explained by answering the five Ws asked in the marketplace.

The first two relate to preferences and endowments: Who cares about a particular piece of information? What are they willing to pay to find it, or what are others willing to pay to pay to reach them? Newspapers can offer different combinations of the four different types of information identified by Downs (1957): entertaining stories; information that helps producers make business decisions; data that help consumers make purchase decisions; and information that helps a person make political decisions. Some publications may specialize in producer information, such as newspapers aimed at financial markets or a particular industry. In the late 1800s, these typically had smaller circulations, higher prices, and were aimed at businessmen. The majority of daily newspapers in the top fifty cities were general circulation publications that carried the local, national, and international news of the day (though the timeliness of the news might vary depending on the cost and reliability of transmission). The type and amount of information provided depended on the willingness of readers to pay for the newspaper, and on the value of those readers as that derived from advertising and political patronage. In some cities papers were segregated by class demographics, with newspapers aimed at middle- or upper-class readers charging more and those aimed at working-class readers charging a lower price (e.g., the "penny press").

Aside from subscriptions or retail purchases, readers also brought newspapers value through advertising and political influence. The role of advertising markedly increased from 1870 to 1900. This stemmed in part from the growth of consumer items sold with national brand names, so that newspapers carried advertising for both local and national goods. Advertisers valued papers with larger circulations for several reasons. An insert in a larger paper reached more potential consumers, and transaction costs were lowered when advertisers dealt with a few larger papers rather than a multitude of smaller ones. At the same time that the number of advertisers was growing, the patronage offered by political parties was waning. With an expanding electorate and more newspapers with mass appeal, funding a party outlet may have been less effective since it might not reach a large audience. The costs of starting a newspaper and number of writers required to maintain the paper also grew tremendously. While an editor and a printing press were sufficient to create a party newspaper in the 1830s, by the 1880s a high speed press cost $80,000 and staffs had expanded to include editors and reporters with specific beats.

A newspaper owner concerned about profit would thus calculate three different values attached to reader demands. The willingness of different demographic groups to pay for a newspaper defined one stream of revenues. The willingness of advertisers to pay to reach potential consumers brought another source of income. The ability of parties and politicians in government to provide subsidies, printing contracts, patronage jobs, and political favors defined an additional source of income.[4] Owners wishing to influence the outcome of partisan elections, and the direction of government policy, might factor in the ideological satisfaction of using the newspaper to achieve political ends. In choosing a partisan or nonpartisan brand identity in the marketplace, the owner would consider each of these demand factors. The revenue stream attached to choosing a Democratic affiliation would depend, for example, on the number of Democrats in the city and the other outlets contending for their attention, the willingness of Republicans and those without a party allegiance to read the paper, the value attached to the demographic groups reading the paper, and the willingness of the party or government to pay for particular coverage in the outlet.

The third and fourth Ws relate to technology and costs: Where can media outlets or advertisers reach people? When is it profitable to provide the information? The large fixed costs in composing and printing the first copy of a day's paper mean there will be a limit on the number of varieties offered in the marketplace. The larger the number of readers in a city, the greater the number of papers whose fixed costs could be covered. Since there is a threshold number of readers for a paper, larger cities may have more varieties since they may be more likely to have a sufficient number of readers with similar tastes. The relative attractiveness of adopting a Republican, Democratic, or independent approach to the news will depend on the number of outlets already serving a particular constituency. New entrants will thus consider current brand locations when staking out their positions. Established papers will also consider changes in market conditions when deciding whether to retain or abandon a particular partisan approach to covering politics.

The relative attractiveness of attaining a large circulation changed with advances in technology during this period. The development of presses with runs of 25,000 sheets or more per hour meant a single newspaper could supply a significant portion of a city's readers. Though these presses had high capital costs, the larger press runs meant that the fixed costs of assembling and producing the paper could be spread across many readers. The decline in average and marginal printing costs, accentuated by a drop in the price of paper, made it possible to reduce the price of the newspaper.[5] This in turn expanded the pool of readers willing to buy the paper. The increasing number of readers garnered by a paper in turn raised the desirability of advertising in the outlet. As more consumer products were developed with brand names supported by national advertising, companies sought to reach consumers through newspaper advertising. Dealing with larger papers reduced the costs of negotiating and placing ads, which reinforced the incentive for papers to become larger. These pressures pushed papers to try to attain sufficient scale to lower production costs and attract both local and national advertisers. The number of party stalwarts placed a boundary on the potential circulations of strongly partisan papers. If a paper adopted a nonpartisan take on political news, it could draw on a larger segment of the population if readers from either party could be attracted to the outlet.

The fifth W, Why is this profitable?, relates in part to institutions that affect the operation of a market. One institutional change during this period is the decline in the patronage provided to papers by parties. Government budgets were increasing during this time period, so to the extent that parties' or politicians' willingness to pay for coverage related to the advantages sought, one might expect increasing pay for partisan coverage.[6] The decline in direct support for partisan papers, however, may be related to changes described by the first four Ws. With the rise of papers supported by advertisers, the economies of scale possible with faster presses, and the drop in subscription costs and expansion of readership, parties may no longer have been able to offer terms attractive enough to win editorial support. Payments did continue throughout this period, especially during election years. The days of party payments guaranteeing the survival of an influential paper manned by a single editor and powered by a small press, however, waned with the rise of mass circulation newspapers.

The five Ws highlight the factors that influence whether a paper would choose a partisan or nonpartisan approach to the news in the period 1870 to 1900: the number of potential readers with a preference for partisan coverage and their willingness to pay for news; the value of particular demographic groups to advertisers or parties; and the economies of scale made possible by changes in printing technology. Economic theories do not offer precise predictions about the number and brand locations of newspapers in given cities over time.[7] Spatial models of product location are sensitive to assumptions about the distribution of preferences of consumers, the interaction of competitors, the number of likely entrants, and the technology of production. The changes in technology that increase the economies of scale in newspaper production and the changes in advertising that generate new sources of revenues would further strain any models of brand location.

The most relevant economic models of content selection are the empirical ones developed by Waldfogel and coauthors to analyze the impact of audience diversity and size on consumption of media products in radio and in newspaper markets. Waldfogel (1999) finds in U.S. local radio markets that larger markets offer more stations and more varieties of stations, consistent with the notion that more potential consumers help cover the fixed costs involved in offering a station. Since consumers vary in their tastes for various radio programs, the likelihood that a particular type of program will be offered will depend on the degree that preferences are shared in the market. If a particular group is only present in a market in small numbers, the radio format that individuals in the group most prefer may not be offered. Waldfogel finds that in radio markets the number of stations targeted toward blacks and the share of blacks listening to the radio increases with the size of the black population. In daily newspaper markets, George and Waldfogel (2000) find that the content positioning of newspapers, and hence the consumption of the paper by different demographic groups, is affected by the racial composition of the city. Blacks are more likely to purchase a daily newspaper in an area with a larger number of blacks; this tendency decreases, however, with the number of whites in the market.

Though the five Ws of media markets and other economic theories of product location do not offer exact predictions about the number and allegiances of papers in an area, they do generate the following hypotheses about the decisions of papers in the top fifty cities to choose partisan or independent affiliations from 1870 to 1900.

Democratic newspapers will garner more readers in cities where voters favor Democrats; Republican papers will fare better where readers are Republican. Newspaper owners concerned with profits will take into account the preferences of potential readers in deciding whether to adopt a partisan viewpoint in interpreting the news. The greater the number of residents favoring Democratic candidates, the larger the potential readership for Democratic newspapers. Note that more Democrats in the city could attract multiple papers to offer Democratic viewpoints. If one of the papers achieved scale economies, these same Democrats could be served by a single Democratic paper. Since newspapers may vary in size, the predictions about paper brand location are not expressed in terms of number of papers adopting a partisan position. Rather, the hypotheses focus on the relationship between the percentage of a city's circulation generated by Democratic papers and the percentage of voters that cast their ballots for Democratic candidates. Since papers can exert influence on the likelihood that residents will vote for a particular presidential candidate, an association between newspaper affiliation and votes for a party could stem from coverage influencing voter choices. To take account of this, the analysis will also focus on the relationship between newspaper circulation and demographic characteristics that relate to party preference but are not influenced by newspaper consumption (such as the percentage of the city population that is foreign-born or black).

Independent newspapers will flourish in larger cities. Cities with larger populations provide more opportunity for a paper to achieve scale economies. Larger presses, with the ability to print thousands of papers rapidly, may be only profitable if there are a large number of readers available in a city. Larger cities will have more local establishments trying to attract customers and will offer national advertisers more potential consumers. Papers will thus be more likely to adopt independent affiliations in larger cities.

Independent newspapers will differ from partisan newspapers in many dimensions; they will have larger circulations, more recent establishment dates, and lower subscription prices. If newspaper owners adopt a nonpartisan approach to covering events in order to achieve economies of scale, then one would expect higher circulations among independent papers. Since the advantages of larger circulations increase over time because of changes in printing technology and in advertising, papers entering a market face higher returns in choosing independent locations. Papers may face costs associated with switching brand locations, so older newspapers established in the earlier era of partisan presses may be more likely to retain their party position. If independent newspapers achieve lower costs through scale economies and attract more advertisers, this may lead them to charge lower prices per square inch.

For a given market size, a paper will be more likely to achieve scale economies if it adopts an independent affiliation. Partisan papers face potential boundaries to their circulations. Democratic voters may be unlikely to consume a newspaper that edits the news to favor Republicans. An independent newspaper, however, may be able to appeal to readers of many different political allegiances by covering current events from a nonpartisan perspective. This will depend on the willingness of party voters to forsake a partisan paper for an independent perspective. If there are enough strong partisans in a city, then a Democratic or Republican paper can achieve a large circulation (defined here as in the top 20% or top 10% of circulations for papers in the sample). If it is easier for independents to build circulation by appealing to a larger segment of a city, then for a given city size one would expect that a paper would be more likely to achieve large-scale circulation if it adopted a nonpartisan brand position.

The advantages conferred by large circulation will increase over time. From 1870 to 1900 advances in printing technology increased the number of issues printed per hour by presses and decreased the cost per paper of producing the paper. As advertising became more important in reaching consumers, newspapers with larger circulations became attractive vehicles because they offered companies the chance to reach significant numbers of potential purchasers. Lower printing costs and greater advertiser support meant papers could charge lower subscription prices, which in turn expanded the number of readers for large-scale papers. These changes in technology and advertising over time mean that there should be a widening gap in the characteristics of large and small daily newspapers. Large papers should have increasingly lower costs per square inch, greater subscription revenues, and larger subscription revenues per square inch.

Papers with larger circulations will charge more per advertisement. Companies will prefer to advertise in larger papers because they may offer lower costs per thousand readers. Larger papers reach more readers, so they may charge more per advertisement. Advertisers will prefer dealing with larger papers than bearing the transaction costs of dealing with many smaller papers. Even though larger papers charge more per advertisement, the overall cost to an advertiser per reader reached may be lower since the larger papers reach significant numbers of consumers.

Independent papers will not stop covering politics; they will simply cover it in a less partisan manner. Independent newspapers will still invest heavily in covering current events. They will pay for correspondents in Washington, D.C. to cover Congress. With larger circulations and revenues from advertising, independent newspapers may be able to afford larger editorial staffs to cover the news.

Viewing editorial content as a product of market forces generates clear hypotheses about the origin and nature of the independent press. Before testing these ideas through statistical analysis, I look for evidence in contemporaneous accounts that the participants in newspaper markets viewed decisions about partisan coverage in economic terms.

What Drives Coverage? Views from the Nineteenth Century

The most remarked upon change in daily newspapers in the period 1870–1900 was the emergence of the independent press. Papers at the time referred to themselves as "independent," though the exact definition of this brand location varied. Independence could mean that a paper did not cover politics closely, or that a paper adopted a neutral stance in describing current events, or even that a paper chose favorites among politicians but did so on the basis of principle rather than party loyalty. These definitions share something in common, the notion that an independent paper is not a partisan outlet directly affiliated with a given party.

Many date the start of the independent press with the founding of penny press newspapers, such as the *Sun* and *Herald* in New York City, in the 1830s. In its first edition in 1835, the *Herald*'s founder James Bennett wrote that, "We shall support no party—be the organ of no faction or coterie, and care nothing for any election or any candidate from president down to constable." He later promised that the *Herald* would "give a correct picture of the world—in Wall Street—in the Exchange—in the Police-Office—at the Theatre—in the Opera—in short, wherever human nature and real life best displays their freaks and vagaries."[8] The partisan press reacted to this new competition by labeling the Independents' coverage of current events, such as crimes and trials, as sensationalism and attacking the editors of the new outlets as immoral.[9]

Some took the focus of the early independent press on events outside of politics as a neutrality of silence. In choosing to establish the *New York Tribune* in 1841, Horace Greeley declared in his autobiography:

> My leading idea was the establishment of a journal removed alike from servile partisanship on the one hand and from gagged, mincing neutrality on the other. Party spirit is so fierce and intolerant in this country that the editor of a non-partisan sheet is restrained from saying what he thinks and feels on the most vital, imminent topics; while, on the other hand, a Democratic, Whig, or Republican journal is generally expected to praise or blame, like or dislike, eulogize or condemn, in precise accordance with the views and interest of its party. I believed there was a happy medium between these extremes,—a position from which a journalist might openly and heartily advocate the principles and commend the measures of that party to which his convictions allied him, yet frankly dissent from its course on a particular question, and even denounce its candidates if they were shown to be deficient in capacity or (far worse) in integrity.[10]

For Greeley, independence meant freely choosing to support a given political position. He explicitly criticized the independent papers that claimed not to take positions in political disputes. He noted in terms of expressing an honest political thought: "... a neutral paper seldom or never can. If it does, it will lose subscribers at every turn. Its only safe course is to avoid political discussion altogether, and thus leave the most important topics wholly untouched.[11]

By the 1870s, editors saw the growth of independent papers as a national trend. An editor in New York wrote in 1872:

> Independent journalism! that is the watchword of the future in the profession. An end of concealments because it would hurt the party; an end of one-sided expositions ...; an end of assaults that are not believed fully just but must be made because the exigency of party warfare demands them; an end of slanders that are known to be slanders ... of hesitation to print the news because it may hurt the party ... of doctoring the reports of public opinion ... of half truths ... that is the end which to every perplexed, conscientious journalist a new and beneficent Declaration of Independence affords.[12]

From the perspective of the editor of the *Springfield Republican* in 1872, the independent newspapers were supplanting partisan outlets: "The Independence, which has been held and despised as Indifference, and the Impersonality, which was denounced as Irresponsibility, are now seen in their higher and broader character, and their reforming and elevating influences are fast possessing the government of the press, and growing in public appreciation. Party Journalism began to fall with the death and retirement of its great representatives.... The growth of Journalism as a business, and the extinction of the old party lines and divisions have united to make ... its emancipation."[13]

Despite the trend toward press independence, some papers still clearly declared their partisan attachments. The New York *World* noted:

> In the year 1872 General Grant's successor is to be chosen; the Forty-third Congress to be elected.... How to influence the people's votes? By the newspaper—for it includes every other agency. It makes known events and facts—among all influences the chief. It assembles the vaster outside audiences which can not gather to the state-house, the pulpit, or the stump. It is the constant interpreter of men's affairs, and of error or truth is the daily seed-sower. Next November is our political harvest-time. As we sow we shall reap. The *World's* seed sowing will be fruitful to the extent that its circulation is widely pushed by those who approve its aim.[14]

In the coming elections, in which the paper noted "the ballot-box is the true battle-field of republics," the paper declared that it would be the organ of the Democratic Party.

In models of brand competition, producers develop products in part by examining the market segments already captured by other products and assessing the prospects for introducing something different. Discussions of entry into the daily newspaper markets during this time period demonstrate that publishers viewed decisions about political affiliation as exercises in market segmentation. James E. Scripps, who established the independent *Detroit News*, noted in 1879: "As a rule, there is never a field for a second paper of precisely the same characteristics as one already in existence. A Democratic paper may be established where there is already a Republican; or vice versa; an afternoon paper where there is only a morning; a cheap paper where there is only a high-priced one; but I think I can safely affirm that an attempt to supplant an existing newspaper ... of exactly the same character has never succeeded."[15] In describing the competition among papers of different affiliations, the editor of the New York *World* wrote a financial backer in 1875 that " independent papers are in the nature of the case nearer and sharper rivals of the paper which represents the dominant political sentiment than of the same paper representing the minority sentiment."[16] The editor of the independent Cleveland *Press* noted in 1879 that a nonpartisan market location brought a higher return than a partisan one. He noted that: "No matter how honorable the editors of the partisan papers may be personally, they are forced to do the dirty editorial work dictated to them by party interests.... We are in the newspaper business for the same purpose as that of most people who go into business—to make money. The independent newspaper is always a more profitable concern than the party organ, no matter how successful the latter may be."[17]

The image of Democratic, Republican, and independent papers contending for readers within a market applied primarily to the larger metropolitan areas, where sizable populations existed within each city to cover the fixed costs of a variety of publications. In an 1891 publication entitled *Making a Country Newspaper*, Augustus J. Munson recommended that publishers in small towns

choose a nonpartisan affiliation. He noted, "newspaper politics belongs to metropolitan journalism where a field sufficiently large to support it can be
found."[18]

Advances in printing technology made large circulation possible for dailies
and increased the pressure on owners to deliver content that generated larger
audiences. In 1846 the *Philadelphia Ledger* made news by adopting a Hoe double cylinder rotary printing press capable of printing 8,000 sheets per hour. By
1875 the Hoe Web printing machine printed 25,000 sheets per hour. In 1893,
the New York *World's* octuple rotary power press produced 96,000 eight-page
newspapers per hour.[19] The founder of the first penny press newspaper in
America, the New York *Sun*, credited the invention of the cylinder press with
making larger circulation newspapers feasible. As Benjamin Day said in a 1851
tribute to Colonel R. M. Hoe (the inventor of the "lightning press"), "Constant
and vexatious complaints of the later delivery of the paper could not be
avoided up to the time . . . [Hoe] came forward with his great invention of setting types upon a cylinder, the success of which . . . has brought gladness to the
hearts of a multitude of newspaper men."[20] The advances in printing technology significantly increased the cost of operating a newspaper. While a new
press in the 1840s could cost $4,000–$5,000, in the 1880s the more sophisticated presses cost $80,000 each.[21]

The increasing costs of establishing a paper effectively raised the cost of running a paper to express an owner's (or party's) worldview. As one editor noted
in 1906: "The immensely large capital now required for the conduct of a daily
newspaper in a great city has had important consequences. It has made the
newspaper more of an institution, less of a personal organ. Men no longer des-
ignate journals by the owner's or editor's name. It used to be Bryant's paper, or
Greeley's paper, or Raymond's, or Bennett's. Now it is simply *Times, Herald,
Tribune*, and so on."[22] Looking back in 1910 at the development of daily newspapers, a critic in the *Atlantic Monthly* noted:

> More and more the owner of the big daily is a business man who finds it hard to see
> why he should run his property on different lines from the hotel proprietor, the
> vaudeville manager, or the owner of an amusement park. The editors are hired men,
> and they may put into the paper no more of their conscience and ideals than com-
> ports with getting the biggest return from the investment. . . . Now that the provider
> of the newspaper capital hires the editor instead of the editor hiring the newspaper
> capital, the paper is likelier to be run as a money-maker pure and simple—a factory
> where ink and brains are so applied to white paper as to turn out the largest possible
> marketable product. The capitalist-owner means no harm, but he is not bothered by
> the standards that hamper the editor-owner. He follows a few simple maxims that
> work out well enough in selling shoes or cigars or sheet-music. "Give people what
> *they* want, not what *you* want." "Back nothing that will be unpopular." "Run the con-
> cern for all it is worth."[23]

The sharing of material across newspapers created some incentives for the creation of nonpartisan content. The rise of the telegraph made it possible for newspapers to share rapidly a story written by a single correspondent in a distant city. L. A. Gobright, the first head of the Associated Press Bureau in Washington, described his charge to provide nonpartisan coverage in this way:

> My business is to communicate facts. My instructions do not allow me to make any comments upon the facts which I communicate. My dispatches are sent to papers of all manner of politics and the editors say they are able to make their own comments upon the facts which are sent them. I, therefore, confine myself to what I consider legitimate news. I do not act as a politician belonging to any school, but try to be truthful and impartial. My dispatches are merely dry matters of fact and detail. Some special correspondents may write to suit the temper of their own organs. Although I write without regard to men or politics, I do not always escape censure.[24]

The ability to sell the same story across many markets, and thus take advantage of the fixed costs of creating and assembling the story, gave rise to newspaper auxiliary companies. These firms would sell country weeklies partially printed paper with news already printed on it; the editors could then add in local news by printing on the blank pages. In later years the newspaper auxiliaries, the forerunners of today's syndication services, would sell newspapers printing plates with stories already composed on them. The demand for different types of news was sufficient so that these auxiliary companies sold stories aimed at different political brand locations. As one company declared in a trade journal advertisement, "our political editions are edited by men identified with the different parties—in full sympathy with their work—and all our editors are familiar by actual experience with the business of editing and publishing country papers. Our news columns are full and comprehensive and contain news up to the time of printing. We supply papers in the same locality with entirely different matter, being particularly careful to prevent interference in this respect."[25]

The growing importance of advertising to newspapers during this time period is evident in discussions of the reader as a potential consumer to sell to other firms. Advertising as a percentage of total national newspaper and periodical revenues grew from 44% in 1879 to 54.5% in 1899.[26] The increase came in part from a rise in population and an increase in brands marketed nationwide, a phenomenon made possible by advances in the coordination of production and distribution of goods. Records from a major advertising firm in the period indicate that in 1878 patent medicines and treatments accounted for 26% of billings, followed by greeting cards and chromos (10.3%) and dry goods and clothing (8.1%). In 1901 the largest billing categories were food and drink (14.8%), fuel (11.2%), and tobacco products (10.9%).[27] The drive to sell readers to advertisers focused newspapers on providing content likely to expand circulation, particularly among the readers desired by advertisers. Describing newspaper assembly in 1896, an editor wrote, "the successful publisher knows what the public demands and serves it to them accordingly, whether he thinks it is what they ought to have or not."[28] An advertising journal in 1899 advised companies that, "The questions always to be asked are: What class of person does this publication reach and are they likely to be purchasers of my goods?"[29] The incentives to bundle stories of interest to different groups of readers, discussed in chapter 1, are evident in discussions of advertising audiences. The rise of advertising and the purchasing decisions made by females in households meant that newspapers offered content expressly designed to attract women. As a trade journal article entitled "Reaching the Men through the Women" put it, in 1892: "The great daily, filled with the bright news of the day to whet the appetite of the readers with its children's columns, its women's column, its column of style, its miscellany, is the paper which has the great circulation and the one which pays the advertiser more to the square inch than any other paper can pay to the square foot. There is not a single case on record of any daily paper succeeding in this or any other country which does not arrange its matter, from editorials to its news, so as to be pleasantly absorbed by the women of the day."[30]

The way that newspapers advertised their own papers to attract potential advertisers provides strong evidence on how publishers viewed the economics of daily papers. N. W. Ayer and Son's *American Newspaper Annual* for 1880 contained a section in which papers paid for advertisements aimed at convincing companies to place ads in their outlets. These ads stressed the brand location of a paper in terms of party affiliation and publishing time (e.g., morning or evening, daily or weekly), circulation size, printing technology, reader demographics, city size, and advertising rates on a line basis and a cost per thousand circulation basis. The largest daily paper in America at the time, *The Sun* (New York), took out the largest ad. The text of the ad captured dimensions important to independent newspapers: coverage of government that was not linked to partisan allegiance; news selected, aside from politics, to draw readers of many different interests; large circulation, important to advertisers; and the ability to translate large circulation and advertising revenues into greater resources devoted to coverage. The text of *The Sun's* advertisement read in part:

> As a newspaper, THE SUN believes in getting all the news of the world promptly, and presenting it in the most intelligible shape—the shape that will enable its readers to keep well abreast of the age with the least unproductive expenditure of time. The greatest interest to the greatest number—that is the law controlling its daily makeup. It now has a circulation very much larger than that of any other American newspaper, and enjoys an income which it is at all times prepared to spend liberally for the benefit of its readers. People of all conditions of life and all ways of thinking buy and read THE SUN; and they all derive satisfaction of some sort from its columns, for they keep on buying and reading it.

In its comments on men and affairs, THE SUN believes that the only guide of policy should be common sense, inspired by genuine American principles and backed by honesty of purpose. For this reason it is, and will continue to be, absolutely independent of party, class, clique, organization, or interest. It is for all, but of none. It will continue to praise what is good and reprobate what is evil, taking care that its language is to the point and plain, beyond the possibility of being misunderstood....

The year 1880 will be one in which no patriotic American can afford to close his eyes to public affairs. It is impossible to exaggerate the importance of the political events which it has in store, or the necessity of resolute vigilance on the part of every citizen who desires to preserve the Government that the founders gave us. The debates and acts of Congress, the utterances of the press, the exciting contests of the Republican and Democratic parties, now nearly equal in strength throughout the country, the varying drift of public sentiment, will all bear directly and effectively upon the twenty-fourth Presidential election, to be held in November.... THE SUN will be on hand to chronicle the facts as they are developed, and to exhibit them clearly and fearlessly in their relations to expediency and right.

Thus, with a habit of philosophical good humor in looking at the minor affairs of life, and in great things a steadfast purpose to maintain the rights of the people and principles of the Constitution against all aggressors, THE SUN is prepared to write a truthful, instructive, and at the same time entertaining history of 1880.[31]

The advertisements of other daily papers also stressed the importance of brand location and circulation. The *New York Star* ad conveyed its market niche in three sentences: "A Democratic daily, published every day in the year. The largest circulation of any Democratic morning newspaper in the state of New York. Its large and constantly increasing circulation makes it a valuable medium for all advertisers."[32]

The difficulties of verifying circulation claims made some newspapers offer their printing technology as a signal for the size of their circulation. The *Kansas City Times* ad said the paper "... is a Western newspaper enjoying a larger daily and weekly circulation than all Omaha, St. Joseph, Atchison, Leavenworth, and Topeka papers combined—a statement that can be verified at any time by personal inspection of our subscription books and subscription lists, and by a visit to our press-rooms where the paper is printed. It is the only paper between St. Louis and San Francisco printed on a Four Cylinder Hoe Press, and with two or three exceptions, the only paper in the West that throws open the doors of its press-rooms to the public, where its mammoth weekly edition of 34,560 copies is printed."[33] Larger papers stressed their greater ability to reach consumers and often translated their advertising prices into a cost "per thousand actual circulation."[34] Papers also highlighted for companies the desirability of advertising in cities with larger populations. The advertisement for *The Minneapolis Morning Tribune* noted that:

As the U.S. Census shows, Minneapolis is now, by many thousands, the largest city in Minnesota or west and North of Chicago and Milwaukee; it is growing faster than any other considerable city in American, and it is the principal business center of the New Northwest, which is advancing in population and wealth more rapidly and substantially than any other section of the United States. *The Tribune* is a first-class metropolitan morning journal, of the same size and form as the New York *Herald*. It is the newspaper representative and exponent of Minneapolis,—the only morning paper published in this city of nearly 50,000, the leading Republican daily northwest of Chicago, and has a general circulation throughout the whole of Minnesota and adjacent portions of Iowa, Wisconsin and Dakota, a region embracing an unusually intelligent population of nearly 1,500,000.[35]

Analyzing the Growth of Press Independence

If you were a businessman in 1880 trying to place advertisements in local papers, what type of information would you be interested in learning about these publications? With travel difficult and terrain expansive, you might not be able to visit each of the cities and counties you wanted to reach with your ad. To allocate your advertising budget, you would want to know facts about a paper such as its circulation, political affiliation, price, establishment date, layout size and number of pages, and advertising rates. You might also want to know about the local market—its population, political composition, and main industries. In the best of all worlds, you could match data on all the publications in an area with its demographic information, make your decisions about ad placement, and have someone execute these purchases with the individual papers across the country. The Philadelphia firm of N. W. Ayer and Son recognized the demand for this service and began in 1880 to publish the *American Newspaper Annual*. The firm acted as a go-between for advertisers and newspapers. By negotiating with multiple newspapers for multiple clients, N. W. Ayer economized on transaction costs and gave firms the ability to reach consumers across a state or region. The information assembled for advertisers in the *American Newspaper Annual* offers a yearly picture of publications in each county in the United States. To analyze the changing nature of the news, I will use the Ayer data and other advertising agent information to describe the market for daily political newspapers in the 50 largest cities in 1870, 1880, 1890, and 1900.[36]

The popularity of independent daily newspapers increased markedly between 1870 and 1880, and continued to grow through 1900. Table 2.1 shows that in 1870 the partisan press still dominated daily newspaper markets in the 50 most populous cities. Democratic papers accounted for nearly a third of all papers and total daily circulations, while Republican papers comprised 54.5%

TABLE 2.1
Political Affiliations of Daily Papers in the Fifty Largest Cities

	Number of Papers	Total Daily Circulation	% of Political Papers	% of Total Circulation
1870				
Democratic	58	429,850	32.6	31.1
Republican	97	597,510	54.5	43.2
Independent	23	357,200	12.9	25.8
Independent+	23	357,200	12.9	25.8
Total Political Papers	178	1,384,560	—	—
1880				
Democratic	72	528,320	28.7	21.8
Republican	89	547,680	35.5	22.6
Independent	74	1,278,570	29.5	52.7
Independent+	85	1,339,190	33.9	55.2
Total Political Papers	251	2,427,730	—	—
1890				
Democratic	84	1,191,050	26.7	21.6
Republican	86	1,360,940	27.3	24.7
Independent	113	2,664,820	35.9	48.3
Independent+	138	2,939,610	43.8	53.3
Total Political Papers	315	5,518,160	—	—
1900				
Democratic	70	1,229,230	21.8	14.9
Republican	91	2,621,120	28.4	31.7
Independent	125	3,623,520	38.9	43.8
Independent+	152	4,382,760	47.4	53.0
Total Political Papers	321	8,275,020	—	—

of papers and 43.2% of circulations. Between 1870 and 1880, however, Independent newspapers jumped from 12.9% of total papers to 29.5%; the share of total daily circulations for independent newspapers grew from 25.8% to 52.7%. If one includes the papers listing themselves as "Independent Democratic" or "Independent Republican" as part of a broader independent brand name category (i.e., the Independent+ group), nonpartisan papers accounted for 33.9% of papers and 55.2% of total circulation in 1880. The attachment of newspapers to partisan loyalties continued to diminish so that by 1900, 47.4% of papers were Independent+. The overall number of political dailies offered grew from 178 in 1870 to 321 in 1900.[37] Newspaper consumption grew even faster than population expansion in the fifty largest cities over this time. In

1870 there were .25 political newspapers circulated each day per person, a figure that increased to .31 in 1880, .50 in 1890, and .55 in 1900.

Most major cities in the United States today have a single local daily newspaper. By contrast in the late nineteenth century there were multiple daily papers covering current events that vied for readers' attentions. In table 2.2, I divide the largest fifty cities into thirds, based on population size, to examine newspaper market averages. In 1870, smaller cities had a Democratic and a Republican newspaper but no independent outlet. The largest cities averaged 6 political daily newspapers, which broke down to 2 Democratic, 3 Republican, and 1 independent. By 1880 independent papers appeared in medium-size cities too, which averaged 1 Democratic, 2 Republican, and 1 independent newspapers. In cities with populations in the top third of the 1880 sample, there were on average 8 daily political newspapers contending for readers. In these largest cities, the mean number of Independent+ papers (3.2) was now greater than the mean number of Democratic (2.4) or Republican (2.5) outlets. By 1900 the mean number of Independent+ papers was 1.5 in small cities, 2.2 in medium, and 5.5 in large cities.[38]

Within each market size category, circulation per resident increased and the concentration of newspaper sales among brands decreased over time. From 1870 to 1900 the number of daily papers circulated per person increased from .20 to .42 in small cities and from .30 to .61 in large cities. This is consistent with the notion that reading the daily newspaper became more prevalent in cities as newspapers became cheaper and papers of different varieties competed for readers' attention.[39] Competition, measured by the spread of sales across papers in a city, increased over this time period too. One way to represent the dispersion of sales among papers in a market is to calculate the sum of the squared market shares of the local political newspapers. This figure, called the Herfindahl-Hirschman Index of market concentration, or HHI, ranges from 0 for competitive markets where individual firms have extremely small market shares to 1 for markets where one firm accounts for all sales. This sales concentration index dropped from .58 to .42 for small markets from 1870 to 1900 and from .38 to .23 in the largest markets. The largest cities had the least concentrated markets, with figures in 1900 of .09 for New York, .11 for Chicago and Pittsburgh, and .12 for Philadelphia.[40]

If newspaper owners chose to produce nonpartisan papers based on economic considerations, then the five Ws predict that independent papers should differ from Republican or Democratic outlets in systematic ways relating to audience size, printing costs, and advertising markets. Table 2.3 confirms these differences. The mean city size for independent papers was higher, consistent with the idea that larger populations offered a greater opportunity to achieve scale-economy size circulations and generated more opportunities for advertising. In terms of audience composition, Republican papers had the highest

TABLE 2.2
Newspaper Market Averages by City Size

City Size	City Population	Number of Political Papers	Number of Democratic Papers	Number of Republican Papers	Number of Independent Papers	Number of Independent+ Papers	Daily Circulation per Person	Circulation Concentration Index
1870								
Small	30,870	2.1	0.8	1.3	0.1	0.1	.20	.58
Medium	53,460	3.3	1.2	1.8	0.3	0.3	.25	.46
Large	267,640	5.9	1.8	3.1	1.1	1.1	.30	.38
1880								
Small	43,310	2.6	0.9	1.0	0.5	0.7	.19	.59
Medium	73,970	4.5	1.1	1.9	1.0	1.3	.24	.39
Large	345,540	8.2	2.4	2.5	2.9	3.2	.30	.25
1890								
Small	68,400	4.2	1.7	1.2	1.1	1.3	.27	.33
Medium	119,100	5.0	1.3	1.5	1.5	2.1	.43	.33
Large	499,310	10.4	2.3	2.6	4.4	5.2	.54	.21
1900								
Small	91,290	3.8	1.3	1.0	1.4	1.5	.42	.42
Medium	144,230	5.1	1.1	1.8	1.6	2.2	.54	.28
Large	669,900	10.7	1.9	2.8	4.5	5.5	.61	.23

Note: For each year, city size categories are defined by dividing the top fifty cities into thirds based on population size.

TABLE 2.3
Mean Characteristics of Daily Papers by Affiliation

	Democratic Papers	Republican Papers	Independent Papers	Independent + Papers
1870				
City Population (000)	209.7	202.5	330.1	330.1
% Democratic Presidential votes	52.5	48.8	54.4	54.4
% Republican Presidential votes	47.5	51.2	45.6	45.6
% Foreign-born Population	29.4	30.6	35.4	35.4
% Black Population	10.1	4.1	6.5	6.5
Paper Pages	4.5	4.3	4.6	4.6
Paper Size (Sq. Inches)	5,070	4,940	4,020	4,020
Circulation	7,540	6,710	16,240	16,240
Annual Subscription Rate ($)	8.92	8.43	8.20	8.20
Subscription Rate ($) per 100 Sq. Inches	0.19	0.19	0.22	0.22
Subscription Revenue ($)	76,170	65,750	137,750	137,750
Subscription Revenue ($) per Sq. Inch	14.03	11.96	38.23	38.23
Establishment Date	1841	1847	1855	1855
1880				
City Population (000)	275.5	247.8	389.1	360.6
% Democratic Presidential votes	52.2	46.3	48.5	48.6
% Republican Presidential votes	46.7	52.4	50.3	50.1
% Foreign-born Population	23.5	26.3	29.5	28.8
% Black Population	8.8	3.3	4.5	5.3
Paper Pages	5.1	5.2	4.7	4.8
Paper Size (Sq. Inches)	5,690	5,790	4,530	4,750
Circulation	8,000	7,020	20,620	18,600
Annual Subscription Rate ($)	8.07	8.09	7.23	7.51
Subscription Rate ($) per 100 Sq. Inches	0.16	0.16	0.18	0.18
Subscription Revenue ($)	62,360	62,600	139,360	128,790
Subscription Revenue ($) per Sq. Inch	12.12	11.53	37.42	33.29
Establishment Date	1854	1850	1861	1861
Advertising Rate ($) Ten Lines, One Month	12.24	12.23	18.85	17.76
Cost per Thousand Readers ($)	2.39	2.60	2.40	2.60
1890				
City Population (000)	296.2	339.2	515.7	481.6
% Democratic Presidential votes	50.6	47.2	50.2	50.2
% Republican Presidential votes	47.7	50.6	47.8	47.8
% Foreign-born Population	22.9	27.7	28.7	28.9

TABLE 2.3 *Continued*

	Democratic Papers	Republican Papers	Independent Papers	Independent + Papers
% Black Population	11.8	2.9	4.3	4.5
Paper Pages	5.9	6.7	5.7	5.9
Paper Size (Sq. Inches)	3,980	4,480	3,930	3,960
Circulation	17,520	16,800	26,650	24,290
Annual Subscription Rate ($)	6.36	6.49	5.46	5.5
Subscription Rate ($) per 100 Sq. Inches	0.17	0.17	0.15	0.15
Subscription Revenue ($)	107,520	111,360	129,060	119,930
Subscription Revenue ($) per Sq. Inch	27.72	26.86	36.84	33.60
Establishment Date	1864	1854	1869	1868
1900				
City Population (000)	523.7	580.3	876.8	798.4
% Democratic Presidential votes	48.9	41.5	44.6	44.1
% Republican Presidential votes	48.6	55.1	52.2	52.7
% Foreign-born Population	20.5	25.8	25.4	25.7
% Black Population	10.1	3.0	4.0	3.9
Paper Pages	9.0	9.5	8.6	8.7
Paper Size (Sq. Inches)	3,720	3,920	3,560	3,610
Circulation	21,190	30,840	35,180	33,970
Annual Subscription Rate ($)	4.79	5.06	4.41	4.56
Subscription Rate ($) per 100 Sq. Inches	0.14	0.15	0.14	0.15
Subscription Revenue ($)	105,950	141,010	155,030	149,060
Subscription Revenue ($) per Sq. Inch	26.41	34.13	36.34	34.61
Establishment Date	1865	1860	1872	1871

percentage of Republican voters in their markets and Democratic outlets operated in cities with the highest percentage of Democratic voters. If one views editorial independence as a middle-of-the-road approach between Republican and Democratic brands, it is interesting to note that independent papers operated in cities midway between the poles established by the partisan outlets. In 1880, 1890, and 1900, the average percentage of Democratic voters in the cities of independent newspapers was midway between the average of Democratic voters for Democratic papers and that for Republican papers. The same pattern emerges for a comparison of Republican votes—independent papers had an average Republican voter percentage in the market that was between the figures for the partisan outlets. Independent papers also had more recent establishment dates than those of either party, which one would expect if changes in printing technology and advertising made new entrants select a nonpartisan brand location to compete with the incumbent partisan papers.[41]

Independent papers did have larger mean circulations throughout this period. For 1870 and 1880, the mean circulation of a nonpartisan paper was twice the figure averaged for a paper with a Democratic or Republican affiliation. Independent papers offered readers a lower annual subscription price, perhaps because of the cost advantages afforded by scale economies or the additional revenues brought by higher advertising. Independent papers were smaller in terms of number of pages and total square inches of newspaper.[42] The lower subscription costs expanded the potential reach of independent papers to readers with lower incomes. The lower prices were offset by higher circulations so that total subscription revenues were higher for independent papers. Subscription revenue per square inch was much higher for these outlets. In 1880, Democratic papers averaged $12.12 per square inch and Republican papers averaged $11.53. Independent outlets, however, garnered $37.42 in annual subscription revenues per square inch. With the high fixed costs of producing a paper's first edition and the low marginal costs of additional copies, these differences in revenue per square inch show the potential for profits attached to reaching higher circulations.

Higher circulations also translated into higher advertising rates. In 1880, independent outlets charged a mean of $18.85 for ten lines of advertising per month, versus $12.24 for Democratic papers and $12.23 for Republicans. Advertisers paid higher prices per ad but got comparable prices on a per-impression basis with the independent papers. The cost of reaching 1,000 subscribers with ten lines of advertising for a month was $2.40 for independent papers and $2.39 for Democratic papers. The cost per thousand readers was higher for Republican outlets ($2.60), which may reflect a higher willingness to pay to reach the audience demographic attracted to these papers.

Changes across time are also evident within each brand location. For papers in each category, nominal annual subscription prices dropped over time. The average cost of an annual subscription to a nonpartisan paper dropped from $8.20 in 1870 to $4.41 in 1900. Though the number of pages in newspapers expanded during this time period, pages became smaller so that the average square inches per paper declined from 1870 to 1900. One way to express the cost of news to a reader is to divide the annual subscription price by the total size of a paper, which yields a price per 100 daily inches of newspaper. This cost declined for each type of paper. For independent outlets, the figure dropped from 22¢ in 1870 to 14¢ in 1900. This is consistent with changes in printing technology and drops in paper costs leading to lower prices for news consumers.[43] During this time period the mean circulation for each type of paper increased. While independent papers were at least twice the size of partisan papers in 1870, by 1900 the size gap had narrowed so that mean circulations were 35,180 for independent, 30,840 for Republican, and 21,190 for Democratic papers.

TABLE 2.4
Mean Financial Characteristics of Daily Papers by Affiliation (1900$)

	Democratic Papers	Republican Papers	Independent Papers	Independent + Papers
1870				
Annual Subscription Rate ($)	5.87	5.55	5.39	5.39
Subscription Rate ($) per 100 Sq.				
Inches	0.13	0.13	0.14	0.14
Subscription Revenue ($)	50,110	43,260	90,630	90,630
Subscription Revenue ($) per Sq.				
Inch	9.23	7.87	25.15	25.15
1880				
Annual Subscription Rate ($)	6.96	6.97	6.23	6.47
Subscription Rate ($) per 100 Sq.				
Inches	0.14	0.14	0.16	0.16
Subscription Revenue ($)	53,760	53,970	120,140	111,030
Subscription Revenue ($) per Sq.				
Inch	10.45	9.94	32.26	28.70
Advertising Rate ($) Ten Lines, One				
Month	10.55	10.54	16.25	15.31
Cost Per Thousand Readers ($)	2.06	2.24	2.07	2.24
1890				
Annual Subscription Rate ($)	5.89	6.01	5.06	5.09
Subscription Rate ($) per 100 Sq.				
Inches	0.16	0.16	0.14	0.14
Subscription Revenue ($)	99,560	103,110	119,500	111,050
Subscription Revenue ($) per Sq.				
Inch	25.67	24.87	34.11	31.11
1900				
Annual Subscription Rate ($)	4.79	5.06	4.41	4.56
Subscription Rate ($) per 100 Sq.				
Inches	0.14	0.15	0.14	0.15
Subscription Revenue ($)	105,950	141,010	155,030	149,060
Subscription Revenue ($) per Sq.				
Inch	26.41	34.13	36.34	34.61

If party affiliation affects a reader's willingness to consume a partisan newspaper, then one would expect the popularity of Democratic or Republican papers in a city to depend on voting patterns in the market. If owners select a nonpartisan brand in the hopes of reaching nonaligned readers and members of both parties to achieve large-scale circulation, city size will be important to the existence and success of nonpartisan outlets since larger cities offer greater possibilities for economies of scale and advertising. Table 2.5 measures the relative success of different types of newspapers in a market by examining how the percentage of newspapers with a given brand location varied by market from 1870 to 1900. For both the Democratic and Republican newspaper categories, the percentage of voters who cast ballots for a Democratic presidential candidate in the most recent presidential election predicts the popularity of the party press. In 1880, for example, an increase in the percentage of Democratic votes in a city by 1 percentage point was associated with an increase of 1.96% points in the Democratic share of newspaper circulation and a 1.5% point decrease in the Republican share of circulation. The percentage of Democratic voters in a market did not influence the success of the independent press, whose fortunes depended on the size of the market. The higher the population of a city, the greater the share of circulation held by independent outlets.

One could argue that the path of causation runs from the newspapers to the voters, so that the Democratic newspapers appear to fare well in Democratic areas because the party newspapers increase the percentage of voters who choose Democratic candidates. To take into account this possibility, I examine in table 2.6 how audience demographics not influenced by reading a newspaper (i.e., percentage of a city's population that is foreign born or black) were associated with the relative success of different categories of papers. The results confirm that particular brands of news coverage appealed to distinct city audiences, and that factors that increased Democratic circulation often decreased Republican circulation. The higher the percentage of blacks in a city, the larger the circulation share earned by Democratic papers. Since Southern cities contained higher percentages of blacks and were strongly Democratic (among white voters) at this time, it is not surprising to find the percentage of a city's black population being associated with success for Democratic news outlets. For independent papers, city size remained a good predictor of the share of circulation earned by nonpartisan papers.

The results for 1900 demonstrate the interactions between audience demographics and newspaper popularity. As the percentage of blacks in a city increased by 1 percentage point, the share of circulation earned by Democratic papers grew by 1.8 percentage points. These gains were balanced out by losses in the other categories. A 1 percentage point increase in black population was associated with a drop of .52 percentage points in the Republican circulation share and 1.36 percentage points in the independent share. As the percentage of a city's population born abroad increased by 1 percentage point, the share of Republican circulation grew by .65 percentage points and the share of independent circulation dropped by 1.25 percentage points. An increase of a city's population size by 10,000 residents increased the independent circulation share by .2 percentage points.

Part of the argument that owners chose nonpartisan affiliation as a business decision rests on the assertion that the independent brand name helped a pa-

TABLE 2.5
Predicting Brand Popularity by Audience Politics

	% Democratic Circulation	% Republican Circulation	% Independent Circulation
1870			
(N = 44 Cities)			
City Population (000)	−0.01	−0.03	0.04*
	(0.03)	(0.03)	(0.02)
% Democratic Presidential Votes	0.71**	−0.60*	−0.11
	(0.30)	(0.32)	(0.22)
Adjusted R^2	0.08	0.08	0.04
Mean % Affiliation Circulation	35.3	56.3	8.5
1880			
(N = 48 Cities)			
City Population (000)	−0.02	−0.02	0.05**
	(0.01)	(0.02)	(0.02)
% Democratic Presidential Votes	1.96***	−1.50***	−0.29
	(0.37)	(0.45)	(0.52)
Adjusted R^2	0.36	0.22	0.07
Mean % Affiliation Circulation	26.7	37.6	29.0
1890			
(N = 47 Cities)			
City Population (000)	−0.02*	2.21e-3	0.02*
	(0.01)	(0.01)	(0.01)
% Democratic Presidential Votes	0.91	−1.27**	0.27
	(0.57)	(0.52)	(0.54)
Adjusted R^2	0.06	0.08	0.04
Mean % Affiliation Circulation	27.9	32.6	31.9
1900			
(N = 47 Cities)			
City Population (000)	−0.01**	8.50e-4	0.01*
	(5.93e-3)	(4.34e-3)	(6.65e-3)
% Democratic Presidential Votes	1.29***	−0.90***	−0.23
	(0.25)	(0.18)	(0.28)
Adjusted R^2	0.38	0.32	0.05
Mean % Affiliation Circulation	26.3	29.9	35.6

Note: Standard errors in parentheses. *** = statistically significant at the .01 level; ** = significant at the .05 level; * = significant at the .10 level. Each specification also included an intercept term.

TABLE 2.6
Predicting Brand Popularity by Audience Demographics

	% Democratic Circulation	% Republican Circulation	% Independent Circulation
1870			
(N = 45 Cities)			
City Population (000)	0.01	−0.04	0.02
	(0.03)	(0.03)	(0.02)
% Foreign-born Population	0.32	−0.69	0.37
	(0.49)	(0.49)	(0.43)
% Black Population	1.02***	−1.23***	0.21
	(0.30)	(0.30)	(0.26)
Adjusted R^2	0.21	0.29	0.01
Mean % Affiliation Circulation	34.5	55.6	9.9
1880			
(N = 48 Cities)			
City Population (000)	0.01	−0.04**	0.04*
	(0.02)	(0.02)	(0.02)
% Foreign-born Population	−0.90*	−0.04	0.58
	(0.48)	(0.50)	(0.59)
% Black Population	0.26	−0.94***	0.39
	(0.33)	(0.34)	(0.40)
Adjusted R^2	0.15	0.23	0.06
Mean % Affiliation Circulation	26.7	37.6	29.0
1890			
(N = 47 Cities)			
City Population (000)	−0.01	−9.01e-3	0.03**
	(0.01)	(0.01)	(0.01)
% Foreign-born Population	0.29	−0.02	−1.01**
	(0.37)	(0.42)	(0.43)
% Black Population	1.57**	−0.97***	−1.03***
	(0.31)	(0.36)	(0.37)
Adjusted R^2	0.48	0.20	0.17
Mean % Affiliation Circulation	27.9	32.6	31.9
1900			
(N = 47 Cities)			
City Population (000)	8.07e-3	6.82e-3	0.02***
	(5.17e-3)	(4.68e-3)	(6.32e-3)
% Foreign-born Population	0.14	0.65**	−1.25***
	(0.36)	(0.32)	(0.43)
% Black Population	1.80***	−0.52*	−1.36***
	(0.29)	(0.27)	(0.36)
Adjusted R^2	0.59	0.32	0.26
Mean % Affiliation Circulation	26.3	29.9	35.6

Note: Standard errors in parentheses. *** = statistically significant at the .01 level; ** = significant at the .05 level; * = significant at the .10 level. Each specification also included an intercept term.

TABLE 2.7

Who Achieves Large-Scale Circulation? Change in Paper's Probability of Achieving Top 20% Circulation

	1870	1880	1890	1900
City Population 10% Above Mean vs. 10% Below Mean	.03***	.02***	.02***	.01***
Independent vs. Partisan	.08	.11**	.09***	.03
Foreign Language vs. English	−.14*	−.15***	−.19***	−.20***

Note: Change in probability = probability of top 20% circulation for paper with first characteristic—probability for paper with second characteristic. Evaluated at the means for all characteristics, the predicted probability of top 20% circulation is .16 for 1870, .12 for 1880, .09 for 1890, and .12 for 1900. *** = statistically significant at the .01 level, ** = .05 significant at the .05 level, * = .10 significant at the .10 level. All regressions included an intercept term.

per achieve large-scale circulation. Table 2.7 explores what factors influenced the ability of a paper to achieve large-scale circulation, which I define as a circulation that would place a paper in the top 20% of newspapers based on circulation in the cities examined. The circulation cutoff for a paper to be included in the top 20% grew across time from 10,000 in 1870, 13,000 in 1880, 30,000 in 1890, and 44,000 in 1900. These larger papers accounted for a significant share of the total newspaper circulations, that is, 64% of all daily circulations in 1870 and 59% of all circulations in 1900. To predict which papers gained enough circulation to land in the top 20%, I estimated a model that included a city's population size, an indicator for whether the paper was independent versus partisan, and a variable for whether the paper was published in a foreign language or in English.[44] City size was a statistically significant predictor of a paper's ability to reach large scale circulation in each of the years examined. The results in table 2.7 indicate that for a paper with mean characteristics, if one compares (in 1870) a paper in a city with a population 10% below the average population with one 10% above that, the likelihood of gaining large-scale circulation would increase by 3 percentage points. The impact of publishing in a foreign language is extremely large. In 1880, for example, the probability a paper would reach large-scale circulation dropped by 15 percentage points if it published in a language other than English. Table 2.7 also indicates that, controlling for city size and language, a paper that chose editorial independence as a brand location was much more likely to achieve economies of scale than a partisan paper in 1880 and 1890. For a paper in a city of mean population size in 1880, if the owners chose an independent affiliation the probability the paper would reach large-scale circulation was 11 percentage points higher.

The benefits of achieving large-scale circulation were increasing throughout this time period. Table 2.8, which translates all dollar figures into 1900 dollars, demonstrates this by comparing the characteristics of papers in the second

TABLE 2.8
Advantages of Large-Scale Circulation (1900 Dollars)

	Means for papers with circulations ranked 21–40% in size percentiles vs. papers ranked 81–100% in size percentiles			
	1870		*1880*	
Annual Subscription Rate ($)	5.41	6.49	6.66	6.76
Subscription Rate ($) per 100 Square Inches	0.14	0.13	0.16	0.15
Subscription Revenue ($) per Square Inch	3.77	32.64	5.25	51.71
Advertising Rate ($) Ten Lines, One Month			7.66	28.49
Cost per Thousand Readers ($)			2.32	0.93
Circulation	2,780	25,300	3,400	35,800
	1890		*1900*	
Annual Subscription Rate ($)	5.79	5.20	4.99	4.49
Subscription Rate ($) per 100 Square Inches	0.16	0.13	0.16	0.10
Subscription Revenue ($) per Square Inch	8.80	80.15	14.17	82.05
Circulation	5,620	63,140	9,360	87,950

quantile of circulations (e.g., those whose circulations ranked in the 21–40 percentiles) with those in the largest quantile (e.g., papers in the top 20% of circulations). Large circulations in theory bring many advantages, such as the opportunity to use press sizes that confer scale economies in cost and the ability to attract more advertisers because of more readers. The evidence in table 2.8 is consistent with these advantages. While prices of larger papers were initially higher than those for papers with smaller circulations, by 1890 the annual subscription price was lower for larger papers. If one defines the price of news to a reader in terms of a subscription rate per 100 square inches of daily news, larger papers delivered the news at lower prices in 1870 (13¢ per 100 square inches) than smaller papers (14¢). Decreasing costs and increasing advertising revenue allowed newspapers in both categories to drop their subscription prices over time. The gap in effective reader prices between large and small papers increased over time because of the increasing importance of scale economies. By 1900, small papers charged readers 16¢ in annual subscription per 100 square inches, while large papers sold at the lower rate of 10¢ per 100 square inches.

The combination of lower subscription prices (made possible by cost advantages and advertiser support) and higher circulations translated into much higher subscription revenues per square inch of newspaper delivered. In 1870 the small papers earned $3.77 per square inch versus $32.64 for larger papers, while in 1900 the gap was $14.17 versus $82.05. The advantages of circulation in advertising are evident from the 1880 data. The larger papers, which had a mean circulation of 35,800, were able to charge $28.49 for ten lines of advertising per month, versus $7.66 per month for the smaller outlets (mean circulation 3,400). The higher ad prices still translated into lower costs for advertisers. The cost of reaching a thousand subscribers for a month with an ad was $2.32 in the smaller papers. Advertisers using the large-scale papers could reach a thousand subscribers at the lower rate of $.93.

If large circulations brought scale economies and these economies were passed on to consumers through lower prices, one would expect prices to drop as circulation increased. Table 2.9 confirms this pattern held for papers in the fifty largest cities in 1870 and 1900. The cost of news to a reader, expressed in annual subscription cost per 100 square inches of newspaper, fell as the circu-

TABLE 2.9
Circulation Impacts on Reader Costs and Paper Revenues

	Subscription Rate ($) per 100 Square Inches	Subscription Revenue ($) per Square Inch
1870		
Paper Circulation (000)	−2.40e-3**	0.80***
	(1.17e-3)	(0.22)
(Paper Circulation (000))^2	3.71e-5**	0.02***
	(1.67e-5)	(3.10e-3)
Foreign-Language Paper	0.04***	1.22
	(0.02)	(2.81)
Adjusted R^2	0.06	0.79
Number of Papers	159	159
1900		
Paper Circulation (000)	−1.31e-3***	1.25***
	(2.96e-4)	(0.07)
(Paper Circulation (000))^2	4.67e-6***	−2.78e-3***
	(1.61e-6)	(3.90e-4)
Foreign-Language Paper	0.08***	4.97**
	(0.01)	(2.52)
Adjusted R^2	0.31	0.75
Number of Papers	277	277

Note: Standard errors in parentheses. *** = statistically significant at the .01 level; ** = significant at the .05 level; * = significant at the .10 level. Each specification also included an intercept term.

lation of a paper increased in 1870. In other words, readers of larger papers enjoyed lower prices for a given amount of reading material. The same pattern still held in 1900—larger papers charged readers lower effective prices per amount of newsprint. In both years foreign language papers charged readers higher prices per 100 square inches. This may reflect higher costs of assembling information, or may indicate that foreign language papers faced lower competition in each market because there were fewer reading options for those who could not read papers in English. In both 1870 and 1900 revenues per square inch increased with circulation, showing that as a paper added readers it added to total subscription revenues. This impact grew at an increasing rate in 1870, but by 1900 (with more papers contending in the local markets) revenues grew with circulation but at a decreasing rate.

In 1880 N. W. Ayer and Son's *American Newspaper Annual* provided information on advertising rates by paper, so one can explore how the market for advertising in daily newspapers worked for that year. Table 2.10 shows that as city size increased, newspapers charged more per ten lines of monthly advertising. Larger cities had more advertisers and were more attractive to regional or national advertisers, so papers could charge more per ad. For a given city size, a newspaper was able to charge more per ten lines if those lines reached a greater number of readers. The results indicate that the ad rate per month grew by 45¢ with a thousand reader increase in circulation. The table indicates that there was no statistically significant impact on ad rates of brand location. For a given level of readers, advertisers did not pay more (or less) to reach those who read independent newspapers versus readers of Democratic or Republican outlets. Foreign language papers did have lower ad prices, which may reflect a lower

TABLE 2.10
The Market for Advertising in Daily Papers, 1880

	Advertising Rate ($) for Ten Lines, One Month	Cost per Thousand Readers ($)
City Population (000)	0.02***	1.50e-3**
	(1.92e-3)	(6.81e-4)
Paper Circulation (000)	0.45***	−0.05***
	(0.04)	(0.01)
Foreign Language Paper	−3.97***	1.35***
	(1.40)	(0.50)
Independent Paper	-0.54	0.28
	(1.30)	(0.46)
Adjusted R^2	0.71	0.11
Number of Papers	220	220

Note: Standard errors in parentheses. *** = statistically significant at the .01 level; ** = significant at the .05 level; * = significant at the .10 level. Each specification also included an intercept term.

TABLE 2.11
Determinants of Editorial Workers per State, 1880

	Editorial Workers Employed in the State, 1880
State Population (000)	0.03***
	(0.01)
Publications	0.57***
	(0.09)
Dailies Subscription Revenues ($000)	0.03
	(0.04)
Dailies Advertising Revenues ($000)	0.08**
	(0.03)
Weeklies/Others Subscription Revenues ($000)	0.08***
	(0.02)
Weeklies/Others Advertising Revenues ($000)	0.23***
	(0.08)
Adjusted R^2	.99
Number of States	45

Note: Standard errors in parentheses. *** = statistically significant at the .01 level; ** = significant at the .05 level; * = significant at the .10 level. Each specification also included an intercept term.

willingness to pay to influence the purchasing decisions of immigrant readers. In terms of the cost of reaching a thousand readers with a month of advertising, advertisers in larger cities were willing to pay more to influence the purchasing decisions of these readers. The cost per reader declined for those advertising in larger papers. The cost of reaching a thousand readers declined by 5¢ for each additional thousand readers of a paper.

How did these changes in news markets from 1870 to 1900 affect the quantity and quality of the news? To explore this question I use the number of journalists working in an area as a proxy for the attention and expenditures devoted to news gathering. For the 1880 census the U.S. government commissioned a special study of the newspaper industry.[45] In table 2.11 I draw upon the data collected there at the state level to show the relationship between resources and reporting. Those states with more population or more publications had more editorial workers involved in producing newspapers (daily and weekly) and other periodicals. Controlling for these factors, states with higher advertising revenues produced by daily or weekly newspapers were able to support more editorial workers. An additional $12,000 in advertising revenues from daily newspapers, or $4,000 in advertising from weeklies, translated into an additional writer or editor covering the news in a state.

In 1870 and 1880 the U.S. Census also collected information on the number of journalists working in each of the top thirty and top fifty cities by popula-

TABLE 2.12
Journalists Employed per City, 1870 and 1880

	Number of Journalists in the City	
	1870	1880
Native-Born Population (000)	0.16	−0.73***
	(0.13)	(0.24)
Foreign-Born Population (000)	0.88***	1.49***
	(0.12)	(0.28)
Black Population (000)	0.06	1.17*
	(0.31)	(0.58)
Farms (00)	−0.69***	−0.50
	(0.23)	(0.39)
Manufacturing Establishments (00)	-1.66***	5.17***
	(0.57)	(1.68)
Adjusted R^2	0.90	0.87
Number of Cities	29	48
	1870	1880
Nonpolitical Papers	10.63***	30.51***
	(3.41)	(7.89)
Democratic Papers	4.95	20.46**
	(10.04)	(8.37)
Republican Papers	9.41	8.02
	(7.59)	(7.51)
Independent + Papers	13.28*	24.64***
	(6.84)	(8.51)
Adjusted R^2	0.53	0.75
Number of Cities	29	48

Note: Standard errors in parentheses. *** = statistically significant at the .01 level; ** = significant at the .05 level; * = significant at the .10 level. Each specification also included an intercept
term.

tion. In table 2.12 I use two different methods to explore the determinants of
the number of journalists covering the news in a given city. The first approach
is based on city demographics. In both years an increase in the number of foreign-born residents resulted in an increase in the number of journalists working in a city. This is consistent with the presence of specialized newspapers
published in foreign languages in areas with larger immigrant populations. In
1880, an increase of two thousand foreign-born residents was associated with
an increase of three journalists working in the city. A one thousand person increase in the black population of a city brought an increase of one journalist,
consistent either with an increase in publications aimed at black readers or a
correlation of black population with readership for Democratic papers in-

creasing employment for reporters. Cities with more farms employed fewer journalists in 1870, as did areas with more manufacturing establishments, perhaps because in this era many papers were aimed at professional or managerial classes. With the growth of lower priced papers aimed at broad readership, however, in 1880 the presence of manufacturing establishments was associated with an increase in the number of journalists working in a city.

The data on working journalists in a city also provides some information on the relative editorial sizes of different types of outlets. If independent papers were larger in circulation and this translated into more resources spent on editorial output, one would expect the addition of an independent newspaper to bring greater growth in journalists' employment than the addition of a partisan paper. Table 2.12 bears this out. In 1870 the addition of another Independent+ newspaper resulted in an increase of thirteen journalists in the city, versus smaller added increments for Democratic or Republican newspapers. By 1880 independent newspapers had higher circulations and brought even more journalists to an area. The addition of an Independent+ outlet resulted in twenty-five more journalists working in a city, compared to twenty-one for a Democratic paper.

Employment of journalists also provides some clues about the relative content of independent versus partisan newspapers. Editorial independence could have several different meanings as a brand location. A newspaper could claim to be nonpartisan if it covered current events in a balanced manner or made its decisions without consideration of party positions on an issue. A newspaper might also avoid partisan disputes by downplaying political events and focusing on other news elements, such as human interest stories or local crime coverage. The evidence presented in table 2.13 indicates that editorial independence did not mean a paper failed to cover politics, at least by one measure of political coverage. The Congressional Directory during this time period listed the names of correspondents covering Congress and listed the papers they represented.[46] I matched these data with the daily newspapers in the top fifty cities to see which outlets employed a correspondent to cover legislative activities in

TABLE 2.13
Who Covered Congress?

	% of Papers in Affiliation Category with at Least One Congressional Correspondent			
	1870	1880	1890	1900
Democratic Papers	12.1	23.6	32.1	34.8
Republican Papers	29.9	23.6	36.0	38.5
Independent Papers	43.5	31.1	26.5	33.6
Independent + Papers	43.5	27.1	27.5	34.2

Washington, D.C. The table indicates that for 1870 and 1880 independent papers were more likely to have dedicated congressional correspondents than those with Democratic or Republican affiliations. By 1900 the percentage of papers with correspondents covering Congress was roughly equal across the affiliation categories. The driving force behind these results is that independent papers had larger circulations, generated more revenues, and thus could spend more on coverage. If one models a paper's decision to employ a congressional correspondent as a function of city size, newspaper circulation, foreign language publication, and independent affiliation, the only variable that is consistently statistically significant across these years is newspaper circulation.[47] The higher the circulation, the greater the likelihood the paper employed a congressional correspondent. In 1880 and 1890, foreign language outlets were less likely, other things being equal, to have a dedicated Washington, D.C. reporter. In the four years studied independent affiliation was only statistically significant in 1890, when independent papers were less likely to have a congressional correspondent than the partisan outlets.

Conclusions

Press independence of party affiliation is a necessary, though not sufficient, part of objective news coverage. Nonpartisan coverage of public affairs is often evoked as an ideal to be honored and a norm to be encouraged. This chapter shows, however, that press independence emerged as commercial product in predictable times and places. The 5 Ws asked in the information marketplace explain how factors, such as innovation in printing technology and the increasing role of advertising, changed the way papers covered politics. The shift from a party press to independence is a story of brand location, market segmentation, economies of scale, technological change, and advertising incentives. The following chapters explore how these same concepts explain the modern segmentation of the market for public affairs information across different media and different styles of coverage. While economics determined how politics was covered in papers at the end of the nineteenth century, by the start of the twenty-first century economic pressures raised the question of whether particular policy questions would be covered at all in many media outlets.

Chapter **3**

News Audiences: How Strong Are the Public's Interests in the Public Interest?

IT IS AN OLD DEBATE: Do the media provide people with the information they want or the information they need? This familiar question ignores the wide content variations in the publications and programs that make up "the media" and the large differences in interests among the demographic groups that constitute "the people." This chapter analyzes the variations in demand for news about government and politics across different types of media outlets and different sets of individuals.[1] The analysis focuses on the implications of the first of the five Ws: Who cares about a particular piece of information?

The basic logic of the spatial model of media content discussed in chapter 1 is clear. Tastes for different types of information vary among individuals. Programs and publications will offer combinations of hard news (e.g., coverage of government decisions) and soft news (e.g., sports or celebrity profiles) to satisfy reader and viewer demands. Interests in information are correlated with the age and gender of consumers. This means that programs targeted at particular information interests may be segmented by age and gender, so that some program audiences will be dominated by particular demographic groups.

These simple assumptions about news audiences generate clear predictions about how economics will influence news content. Consider the case of the network evening news programs. The audience for these programs consists largely of viewers aged 50+. Advertisements for products on those programs are used disproportionately by consumers aged 50+. When producers on these programs are making decisions about what stories to cover, however, it is the interests of younger viewers (particularly younger female viewers) that matter. Two economic concepts, advertiser value and marginal viewers, help explain this. Advertisers are often willing to pay more for viewers 18–34 or 35–49 for a variety of reasons. Their purchasing decisions may be more easily influenced, and they may be harder to reach since they watch less television than older viewers.[2] Since females 18–34 are particularly likely to make the purchasing decisions in their households, they are a highly valued demographic group by advertisers. This means that programmers will try to attract younger viewers to the network evening news, in part to increase news advertising revenues and in part to add these viewers to the audience that stays with the network into the prime-time schedule.

Though viewers 18–34 make up 18.3% of the regular viewers of network evening television, they constitute 38.1% of the marginal viewers (i.e., those who report that they sometimes watch the programs). In the provision of news stories, programmers may often take the interests of the average viewer for granted since these (generally older) viewers are unlikely to go elsewhere. In models of product quality, it will often be the desires of the marginal consumers that producers pay attention to since those consumers are by definition making a close decision about consuming the product.[3] This means that at the margin, network evening news producers will consider the interests of viewers 18–34 in determining what topics to cover in the news. The results in this chapter bear out these predictions about the demand for news. In terms of the number of stories presented about a set of public affairs topics in 2000, or time devoted to these topics, the networks focused on stories that interested particular demographic groups. The higher the interest in a topic among those 18–34, especially women, the greater the number of stories or time devoted by the network evening news shows. Economics predicts that the networks will factor in who cares about a topic when deciding whether it is newsworthy, since advertisers place different values on individuals and since particular individuals are likely to be the marginal viewers. The evidence presented here confirms this link between viewer interests and content selection.

The segmentation of news audiences by interests, the correlation of these interests with age and gender, and the targeting of demographic groups by news outlets and advertisers also help explain many popular criticisms of the media. When asked whether "people who decide what to put on TV news or in the newspapers are out of touch with people like me," people 50+ are more likely to agree with this than younger readers or viewers, and men are more likely to agree than women. Young women are the least likely to agree with this statement, while older men are the most likely to agree. In a world where advertisers place a higher value on attracting the attention of women than of men and pay more for audiences filled with younger rather than older consumers, one would expect that at the margin news outlets will offer content of more interest to young women than older men. This should mean that young women will be the least likely to say that the media are not responsive to their interests. In the survey data, this translates into 10.7% of women 18–34 reporting that the news media are "out of touch" with their interests versus 23.9% of men 50+.

Perceptions of media bias also have roots in economic concerns. When individuals are asked to place themselves on a scale of liberalism and conservatism, those 18–34 are more liberal than those 50+, women are more liberal than men, and women 18–34 report the highest ratings as liberals. If a media outlet selects or covers issues to attract younger or female viewers, one can expect that content will on the margin relate to liberal concerns. Survey responses again bear out these predictions. Younger viewers and female viewers are less likely to report that they see political bias in news coverage. Women 18–34 are the least likely to report that they see political bias, which is what one would expect if some news outlets were shaping content to attract these particular viewers. Of those survey respondents who identify themselves as "very liberal," only 25.3% perceive a "great deal" of political bias in news coverage. In contrast, among those who say they are "very conservative," 44.5% report there is a great deal of bias.

Political bias in media content is similar to product differentiation.[4] The survey data in this chapter do not provide a direct measure of how media content varies. The surveys do ask individuals to rate themselves on a conservative-liberal scale, with 1 being very conservative and 6 being very liberal. The respondents also rated particular programs on a scale ranging from very biased to completely objective. To construct an indirect measure of media content, I calculate the mean ideological ratings of the program audiences. By treating the ideology of the audience as an indicator of the ideological content of the program, I develop an indicator of where programs are located on the ideological spectrum. In this sense media outlets can be seen as choosing an ideological location, much like firms in other industries choose particular combinations of attributes to differentiate their products. If the audience ideology is a proxy for the "ideological content" of the program, then the audience means should capture how dispersed news outlets are in terms of political ideology. If readers and viewers define bias by the distance between a program's content and their ideology, then they should be more likely to see a program as biased if its audience's ideology is farther from their own political beliefs.

The analyses of audience ideologies suggest that media outlets do differ in their ideological content and that viewers react to this based on their own political beliefs. If programs are defined by the mean ideology ratings of their consumers, in one survey concerning sources of information about campaigns and candidates, the most conservative audience belongs to religious radio programs such as *Focus on the Family* and the most liberal audience is for late night talk shows such as those hosted by David Letterman and Jay Leno. In another survey, audience ideologies range from Fox News Cable Channel as the most conservative to magazines such as *The Atlantic Monthly*, *Harper's*, or *The New Yorker* as the most liberal. Many of the mean audience ideologies for the mass media outlets are clustered near the value for the national audience. The mean ideology on a 1–6 scale for the national nightly network news audience was a 3.28, which mirrors the mean rating of the survey respondents.

Readers and viewers respond to programs and publications as if they view media bias as a function of how different a program is from their ideology. With most of the media outlets registering a mean ideology in the 3s, it is not surprising that survey respondents who rate themselves as a 3 on the ideological scale do not view these programs as very biased. Respondents who rate themselves as very conservative (1) or very liberal (6) are much more likely to view the outlets as very biased. For a given program, those who are very conser-

vative are more likely than those who are very liberal to rate the program as
biased. This is consistent with the earlier suggestion that programs may tilt
content toward liberal views to gain marginal consumers who are younger
(and therefore more liberal). As the mean ideology of a program audience
grows more liberal, respondents who rate themselves as very liberal are less
likely to view the source as very biased. This suggests that perceptions of media bias do relate to different brand locations outlets choose when they cover
politics.

Variations in tastes in most markets do not attract public scrutiny; whether
consumers prefer khakis to blue jeans is not often a question covered in policy
debates. Differences in tastes in news coverage, however, attract more attention
since they are related to differences in political activity. The audience data analyzed here show that interests in politics are correlated with actions in politics.
Some news outlets provide high levels of public affairs information and attract
viewers who are active in politics. Among those who are regular consumers of
NewsHour with Jim Lehrer on PBS, 60.8% reported that they always vote,
41.5% indicated they were following the 2000 presidential election closely, and
55.9% were able to identify correctly Alan Greenspan as the chairman of the
Federal Reserve. Among those who are regular consumers of *Cops* or *America's
Most Wanted*, 31% reported that they always vote, 20% indicated they were following the 2000 presidential election closely, and 24.7% were able to identify
Alan Greenspan correctly. These differences are indicative of the segmentation
of the audiences for public affairs information. Individuals who report that
they regularly vote indicate that they follow news about government closely.
People who vote some of the time follow news about politics some of the time,
while those who rarely vote are the least likely to follow such news.

How to evaluate the links between the market for news and the operation of
politics is the topic of chapter 9. This chapter (3) provides analyses on three related questions: the overlap between the interests of marginal voters and marginal viewers; the ability of marginal voters to draw a political map of where
candidates stand in politics; and the degree that less-informed voters are satisfied with their political choices after they are made. The analysis here shows
that marginal voters are interested in news about crime, health, or the local
community more than they are interested in news about political figures and
events in Washington. To attract the attention of marginal consumers, most
news outlets face greater incentives to cover crime, health, local community
events, and even entertainment news rather than news about political events.
The good news is that the interests of marginal voters often coincide with the
interests of the marginal consumers that news outlets are trying to attract. The
bad news, from the perspective of informed discourse, is that these interests do
not focus on public affairs.

Though many survey respondents do not express a strong interest in politics, they still may learn enough about politics to make "informed" political de-

cisions.[5] The analysis here shows that marginal voters are able to determine who stands where in politics. When respondents were asked to rate politicians such as Clinton, Gore, Bradley, Jackson, Bush, McCain, and Buchanan on a 6-point ideology scale, the candidate ratings reported by regular voters were nearly the same as those reported by marginal voters. The only statistically significant difference in the mean ratings was the placement of Bill Bradley, who was given a 3.88 by regular voters and a 3.55 by marginal voters. The differences in ratings between those who were following the 2000 election very closely, versus only fairly closely, were similarly small. This suggests that even in a world where readers and viewers consume programs with great differences in hard news content, those who make some attempt to learn about politics or take some action to participate may possess enough information to place candidates on a left-right political scale.

Another way to view the operation of the political information market is to see whether less-informed voters regret their decisions. It could be the case that voters without much political information choose candidates whose actions later disappoint them. If voters had been better informed, the reasoning goes, they would have made different selections and hence been less likely to be surprised or disgruntled when politicians are elected and choose policies. The survey data here indicate that less-informed voters are not more likely to be disappointed. The analysis examines those respondents who indicated that they voted for President Clinton in 1996. If this set of voters is divided into groups based on levels of political information (i.e., ability to identify Bush, Bradley, and McCain), those who are least knowledgeable did not report higher levels of disapproval for Clinton's performance. They were less likely to register a response to the question of approval or disapproval, which would be consistent with their lack of political knowledge overall.

In markets where consumers have widely divergent preferences, one often hears the phrase "there's no accounting for tastes." While this may be true, in a news market where accountants track tastes it does matter who cares about what types of information. This chapter explores the differences in audience interests for types of news and analyzes the implications of the variations of news interests across demographic groups.

Tastes across Programs and Demographic Groups

Managers in broadcasting and print outlets have many data sources on who follows particular types of news: Nielsen Media Research ratings reports; other surveys of local or national viewers; studies done by media consulting firms; and information from focus group discussions about how readers and viewers react to a given program or publication. Most of these data never emerge in the public domain. Fortunately, the Pew Research Center for the People and the

Press conducts regular surveys on media consumption and makes the individual-level survey responses available through the Internet. This chapter uses three Pew surveys conducted in 1999 and 2000 to explore patterns in media consumption and reactions to the media.[6]

A basic assumption in the spatial competition model of news provision is that consumers have different interests in types of news and that news outlets will form to cater to these different interests. Table 3.1 shows that media outlets serve audiences that vary widely in interests. The table reports how the percentage of respondents following a given type of news differs across news audiences.[7] Media outlets are clearly segmented by reader or viewer interests. In terms of following political figures and events in Washington, D.C., outlets with reputations for hard news content and analysis have audiences with the highest percentage following this type of news; C-SPAN (48.6%); *NewsHour with Jim Lehrer* (39.6%); and magazines such as *The Atlantic Monthly, Harper's*, or *The New Yorker* (39.1%). Programs with reputations for soft news have audiences with some of the lowest percentage of readers or viewers following events in Washington: *The National Enquirer, Sun*, and *Star* (21.5%); daytime talk shows such as *Ricki Lake* or *Jerry Springer* (21.1%); programs such as *Cops* or *America's Most Wanted* (21.0%); and other daytime talk shows such as *Rosie O'Donnell* or *Oprah* (19.1%).

Outlets with audiences interested in following international affairs very closely are similarly predictable. Those with the highest fraction interested in international affairs were *NewsHour with Jim Lehrer* (40.1%), C-PSAN (38.5%), and magazines such as *The Atlantic Monthly, Harper's*, or *The New Yorker* (36.0%). Outlets whose audiences expressed the least interest in international affairs were those for personality magazines such as *People* (16.1%), courtroom programs such as *Judge Judy* or *Divorce Court* (15.9%), and daytime talk shows such as *Rosie O'Donnell* or *Oprah* (11.8%). The gaps in audience interests are even stronger for business and finance news. Programs and publications with a brand image specializing in business and economics have the highest audience percentages that follow this information very closely. For business magazines such as *Fortune* or *Forbes*, 56.5% of regular consumers report they follow business and finance news very closely. For CNBC, which offers cable viewers programs covering Wall Street and other business topics, 34.2% of the regular viewers follow this type of news very closely. At the other end of the interest spectrum, viewers of daytime talk shows such as *Ricki Lake* or *Jerry Springer* (12.1%) or *Rosie O'Donnell* or *Oprah* (10.8%) report very little interest in business and finance news.

A high percentage of audience members across different media outlets report that they follow news about people and events in the local community very closely. The wide variation in the nature of events one might follow in a local community may mean this category signifies different things to particular survey respondents. A high percentage of viewers of *Cops* or *America's Most*

TABLE 3.1
Media Audience Tastes

Regular Consumers of	% of Row Respondents Following a Type of News Very Closely							
	Political Figures/ Events in D.C.	International Affairs	Business/ Finance	People/Events in Local Community	Crime	Health	Entertainment	Culture/ Arts
Daily Newspaper	21.1	17.2	17.5	30.5	32.0	32.6	16.6	11.6
National Nightly Network News	28.4	22.6	19.7	35.0	38.9	40.4	17.3	11.8
Local TV News	20.3	16.5	14.8	35.1	38.6	34.9	16.9	9.9
CNN	27.4	24.3	23.6	33.9	39.6	35.6	18.8	14.5
C-SPAN	48.6	38.5	26.4	32.8	40.7	46.1	21.8	21.9
National Public Radio	22.0	24.0	20.4	31.5	27.6	34.9	17.2	17.5
NewsHour with Jim Lehrer	39.6	40.1	21.2	42.4	47.9	47.0	23.5	21.8
News Magazine Shows Such as 60 Minutes, 20/20, Dateline	23.9	18.8	15.4	34.8	40.8	39.8	18.5	11.5
Shows Such as Cops, America's Most Wanted	21.0	20.0	12.6	43.2	56.4	38.3	30.3	11.5
CNBC	31.1	27.5	34.2	33.5	40.9	46.2	20.2	15.6
Fox News Cable Channel	26.2	22.0	18.3	37.8	46.7	34.9	22.4	11.4
MSNBC	33.2	27.1	30.2	32.7	39.9	41.4	18.9	13.1
Shows Such as Entertainment Tonight, Access Hollywood	27.7	19.9	14.9	43.2	54.9	36.1	52.5	15.7

Today Show, Good Morning America, Early Show	23.5	17.7	14.4	37.7	37.6	42.3	18.2	12.4
Weather Channel	20.5	16.3	15.5	33.8	39.2	37.3	19.7	10.7
Sports News on ESPN	22.5	18.0	19.5	31.9	37.7	31.6	23.9	12.4
Documentaries on Channels Such as History Channel, Discovery Channel	20.2	19.1	16.6	29.0	35.3	32.3	16.5	13.5
Daytime Talk Shows Such as *Ricki Lake, Jerry Springer*	21.1	16.5	12.1	40.9	58.4	36.3	42.4	14.2
Daytime Talk Shows Such as *Rosie O'Donnell, Oprah*	19.1	11.8	10.8	42.4	43.7	45.6	27.6	11.4
Courtroom Shows Such as *Judge Judy, Divorce Court*	22.9	15.9	13.4	44.1	55.5	42.6	28.6	14.4
News Magazines Such as *Time, U.S. News, Newsweek*	28.9	29.5	24.2	31.9	32.5	40.9	17.0	22.3
Business Magazines Such as *Fortune, Forbes*	34.4	33.8	56.5	32.8	30.8	33.1	15.6	18.8
The National Enquirer, Sun, Star	21.5	19.5	15.1	38.8	46.4	46.3	44.8	14.4
Personality Magazines Such as *People*	23.8	16.1	13.3	39.4	48.5	45.2	40.4	18.5
Magazines Such as *The Atlantic Monthly, Harper's, The New Yorker*	39.1	36.0	26.7	38.0	27.0	45.7	20.2	42.1

Wanted (43.2%) and courtroom shows such as *Judge Judy* or *Divorce Court* (44.1%) report a strong interest in local people and events, which for these viewers may involve stories about local conflicts and disputes. Consumers of daytime talk shows such as *Rosie O'Donnell* or *Oprah* (42.4%) or *Ricki Lake* or *Jerry Springer* (40.9%) may be interested in local human interest stories. Regular viewers of *NewsHour with Jim Lehrer* (42.4%) also follow local events closely, though these may be events that fall into hard news categories.

Crime news rates highly among nearly all media audiences. The programs with the highest percentages of audience members who report they follow crime news very closely are those associated with soft news or entertainment: daytime talk shows such as *Ricki Lake* or *Jerry Springer* (58.4%); programs such as *Cops* or *America's Most Wanted* (56.4%); courtroom programs such as *Judge Judy* or *Divorce Court* (55.5%); and shows such as *Entertainment Tonight* or *Access Hollywood* (54.9%).[8] The outlets with the lowest audience interest in crime news are National Public Radio (27.6%) and magazines such as *The Atlantic Monthly*, *Harper's*, or *The New Yorker* (27.0%). Health news is of strong interest to readers and viewers across the hard news/soft news spectrum. Viewers of *NewsHour with Jim Lehrer* (47%), CNBC (46.2%), and C-SPAN (46.1%) follow health news very closely. Consumers of *The National Enquirer*, *Sun*, or *Star* (46.3%), daytime talk shows such as *Rosie O'Donnell* or *Oprah* (45.6%), and personality magazines such as *People* (45.2%) also express a strong interest in health news.

The choice of some outlets to specialize in soft news, drama, and entertainment is evident in the high percentage of audience members for these programs following entertainment news. As implied by the program titles, *Entertainment Tonight* and *Access Hollywood* attract regular viewers with the highest interest in entertainment news; 52.5% of their regular viewers report that they follow this type of information very closely. Outlets with similarly intense audience interest in entertainment news include *The National Enquirer*, *Sun*, or *Star* (44.8%), daytime talk shows such as *Ricki Lake* or *Jerry Springer* (42.4%), and personality magazines such as *People* (40.4%). Programs and publications with the lowest interest in entertainment news include National Public Radio (17.2%), daily newspapers (16.6%), and business magazines (15.6%). Interest in culture and arts news is relatively lower across outlets, reaching its lowest expression among regular viewers of local news (9.9%). The exception is for the publications that provide coverage of culture and the arts. Among regular consumers of magazines such as *The Atlantic Monthly*, *Harper's*, or *The New Yorker*, 42.1% follow culture and arts news very closely.

These results show that tastes for different types of news vary widely across media outlets. To examine whether preferences for a given type of news lead to the consumption of a particular news outlet, I conducted the following analysis. For each news program or publication in the survey I developed a model of an individual's decision to consume the outlet as a function of whether the person reported following very closely different types of news: news about political figures and events in Washington, sports, business and finance, international affairs, local government, religion, people and events in the local community, entertainment, consumer news, science and technology, health, crime, and culture and the arts. I divided the survey respondents into six subsamples based on the age and gender categories frequently used in the media industry: females 18–34, 35–49, and 50+, and the same for men. I then ran for each subsample a logit model for each media outlet predicting whether a person consumed the program or publication based on the types of news the individual followed very closely.

In Table 3.2, I report which news variable types had coefficients that were positive and statistically significant at the .10 level (or better) in predicting consumption in at least five of the six demographic groups. This is a stringent screen for capturing what interests lead to consumption of a media product. The theory in chapter 1 indicates that some media outlets provide a portfolio of information types. They do not develop a reputation for providing predominantly a single type of news. Different demographic groups may consume the product for different reasons, for example, one set of readers may consume the daily newspaper for sports coverage while another reads it for local community news. The question I examine in table 3.2 is whether there are interests across demographic groups that are associated with consumption of a product. The outlets that are television channels provide a variety of programs, so one would not expect them to have a particular news category that consistently predicts their consumption. Thus for the CNN, CNBC, Fox News Cable Channel, and MSNBC there is no particular news category that predicts their consumption. Daily newspapers and National Public Radio provide a portfolio of stories, so again there is no particular type of news interest that predicts their consumption across all demographic groups.

The link between audience interest and consumption across demographic groups is evident for a number of programs in table 3.2. Those who follow political figures and events in Washington, D.C. are more likely, controlling for other interests, to consume the network nightly news and C-SPAN. Interest in people and events in the local community predicts consumption of local news, local all-news cable, *Today Show*, *Good Morning America*, and *Early Show*, and programs such as *Cops* or *America's Most Wanted*. The broad popularity of health news is evident in the link between a strong interest in health news and consumption of the network nightly news and the network morning programs. Though local news programs are often criticized for their coverage of crime, table 3.2 shows that for at least five of the six demographic groups examined those who follow crime closely are more likely to consume local news regularly. Audience preferences for some type of crime news were thus linked to consumption of this product.

TABLE 3.2
News Interests That Predict Media Product Consumption

Media Product	*Type of News Followed Very Closely*
Daily Newspaper	
TV News Program	
News on Radio	
National Nightly Network News	Political Figures and Events in Washington, D.C., Health
Local TV News	People and Events in the Local Community, Crime
CNN	
Local All News Cable	People and Events in the Local Community
C-SPAN	Political Figures and Events in Washington, D.C.
National Public Radio	
NewsHour with Jim Lehrer	
News Magazine Shows Such as *60 Minutes, 20/20, Dateline*	
Today Show, Good Morning America, Early Show	People and Events in the Local Community, Health
Shows Such as *Cops, America's Most Wanted*	People and Events in Local Community, Crime
CNBC	
Fox News Cable Channel	
MSNBC	
Weather Channel	
Sports News on ESPN	Sports
Documentaries on Channels Such as History Channel, Discovery Channel	Science and Technology
Shows Such as *Entertainment Tonight, Access Hollywood*	Entertainment
Daytime Talk Shows Such as *Ricki Lake, Jerry Springer*	Crime
Daytime Talk Shows Such as *Rosie O'Donnell, Oprah*	
Courtroom Shows Such as *Judge Judy, Divorce Court*	Entertainment, Crime
News Magazines Such as *Time, US News, Newsweek*	
Business Magazines Such as *Fortune, Forbes*	Business and Finance
The National Enquirer, Sun, Star	Entertainment
Personality Magazines Such as *People*	Entertainment
Magazines Such as *The Atlantic Monthly, Harper's, The New Yorker*	Culture

Note: Within each demographic group, a logit was run predicting program consumption by an individual based on indicators for 13 different news interests. The interests whose coefficients were positive and statistically significant at the .10 level or lower in at least 5 of the 6 demographic group samples are reported here.

An interest in crime news is also a predictor of regular viewing for a number of programs with brand name reputations for showing acts of violence or verbal conflicts. People interested in crime news were more likely to be regular consumers of programs such as *Cops* or *America's Most Wanted*, daytime talk shows such as *Ricki Lake* or *Jerry Springer*, and courtroom shows such as *Judge Judy* or *Divorce Court*. Interest in entertainment news also broadly predicted consumption of a number of soft news outlets such as *Entertainment Tonight* or *Access Hollywood*, *The National Enquirer*, *Sun*, or *Star*, personality magazines such as *People*, and courtroom programs.

There were also news interests in the survey that were only associated with predicting consumption of outlets targeted to appeal to specialized audiences. Following business and finance news predicted consumption of business magazines across the demographic groups analyzed. An interest in science and technology predicted viewership of documentaries on the History Channel or Discovery channel. Regularly viewing ESPN was, unsurprisingly, predicted by a strong interest in sports news. Though the number of respondents saying that they followed culture and arts news very closely was relatively low, those who did were more likely to consume magazines such as *The Atlantic Monthly*, *Harper's*, or *The New Yorker*.

Taken together, tables 3.1 and 3.2 show that interests in news categories vary widely across media outlets. Consumption of some programs is predicted across demographic groups by a strong interest in a given type of news. Within each demographic group, for example, a person interested in sports would be more likely to view ESPN or a person interested in crime would be more likely to watch *Cops* or *America's Most Wanted*. The proportions of individuals across the age and gender categories that have specific interests in crime or sports vary in systematic ways. Men of all age groups register higher interest in sports, for example, and women are more likely to follow health news. The correlation of news interests and political interests with age and gender forms the second part of the story of how audience demands affect news content.

Advertisers divide the adult population into groups based on age and gender. They often place a higher value, other things being equal, on reaching younger viewers or female viewers. Table 3.3 analyzes the variations in news interests by the demographic categories used by programmers and advertisers.[9] Of the thirteen types of news covered in the Pew survey, four attracted sufficient attention so that at least a quarter of the respondents reported they followed the news category "very closely." Crime news was the most popular news category, with 29.6% of the total respondents saying they followed this very closely. This was followed in overall popularity by health (28.6%), sports (26.9%), and people/events in the local community (25.8%). News about political figures and events in Washington came in eighth in overall interest, with 16.8% of respondents saying they followed this type of information very closely. International affairs news came in tenth, attracting the close attention of 14.5% of the overall audience.[10]

When readers and viewers are considered as a total audience, strong interests in crime and health news and moderate interests in domestic and international affairs are apparent. This way of analyzing the audience for news misses, however, the great differences in interests across age and gender categories. Table 3.3 shows that for interests in political events in Washington or international affairs, older respondents are more likely to follow this type of news than younger viewers and men are more likely to report they are following these categories then women. Only 8.4% of women 18–34 indicate that they follow political news from Washington very closely, versus 26.6% of men 50+. The same pattern of stronger interest among older respondents and among male respondents holds for business and finance news. Interests range from 5.6% of women 18–34 following this type of news very closely versus 24.7% of men 50+.

TABLE 3.3
News Interests by Demographic Groups

| | % of Column Respondents Following a Type of News Very Closely | | | | | |
	Total	Females 18–34	Females 35–49	Females 50+	Males 18–34	Males 35–49	Males 50+
Political Figures/Events in Washington, D.C.	16.8	8.4	9.1	21.0	13.4	21.0	26.6
Sports	26.9	17.3	10.4	14.4	48.7	38.4	35.7
Business/ Finance	13.7	5.6	8.1	10.6	13.5	20.6	24.7
International Affairs	14.5	7.1	8.2	13.4	14.1	19.8	24.6
Local Government	20.5	11.3	18.3	25.5	11.3	24.1	31.0
Religion	21.2	14.6	19.7	32.6	14.9	21.0	21.3
People/Events in Local Community	25.8	25.5	26.6	32.6	16.4	25.6	26.5
Entertainment	15.3	21.7	12.0	13.2	22.4	12.0	10.8
Consumer News	12.0	10.8	10.1	12.1	8.9	14.3	15.7
Science and Technology	18.4	10.9	11.9	11.2	27.3	25.6	25.3
Health	28.6	31.8	32.0	40.4	14.8	22.6	26.8
Crime	29.6	37.6	31.0	29.0	25.0	29.1	26.4
Culture/Arts	9.8	10.3	10.2	11.0	10.1	9.1	7.5

For other types of news different patterns of age and gender interests emerge. Men are much more interested in sports than women, and younger viewers more interested than older respondents. Men 18–34 report the highest percentage (48.7%) following sports news closely. For news about the local community, women are more likely to follow this type of information closely than men. Entertainment news attracts the attention primarily of younger viewers, while science and technology is much more popular among men than women. For health news, women report higher interests than men and older viewers register more interest than younger respondents. Among those 18–34, 31.8% of females versus 14.8% of males follow health news closely. Women 50+ report the highest percentage (40.4%) following health information closely. While crime coverage is popular among all demographic groups, it is followed most closely by female viewers. It is the only news category where women 18–34 report the highest percentage (37.6%) of viewers following a topic very closely.

The differences in absolute levels of interests and ranking of interests are most apparent when one compares the preferences of women 18–34 to those of men 50+. For women 18–34 there are four news categories for which 20% or more of the respondents follow the type of news very closely. For nine of the thirteen news categories examined at least 20% of men 50+ reported they followed the news category very closely. The top four news categories for women 18–34 were (in order) crime, health, people/events in the local community, and entertainment. The top four news categories for men 50+ were sports, local government, health, and political figures/events in Washington.

Table 3.4 explores in more depth how tastes for political news vary. When asked whether they followed what was going in government and public affairs, 17.3% of women 18–34 indicated they did this most of the time. For men 50+, 63.0% reported following government news most of the time. Within each age group category, the percentage of women following political news most of the time was at least ten percentage points lower than the percentage of men who reported this. Older respondents in general were much more likely to say they followed the news about government and public affairs most of the time. Women 50+ reported the second highest percentage (48.5%) of respondents following this news most of the time. For females 18–34, females 35–49, and males 18–34, a plurality of respondents reported that they followed government news "some of the time." Nearly a quarter of men 18–34 and women 18–34 reported that they followed news about government and public affairs "only now and then."

These differences in attention to political news translate into markedly different levels of knowledge about some aspects of politics.[11] When asked to identify which party had a majority in the U.S. House of Representatives, older respondents and males were more likely to know that it was the Republican

TABLE 3.4
Who Follows Political News?

		% of Column Respondents					
	Total	Females 18–34	Females 35–49	Females 50+	Males 18–34	Males 35–49	Males 50+
Would you say you follow what is going on in government and public affairs?							
Most of the time	39.6	17.3	32.4	48.5	28.7	46.4	63.0
Some of the time	34.8	41.5	40.5	33.8	36.0	32.3	24.6
Only now and then	16.7	25.8	18.2	12.5	22.3	14.9	7.4
Hardly at all	8.6	15.4	8.9	4.7	12.5	6.3	4.4
Do you happen to know which political party has a majority in the U.S. House of Representatives?							
Republican Party	54.8	42.0	45.0	52.9	48.8	66.2	73.8
Number of correct answers to 3 questions about which presidential candidate is governor of Texas, a former senator from New Jersey, or cosponsor of a campaign finance reform bill:							
0	30.3	52.2	28.6	29.9	35.8	28.3	7.8
1	36.1	32.2	40.6	41.0	35.2	30.9	35.7
2	20.9	12.4	21.8	15.9	20.5	25.5	29.9
3	12.7	3.2	9.0	13.2	8.5	15.3	26.7

party. Among women 18–34, 42% gave the correct answer versus 73.8% of men 50+. Table 3.4 also shows the results of a news quiz of three questions requiring respondents to identify George W. Bush as the governor of Texas, Bill Bradley as a former senator from New Jersey, and John McCain as a cosponsor of campaign finance reform legislation. Older respondents were more likely to answer these questions correctly than younger respondents; men were more likely to identify the candidates correctly than women. More than half of women 18–34 (52.2%) failed to identify any of the three candidates correctly, versus 7.8% of men 50+. Among males 50+, 26.7% identified all three candidates correctly, compared with 3.2% of women 18–34.

Aside from variations in the attention paid to public affairs, demographic groups based on age and gender also differ in the worldviews they use to analyze political events. When asked to place themselves on the six point scale (where 1 is very conservative and 6 very liberal), a plurality of each demographic group responded by choosing a 3 on this scale. Yet there are clear ideological differences across these groups (see table 3.5). Only 7.7% of women 18–34 rated themselves as very conservative, compared to 18.2% of women 50+. Females 18–34 reported the highest percentage of respondents (15.0%) identifying themselves as very liberal, followed by males 18–34 (13.9%). People over 50 were the least likely to identify themselves as very liberal.

Ideological differences based on age and gender were also apparent in the percentages of respondents who identified themselves as supporters of particular issues. Table 3.5 reports the percentage of a demographic group that indicated a particular description was "perfect" for them. Within each age group women were more likely than men to say they were supporters of the women's movement. Among females, 30.9% of women 18–34 reported they were supporters of the women's movement versus 20.0% of women 50+. Women were more likely than men to say they were supporters of the pro-life movement. Within each age grouping, men were much more likely to identify themselves as supporters of the National Rifle Association. Identification as a supporter of the civil rights movement was higher among younger survey respondents and

TABLE 3.5
Distribution of Ideologies across Demographic Groups

| | | *% of Column Respondents* | | | | | |
	Total	*Females 18–34*	*Females 35–49*	*Females 50+*	*Males 18–34*	*Males 35–49*	*Males 50+*
Self-Rating:							
1 Very Conservative	13.5	7.7	15.0	18.2	12.0	15.4	11.7
2	14.7	13.8	8.7	13.3	17.8	16.7	17.8
3	28.2	22.8	28.7	28.2	29.7	27.2	32.6
4	15.3	17.4	14.9	12.0	15.6	18.8	13.9
5	9.5	14.0	14.9	9.0	6.4	7.8	5.2
6 Very Liberal	11.2	15.0	12.0	7.5	13.9	10.5	9.0
Self description as:							
Supporter of the women's movement	20.8	30.9	24.3	20.0	15.9	16.4	17.5
Supporter of the pro-life movement	22.7	24.8	26.3	25.6	17.2	22.4	19.4
Environmentalist	17.3	13.5	17.9	22.7	15.7	17.6	15.1
National Rifle Association supporter	15.5	8.8	8.3	13.6	21.3	22.6	18.8
Supporter of the civil rights movement	26.0	32.3	29.8	24.9	26.4	22.8	19.9
Patriot	34.1	17.4	30.7	44.0	28.5	39.4	42.1

among women. Females 18–34 registered the highest percentage identifying as supporters of the civil rights movement (32.3%), while males 50+ reported the lowest percentage (19.9%). Older respondents were much more likely to say that "patriot" was a perfect self-description. Among those 50 or older, 44.0% of women and 42.1% of men said they were patriots. This compares to 17.4% of women 18–34 and 28.5% for men 18–34.

The Pew survey results show that the audiences of media outlets vary by news interests and that interests in news (and views of the world) vary by age and gender. Putting these results together implies that media audiences will show some segmentation by age and gender. The demographic breakdown of respondents in the Pew (2000b) media survey was 16.0% female 18–34, 15.6% female 35–49, 20.4% female 50+, 15.9% male 18–34, 15.8% male 35–49, and 16.2% male 50+. Table 3.6 reveals that some media outlets and programs have audiences whose composition resembles the general population. Local television news programs appeal to all demographic groups, so the demographic breakdown of the local news audience is similar to that of the full sample. This is also true to a degree for National Public Radio, the Fox News Cable Channel, MSNBC, and news magazines such as *Time, U.S. News and World Report*, and *Newsweek*. All these outlets provide a portfolio of stories or program types, with the end result that they attract audiences across age and gender categories.

Table 3.6 shows that programs that have brand reputations for providing particular categories of news are segmented by age and gender. The audience for the *NewsHour with Jim Lehrer*, which has a strong reputation for providing hard news, draws the majority of its viewers from those over 50. Women 50+ comprise 33.1% of its audience, with the next most numerous group being males 50+ (24.2%). C-SPAN has a similarly high fraction of older viewers (25.8% females 50+, 23.7% males 50+). The national network nightly news programs also draw a majority of their viewers from females 50+ (32.1%) and males 50+ (22.7%). Programs that skew younger tend to focus on entertainment or conflict. The audience for shows such as *Entertainment Tonight* and *Access Hollywood* contains 23.7% females 18–34 and 18.5% males 18–34. Daytime talk shows such as *Ricki Lake* and *Jerry Springer* garner the majority of their viewers from those between 18–34, with females 18–34 comprising 28.5% of the audience and males 18–34 accounting for 26.9%. The outlets with the highest percentage of females 18–34 in their audiences (31.1%) are personality magazines such as *People*.

Gender segments other media audiences. The audience for sports news on ESPN is largely male. Males 18–34 comprise 29.2% of the ESPN news audience, followed by males 35–49 (24.0%) and males 50+ (21.0%). The readership of business magazines such as *Fortune* and *Forbes* is predominately male (23.0% males 18–34, 23.3% males 35–49, and 23.8% males 50+), though the presence of younger females in the business workplace is reflected in the fact that women 18–34 comprise 15.9% of the business magazine audience. The

TABLE 3.6
Media Audience Demographics

Regular Consumers of	% of Row Product's Regularly Consuming Audience Accounted for by Demographic Group					
	Females 18–34	Females 35–49	Females 50+	Males 18–34	Males 35–49	Males 50+
Daily Newspaper	12.9	14.7	22.5	14.0	16.5	19.4
TV News Program	15.0	15.3	23.4	13.4	15.3	17.7
News on Radio	14.4	17.5	16.8	14.2	20.1	17.1
National Network Nightly News	9.1	12.7	32.1	9.2	14.2	22.7
Local TV News	14.1	15.4	23.8	12.5	15.5	18.8
CNN	12.2	13.9	21.0	14.3	19.2	19.4
Local All News Cable	16.2	15.1	26.2	12.3	13.3	16.9
C-SPAN	7.0	9.0	25.8	15.5	19.0	23.7
National Public Radio	12.8	17.3	17.4	14.3	19.3	18.9
NewsHour with Jim Lehrer	8.0	6.8	33.1	11.5	16.4	24.2
News Magazine Shows Such as *60 Minutes, 20/20, Dateline*	14.7	18.2	27.5	9.5	12.7	17.5
Today Show, Good Morning America, Early Show	14.1	20.6	29.9	8.1	12.9	14.3
CNBC	9.0	12.9	21.2	16.7	20.1	20.1
Fox News Cable Channel	15.2	13.7	21.0	13.1	19.6	17.5
MSNBC	15.8	15.1	17.4	13.6	18.1	20.1
Weather Channel	11.8	12.9	23.5	12.9	17.8	21.1
Sports News on ESPN	9.5	7.7	8.5	29.2	24.0	21.0
Documentaries on Channels Such as History Channel, Discovery Channel	14.6	15.0	15.2	16.1	19.6	19.5
Shows Such as *Cops, America's Most Wanted*	16.1	16.6	20.7	18.6	18.3	9.7
Courtroom Shows Such as *Judge Judy, Divorce Court*	13.6	16.9	30.2	13.0	11.5	14.8
Shows Such as *Entertainment Tonight, Access Hollywood*	23.7	12.4	20.8	18.5	13.2	11.4
Daytime Talk Shows Such as *Ricki Lake, Jerry Springer*	28.5	11.4	9.9	26.9	9.9	13.5
Daytime Talk Shows Such as *Rosie O'Donnell, Oprah*	25.3	21.3	31.9	5.4	9.0	7.1
News Magazines Such as *Time, U.S. News, Newsweek*	17.3	15.0	18.7	15.0	13.3	20.8
Business Magazines Such as *Fortune, Forbes*	15.9	7.3	6.7	23.0	23.3	23.8
The National Enquirer, Sun, Star	17.7	14.8	35.0	6.9	14.2	11.4
Personality Magazines Such as *People*	31.1	18.5	23.7	12.6	7.2	7.0
Magazines Such as *The Atlantic Monthly, Harper's, The New Yorker*	10.9	11.2	23.7	8.2	28.2	17.8

viewers of daytime talk shows such as *Rosie O'Donnell* and *Oprah* are predominantly female (25.3% females 18–34, 21.3% females 35–49, and 31.9% females 50+). News magazine programs such as *60 Minutes* and *20/20* contain a high proportion of women 50+ (27.5%) and women 35–49 (18.2%). A similar pattern holds for the network morning programs *Today Show, Good Morning America,* and *Early Show,* where women 50+ comprise 29.9% of the audience and women 35–49 account for 20.6%. Females 50+ also account for a large fraction of the audience of courtroom shows such as *Judge Judy* and *Divorce Court* (30.2%) and of the readership of the *National Enquirer, Sun,* and *Star* (35.0%).

Table 3.7 offers another way to examine the same data by exploring what percentage of each demographic group consumes a particular media product. Some news outlets are part of the regular consumption patterns for all age and gender groups. Within each of the six demographic categories, at least 40% of respondents report that they are regular consumers of a daily newspaper, watch television news programs, listen to news on the radio, or watch local television news programs. Within these products, consumption by older respondents is still higher. For daily newspapers, 50.3% of females 18–34 are regular consumers versus 69.0% for females 50+ and 75.0% for males 50+. For local television news programs, 43.8% of men 18–34 are regular viewers versus 64.8% of males 50+ and 65.1% for females 50+. The network nightly news still captures at least 40% of viewers over 50. Among females 50+ 47.1% regularly watch the network nightly news, as do 41.9% of males 50+. Viewing the national news is not a part of most younger respondents' lives. For females 18–34 16.9% report regularly watching the network evening news, which is similar to the 17.3% figure for men 18–34.

Some products can attract at least a quarter of the viewing audience among one demographic while failing to reach this level of viewership in others. Sports news on ESPN is a regular part of media consumption by males. Among males 18–34, 41.5% report regularly viewing the sports news on ESPN, as do 35.0% of males 35–49 and 28.5% of males 50+. The highest consumers among females are those 18–34, where 13.3% regularly watch ESPN news. News magazines such as *60 Minutes* and *20/20* have a regular audience among females 35–49 (35.8%), females 50+ (41.4%), and males 50+ (33.2%). The morning network shows are similarly popular among women 35–49 (26.1%) and females 50+ (29.0%).

A diverse set of products generates moderate consumption levels across demographic groups. National Public Radio is consumed by between 12% and 19% of each demographic group. Programs such as *Cops* or *America's Most Wanted* garner close to 18% of each demographic group, except males 50+ (11.0% of whom regularly watch these programs). There are small percentage point variations across demographic groups for some products because they are only consumed by a small percentage of the audience. These include C-SPAN and magazines such as *The Atlantic Monthly, Harper's,* and *The New Yorker.*

TABLE 3.7
Percentage of Demographic Group Regularly Consuming Media Product

Regular Consumers of	Total	Females 18–34	Females 35–49	Females 50+	Males 18–34	Males 35–49	Males 50+
				% of Column Respondents			
Daily Newspaper	62.5	50.3	58.8	69.0	55.0	65.1	75.0
TV News Program	74.7	69.7	72.8	85.6	62.9	72.1	82.0
News on Radio	46.4	41.6	52.0	38.2	41.3	58.9	49.1
National Network Nightly News	29.9	16.9	24.4	47.1	17.3	26.8	41.9
Local TV News	55.8	48.9	54.9	65.1	43.8	54.6	64.8
CNN	21.1	16.1	18.8	21.7	18.9	25.7	25.3
Local All News Cable	29.2	29.5	28.2	37.5	22.5	24.6	30.5
C-SPAN	3.8	1.7	2.2	4.8	3.7	4.6	5.6
National Public Radio	15.3	12.3	16.9	13.1	13.8	18.7	17.9
NewsHour with Jim Lehrer	4.6	2.3	2.0	7.5	2.4	4.8	6.9
News Magazine Shows Such as 60 Minutes, 20/20, Dateline	30.7	28.1	35.8	41.4	18.2	24.7	33.2
Today Show, Good Morning America, Early Show	19.8	17.5	26.1	29.0	10.0	16.2	17.5
CNBC	11.2	6.3	9.4	11.7	11.7	14.5	13.5
Fox News Cable Channel	17.9	17.0	15.9	18.5	14.6	22.5	18.7
MSNBC	9.8	9.6	9.6	8.4	8.3	11.4	11.7
Weather Channel	31.7	23.2	26.6	36.6	25.6	36.3	39.9
Sports News on ESPN	22.6	13.3	11.3	9.5	41.5	35.0	28.5
Documentaries on Channels Such as History Channel, Discovery Channel	37.2	33.8	36.3	27.8	37.5	46.8	43.4
Shows Such as Cops, America's Most Wanted	17.7	17.8	18.6	17.9	20.7	20.2	11.0
Courtroom Shows Such as Judge Judy, Divorce Court	11.9	10.1	12.8	17.6	9.7	8.7	10.9
Shows Such as Entertainment Tonight, Access Hollywood	8.6	12.7	6.9	8.8	9.9	7.3	5.8
Daytime Talk Shows Such as Ricki Lake, Jerry Springer	7.5	13.3	5.4	3.6	12.6	4.7	6.2
Daytime Talk Shows Such as Rosie O'Donnell, Oprah	10.4	16.4	14.2	16.3	3.5	5.9	4.6
News Magazines Such as Time, U.S. News, Newsweek	12.5	13.4	12.0	11.4	11.7	10.4	16.0
Business Magazines Such as Fortune, Forbes	4.7	4.7	2.2	1.6	6.9	7.0	7.0
The National Enquirer, Sun, Star	2.8	3.0	2.6	4.7	1.2	2.5	1.9

TABLE 3.7 *Continued*

Regular Consumers of	Total	% of Column Respondents					
		Females 18–34	Females 35–49	Females 50+	Males 18–34	Males 35–49	Males 50+
Personality Magazines Such as *People*	6.2	11.9	7.3	7.2	4.9	2.8	2.7
Magazines Such as *The Atlantic Monthly, Harper's, The New Yorker*	2.2	1.5	1.6	2.5	1.1	3.9	2.4

Outlets focused on entertainment or human interest stories often have the highest percentage of consumption among females 18–34. This group has the highest percentage of regular consumers for programs such as *Entertainment Tonight* and *Access Hollywood* (12.7%), daytime talk shows such as *Ricki Lake* or *Jerry Springer* (13.3%), daytime talk programs such as *Rosie O'Donnell* or *Oprah* (16.4%), and personality magazines such as *People* (11.9%). This demographic also registers the second highest readership of news magazines such as *Time, US News,* and *Newsweek* (13.4%).

Targeting Viewers through Content Selection

What do you need to know to cast an informed vote for president ? What happened in your local community today? Did your favorite sports team win? What did the television actor you watch each week do at his movie premiere? The Pew survey data show that interests in these questions vary widely across demographic groups and that media outlets vary in the types of audience interests they serve. To see how economic considerations affect the selection of topics covered in the media, consider the case of the national network evening news programs. The high fixed costs of gathering and assembling news means that you cannot turn on the television and receive a broadcast tailored only to your interests. The current technology of broadcasting also means that stories offered on a program such as *NBC Nightly News with Tom Brokaw* are offered in the same sequence to all viewers. A news director trying to assemble stories based on what viewers need to know faces the difficulty of defining what political and social issues are important in the decisions viewers will face. A news director driven ultimately by profit faces a similarly difficult balancing act in answering the question, What combination of topics will yield the most valuable audience for my program? Two economic concepts, marginal viewers and advertiser value, help explain the way audience demands affect content selection in network news.

The network evening news programs have a core audience of faithful viewers and a set of marginal viewers, those who may tune into the news or choose another program depending on what has happened in the world or what types of news the networks choose to focus on. In some sense the news directors can take the interests of average viewers for granted. If the news programs do not stray too far from the expected presentation of hard and soft news, the average viewers will remain with the program. The problem for the network news programs is how to attract the marginal viewers, those by definition that do not like the presentation of news enough to tune in regularly. The news directors will select a mix of stories aimed at capturing the marginal viewers while not alienating the average viewers. The result will be a mix of news stories that may leave average viewers somewhat frustrated and marginal viewers somewhat placated.

Table 3.8 shows the tension between the interests of average and marginal viewers for the nightly network news shows. In this table I call those who say they regularly view the network news the average viewers, while those who say they sometimes view are called the marginal viewers. A majority of the regular viewers are over 50 (54.8%) and female (53.9%).[12] The marginal viewers are much younger. Females 18–34 account for 20.6% of those who sometimes view the national news, and males 18–34 account for 17.5% of these sometime viewers. In contrast, females 18–34 are only 9.1% of the regular audience and males 18–34 only 9.2% of the regular viewers. These demographic differences translate into predictable and sharp differences between the interests of marginal and average viewers. The marginal viewers are not as attached to the news. When asked how much they enjoyed keeping up with the news, 68.1% of average viewers responded that they did "a lot" versus only 37.0% for the marginal viewers. A majority of marginal viewers said that they followed national or international news closely "only when something important or interesting is happening." Marginal viewers were also more likely to report that they watched the news with "my remote in hand" and switched channels when they were not interested in a topic.

What captures the interests of occasional viewers differs from the type of news favored by loyal viewers. The marginal and average viewers have the same top-two news interests, crime and health, which may explain the prevalence of these news categories on the network evening news. The two sets of viewers differ markedly, however, in their interest in politics. For the average viewer of network news, news about political figures and events in Washington ranked fifth out of thirteen news types. This same category of news ranked tenth among marginal viewers. Political news about Washington was followed very closely by 28.4% of the average viewers, versus 12.3% of the marginals. Sports ranked sixth and entertainment news ranked twelfth among the regular viewers. These topics ranked much more highly among marginal viewers, who ranked them third and eighth among the thirteen news topics. When politics is covered on the nightly news, the worldviews with which audiences react to stories also differ slightly across the average and marginal audiences. The occasional viewers are slightly more likely to report that they are moderate or very liberal than those who watch the programs regularly.

If news directors are assembling an audience by selecting topics, economics predicts they may at the margin try to pull in the occasional viewer rather than try to make the core viewer happier. A second reason news directors may treat viewers differently is because of the different values that advertisers place on individuals. In the television advertising market, companies are often willing to pay more to reach young adults (e.g., 18–34) than older adults (e.g., 50+) and more to reach women than men. Women 18–34 command a high advertising premium, in part because they frequently make the purchasing decisions of their households, as I've noted previously. When news directors are assembling stories, they may take advertiser values into account when deciding which marginal viewers to try and attract. The value of attracting ten thousand more viewers age 35–49 versus 50+ depends in part on the price they can charge for these different sets of viewers and the degree that advertisers may change what products they advertise on a show when the audience changes. For example, ten thousand viewers age 35–49 might not raise the amount that a company with a product used by those age 65 or higher would pay to advertise on the program. That advertiser would prefer to reach ten thousand more viewers age 65 on the evening news. At some point, however, ten thousand more viewers age 35–49 might make companies aiming at these consumers willing to advertise on the evening news. The network would also prefer ten thousand more viewers age 35–49 than ten thousand more viewers 65+ to remain in the audience for the prime-time schedule, since this is a demographic targeted by advertisers in prime time.

Though the weekday network evening news programs have a combined average audience of 30.3 million, a particular advertiser may only be interested in reaching a segment of that viewing audience. An advertiser purchases the attention of the audience members likely, with a nudge, to buy their product. Table 3.9 contains information about who consumes the products marketed on network evening news programs. For 1999 I picked a random weekday in each month and used the Vanderbilt Television News Archive to determine what products were advertised on the three national network evening news programs.[13] I then matched these products with information from Mediamark Research 1998 survey reports that describe who consumes particular products. For the 521 ads that I could match with consumer demographics, table 3.9 reports the mean percent of a product's consumers that come from a particular demographic group. The table also reports the percentage of ads where the percentage of product users in the demographic group is higher than the percentage of that group in the overall survey pool.

TABLE 3.8
Average versus Marginal Viewers of Network Nightly News

	Females 18–34	Females 35–49	Females 50+	Males 18–34	Males 35–49	Males 50+
			% of Row Respondents			
Regularly View	9.1	12.7	32.1	9.2	14.2	22.7
Sometimes View	20.6	17.4	16.2	17.5	16.6	11.8

	Very Conservative	Conservative	Moderate	Liberal	Very Liberal	Don't Know/ Refused
Regularly View	7.2	32.5	37.4	14.0	4.9	4.0
Sometimes View	5.1	30.3	39.3	13.0	6.3	3.0

Follow Type of News Very Closely

	Political Figures/Events in DC	Sports	Business/ Finance	International Affairs	Local Government	Religion	People/Events in Local Community
Regularly View	28.4	28.4	19.7	22.6	30.3	25.0	35.0
Sometimes View	12.3	26.8	11.6	12.7	18.0	22.4	24.6

	Entertainment	Consumer News	Science and Technology	Health	Crime	Culture/Arts
			% of Row Respondents			
Regularly View	17.3	18.2	20.5	40.4	38.9	11.8
Sometimes View	15.7	9.5	16.8	28.8	29.0	9.3

	How much do you enjoy keeping up with the news? A lot.	I follow intl. news closely only when something important/interesting is happening.	I follow natl. news closely only when something important/interesting is happening.	I follow the local community news closely only when something important/interesting is happening.	I often watch the news with my remote in hand, flipping to other channels when I'm not interested.
Regularly View	68.1	55.1	34.2	30.0	29.7
Sometimes View	37.0	66.3	51.7	40.7	37.1

TABLE 3.9
Consumption of Products Advertised on Network Television News

Demographic Group	Mean % of a Product's Consumers Accounted for by Consumers in a Particular Demographic Group	% of Ads with a Higher % of Product Consumers in a Particular Demographic Group than the Survey % in the Group	% Survey Respondents in a Particular Demographic Group
Age			
18–24	8.7	11.7	12.7
25–34	18.5	27.4	21.0
35–44	22.3	42.2	22.3
45–54	18.7	59.7	16.7
55–64	12.6	50.5	10.9
65+	19.3	41.7	16.4
18–34	27.1	21.8	33.7
18–49	59.8	36.5	65.5
Male	35.2	25.1	47.9
Female	64.8	55.1	52.1
Income			
<$10K	7.2	30.2	8.1
$10K–19K	13.4	31.4	13.7
$20K–29K	13.3	29.1	13.9
$30K–39K	12.4	34.3	12.9
$40K–49K	10.8	33.4	11.3
$50K–59K	9.8	45.7	9.6
$60K–74K	12.0	61.7	10.7
$75K+	21.3	45.2	19.6
Education			
Not HS Graduate	16.8	22.5	18.6
HS Graduate	33.9	47.8	33.2
Attended College	26.5	43.5	26.4
College Graduate	22.8	41.2	21.7

Note: Based on a sample of 521 ads shown during the evening news programs on ABC, NBC, and CBS in 1999. Product usage demographics come from Mediamark Research 1998 survey reports.

The data in table 3.9 suggest that advertisers on the network evening news programs are targeting older consumers, females, those with moderate-to-high incomes, and viewers with relatively higher educations. If one compares the mean percentage of a product's users with those in the general survey population, it becomes clear that the consumers of products advertised on the evening news are likely to be older. The mean percentage of product users in the category 65+ was 19.3%, versus 16.4% of survey respondents in this category overall. The age categories 45–54 and 55–64 also had a higher mean percentage of advertised product users than their percentage in the survey population. On average the purchasers of products advertised on the network news were female; the mean percentage of female product users was 64.8%. For the income categories $50,000–59,999, $60,000–74,999, and $75,000,+ the mean percentage of product users in these categories was higher than the general population percentage. This was also true for the percentage of product users who attended college or graduated from college.

Another way to see the association between advertising and targeted viewers is to calculate the percentage of ads where the fraction of product users in a demographic group is higher than the fraction in the general population. The second column in table 3.9 reports this calculation. This makes clear that while older consumers are a target demographic, consumers in slightly younger demographics are also the target of some advertisements on these programs. For those age 35–44, 42.2% of the ads were for products where this age group accounted for a higher percentage of users than they did for the general population. For nearly 60% of the ads, consumers 45–54 accounted for a higher percentage of product users than they did of the general population. For those 55–64 this percentage was 50.5%, and for those 65+ it was 41.7%. Of the network ads analyzed, 55.1% had a higher percentage of female users than the percentage of females in the survey respondents. At least 45% of the ads had higher product user percentages for the income groups $50–59,999, $60–74,999, and $75,000+. At least 40% of the products had higher percentages of product users than percentage of survey respondents for high school graduates, those who attended college, and college graduates.

If news directors worry about marginal viewers and advertiser values, then the identity of who cares about a particular story will matter as the network evening programs are assembled. The concentration of occasional viewers among those 18–34 and the value, especially of females 18–34, of these consumers to advertisers suggests that their interests will influence content choices. One way to forge a compromise between the interests of average viewers, who are interested in politics, and marginal viewers, who are less interested, is to cover the political issues of interest to younger viewers. Tables 3.10 and 3.11 explore demographic interests across issues by reporting the percentage of a demographic group listing a particular policy area as a top priority for the president and Congress in 2000. Table 3.11 gives the percentage of respondents for

TABLE 3.10
Ranking of Topics as Top Priorities by Demographic Group

	Total	Females 18–34	Females 35–49	Females 50+	Males 18–34	Males 35–49	Males 50+
Improving the educational system	1	1	1	6	1	1	1
Keeping the economy strong	2	3	4	4	2	2	3
Reducing crime	3	2	5	1	3	7	6
Taking steps to make the Social Security system financially sound	4	9	2	2	4	3	2
Taking steps to make the Medicare system financially sound	5	5	3	5	6	4	4
Regulating HMOs and health care plans	6	10	6	10	12	10	7
Dealing with the problems of the poor and needy people	7	7	9	7	9	11	13
Providing health insurance to the uninsured	8	6	7	8	17	8	9
Adding prescription drug benefits to Medicare coverage	9	12	10	3	10	13	10
Protecting the environment	10	11	14	11	5	6	14
Reducing federal income taxes for the middle class	11	15	13	12	11	5	5
Dealing with the problems of families with children	12	4	12	16	8	9	15
Dealing with the moral breakdown of the country	13	14	16	9	15	14	11
Working to reduce racial tensions	14	13	11	14	14	15	16
Strengthening gun control laws	15	8	8	13	16	18	19
Paying off the national debt	16	18	17	15	13	12	12
Improving the job situation	17	16	15	17	7	17	20
Increasing the minimum wage	18	17	18	19	19	19	18
Reforming the campaign finance system	19	20	20	18	20	16	8
Dealing with global trade issues	20	19	19	20	18	20	17

TABLE 3.11
Percentage of Demographic Group Rating Topic as a Top Priority

		% of Column Respondents					
	Total	Females 18–34	Females 35–49	Females 50+	Males 18–34	Males 35–49	Males 50+
Improving the educational system	77.0	84.2	84.8	67.4	76.6	70.0	80.7
Keeping the economy strong	70.7	69.7	70.3	70.9	75.7	64.9	72.6
Reducing crime	69.6	77.7	66.5	80.3	68.9	59.3	61.5
Taking steps to make the Social Security system financially sound	68.6	58.5	72.7	77.4	62.0	64.8	74.7
Taking steps to make the Medicare system financially sound	63.9	62.6	71.4	69.6	50.0	63.2	66.0
Regulating HMOs and health care plans	55.5	57.0	61.4	60.0	42.0	51.6	60.1
Dealing with the problems of the poor and needy people	54.7	61.5	57.0	66.7	44.3	51.5	46.2
Providing health insurance to the uninsured	54.7	62.0	59.3	64.9	34.3	54.3	52.8
Adding prescription drug benefits to Medicare coverage	54.6	52.7	56.3	71.9	42.9	50.3	48.7
Protecting the environment	54.3	54.5	45.8	58.8	60.6	60.0	44.9
Reducing federal income taxes for the middle class	53.7	45.5	49.1	58.7	42.1	60.9	64.6
Dealing with the problems of families with children	52.4	65.6	55.0	50.2	47.4	52.8	44.2
Dealing with the moral breakdown of the country	48.2	48.5	44.0	62.3	37.2	47.3	48.2
Working to reduce racial tensions	46.3	48.5	55.3	52.9	38.0	39.4	43.5
Strengthening gun control laws	46.1	60.2	57.1	55.3	35.4	36.1	29.9
Paying off the national debt	43.6	29.1	39.9	52.6	38.8	50.7	47.8
Improving the job situation	41.5	45.0	45.7	47.2	50.0	37.4	22.4
Increasing the minimum wage	34.4	40.6	38.5	34.7	26.1	35.6	31.0
Reforming the campaign finance system	32.1	16.1	21.7	37.8	18.2	38.8	58.3
Dealing with global trade issues	30.1	24.9	26.3	31.4	26.3	29.7	41.6

the total sample and for each demographic group rating each issue as a top priority, while table 3.10 uses these percentages to rank the twenty issues by order of priority for each of the groups. Improving the educational system ranked as the top priority in the total sample and among five of the six demographic groups, with 77.0% of those surveyed listing it as a top priority. Dealing with global trade issues garnered the lowest percentage in the overall sample listing it as a top priority (30.1%) and ranked near the bottom in each demographic group.

Though respondents across demographic groups agree that improving the education system is a top priority for the president and Congress and dealing with global trade issues is not, there are wide variations across demographic groups in their rankings of areas as top priorities. For women 18–34 reducing crime ranked second in the percentage of that demographic rating the issue as a top priority. Women 50+ ranked reducing crime as the top issue. The relative concern for men about crime is lower, with males 35–49 ranking this seventh among their priority list and males 50+ ranking it sixth. Differences in priorities are very evident across age groups. Taking steps to make the social security system sound ranked second for males and females 50+, while women 18–34 placed this ninth on their list. Adding prescription drug benefits to Medicare garnered the third highest percentage listing it as a top priority among females 50+, while this ranked twelfth for females 18–34. Dealing with the problems of families with children was fourth on the list for women 18–34, but ranked sixteenth for women 50+ and fifteenth for men 50+.

Differences in opinion across gender categories are also evident in table 3.10. Females 18–34 and 35–49 placed strengthening gun control laws as eighth out of the twenty issues examined. Men 18–34 ranked this issue sixteenth and men 35–49 placed it eighteenth. Improving the job situation was seventh for men 18–34 and sixteenth for women 18–34. Dealing with the problems of the poor and needy was seventh among women 18–34 and thirteenth among males 50+. Reforming the campaign finance system was nineteenth in the overall sample and twentieth among women 18–34 or 35–49. Men 50+, however, placed this issue eighth overall in their rankings.

If viewers are more interested in seeing stories about issues they feel are a top priority and if program directors care about attracting particular viewers, the issue rankings provide evidence about what topics may attract particular demographic groups. Females 18–34 care relatively more about reducing crime, dealing with the problems of families with children, and strengthening gun control laws. News directors in search of these viewers will add more stories or devote more time to the issues they care about. Table 3.12 confirms the prediction that the network evening news programs select stories in part based on the interests of those marginal viewers highly valued by advertisers, particularly women 18–34. For each of the twenty issues examined in table 3.10 I counted the number of stories and total time devoted to these stories, in 2000, on each of the three network evening news broadcasts. I then modeled the number of stories and story time devoted to each area as a function of the percentage of each demographic group listing the issue as a top priority for the president and Congress. I combined the twenty observations for each network so that the sample totaled sixty observations. I included dummy variables for ABC and NBC (with the omitted network being CBS) in case there were persistent differences in how each network treated policy issues.

Table 3.12 suggests that networks do base story decisions on audience interests, and that they do select stories in part based on which demographic group may be interested in the policy area. In terms of total stories, the higher the percentage of women or men 18–34 who list an issue as a top priority the greater the number of stories devoted by a network evening news program to the area in 1999. An increase in one percentage point of women 18–34 listing the issue as a top priority translates into 1.28 more stories about the issue on the evening news broadcast, while a one percentage point increase in the percentage of men 18–34 listing the issue as a top priority generates .89 more stories. It may be the case that greater coverage causes individuals to rank an issue as a top priority.[14] To guard against this effect, I separate the sample into those who view the network news regularly and those who do not (i.e., the non-network news viewers). Differences between these two samples can also be interpreted as the reaction of programmers to the interests of regular network news viewers and potential network news viewers (i.e., marginal viewers). For both the network news viewers and the non-network news viewers, higher interest among women and men 18–34 translates into more stories. In all three analyses, higher interest among women 50+ translates into less coverage. This may reflect the tight time constraint of twenty-two non-advertising minutes that each half-hour news program faces, so that adding stories of interest to older women would crowd out more profitable stories of interest to other demographic groups.

A similar pattern of coverage catering to the interests of young viewers holds when the total time devoted to each issue in 2000 is examined. For the full sample, a one percentage point increase among females 18–34 listing an issue as a top priority translates into 3.08 more minutes of coverage about the topic on a network evening news broadcast. A one percentage point increase among males 18–34 translates into 2.59 more minutes. Higher interest among women 50+ results in less time devoted to the issue. When the sample is divided into network news viewers and non-network news viewers, the same pattern (made apparent with story counts) appears for total story time. Among the regular network news audience, higher interest among females and males 18–34 results in more time devoted to the issue. Among non-network viewers, the same is true, perhaps because these are the most prized of the potential viewers. Higher interests among females 50+ results in less time devoted to an issue.

TABLE 3.12
Impact of Viewer Interests on Network Evening News Content

	Total Stories on Network about Topic, 2000 (N = 60)		
	(1) Full Sample	*(2)* Network News Viewers	*(3)* Non-Network News Viewers
% Top Priority for:			
Females 18–34	1.28***	0.56*	1.29***
	(0.44)	(0.29)	(0.44)
Females 35–49	−0.85	−0.42	−0.90
	(0.53)	(0.36)	(0.56)
Females 50+	−0.84**	−0.73*	−0.84**
	(0.35)	(0.38)	(0.35)
Males 18–34	0.89***	1.17***	0.89***
	(0.31)	(0.33)	(0.31)
Males 35–49	0.20	−0.28	0.27
	(0.59)	(0.50)	(0.49)
Males 50+	0.17	0.11	0.14
	(0.32)	(0.29)	(0.25)
ABC	3.58	4.60	3.58
	(6.02)	(6.46)	(6.02)
NBC	3.20	3.20	3.20
	(6.01)	(6.45)	(6.01)
Adjusted R^2	0.45	0.37	0.45
	Total Story Minutes on Network about Topic, 2000 (N = 60)		
	(4) Full Sample	*(5)* Network News Viewers	*(6)* Non-Network News Viewers
% Top Priority for:			
Females 18–34	3.08**	1.40*	3.04**
	(1.26)	(0.82)	(1.27)
Females 35–49	−1.81	−0.90	−1.84
	(1.53)	(1.03)	(1.62)
Females 50+	−2.48**	−2.06*	−2.49**
	(1.01)	(1.10)	(1.01)
Males 18–34	2.59***	3.19***	2.59***
	(0.89)	(0.94)	(0.90)
Males 35–49	0.62	−0.49	0.94
	(1.69)	(1.42)	(1.40)
Males 50+	0.49	0.26	0.31
	(0.94)	(0.84)	(0.72)
ABC	17.12	20.52	17.11
	(17.24)	(18.55)	(17.26)
NBC	23.97	23.97	23.97
	(17.21)	(18.52)	(17.23)
Adjusted R^2	0.46	0.37	0.45

Note: Dependent variable in the OLS regressions 1, 2, and 3 is the total number of stories in 2000 about a topic on a particular network evening newscast (i.e., ABC, NBC, or CBS). Specifications 4, 5, and 6 use the total number of minutes devoted to a topic during 2000 by a network evening newscast. Each specification also included an intercept. Standard errors are in parentheses. *** = statistically significant at the .01 level, ** = statistically significant at the .05 level, * = statistically significant at the .10 level.

Audience Reactions

The correlation of audience interests with age and gender, the different advertiser values placed on the attention of specific demographic groups, and the
targeting of content based on economics help explain the reactions to the media by age and gender listed in table 3.13. The analysis of the evening network
news suggests that news directors pay particular attention to the interests of females 18–34 in fashioning political coverage. The greater value in general attached to younger versus older consumers and females versus males suggests
that satisfaction with the media should vary by demographic group. When
asked whether the "people who decide what to put on television news or in the
newspapers are out of touch with people like me," women 18–34 are the least
likely to agree completely with this statement (only 10.7% register this opinion). Males 50+ were the most likely to agree completely with this statement,
with 23.9% voicing this sentiment. The difficulty of holding the attention of
younger viewers is reflected in the percentage of respondents agreeing that they
often watch the news with a remote control in hand and switch channels when
not interested in a news topic. Females 18–34 had the highest percentage of
complete agreement with this statement (45.3%), followed by males 18–34
(44.7%). Females 18–34 also reported the highest percentage for wishing they
had more time to follow the news (30.6%).

When asked whether they "enjoy keeping up with the news," the preferences
evident from the earlier audience analysis emerge again. Older readers and
viewers are more likely to respond that they enjoy keeping up with the news a
lot, and men are more likely to report this than women. For males 50+, 59.9%
say they enjoy this a lot, as do 54.4% of females 50+. This compares to 32.7%
for males 18–34 and 28.9% for females 18–34. Younger respondents and females are more likely to say that they only follow the news when "something
important or interesting is happening." For international news a majority in
each demographic group, with the exception of men 50+, report they only follow this type of news closely when something important or interesting is happening. This is true for 75.3% of women 18–34 versus 48.8% of men 50+. The
age and gender gap is also evident for national news. For females 18–34, 62.5%
say they only follow national news closely when something important or interesting is happening, versus 39.2% of males 50+. Only males 18–34 report a
majority (53.1%) saying that they follow local news closely only when something important or interesting is happening.

Media Bias as Product Differentiation?

Chapter 2 emphasized that nonpartisan coverage in nineteenth-century newspapers emerged as a commercial product. By assembling a larger audience a news-

TABLE 3.13
Media Satisfaction

		% of Column Respondents					
	Total	Females 18–34	Females 35–49	Females 50+	Males 18–34	Males 35–49	Males 50+
How much do you enjoy keeping up with the news? A lot	44.9	28.9	42.7	54.4	32.7	47.5	59.9
Do you feel overloaded, or do you like having so much information available? Overloaded	29.4	23.2	28.4	38.3	19.9	27.7	36.5
% who completely agree that:							
I find that I often watch the news with my remote control in hand, flipping to other channels when I'm not interested in the topic.	35.9	45.3	31.1	26.5	44.7	37.8	32.8
I wish I had more time to follow the news.	20.6	30.6	25.2	18.2	18.3	19.8	12.5
People who decide what to put on TV news or in the newspapers are out of touch with people like me.	18.1	10.7	15.0	20.8	15.4	21.6	23.9
% who say I . . .							
Follow international news closely only when something important or interesting is happening	64.5	75.3	70.2	61.7	68.4	63.5	48.8
Follow national news closely only when something important or interesting is happening	49.7	62.5	54.6	42.4	59.8	42.2	39.2
Follow the local community news closely only when something important or interesting is happening	40.3	45.9	37.1	33.3	53.1	38.7	35.9

paper could charge advertisers higher rates and take advantage of economies of scale in paper production. Though objectivity now forms part of the creed of modern journalism, perceptions of media bias still persist. Often complaints about media bias are expressed in terms of conspiracy, corporate control, or class conflict. The evidence presented here on audience interests and the targeting of demographic groups provide another explanation, that perceptions of media bias arise in part from the economics of news markets. When asked to place themselves on a scale of liberalism and conservatism, individuals age 18–34 are more likely to say they are very liberal than those age 50+. Women in each age category on average are more liberal than men. Females 18–34 report the most liberal mean ideology rating for the six adult demographic groups examined. This implies that if news outlets try to attract younger, female, or especially young female readers/viewers, they may end up covering issues or adopting perspectives that are attractive to liberals.

The opinions of media bias reported in tables 3.14 and 3.15 are consistent with media bias arising from economic targeting of content to attract liberal demographic groups. Younger survey respondents are less likely to say there is a "great deal" of political bias in news coverage. Females in each age group are slightly less likely then men to see a great deal of political bias. Young females 18–34 are the least likely demographic to report that there is a great deal of political bias in news coverage. Those who report that they are very conservative

TABLE 3.14
Media Bias Opinions

	% of Row Respondents to the Question: To what extent do you see political bias in news coverage?			
	A Great Deal	A Fair Amount	Not Too Much	Not at All
Ideology Rating				
1 Very Conservative	44.5	33.7	14.3	7.5
2	39.4	36.0	20.6	4.1
3	34.6	39.9	21.0	4.4
4	27.9	46.3	21.8	4.0
5	30.5	43.6	21.3	4.6
6 Very Liberal	25.3	43.5	23.1	8.1
Demographic Group				
Females 18–34	29.0	43.7	22.7	4.6
Females 35–49	35.0	40.3	16.4	8.4
Females 50+	34.0	32.1	25.8	8.2
Males 18–34	31.5	45.7	18.1	4.7
Males 35–49	37.5	35.1	20.3	7.2
Males 50+	34.4	40.1	21.3	4.2

TABLE 3.15
Perceived Bias in Presidential Race Coverage

| | % of Row Respondents to the Statement: Coverage of presidential race by news organizations shows . . . | | |
	Democratic Bias	Republican Bias	No Bias
Republicans	43.4	7.9	48.7
Democrats	9.9	24.1	66.1
Independents	20.3	16.9	62.8

are the most likely to see bias in the media (i.e., 44.5% see a "great deal"). Survey respondents who identify themselves as very liberal are least likely to see a great deal of political bias in news coverage and are most likely to report that there is "not too much" or "not at all."

If news outlets are using certain political issues to target young female viewers, the analysis in table 3.10 suggests they will cover issues such as reducing crime, dealing with the problems of families with children, and strengthening gun control laws. Coverage of these issues, some of which are traditionally associated with Democratic candidates, can further lead some viewers to conclude that the media are biased.[15] Table 3.15 indicates that among Republicans, 43.4% reported in January 2000 that coverage of the presidential race to that point by news organizations showed a Democratic bias. Among Democrats, 24.1% saw a Republican bias in news coverage of the presidential race. Independents are slightly more likely to see a Democratic bias (20.3%) than a Republican bias (16.9%). A plurality of each group (48.7% for Republicans, 66.1% for Democrats, and 62.8% for independents) saw no bias overall in coverage.

Political bias in media content can be seen as akin to product differentiation. Individuals may have worldviews or ideologies, which we can think of as their political preferences. Media outlets choose combinations of topics and approaches to issues that may reflect these worldviews. To an individual, a media outlet will develop a reputation for presenting the news in a manner that may be close or distant from the individual's ideology. The farther a product is from an individual's worldview, the more likely the person will be to say that the media outlet is biased. The Pew survey data do not provide direct measures of media content. The survey did ask respondents to rate themselves on a 1–6 conservative-liberal scale where 1 represents very conservative and six represents very liberal. The same survey had respondents rate particular publications and programs on a scale that ranged from very biased to completely objective. I use these two measures to explore how distance from a program's approach to politics affects a person's view of that program's objectivity. To construct a proxy for a program's ideology, I calculate the average of the ideology ratings re-

ported by its audience members. This allows me to construct a spectrum showing the ideological location of particular programs. If readers and viewers define bias by how distant they are from a show's ideological location, then they
should be more willing to say that a program is biased if the program's mean
ideology is farther from their own worldviews.

Tables 3.16 and 3.17 show that there is a dispersion among the audience ideologies of programs that corresponds to the brand images outlets have in their
approach to politics. In the survey where respondents ranked their ideologies
on a six-point scale, the program audience for religious radio shows such as *Focus on the Family* had the most conservative rating (a mean of 2.95) and the
late-night talk shows such as those hosted by David Letterman and Jay Leno
had the most liberal rating (3.62).[16] The audience for a program here is defined
by those who say they regularly learn about a presidential campaign/candidate
from the outlet. Note that the percentage saying they learn about the presidential race from the late-night talk shows (9.5%) is similar to the percentage saying that they learn about the race from National Public Radio (11.7%). The
mean audience ideology for the network news, 3.28, is the same as that for the
total respondents. This is also true for other mass media outlets such as CNN
and MSNBC. Younger respondents report more liberal ideologies than older
ones, women in general are more liberal than men, and young females 18–34
have the most liberal rating (3.68).

Table 3.17 shows a similar dispersion when survey respondents rated themselves on a five-point scale. The outlet with the most conservative audience was
the Fox News Cable Channel (2.66), while magazines such as *The Atlantic
Monthly, Harper's,* or *The New Yorker* had the most liberal audience mean
(3.29). Mass media outlets such as the daily newspaper or morning television
programs such as *Today Show* or *Good Morning America* had mean audience
ratings (2.81) equal to the mean for the sample as a whole (2.81). Outlets with
younger or more female audiences predictably had audience means that were
closer to the liberal side of the spectrum. Personality magazines such as *People*
and daytime talk shows such as *Rosie O'Donnell* or *Oprah,* for example, had audience means of 2.91.

The parallel between media bias and product differentiation depends on two
"ifs": 1) If the mean ideology of its audience describes a program's approach to
politics, then one can use the audience ratings to describe a program's ideological location and 2) If individuals define media bias by the distance of an outlet
from their own ideology, then views about whether a program is biased or objective should depend on the ideology of the respondent and the location of
the program. Table 3.18 shows that perceptions of media bias do operate as if
there are ideological differences among media outlets. The media outlets listed
in the table are ordered by the audience ideology mean reported in Table 3.16.
The average audience ideology ratings range from 3.17, for the Sunday network talk shows such as *This Week* and *Meet the Press,* to 3.57 for cable political

TABLE 3.16
Ideological Ratings by Media Audience

	Audience Mean of Ideology Scale Rating (1–6)	% Adults Regularly Learning about Presidential Campaign/Candidate from Outlet
Religious Radio Shows Such as		
Focus on the Family	2.95	6.7
Talk Radio	3.16	15.3
Sunday NetworkTalk Shows Such as		
This Week, Meet the Press	3.17	15.4
MTV	3.21	4.7
Daily Newspaper	3.21	40.0
Local TV News	3.22	47.6
PBS Shows Such as NewsHour with Jim Lehrer, Washington Week in Review	3.27	12.3
Cable News Networks Such as CNN, MSNBC	3.28	34.5
National NightlyNetwork News	3.28	44.6
National Public Radio	3.31	11.7
Morning TV Programs Such as Today Show, Good Morning America	3.34	17.8
News Magazines Such as Time, U.S. News, Newsweek	3.38	14.7
Comedy Shows Such as Saturday Night Live, Politically Incorrect	3.39	6.0
C-SPAN	3.44	9.2
Internet	3.45	9.2
News Magazine Shows Such as 60 Minutes, 20/20, Dateline	3.46	29.1
Cable Political Shows Such as Crossfire, Hardball	3.57	14.4
Late Night TV Shows Such as David Letterman, Jay Leno	3.62	9.5
Females 18–34	3.68	
Females 35–49	3.44	
Females 50+	3.03	
Males 18–34	3.30	
Males 35–49	3.19	
Males 50+	3.11	
Total Sample	3.28	

TABLE 3.17
Ideological Ratings by Media Audience

	Audience Mean of Ideology Scale Rating (1–5)	% Adults Regularly Consuming
Fox News Cable Channel	2.66	17.6
Business Magazines Such as *Fortune, Forbes*	2.71	4.8
News on Radio	2.75	46.3
C-SPAN	2.76	3.8
Local TV News	2.76	55.6
National Nightly Network News	2.76	30.0
Weather Channel	2.77	31.5
CNN	2.77	21.2
CNBC	2.77	11.2
News Magazines Shows Such as *60 Minutes, 20/20, Dateline*	2.77	30.6
Documentaries on Channels Such as History Channel, Discovery Channel	2.78	36.7
Local Cable News	2.80	29.1
Daily Newspaper	2.81	62.4
Today Show, Good Morning America, Early Show	2.81	19.9
The National Enquirer, Sun, Star	2.82	2.7
MSNBC	2.86	9.8
Sports News on ESPN	2.86	22.2
Courtroom Shows Such as *Judge Judy, Divorce Court*	2.89	11.8
News Magazines Such as *Time, US News, Newsweek*	2.89	12.4
Shows Such as *Entertainment Tonight, Access Hollywood*	2.90	8.5
Personality Magazines Such as *People*	2.91	6.1
Daytime Talk Shows Such as *Rosie O'Donnell, Oprah*	2.91	10.3
Shows Such as *Cops, America's Most Wanted*	2.92	17.7
National Public Radio	2.95	15.3
NewsHour with Jim Lehrer	3.00	4.7
Daytime Talk Shows Such as *Ricki Lake, Jerry Springer*	3.13	7.4
Magazines such as *The Atlantic Monthly, Harpers,* or *The New Yorker*	3.29	2.2

TABLE 3.17 *Continued*

	Audience Mean of Ideology Scale Rating (1–5)	% Adults Regularly Consuming
Females 18–34	3.07	
Females 35–49	2.83	
Females 50+	2.72	
Males 18–34	2.98	
Males 35–49	2.71	
Males 50+	2.60	
Total Sample	2.81	

TABLE 3.18
Media Bias Evaluations by Ideology of Respondent

Outlet	% of Column Respondents Rating Outlet as Very Biased		
	1 Very Conservative	3	6 Very Liberal
Sunday Network Talk Shows Such as *This Week, Meet the Press*	25.9	11.4	25.8
Daily Newspaper	29.0	18.5	25.3
Local TV News	30.9	9.0	21.0
PBS Shows Such as *NewsHour with Jim Lehrer, Washington Week in Review*	27.4	8.1	22.3
Cable News Network Shows Such as CNN, MSNBC	25.7	5.9	15.0
National Nightly Network News	37.4	10.3	16.6
National Public Radio	30.0	10.3	17.3
Morning TV Programs Such as *Today Show, Good Morning America*	29.1	9.6	16.3
News Magazines Such as *Time, U.S. News, Newsweek*	39.9	15.5	22.1
C-SPAN	27.9	4.7	18.4
TV Magazine Shows Such as *60 Minutes, 20/20, Dateline*	25.6	12.1	18.4
Cable Political Shows Such as *Crossfire, Hardball*	26.8	20.8	33.3

shows such as *Crossfire* and *Hardball*. With all of the outlets registering an audience mean ideology in the 3s, respondents who rate themselves as a 3 on the
scale do not view most of these outlets as very biased. Individuals who rate
themselves as very conservative (1) or very liberal (6) are much more likely to
rate programs averaging a 3 as very biased.

For nearly every program, those who are very conservative are more likely
than those who are very liberal to rate the program as very biased. One would
expect this if programs trying to garner younger or female consumers used liberal content to attract these viewers. This pattern is evident in reactions to the
network nightly news. Only 10.3% of respondents rating themselves as a 3
viewed the network news as very biased. Among very liberal respondents
16.6% shared this view. For those who said they were very conservative, however, 37.4% rated the network news as very biased. As the mean ideology of a
program's audience increased (i.e., became more liberal), liberals were less
likely to see the program as very biased. The one outlet that was viewed as very
biased by at least 20% of all three groups were cable political shows such as
Crossfire and *Hardball*. Even though this set of shows attracted the most liberal
viewing audience for those evaluated in the table, 33.3% of the very liberal respondents saw these outlets as very biased. Overall, these results suggest that
perceptions of media bias relate to the ideological brand locations that outlets
choose when they cover political issues.

Viewing and Voting

In idealized descriptions of democracy all citizens take an active role in keeping
up with public affairs and voting. Voter turnout rates in presidential elections
and Nielsen ratings for hard news programming show that voting and viewing
fall short of this idealized world. The good news from table 3.19 is that relative
rates of following political news are related to relative rates of political participation and learning. It is the case that those who participate more in politics
are more likely to consume news about politics. Among those who report that
they always vote, 58.8% say that they follow what is going on in government
and politics most of the time. Among those who say that they vote "nearly
always," the group I refer to as marginal voters, 38.8% report following govern-
ment/politics news most of the time and 41.5% some of the time. As participation in voting drops off, interest in the news also declines. For those who vote
part of the time, a majority say they follow news about government and public
affairs some of the time or now and then. Among those who seldom or never
vote, a majority say they follow government and public affairs news only now
and then or hardly at all. Those who follow politics more are also more likely to
know more. When asked to identify the political party that had a majority in
the U.S. House of Representatives in 1999, 64.8% of those who always vote and

TABLE 3.19
Political Interests and Actions

	% of Column Respondents				
	How often would you say you vote?				
	Always	Nearly Always	Part of the Time	Seldom	Never
Would you say you follow what is going on in government and public affairs?					
Most of the time	58.8	38.8	20.2	12.1	10.7
Some of the time	28.8	41.5	43.8	33.4	27.7
Only now and then	9.4	15.5	26.5	30.9	24.7
Hardly at all	2.8	4.2	8.8	22.6	36.3
Do you happen to know which political party has a majority in the U.S. House of Representatives?					
Republican Party	64.8	61.8	42.6	38.0	23.8
Demographic Group					
Females 18–34	9.2	14.9	21.1	28.7	29.9
Females 35–49	14.6	19.1	14.8	15.6	15.9
Females 50+	29.2	17.6	10.0	7.0	10.3
Males 18–34	9.8	13.7	22.5	30.7	28.6
Males 35–49	15.4	20.7	18.2	11.8	11.1
Males 50+	21.8	14.0	13.4	6.3	4.3

61.8% of those who vote nearly always gave the correct answer of the Republican Party. There is a sharp drop-off for those who vote only part of the time (42.6%), seldom (38.0%), or never (23.8%).

The same demographic patterns evident in interests in political news appear in voting. Those 50+ makeup a majority of those who say that they always vote. Men and women 18–34 make up a majority of those who seldom vote or never vote. Among the marginal voters (i.e., those who say they nearly always vote), males 35–49 constitute the highest demographic percentage (20.7%) followed by females 35–49 (19.1%). Though females 18–34 constitute 9.2% of those who always vote and males 18–34 comprise just 9.8%, these young adult demographic groups constitute a higher percentage of marginal voters. Women 18–34 are 14.9% of marginal voters, and men 18–34 constitute 13.7%.

The segmentation of the media market into news outlets that offer widely different types of news means that there are clear differences in the political interests and activities of program audiences.[17] Table 3.20 shows that programs associated with hard news content attract audiences that are politically active and knowledgeable, while those associated with soft news attract viewers who are less interested in and active in politics. Only two outlets had at least 40% of their audiences report that they were following the presidential election very closely, C-SPAN (46.1%) and *NewsHour with Jim Lehrer* (41.5%). These outlets, which concentrate on politics, are notable because they are noncommercial and because they only appeal to a small segment of viewers (i.e., 3.8% of respondents are regular C-SPAN viewers, and 4.6% regular viewers of the PBS evening news program). C-SPAN also registered the highest percentage of viewers able to identify Alan Greenspan as the chairman of the Federal Reserve system (71.5%).

NewsHour with Jim Lehrer and C-SPAN also had the top two percentage of audience members that reported they always voted (60.8% and 54.3% respectively). The other outlets where at least 50% of audience members said they always voted included news magazines such as *Time, U.S. News and World Report*, and *Newsweek*, business magazines such as *Fortune* and *Forbes*, and MSNBC and National Public Radio. The percentage of audience members who said that they followed the presidential election very closely for most of these outlets was 30%. A high percentage of the audiences members could identify Alan Greenspan (e.g., 67.9% of the readers of the business magazines).

At the other end of the news spectrum there are a set of programs and publications where audience members do not consistently vote, are less interested in election news, and do not know who Alan Greenspan is. Outlets where less than 35% of the audience members report that they always vote are personality magazines such as *People* (34.0%), *The National Enquirer, Sun,* and *Star* (33.2%), shows such as *Cops* and *America's Most Wanted* (31.0%), and daytime talk shows such as *Ricki Lake* or *Jerry Springer* (26.9%). These outlets have a lower percentage of audience members who say they follow the presidential election news very closely. Personality magazines such as *People* register the lowest percentage of audience members (19.6%) following the election very closely. Readers and viewers of these outlets are much less likely to know who Alan Greenspan is. Viewers for daytime talk shows such as *Ricki Lake* or *Jerry Springer* are the least likely to be able to identify the chairman of the Federal Reserve system, with only 18.0% correctly identifying him.

The audience data here demonstrate that with a wide variety of news outlets, some readers and viewers choose programs where audiences express an interest in politics, participate through voting, and know about the details of government. Other readers and viewers choose to consume outlets whose audiences do not follow politics, do not vote as often, and do not know as much about the government. Evaluating the relationships between the economics of the news

TABLE 3.20
Political Action by Program Audience

Regular Consumers of	% of Row Respondents			
	Always Vote	Nearly Always Vote	Follow Presidential Election Very Closely	Can Identify Alan Greenspan
Daily Newspaper	44.5	25.0	21.6	51.0
National Nightly Network News	49.0	27.4	30.9	53.2
Local TV News	42.2	25.5	22.1	46.0
CNN	48.4	24.2	28.4	56.4
C-SPAN	54.3	26.4	46.1	71.5
National Public Radio	50.7	22.6	22.9	51.7
NewsHour with Jim Lehrer	60.8	18.6	41.5	55.9
News Magazine Shows Such as 60 Minutes, 20/20, Dateline	45.9	24.8	25.1	47.1
Shows Such as Cops, America's Most Wanted	31.0	23.0	20.0	24.7
CNBC	46.2	24.5	26.5	54.4
Fox News Cable Channel	46.7	20.6	26.0	37.8
MSNBC	50.9	22.3	29.0	52.5
Shows Such as Entertainment Tonight, Access Hollywood	35.5	24.5	29.6	25.9
Today Show, Good Morning America, Early Show	43.5	27.7	24.6	45.0
Weather Channel	43.4	20.9	20.7	38.6
Sports News on ESPN	43.7	23.3	27.5	45.0
Documentaries on Channels Such as History Channel, Discovery Channel	43.3	26.6	22.4	46.8
Daytime Talk Shows Such as Ricki Lake, Jerry Springer	26.9	16.3	20.9	18.0
Daytime Talk Shows Such as Rosie O'Donnell, Oprah	42.1	20.7	21.3	31.0
Courtroom Shows Such as Judge Judy, Divorce Court	39.1	20.2	23.5	28.1

TABLE 3.20 *Continued*

Regular Consumers of	% of Row Respondents			
	Always Vote	*Nearly Always Vote*	*Follow Presidential Election Very Closely*	*Can Identify Alan Greenspan*
News Magazines Such as *Time, US News, Newsweek*	53.6	24.2	31.2	62.6
Business Magazines Such as *Fortune, Forbes*	51.2	27.5	30.0	67.9
The National Enquirer, Sun, Star	33.2	21.6	26.5	22.7
Personality Magazines Such as *People*	34.0	22.8	19.6	37.9
Magazines Such as *The Atlantic Monthly, Harper's, The New Yorker*	48.6	29.3	30.5	69.1

market and the operation of politics is the topic of chapter 9. The Pew audience data here do allow me to analyze three relevant questions: 1) How do the interests of marginal voters versus marginal viewers overlap? 2) Do marginal voters know who stands for what in politics? and 3) Are less informed voters satisfied with their political choices after they are made.

News programmers select topics to attract marginal viewers. Campaigns choose issues to attract marginal voters. Table 3.21 examines the degree that the interests of marginal viewers and voters coincide for different news programs. The table lists the percentage of respondents following a particular type of news very closely for six different news types. The results demonstrate that for most programs the things that marginal consumers are interested in also reflect the interests of marginal voters. Since marginal voters are by definition those who may or may not vote, it is not surprising that following political events in Washington, D.C. is not high on their list of interests. Among marginal voters and the marginal consumers of all seven outlets examined, crime and health are the top-two types of news followed most closely and news about local people and events rank third. In terms of political events in Washington, this ranks fourth in interest level for marginal voters. This also ranks fourth among NPR and *NewsHour with Jim Lehrer* marginal consumers. These two outlets face relatively higher incentives to talk about political events in Washington, D.C. than the other news outlets, with 20.2% and 29.6% of their mar-

TABLE 3.21
The Interests of Marginal Voters and Marginal Viewers

| | | % of Column Respondents Following a Type of News Very Closely | | | | | | |
| | | Marginal Consumers of | | | | | | |
	Marginal Voters	National Nightly Network News	Local TV News	CNN	National Public Radio	NewsHour with Jim Lehrer	News Magazine Shows Such as 60 Minutes, 20/20, Dateline	Today Show, Good Morning America, Early Show
Political Figures/Events in Washington, DC	15.6	12.3	11.6	17.7	20.2	29.6	14.0	14.7
International Affairs	13.5	12.7	10.7	13.9	18.7	25.1	12.2	13.3
People/Events in Local Community	24.7	24.6	15.5	26.3	30.0	29.7	25.6	27.5
Entertainment	14.5	15.7	13.2	16.6	14.4	18.5	15.9	17.0
Health	28.6	28.8	23.1	30.5	31.9	37.4	25.9	32.0
Crime	27.4	29.0	20.9	31.0	32.3	30.3	27.5	31.9
2000 Presidential election	16.1	13.6	13.7	18.2	22.4	29.5	16.3	17.8
Stock market ups and downs	18.7	15.6	14.4	20.0	20.8	28.7	17.2	15.7
Debate over whether Elian Gonzales should be returned to his father	26.7	23.3	17.1	32.6	29.0	42.6	31.7	31.1
Elian Gonzales being returned	27.8	27.0	21.4	30.8	29.5	39.9	27.4	34.4
One-year anniversary of shootings at Columbine High School	14.0	21.0	14.6	18.3	17.3	23.6	17.2	23.2
Protests at World Bank and International Monetary Fund	4.2	6.2	3.7	3.8	6.6	9.9	3.6	8.4
Government recommendation to break up Microsoft	15.2	12.5	14.1	15.2	22.8	27.7	14.0	17.6

ginal consumers following this type of news very closely. Among marginal voters, 15.6% follow political events in Washington very closely. The marginal consumers of the network nightly news and local television news express less interest in politics than the marginal voters. Political events in Washington rank sixth among network news marginal viewers (12.3% following very closely) and fifth among local news marginal consumers (11.6%). For all outlets except NPR and *NewsHour*, the percentage of marginal consumers following health or crime is nearly double the percentage following political news from Washington.

The particular stories followed by marginal consumers also reflect the low interest in electoral politics among marginal voters and the marginal viewers of most programs. Relative to marginal voters, the marginal consumers of NPR and *NewsHour with Jim Lehrer* report higher interest in hard news topics such as the 2000 presidential election, stock market movements, protests at the World Bank, and the Microsoft antitrust case. Lower percentages of the marginal consumers of network evening news and local television news report following the presidential election, stock market, or Microsoft case than the percentages of marginal voters following these stories. The Elian Gonzales case generated the highest interest among each of the viewing groups examined.[18] Among network evening news marginal viewers, 27% reported following the return of Elian Gonzales very closely versus 13.6% following the 2000 presidential election. Overall these results indicate that for most news outlets the interests of marginal consumers are similar to those of marginal voters, so that programmers trying to give marginal viewers what they want will also provide marginal voters with stories they like. This means incentives for providing political news about Washington will be relatively lower, however, since marginal viewers and voters express less interest in these stories. NPR and *NewsHour with Jim Lehrer* are exceptions to this pattern, since their marginal consumers express relatively higher interest in political news. The survey data indicate overall that few viewers choose regularly to watch these outlets.

Even if readers and viewers are not following the news of politics very closely, the aggregate amount of coverage across different outlets they consume, their conversations with friends, and the paid political advertising they observe may give them enough information to participate well in politics. Table 3.22 offers evidence on a rough test of political knowledge—Can a person sort out who stands for what in American politics? When asked to rate seven political figures on a six-point scale (where 1 was very conservative and 6 very liberal), respondents were remarkably consistent in their placement of the politicians. Those who followed news about the candidates in the 2000 presidential election "very closely" and "fairly closely" ranked the candidates in the same order from right to left: Buchanan, Bush, McCain, Bradley, Gore, Clinton, Jackson. Those who said they followed the election "not too closely" came up with a similar ranking, though they ranked Clinton as more liberal than Jack-

TABLE 3.22
Maps of Politics by Interest and Activity

	Mean Ideological Ratings by Row Respondents of							
	Clinton	Gore	Bradley	Jackson	Bush	McCain	Buchanan	Self
A. Follow news about candidates for the 2000 presidential election								
Very Closely (N = 205)	4.17	3.97	3.93	4.65	2.86	2.92	2.75	3.25
Fairly Closely (N = 347)	4.28	3.96	3.70*	4.36*	2.97	3.09	2.62	3.16
Not Too Closely (N = 265)	4.34	3.79	3.68**	4.18***	3.12**	3.17*	2.65	3.36
Not at All Closely (N = 148)	4.22	3.65	3.35	4.11	3.12	3.25	3.21	3.41
B. How often would you say you vote?								
Always (N = 406)	4.32	3.92	3.88	4.50	3.02	3.12	2.62	3.17
Nearly Always (N = 303)	4.32	3.94	3.55***	4.37	2.94	2.96	2.75	3.27
Part of the Time (N = 133)	4.07	3.70	3.61*	4.02***	3.04	3.18	2.85	3.32
Seldom (N = 58)	4.43	3.76	3.48	4.07	2.83	3.12	2.77	3.23
Never (N = 60)	3.88	3.70	3.97	3.75	3.53	3.45	3.31	3.69

Note: For each rating in A, the mean for respondents following the election very closely was compared to that for those following fairly closely and those following not too closely. In B, the mean for respondents who report they always vote was compared to those who vote nearly always and those who vote part of the time. In these difference of mean tests, *** = statistically significant at the .01 level, ** = statistically significant at the .05 level, * = statistically significant at the .10 level.

son. If I compare the mean ideological ratings of each candidate for those who follow the election very closely versus fairly closely, the only two that show statistically significant differences are those for Bradley and Jackson.

The political roadmaps used by people who always vote versus those who "nearly always vote," the group I call the marginal voters, are also remarkably similar. Voters and marginal voters rank the seven politicians in the same order from right to left. In difference of means tests, only the mean ideological rating for Bill Bradley shows a statistically significant difference between the evaluations of voters and marginal voters. For those who report that they vote only "part of the time," their ranking of candidates is the same as that of those who always vote, except that those who participate less rate Clinton as more liberal than Jackson. In terms of differences of means for ideological ratings between those who always vote and those who vote only part of the time, there were only two differences that were statistically significant (i.e., Bradley and Jackson). These results indicate that relative to those who follow elections very closely or always vote, those who demonstrate less enthusiasm for political news or vote less frequently can still draw a map of where candidates stand on a conservative-liberal spectrum.

Another way to judge how well the market for political information works is to see if less-informed voters express more dissatisfaction with their choices after the fact. If there are problems with the amount of knowledge that voters have when they make their candidate selection, those with less information might be more likely to choose candidates that disappoint them once in office. The Pew data in table 3.23 indicate that the less informed are not more likely to be less satisfied in their political decisions. Those respondents who reported voting for Clinton in 1996 are sorted into four categories based on the number of correct survey answers given in identifying Bush, Bradley, and McCain. When asked in January 2000 whether they approved of the way Bill Clinton

TABLE 3.23
Ex Post Regret among Clinton Voters

	% of Column Respondents			
	Number of Correct Answers Given Identifying Bush, Bradley, and McCain			
	0	1	2	3
Do you approve or disapprove of the way Bill Clinton is handling his job as President?				
Approve	72.1	86.1	86.1	86.4
Disapprove	8.3	9.4	9.7	11.7
Don't Know/Refused	19.6	4.6	4.2	1.9

was handling his job as president, the percentage of respondents reporting disapproval was very similar across all respondent knowledge categories. Those who failed to get any candidate identifications correct reported the lowest percentage disapproving (8.3%), while those who got all identifications correct reported the highest percentage disapproving (11.7%). It is the case that those with the least knowledge had a lower percentage registering approval for the president, but this is because they had the highest percentage who responded "don't know" to this question. This unwillingness to rate the president may reflect the lack of political knowledge made evident on the candidate test. It is still the case that the Clinton voters with the least political knowledge do not express more regret, that is, disapproval of his job handling.

Conclusions

Tastes vary by age and gender. Differences in preferences for clothing or cars between women 18–34 and males 50+ do not generate headlines or public debates. Differences in tastes for news across demographic groups do generate public debate. The high fixed costs of gathering, producing, and distributing news mean that the varieties of information products offered in the market will be limited. In this sense, the tastes of others will affect the categories and combinations of news available to you.[19] Individuals also care about the media consumption of others because of the potential for news consumption to influence political beliefs and actions.

   This chapter makes apparent the importance of who cares about a particular piece of information. The highly segmented media market offers a wide variety of combinations of hard and soft news. The competition for marginal consumers among outlets, and the value placed on younger or female viewers by advertisers, helps explain a number of criticisms of the media. Network news programs target the issues they cover to attract young viewers. This leaves older viewers less satisfied with coverage than younger viewers. Since the issues used to attract young female viewers may be those associated with liberalism, this means that programs driven by profit maximization may appear to be biased because of attempts to attract viewers highly valued by advertisers. Though readers and viewers express more interest in crime, health, and local events than in the political news from Washington, D.C., enough information appears to seep through so that regular and marginal voters can draw similar roadmaps of where candidates stand in politics. The following chapter explores further how the differences in interests across demographic groups affect media content in the national television market.

Chapter **4**

Information Programs on Network Television

60 Minutes is appointment viewing. At 7 P.M. on Sunday evenings millions of viewers tune in to watch this venerable CBS news magazine. Nielsen data for the fall 1999 sweeps period tell a familiar tale about the show's popularity. During November 1999 Nielsen tracked a total of ninety-six informational programs on the broadcast television networks. *60 Minutes* attracted the largest average audience among these programs by many measures. The program garnered the most viewing households (12,397,000), most adult women (9,073,000), and most adult men (7,679,000). For some categories of viewers, however, *60 Minutes* did not even make the top ten most frequently viewed informational programs. For women 18–34, the NBC program *World's Most Amazing Videos* attracted the largest audience (1,772,000 viewers) among informational programs by showing footage of accidents and explosions. For men 18–34, the Fox offering entitled *When Good Pets Go Bad 2* was the most popular informational program (1,543,000 viewers).[1] The differences in content and viewer demographics between a program about violent (i.e., bad) pets and a program with interviews and investigations such as *60 Minutes* highlight how varied information programs can be on television.

The spatial model discussed in chapter 1 predicts that media content will depend in part on who cares about a particular piece of information, what they are willing to pay for information or others (advertisers) are willing to pay for their attention, and where they can be reached by media outlets and advertisers. This chapter uses the computer software program DICTION to show how these three factors (which are three of the five Ws) work in describing content in a particular market, the informational programs on broadcast network television. DICTION compares a text with a dictionary of ten thousand words and calculates forty different indicators based on the frequency of particular types of words. By taking a sample of the transcripts of network informational programs from November 1999 available on Lexis and running them through the DICTION program, I can describe the degree that news programs vary based on the types of words they employ.

The DICTION results show the many dimensions that differentiate the way that news is covered in different types of programming available during a viewing day. A rough way to contrast the morning network programs, such as *Today Show*, with the evening newscasts would be to say that the morning programs

TABLE 4.1
Top Ten Broadcast Network Informational Programs, Fall 1999

	Total Households			Women 18+	
Rank	Program	Audience (thousands)		Program	Audience (thousands)
1.	60 Minutes	12,397		60 Minutes	9,073
2.	60 Minutes II	9,786		60 Minutes II	7,795
3.	Dateline Tuesday	9,233		Dateline Friday	7,486
4.	Dateline Friday	8,927		Dateline Friday (Special)	7,483
5.	20/20 Friday	8,715		Dateline Tuesday	7,203
6.	48 Hours (Special)	8,714		20/20 Friday	7,033
7.	NBC Nightly News	8,409		48 Hours (Special)	6,903
8.	Dateline Friday (Special)	8,359		Dateline Monday	6,574
9.	Dateline Monday	8,217		NBC Nightly News	6,189
10.	20/20 Wednesday	8,157		20/20 Wednesday	6,140

	Women 18–34			Women 18–49	
Rank	Program	Audience (thousands)		Program	Audience (thousands)
1.	World's Most Amazing Videos (Special)	1,772		Dateline Tuesday	3,850
2.	Dateline Friday (Special)	1,627		Dateline Friday	3,828
3.	Dateline Tuesday	1,575		20/20 Wednesday	3,568
4.	20/20 Wednesday	1,493		World's Most Amazing Videos (Special)	3,476
5.	Dateline Monday	1,387		20/20 Friday	3,391
6.	When Good Pets Go Bad 2	1,324		Dateline Monday	3,346
7.	20/20 Friday	1,280		48 Hours (Special)	3,000
8.	Cops 4 (Special)	1,224		Dateline Friday	2,955
9.	America's Most Wanted: America Fights Back	1,154		When Good Pets Go Bad 2	2,704
10.	48 Hours (Special)	1,142		60 Minutes	2,695

	Teens 12–17			Men 18+	
Rank	Program	Audience (thousands)		Program	Audience (thousands)
1.	World's Most Amazing Videos (Special)	848		60 Minutes	7,679
2.	World's Sexiest Commercials	795		60 Minutes II	5,437
3.	World's Deadliest Earthquakes	724		World's Most Amazing Videos (Special)	4,935

TABLE 4.1 *Continued*

	Teens 12–17			Men 18+	
Rank	*Program*	*Audience (thousands)*		*Program*	*Audience (thousands)*
4.	When Good Pets Go Bad 2	723		Dateline Tuesday	4,825
5.	Busted on the Job 4	674		NBC Nightly News	4,657
6.	20/20 Friday	559		When Good Pets Go Bad 2	4,572
7.	World's Most Amazing Videos	486		Dateline Friday	4,438
8.	America's Most Wanted: America Fights Back	464		ABC World News Tonight (Special)	4,403
9.	20/20 Friday (Special)	464		ABC World News Tonight	4,360
10.	20/20 Wednesday	458		20/20 Wednesday	4,098

	Men 18–34			Men 18–49	
Rank	*Program*	*Audience (thousands)*		*Program*	*Audience (thousands)*
1.	When Good Pets Go Bad 2	1,543		World's Most Amazing Videos (Special)	3,487
2.	World's Most Amazing Videos (Special)	1,528		When Good Pets Go Bad 2	3,266
3.	Busted on the Job 4	1,340		60 Minutes	2,775
4.	World's Sexiest Commercials	1,252		Dateline Tuesday	2,648
5.	Cops 3 (Special)	1,208		Cops 4 (Special)	2,639
6.	Cops 4 (Special)	1,190		Cops 3 (Special)	2,624
7.	Dateline Tuesday	1,152		World's Sexiest Commercials	2,531
8.	World's Most Amazing Videos	1,107		Busted on the Job 4	2,504
9.	Cops	998		20/20 Wednesday	2,362
10.	America's Most Wanted: America Fights Back	911		World's Most Amazing Videos	2,305

Note: Audience numbers (expressed in 000s) are based on average national audiences for each program during the November 1999 sweeps period.

focus on soft news and the evening ones contain more hard news. DICTION allows one to be more precise in describing the ways these programs approach information provision. The analysis for November 1999 reveals that the morning programs score higher than the evening news on DICTION indicators for human interest, optimism, and self-references. The nightly news programs are more likely to use numerical terms, focus on collective concerns, and employ more complex language.

Matching viewer data with DICTION content indicators allows me to investigate how ratings among particular demographic groups respond to variations in content. For the sample of informational programs I analyzed for November 1999, there were clear differences between the sexes in factors that attracted viewers to programs. Controlling for how popular programs were overall, I examined what factors particularly increased the ratings among demographic groups defined by age and gender. In many cases the news dimensions measured by DICTION had opposite effects on the ratings for adult men and women. Programs that scored higher on self-references, use of collective terms, and language complexity had lower ratings among females 18+, while these factors increased ratings among males 18+. Programs that used more human interest language gained higher ratings among women 18+, though this language resulted in lower ratings among men 18+. Since demographic groups vary in their value to advertisers, I expected differences in DICTION content measures to translate into differences in advertising rates. I found that overall an increase in human interest language or self-references resulted in higher advertising rates for an informational program. Measures relating to language complexity, variety of terms, or analysis of collective concerns had no statistically significant impact on advertising rates.

To explore directly how advertising rates follow demographics, I divided up the informational programs on the four broadcast networks into two subsamples, news programs and news magazine/documentary programs. The mean price for a thirty-second ad during the news programs was $24,050. Increasing a news program's audience by ten thousand men age 18–49 increased the ad rate by $210, while increasing the number of females 18–49 watching by ten thousand caused the ad rate to increase by $160. The number of viewers age 50+ had no statistically significant impact on ad rates for news programs. The story is different for news magazines/documentaries. Here the number of men 18–49 had no statistically significant impact on advertising rates, which averaged $85,260. Increasing the number of women 18–49 watching a news magazine by ten thousand increased the ad rate by $260, while increasing the number of men and women 50+ watching by ten thousand caused the ad rate to increase by $80. These results provide additional confirmation of the value to the broadcast networks of attracting viewers 18–49, particularly women 18–49, to informational programming.

Relative Popularity of Information Programs

Television networks and advertisers divide up the programming on television by genre when they analyze the sale of viewers to advertisers. Companies in search of a particular consumer demographic may compare prices for shows in categories such as situation comedy, private detective, or adventure. In reporting the sale of advertising time on television, Nielsen Media Research uses a broad program classification called "total informational," which includes five smaller program types: conversations/colloquies; news documentary; general documentary; instructions/advice; and news. Programs in the news documentary category are generally news magazines such as *Dateline* or *60 Minutes*. General documentary shows are better known as reality programming and include *Cops, America's Most Wanted: America Fights Back,* and *Busted on the Job 4.* Conversations/colloquies include Sunday morning public affairs programs such as *Meet the Press* or *Face the Nation.* The news category includes the morning network programs such as *Today Show* or *Good Morning, America* and the three network evening newscasts. For the November 1999 sweeps period I found in Nielsen advertising data ninety-six broadcast network programs in the broad informational category.[2] In this section I analyze these information programs to show the relative popularity of different types of news.

Table 4.1 explores the top ten informational programs in the November 1999 sweeps by demographic group. News magazines garner the largest audiences in terms of total viewing households. Nine of the top ten programs in total household audiences are news magazines such as *Sixty Minutes, Dateline Tuesday,* and *20/20*. A similar story holds for informational program viewing by adult women. Among women 18+, news magazines accounted for nine of the top ten informational programs. *NBC Nightly News* (ranked ninth) was the only hard news program in women's top ten. For men 18+ the top ten most frequently viewed programs included five news magazines, three evening news programs, and two reality programs.

Breaking down the program audiences by age shows that reality programming is particularly popular among younger viewers. For women 18–49 the top ten informational programs included *World's Most Amazing Videos* (fourth) and *When Good Pets Go Bad 2* (ninth). The former focuses on video footage of accidents, while the latter shows scenes of animal violence. Among men 18–49, reality programs account for seven of the top-ten informational programs. *World's Most Amazing Videos* and *When Good Pets Go Bad 2* were the top two programs among men 18–49. Women 18–34 prefer a mix of news magazine shows (six of the top ten) and reality programs (four of top ten). Their top informational program was *World's Most Amazing Videos.* The preferences among males 18–34 for reality or documentary programs featuring accidents, violence, and sex are clear. The top programs in order for this age group are *When Good Pets Go Bad 2, World's Most Amazing Videos, Busted on the Job 4, World's Sexiest Commercials, Cops 3,* and *Cops 4.* The viewing rankings of teens 12–17 are very similar to those for men 18–34, with the exception that for teens *World's Deadliest Earthquakes* ranks number three.

News programs with a reputation for hard news content are generally absent

from these top ten lists. To see the relative popularity of news shows, consider the
rankings among different demographic groups of three NBC news programs:
NBC Nightly News, Today Show, and *Meet the Press.* Among women 18+ the
rankings for these shows were 9th, 27th, and 49th out of 96 informational programs. For men 18+ the rankings were 5th, 40th, and 48th. For women 18–34
these three NBC programs were 29th, 30th, and 54th. For men 18–34, the shows
were 28th, 40th, and 45th. For women 18–49 the programs ranked 26th, 27th,
and 54th, while among men 18–49 the rankings were 27th, 40th, and 49th. Consider also the absolute sizes of these audiences for hard news. Among women
(18–49) 3,476,000 watched *World's Most Amazing Videos,* compared with
1,856,000 for *NBC Nightly News.* For men (18–49) 3,487,000 tuned in for *World's
Most Amazing Videos,* versus 1,588,000 for *NBC Nightly News.*

These audience figures confirm the patterns evident in the survey data in
chapter 3. Older viewers prefer news programs, younger viewers flock to reality
programming, and women watch news magazines in large numbers. Determining the specific features of these different informational programs that attract different viewing audiences requires a way to analyze content across programs. In the following section I measure the relative use of different types of
words to explore what dimensions attract demographic groups to particular
types of informational programs.

Content Analysis of News Programs

The style and content of information programs on broadcast network television vary with the time of day and day of the week. Morning programs such as
Today Show start with brief news headlines and then segue into lifestyle stories,
celebrity interviews, health updates, and music performances. The dinner-
hour evening news programs contain hard news stories about politics or government, investigative reports, and lighter human interest stories. News magazines in prime time focus on the dramatic—crime, scandal, and accidents.[3] The
Sunday public affairs programs such as *Meet the Press* provide time for more
in-depth discussions with policymakers and pundits. Each of these genres of
information programs has implicit rules about what topics to cover and how to
present ideas and information. Viewers do not know the rules of thumb used
by producers, reporters, and anchors to fashion these news programs. Yet viewers do have distinct expectations about what each type of program will offer
when they turn on the television. These expectations are the brand images consumers have about these products. Uncovering how viewers map the expected
content of programs is very difficult. In this section I try to measure indirectly
some of the dimensions that give rise to these expectations. The raw data I use
in table 4.2 are from the transcripts of news programs, and the analytical tool
employed is the software program DICTION.

Roderick Hart developed DICTION to study the language of politics.[4] The program takes a five-hundred word sample of text and compares the words used with approximately ten thousand terms that are divided into thirty-three different lists. The program reports the relative frequency that words from each of the thirty-three different lists are used, combines these counts into five summary measures of content, and calculates two additional language measures (a complexity count based on average word length and a variety count based on number of different words used). Each five-hundred word sample run through DICTION thus produces forty statistical indicators. The thirty-three word lists are derived from research in communications and politics and correspond to product dimensions. The self-reference indicator, for example, counts the use of first-person language such as "I," "me," or "mine." The human interest measure reflects the use of words relating to people, such as personal pronouns (his, them), family terms (wife, grandchild), and words such as "baby" or "friend." The collectives indicator tracks the use of words relating to social groups (e.g., crowd, team), organizations (e.g., congress, army), and countries (e.g., county, republic). The thirty-three relative word counts and two measures of complexity and variety are combined into five summary indicators meant to reflect certainty, optimism, activity, realism, and commonality (e.g., values common in a group).

Though the sounds and pictures of television news are ephemeral, the transcripts of these programs live on in the Lexis database. To study how the language of information programs varies, I downloaded the transcripts of all broadcast network informational programs on Lexis for the week of November 7–13, 1999. This yielded a sample of twenty-seven programs, some of which had multiple episodes during the week.[5] Dividing the transcripts into five-hundred word segments and running each text segment through DICTION yielded an initial data set of 1,207 observations, where each observation contains the forty DICTION content measures for a text segment. After dropping the DICTION results for segments of less than four-hundred words and eliminating the texts of early morning (e.g., 2 A.M.) broadcasts, I analyzed a sample of 1,010 observations. These corresponded to the DICTION results for 1,010 news segments, which when combined contained 502,400 words.[6]

Table 4.2 reports the mean values calculated for each of the DICTION content measures for four different categories of news programming in the November 1999 sample: morning news programs, evening (i.e., dinner hour) news programs, news magazines, and Sunday public affairs programs. The overall patterns of word use suggest that morning news shows and news magazines both differ from the evening news programs, and do so in similar ways. In terms of summary scores, the evening news appears to differ more from the magazine programs than from the morning news. The differences between the Sunday public affairs programs and the evening news are generally in the same direction as those between the morning or magazine programs and the evening

TABLE 4.2
Language Use by Type of Network News Program

DICTION Dimension	Morning News Program Mean	Evening News Program Mean	News Magazine Mean	Sunday News Program Mean	Difference of Means			
					Morning-Evening	Magazine-Evening	Morning-Magazine	Sunday-Evening
Certainty								
Tenacity	41.7	29.4	37.1	42.0	12.2***	7.7***	4.6***	12.6***
Leveling	7.7	5.8	7.0	6.9	1.9***	1.2***	0.7*	1.1**
Collectives	4.0	7.7	4.6	7.5	-3.7***	-3.2***	-0.6*	-0.2
Insistence	26.7	33.6	20.8	27.9	-6.9***	-12.8***	5.9***	-5.6*
Numerical Terms	9.7	13.6	9.2	6.4	-3.9***	-4.4***	0.4	-7.2***
Ambivalence	17.7	14.7	18.8	23.7	2.9***	4.1***	-1.1*	9.0***
Self-Reference	11.2	3.0	11.7	12.0	8.1***	8.7***	-0.5	9.0***
Variety	0.5	0.6	0.5	0.5	-0.1***	-0.05***	-0.02***	-0.1***
Optimism								
Praise	7.9	4.2	5.4	6.5	3.7***	1.2***	3.4***	2.3***
Satisfaction	5.3	2.8	3.4	3.4	2.5***	0.6**	2.5***	0.7*
Inspiration	1.7	2.4	1.6	2.6	-0.7***	-0.7***	0.1	0.2
Blame	1.9	2.3	3.1	2.2	-0.4**	0.8***	-1.1***	-0.1
Hardship	3.1	6.8	7.3	3.1	-3.7***	0.5	-4.2***	-3.8***
Denial	7.3	5.4	9.1	8.8	1.9***	3.7***	-1.8***	3.4***
Activity								
Aggression	3.6	6.7	5.4	3.7	-3.2***	-1.3***	-1.9***	-3.1***
Accomplishment	6.6	10.2	7.3	9.2	-3.6***	-2.9***	-0.7**	-0.9
Communication	8.1	7.2	10.1	11.3	0.9**	2.9***	-2.1***	4.1***

Motion	5.4	4.6	4.7	4.0	0.9**	0.1	0.8**	-0.6
Cognitive Terms	9.8	8.2	10.4	16.1	1.5***	2.2***	-0.6	7.9***
Passivity	3.5	3.6	4.4	4.0	-0.1	0.8***	-0.9***	0.4
Embellishment	0.6	0.5	0.6	0.5	0.0	0.0	0.0	0.0
Realism								
Familiarity	117.8	127.4	116.2	125.6	-9.6	-11.2***	1.6	-1.8
Spatial Awareness	8.4	12.6	8.1	8.3	-4.2***	-4.5***	0.3	-4.2***
Temporal Awareness	18.4	21.5	16.0	12.0	-3.1***	-5.5***	2.4***	-9.5***
Present Concern	14.6	11.4	11.7	15.6	3.2***	0.3	2.9***	4.2***
Human Interest	33.7	18.1	42.0	31.3	15.6***	23.9***	-8.2***	13.2***
Concreteness	17.3	26.4	20.0	19.5	-9.1***	-6.4***	-2.7***	-6.9***
Past Concern	4.9	3.6	6.4	4.2	1.2***	2.7***	-1.5***	0.5
Complexity	4.3	4.6	4.3	4.4	-0.4***	-0.3***	-0.1***	-0.3***
Commonality								
Centrality	1.9	2.1	1.7	2.8	-0.3	-0.4**	0.2	0.7**
Cooperation	2.0	2.7	2.0	2.1	-0.7***	-0.7***	0.0	-0.6*
Rapport	1.1	1.6	1.1	1.6	-0.5***	-0.5***	0.0	0.0
Diversity	1.4	1.7	1.5	1.4	-0.3*	-0.3	-0.1	-0.3
Exclusion	1.3	2.2	2.0	1.6	-0.8***	-0.2	-0.7***	-0.6**
Liberation	1.0	1.1	1.2	1.3	-0.2	0.0	-0.2**	0.1
Summary Scores								
Certainty	47.8	45.9	46.3	47.8	1.9***	0.4*	1.5***	1.9***
Optimism	50.7	48.4	47.4	49.3	2.3***	-1.0***	3.4***	1.0**
Activity	51.1	52.0	51.3	50.0	-0.9***	-0.7**	-0.2	-1.9***
Realism	50.1	50.2	49.2	49.9	-0.1	-1.1***	1.0***	-0.3
Commonality	49.1	49.0	48.6	49.5	0.1	-0.4*	0.5***	0.5*
Number of segments	397	122	158	59				

Note: *** = statistically significant at the .01 level; ** = significant at the .05 level; * = significant at the .10 level.

news. This is consistent with morning programs containing a mix of hard and soft news, evening programs focusing on current events, news magazines delivering a brand of soft news focused on melodrama, and the Sunday shows offering the opinions of pundits rather than hard news analysis. The multiple categories used in DICTION allow one to explore how these impressions of hard versus soft news coverage translate into different styles and content across information programs.

The greater hard news focus on the evening news programs is apparent across multiple dimensions. The evening news programs score higher than the morning news or news magazines on the use of collective terms (e.g., those that refer to groups or organizations). Numerical terms appear more frequently in the evening news broadcasts than in the language used in the morning programs, news magazines, or Sunday public affairs shows. Discussion relating to values such as cooperation or exclusion is higher in the evening news programs. The activity score, which reflects movement or change, is greater for language in the evening news, which is not surprising since the shows often focus on a day's new events. The discussion of wars, crime, and legislative battles translates into more frequent use of terms relating to aggression on the nightly news. The evening news programs also use more complex (i.e., longer) words than the three other types of news programs.

A soft news focus is evident in the data for morning news shows and news magazines. News magazines scored highest on the use of human interest terms, followed closely by the morning news and Sunday public affairs programs. All three of these programs had greater use of human interest language than on the nightly news. Self-references are used more frequently on news magazines (which focus on personal dramas), morning programs (where entertainers or celebrities are interviewed), and the Sunday morning public affairs programs (where pundits offer their personal opinions or predictions about politics). On evening news broadcasts, journalists often spend time researching a story and developing the facts about a case. In the morning news programs, news magazines, and Sunday programs opinions and predictions may replace pronouncements of fact. This translates into higher levels of ambivalent language (e.g., allegedly, perhaps, could, suppose) used in the morning, news magazine, and Sunday programming than on the evening news. At the same time, the language used on morning and public affairs program conveys more certainty in the sense that views are expressed in a more resolute or inflexible manner than those on the evening news. This translates into higher certainty scores for these news shows than for the evening news.

The different style and content of information programs across the day also appear in word uses relating to dispositions and demeanors. The morning news programs score higher on the optimism score compared to evening news or news magazines. The morning programs, news magazines, and Sunday shows are more likely to use words of praise than the evening news shows.

These three programming niches also score higher on the use of language that conveys satisfaction. DICTION also measures language related to hardship, which includes words relating to accidents, crimes, and other adverse outcomes. The evening news programs score higher on the hardship indicator than each of the three other programming genres.

To explore how the popularity of different dimensions of information provision varies across groups, I combined the DICTION content analysis with Nielsen ratings data. For each of the transcript segments in the November 1999 information program sample I matched the DICTION indicators with the Nielsen rating for the program among different demographic groups. As variables in a model predicting a program's rating I chose DICTION measures from each of the five major content categories. The model also included the total household rating for a program. This allowed me to examine which types of content particularly drive the ratings for a given demographic group, controlling for how popular a program is in general.

The results in table 4.3 show there are distinct differences in the factors that draw men and women to information programming.[7] Men 18+ have higher ratings for programs that use self-reference terms more frequently, while an increase in self-references lowers ratings among females. Programs that use more collective terms (e.g., groups, organizations, countries) attract more men 18+. Shows that focus more on collectives earn lower ratings among women 18+, and among women 18–34 and 18–49. The greater the complexity of words (as measured by word length), the higher the rating among men 18+. The rating for women 18+ declines with the increase in the complexity score for a program. Women 18+ turn out in larger numbers for programs using human interest language (e.g., personal or family terms), while the ratings for men 18+ decline as the human interest score increases. The lower ratings among males for human interest may be driven by the lack of expressed interest by older males. For males 18–34 and 18–49, higher human interest scores translate into higher ratings. Women 18–34 and 18–49 also are drawn to human interest programming.

Some types of content draw viewers across many age groups. The hardship indicator tracks language relating to disasters, violence, tragedy, and other adverse outcomes. The higher the hardship indicator the greater the rating among each demographic group, except for the broad category of men 18+. The communication indicator measures the use of terms relating to personal interactions (e.g., listen, speak) and media experiences (e.g., film, broadcast). The higher the communication score the greater the ratings among five of the six demographic groups. For each of the six groups, the cognitive terms indicator tracking language relating to mental activities or intellectual challenges was not statistically significant in predicting ratings. These results provide additional evidence on the drawing power of danger and disappointment versus discussions of a cerebral nature.

TABLE 4.3
Impact of Program Content on Ratings for Informational Programs, Fall 1999

	Females 18+	Females 18–34	Females 18–49	Males 18+	Males 18–34	Males 18–49
Self-Reference	-3.21e-3***	-1.31e-3	-2.56e-3	3.49e-3*	1.96e-3	3.04e-3
	(9.83e-4)	(3.00e-3)	(3.19e-3)	(1.99e-3)	(2.01e-3)	(1.93e-3)
Collectives	-9.28e-3***	-2.46e-2***	-2.87e-2***	1.67e-2***	-5.24e-3	-9.51e-4
	(1.72e-3)	(5.26e-3)	(5.59e-3)	(3.50e-3)	(3.53e-3)	(3.39e-3)
Blame	1.51e-3	1.55e-2*	3.28e-3	1.04e-2*	1.46e-2**	8.26e-3
	(3.07e-3)	(9.37e-3)	(9.95e-3)	(6.23e-3)	(6.28e-3)	(6.04e-3)
Hardship	5.39e-3***	2.73e-2***	2.43e-2***	1.39e-3	2.01e-2***	1.52e-2***
	(1.64 e-3)	(5.02e-3)	(5.33e-3)	(3.33e-3)	(3.36e-3)	(3.23-3)
Communication	2.91e-3**	1.29e-2***	1.58e-2***	-4.17e-3	7.71e-3***	6.24e-3**
	(1.30e-3)	(3.97e-3)	(4.22e-3)	(2.64e-3)	(2.66e3)	(2.56e-3)
Cognitive Terms	1.63e-3	2.94e-3	2.37e-3	-3.71e-3	-2.17e-3	-2.45e-3
	(1.16e-3)	(3.55e-3)	(3.77e-3)	(2.36e-3)	(2.38e-3)	(2.29e-3)
Human Interest	1.37e-3***	1.04e-2***	1.19e-2***	-2.15e-3*	7.15e-3***	6.52e-3***
	(5.78e-4)	(1.76e-3)	(1.87e-3)	(1.17e-3)	(1.18e-3)	(1.14e-3)
Familiarity	-2.06e-3***	-1.68e-3	-6.90e-4	1.91e-3*	2.35e-3**	2.42e-3**
	(5.12e-4)	(1.56e-3)	(1.66e-3)	(1.04e-3)	(1.05e-3)	(1.01e-3)
Diversity	-1.64e-3	-6.75e-3	-7.65e-3	-1.17e-2	-9.60e-3	-1.30e-2*
	(3.55e-3)	(1.09e-2)	(1.15e-2)	(7.21e-3)	(7.28e-3)	(7.003-3)
Variety	.23	-.36	-0.65	1.00***	.14	.56*
	(.17)	(.52)	(.55)	(0.35)	(.35)	(.34)
Complexity	-7.25e-2*	-5.53e-3	-7.59e-2	.14*	6.76e-2	.10
	(4.28e-2)	(.130)	(.139)	(8.67e-2)	(8.75e-2)	(8.41e-2)
Adjusted R^2	.99	.78	.84	.96	0.79	.90

Note: Dependent variable is the November 1999 rating for the program which contained the segment. Sample consists of 992 transcript segments from broadcast network informational programs shown from November 7–13, 1999. Each specification also included an intercept term and a total households ratings term. Standard errors are in parentheses. *** = statistically significant at the.01 level; ** = significant at the .05 level; * = significant at the .10 level.

Age also plays a role in the ability of some content indicators to predict program popularity. Controlling for how many households a show attracts, I find that programs that use more language associated with blame (e.g., mean, stupid, rash, painful, cruel) score higher ratings among women 18–34 and men 18–34. The familiarity score captures the use of some of the most commonly used words (e.g., across, that, for). Programs that score higher on the familiarity indicator attract higher ratings among males 18–34 and 18–49; "familiarity" was not statistically significant in determining the ratings of women 18–34 or 18–49. Variety of expression, measured by the ratio of unique words in a text segment to total words, is meant in part to measure the precision of expression. Greater variety in expression does not increase ratings among males 18–34. For men 18–49 and men 18+ (the measure that includes men over 50), programs with more variety of expression score higher ratings. Variety did not influence the ratings among any of the three female demographic groups examined.

The spatial model of media competition implies that the content provided by media outlets will vary with consumer tastes.[8] The DICTION analysis of informational programs here defines differences in news program content by word use. The ratings analysis reveals which dimensions are particularly effective in attracting specific demographic groups defined by gender and age. Since advertisers care about the size and demographic composition of a viewing audience, the relative popularity of particular types of content among viewers should translate into different advertising returns for specific types of content. Table 4.4 shows how advertising prices the networks charge for informational programs vary with the product dimensions measured by DICTION. To conduct the analysis I matched each text segment from the November 1999 informational program sample with the average price for a thirty-second ad on the show.[9] The results indicate that overall elements associated with soft news content result in higher advertising rates. The greater the use of self-reference terms, the larger the advertising rate charged by the broadcast networks for a program. Shows using more human interest terms, which are particularly popular among female and younger viewers, also command a premium in the advertising marketplace. The language of hardship, which covers disasters, violence, and tragedies, attracts viewers in numbers that translate into higher advertising prices. Programs higher in communication terms (e.g., film, broadcast) also register higher advertising prices.

Product dimensions that one might associate with hard news provision do not in general have a statistically significant impact on advertising prices. The use of collective terms had no statistically significant impact on ad rates. Complexity of word use, as measured by word length, did not have an impact. Variety of expression was not statistically significant in explaining the ad prices on information programs. Shows that scored higher on cognitive terms did, however, garner higher advertising prices.

Table 4.5 reinforces the points that informational programs are targeted at specific demographic groups and that the willingness of advertisers to pay for

TABLE 4.4
Impact of Program Content on Advertising Rates, Fall 1999

Intercept	−35.49*
	(19.64)
Self-Reference	0.21**
	(0.10)
Collectives	−0.02
	(0.18)
Blame	0.34
	(0.12)
Hardship	0.48***
	(0.17)
Communication	0.61***
	(0.14)
Cognitive Terms	0.33***
	(0.12)
Human Interest	0.41***
	(0.06)
Familiarity	0.08
	(0.05)
Cooperation	−0.03
	(0.28)
Variety	1.20
	(17.42)
Complexity	−2.00
	(4.49)
Adjusted R^2	0.78

Note: Dependent variable is the November 1999 advertising rate (in $000) for a thirty-second ad during the program which contained the segment. Sample consists of 1,010 transcript segments from broadcast network informational programs shown from November 7–13, 1999. Standard errors are in parentheses. *** = statistically significant at the .01 level; ** = significant at the .05 level; * = significant at the .10 level.

the attention of viewers varies with their age and gender. For the full set of eighty-two informational programs on the four major broadcast networks in November 1999, the mean price for a thirty-second advertisement was $44,950. The mean number of viewers for the set of eighty-two programs was 1,112,000 men 18–49, 1,344,000 women 18–49, and 2,922,000 men and women age 50+. While viewers over 50 account for more than half of the average audience for an informational program, the networks are rewarded less by advertisers for attracting their attention. For the full sample of informational programs, adding an additional ten thousand female viewers 18–49 increases the advertising rate by $290. Attracting an additional ten thousand viewers age 50+ only increases the advertising rate by $42. Note that for informational pro-

TABLE 4.5
Determinants of Advertising Rates on Broadcast Network Informational Programs,
Fall 1999

	All Informational Programs (N = 82)	News Programs (N = 50)	News Magazine/ Documentary Programs (N = 28)
Intercept	−3.75	0.82	3.79
	(3.60)	(2.87)	(19.2)
Men 18–49			
Viewing (000)	−2.27e-3	2.10e-2***	−8.03e-3
	(5.37e-3)	(7.08e-3)	(9.61e-3)
Women 18–49			
Viewing (000)	2.91e-2***	1.59e-2**	2.59e-2***
	(5.07e-3)	(6.24e-3)	(8.69e-3)
Men and Women			
50+ Viewing (000)	4.16e-3***	−5.59e-4	7.90e-3***
	(1.22e-3)	(1.52e-3)	(2.32e-3)

Note: Dependent variable is the November 1999 advertising rate (in $000) for a thirty-second ad during the program. Standard errors are in parentheses. *** = statistically significant at the .01 level; ** = significant at the .05 level; * = significant at the .10 level.

grams overall, the number of men 18–49 did not have a statistically significant impact on ad rates.

The targeting of demographic groups is also apparent when the sample is divided by programming genre into news shows (N=50) and news magazine/documentary programs (N=28). The mean advertising price for a thirty-second ad was $24,050 for the news programs and $85,260 for the news magazines/documentaries. Although news programs are highly popular among those over 50, the analysis of advertising data indicates that it is the viewership of those 18–49 that drives advertising rates. An additional ten thousand men 18–49 increases the price for a thirty-second ad on a news program by $210. Increasing the number of women 18–49 watching by ten thousand raises the ad price by $160. The number of viewers age 50+ was not statistically significant in determining the advertising rate on news programs. A different picture emerges in the sale of audiences for news magazines/documentaries. There the viewing of men 18–49 is not a statistically significant factor in modeling ad prices. Increasing the number of women 18–49 watching by ten thousand results in a $260 increase in the advertising rate. Attracting ten thousand more viewers age 50+ also increases the ad rate, but by a smaller amount ($80). These results confirm the value of viewers 18–49, especially women 18–49, to broadcasters seeking to assemble audiences to sell to advertisers.

Conclusions

The market for information programs on television convenes daily as viewers turn on their sets. On an average night during the November 1999 sweeps, sixty-three million households had their televisions turned on between 8 P.M. and 9 P.M.[10] Fashioning a program to attract a significant number of these viewers represents a tremendous challenge for programmers, who must consider many variables: the relative interests of viewers; the value of particular viewers to advertisers; and the plans of competitors to offer shows aimed at specific demographic groups. The results here show that when the networks offer information programs the content they choose favors the provision of soft news over hard news. The DICTION software analysis provides a way to quantify these choices. Relative to the evening news programs, for example, the morning programs and news magazines are more likely to use language that focuses on human interest, uses self-references, and contains shorter words. These genres are also less likely to use the collective terms or numerical phrases that are employed on the nightly news programs.

Differences in the style and content of information programs translate readily into distinct differences in audience composition. Controlling for the general popularity of a program, I find that ratings are higher among women where human interest language is used more frequently. Ratings among men increase where collective terms are used or self-references employed. Younger viewers of both sexes turn out for shows that score higher on the language of blame or focus on human interest. The differences in audiences translate into different advertising rates for programs. Shows that score higher on human interest and self-reference charge more for thirty-second ads. Dimensions such as use of collective phrases, complexity of terms, or variety of word use did not have a statistically significant impact on ad rates. The variation of ad prices with viewer demographics shows the strong returns to attracting viewers 18–49, particularly women, to many types of information programming. Overall, the analysis of information programs on network television reinforces that news interests segment by age and gender and that the market rewards outlets differently for gaining the attention of specific demographic groups. The next chapter focuses on how the spatial model helps explain outcomes in two sets of relatively smaller markets, local newspaper and local television markets.

Chapter **5**

What Is News on Local Television Stations and in Local Newspapers

LOCAL NEWS is often crafted and marketed as a personalized product. Local television stations promise to be "your eyewitness news team," to be "on your side," or to deliver "news you can use." Local newspapers stress their ties to the community in statements or slogans on their mastheads and editorial pages. Internet versions of these papers often invite readers to "personalize" the newspaper by selecting the types of news they wish to see. The large fixed costs of creating a news story means that individuals will not find a story to match their every interest. The likelihood that you are the "You" in television and newspaper advertising campaigns depends on local demographics. How many local residents share your interests? How attractive are you to advertisers? How many outlets are clamoring for your attention? This chapter explores the impacts on content of local demand for information and the supply of contending media outlets. The results overall demonstrate the influence of local consumers' tastes and of owners outside the community on the types of news delivered.

The spatial location model described in chapter 1 offers a number of predictions about how local television stations will shape their news broadcasts. Within a given market, some news directors will attempt to capture younger or female viewers with news programs that feature less hard news and more soft news. Across markets, stations in cities where viewers exhibit a greater interest in public affairs information will be more likely to include national or international hard news stories in their local news broadcasts and more likely to cover local and state officials. News programs in markets where people have a stronger preference for soft news will be more likely to cover topics such as entertainment news. Stations owned by group owners may be more likely to provide news from outside the local area because of the low costs of transmitting information developed by affiliated stations. In this sense, group ownership can translate into less time for coverage of local or state officials. The affiliation of a station with a particular network will also influence the local news content. A station may be more likely to include stories about its affiliated network's programs or stars, both because this reinforces demand for the station's entertainment programming and because the network is likely to offer prepackaged stories for free about a program or star to its local news outlets.

The theory of information bundling outlined in chapter 1 provides insight into how local newspapers will tailor their coverage. Television news directors have to worry about the impact of each story on all viewers, since stories have to be presented in the same fashion to all of the program's consumers. The nature of a newspaper as a portfolio of stories allows readers to make choices about what stories to consume. This means that newspapers can add stories of less-than-universal interest without alienating the majority of readers, since a paper's consumers can choose which sections and articles to peruse.[1] Audience demand will still influence the bundle of stories editors choose to offer, with greater interest in hard news in a city resulting in more hard news content in the local paper. In adding stories with limited appeal, the editors will still calculate the number of potential readers to decide what specialized coverage gets added to the news product. If the real-world incidence of a problem interests a newspaper's target readers, then the extent of a policy problem in a city will be a good predictor of its coverage. If a paper's target audience, which will generally be an area's more affluent and educated residents, is less interested in a problem, then the prevalence of that problem in a city will not affect its coverage.[2] There is a market-induced limit on the impact of some local tastes on content. Many papers will endorse presidential candidates in their editorials. The endorsements may arise from a desire of owners to express their ideology, or an attempt by papers to satisfy audience demand for political expression. The profitability of objective coverage in news coverage discussed in chapter 2, however, should mean that a paper's editorial endorsement will not affect how it covers national political events such as the race for the presidency.

This chapter explores the workings of local television news markets by taking a snapshot of local news programs in the top fifty television markets in November 1999. The results largely bear out the predictions of the spatial news model. Programs targeted at specific demographics do vary their news contents. Local television news shows with a higher percentage of female viewers were less likely to show hard news stories dealing with national and international affairs and less likely to do stories about state and local political officials. Programs in markets with higher viewer interest in hard news carried a higher number of national hard news stories and local political stories. In areas where viewers demonstrated a greater taste for entertainment news, news directors added more soft news stories to local news broadcasts. Stations owned by group owners carried fewer hard news stories and fewer stories about a state's U.S. Senators. Network affiliation also influenced which celebrities and television programs were discussed on local television news broadcasts. Fox stations were more likely to carry stories about the Fox program *Greed*. ABC stations were more likely to talk about Monica Lewinsky during the time when the network's star Barbara Walters became the first person to interview in-depth the former intern about her relationship with President Clinton. ABC affiliates were also more likely to air segments in their newscasts about the highly successful quiz program *Who Wants to Be a Millionaire?*.

The analysis of local newspaper markets focuses on the content of daily newspapers in the top fifty cities in samples of coverage from 1998 through 2000. Using the same soft news stories from November 1999 examined in the television analysis, I find that the overall interests of readers had no statistically significant impact on the number of soft news stories carried in the daily newspapers. For particular hard news topics in 1998 and 1999 I am able to measure the local incidence of the problems. For stories such as poverty, Medicaid, and campaign finance reform, I find that local interest in hard news translates into more stories on these topics in the local daily newspapers. In terms of local incidence of problems, areas with greater levels of food stamps or family assistance spending actually have fewer articles written about these topics. For topics likely to be of interest to a paper's target readers, such as computers or soft money contributions in politics, the greater the real-world incidence of these topics in the community the larger the number of stories about the topic in the paper. In contrast, local crime rates have almost no statistically significant impact in explaining the amount of coverage devoted to particular types of crime in a city. Crime coverage appears to be more related to reader interest than real-world incidence. An area where coverage appears divorced from local preferences is news coverage of the presidential campaign. Analysis of the coverage of the convention speeches by Al Gore and George Bush in 2000 shows that there were almost no differences based on the editorial politics of a paper. Newspapers covered Gore's speech in similar ways regardless of which candidate the editorial page endorsed. The same pattern held for coverage of Bush's speech.

A key decision in analyzing media coverage of hard and soft stories in local news markets lies in defining hard and soft news.[3] The following sections lay out the definitions of these terms and explore how local television stations and newspapers make their content selections based on audience interests in different topics.

Local Television News Programs

Local television news programs can cover the world. The primary focus of news programs produced by local stations remains local, including local weather, sports, crimes, and accidents. The easy availability of satellite feeds and the stream of stories generated by news services and the networks means that local news directors also have the ability to include national or international stories in their broadcasts. The resources devoted by entertainment companies to publicizing film releases and television programs means that local news programs can easily carry stories about celebrities and their work. While community events that can be covered will vary widely across cities, local television news directors in different markets face the same potential pool of national hard news stories and same potential set of national entertainment celebrities to cover. It could be the case that decisions about whether to include a national hard or soft news story in a local news broadcast depend on a news director's vision of what local viewers need to know. If the self-interest of broadcasters drives the selection of stories, however, the interests of local viewers and structure of the local broadcasting market will influence the content decisions in local news programs.[4]

To test the impact of market forces on local television news programs I took a snapshot of decisions made in the top fifty local television markets during November 1999 about how to cover national hard and soft news stories. The sample of hard news stories was defined as those stories during the month that were included in the end of the program summary on the broadcasts of the *NewsHour with Jim Lehrer* on PBS. This definition yielded a total of thirty-eight hard news stories, including reports about the stock market, budget bill debates, an earthquake in Turkey, and the Microsoft antitrust case. For soft news stories, I analyzed the stories promoted in the opening segments of the entertainment/tabloid television programs *Entertainment Tonight, Access Hollywood,* and *Inside Edition.* This generated a sample of ninety-six soft news topics, including Carmen Electra, Tom Hanks, Sylvester Stallone, *Who Wants to Be a Millionaire?,* and the World Wrestling Federation. To measure the coverage of state and local public affairs, I used the names in each respective television market of the U.S. senators, the governor, and the mayor(s). Searching the abstracts in Lexis of local television news programs allowed me to count the number of stories about these topics on a specific news program during its broadcasts in November 1999. At least twelve broadcasts of a given news program had to be abstracted for the program to be included in the analysis. The availability of news abstracts in Lexis resulted in a sample of 707 local television news programs spread across forty-nine of the top fifty television markets.

If local news directors decide what is news based on audience demand, program content should vary across and within markets in predictable ways. Areas where residents have a strong interest in public affairs should get more hard news stories included in their local news. Within a given market, a station targeting demographic audiences interested in government should include more national hard news stories and fewer national soft news stories. To measure the variation (across cities) in tastes for particular types of information, I use figures based on the percentage of households in the television market that subscribe to four magazines: *Time* (reflects interest in hard news); *People* (reflects tastes for entertainment/celebrity stories); *Modern Maturity* (denotes interests of residents age 50+); and *Playboy* (captures interest of younger men in sexual content).[5] Since the age and gender composition of television audiences varies by time of day, I control for attempts to target particular demographic groups by noting when a program aired. Nielsen ratings data on the percentage of a given program's adult viewers who were 18–49 in November 1999 and on the percentage that were female also allow me to test specifically how shows with particular demographics target their content. The brand position of a local news program may also relate to its network affiliation, since the lead-in audience for news programs will depend on the viewers watching the previous entertainment programs. News directors at Fox affiliate stations, for example, may choose stories aimed at younger viewers since the audience for Fox entertainment shows are often younger than those for the other major broadcast networks.[6]

On the supply side, I include the number of broadcast stations in a market to examine how increased competition affects news decisions. Nearly all (96%) of the programs in the sample air on stations controlled by group owners, defined as companies that own more than one station. To see how the type of media company that owns a station may affect local news decisions, I include controls for whether a station is controlled by a group owner, the total number of stations held by the owner, and the number of newspapers held by the owner.[7]

The results in table 5.1 indicate that patterns of hard and soft news coverage across markets vary predictably based on audience interests and market structure. Competition appears to generate higher story totals for national hard news, national soft news, and state and local officials' stories. This may be because as the number of broadcast stations in a market increases, the pressure to hold viewer attention generates shorter stories (and hence more stories per broadcast). As market size increases, stations are more likely to increase soft news coverage and less likely to include stories about national hard news topics or state/local officials. Strong evidence that local news directors make content decisions based on audience demand appears in the link between program content and magazine circulation in the area. Stations in cities with higher circulations for *Time* are more likely to cover hard news stories. A one percentage point increase in *Time* magazine circulation in a city translates into 2.78 more national hard news stories covered on a local news program in the market during the month. Markets with higher circulations for *People* magazine also carry more hard news stories, with a one percentage point increase in the *People* magazine circulation resulting in 1.65 more hard news stories.[8] For soft news coverage, areas with higher *Time* magazine circulations have fewer soft news stories. A one percentage point increase in *Time* circulation results in 3.48 fewer stories about national entertainment topics or celebrities. News directors in cities where *People* magazine is popular are more likely to add soft news stories to local news broadcasts. A one percentage point increase in the *People* circulation results in 4.24 more soft news stories covered in a program. Soft news coverage is lower in areas with higher circulation for *Playboy*, which may be because soft news is generally targeted at female viewers and higher *Playboy* circulations may represent more young males in a market.[9] Coverage of state and local officials also responds to audience demand, with a one percentage point increase in *Time* magazine circulation generating .6 more stories about the U.S. Senators, the governor, or mayors in a market.

TABLE 5.1
Determinants of Local News Broadcast Content

	Hard News Story Totals	Soft News Story Totals	State and Local Officials Story Totals
Total Television Households (000)	−1.74e-3**	1.80e-3***	−1.54e-3***
	(7.08e-4)	(6.44e-4)	(2.56e-4)
No. Broadcast Stations	0.47**	0.53**	0.69***
	(0.42)	(0.22)	(0.09)
Broadcast Length 30 Minutes	−8.56***	−8.33***	−1.25***
	(1.01)	(0.92)	(0.36)
No. Days in Sample	0.75***	0.37***	0.16***
	(0.13)	(0.12)	(0.05)
Program Starts 4–5:30 PM	−5.47***	−1.23	0.50
	(1.08)	(0.98)	(0.39)
Program Starts 6–7 PM	−11.45***	−6.46***	1.13***
	(1.20)	(1.10)	(0.43)
Program Starts 9–11:30 PM	−4.52***	−0.07	0.82
	(1.21)	(1.10)	(0.43)
Time Circulation, %	2.78***	−3.48***	0.60**
	(0.82)	(0.74)	(0.30)
People Circulation, %	1.65**	4.24***	0.28
	(0.81)	(0.74)	(0.29)
Modern Maturity Circulation, %	−0.10	−0.20**	−0.08**
	(0.11)	(0.10)	(0.04)
Playboy Circulation, %	−1.66	−1.90**	0.06
	(1.05)	(0.95)	(0.40)
Group Owned Station	−4.19*	−2.90	−0.20
	(2.15)	(1.96)	(0.77)
No. TV Stations Held by Station Owner	0.07	−0.01	0.03
	(0.06)	(0.06)	(0.02)
No. Newspapers Held by Station Owner	−7.24e-3	−0.02	−0.01*
	(0.02)	(0.02)	(6.34e-3)
ABC Affiliate	3.88*	7.20***	1.54*
	(2.27)	(2.07)	(0.81)
CBS Affiliate	3.58	4.26**	1.16
	(2.26)	(2.06)	(0.81)
FOX Affiliate	6.59***	8.77***	1.14
	(2.47)	(2.25)	(0.88)
NBC Affiliate	4.01*	3.63*	0.97
	(2.24)	(2.04)	(0.80)
Election, Governor			1.93
			(0.94)
Election, U.S. Senator			7.97***
			(1.06)

TABLE 5.1 *Continued*

	Hard News Story Totals	Soft News Story Totals	State and Local Officials Story Totals
Election, Mayor			−0.08**
			(0.29)
Adjusted R^2	0.32	0.37	0.21

Note: Standard errors in parentheses. *** = statistically significant at the .01 level; ** = significant at the .05 level; * = significant at the .10 level. Each specification also included an intercept term. Totals are for November 1999 broadcasts of 672 local news programs.

Group ownership also affects story selection. Stations owned by a company with more than one broadcast station are less likely to provide hard news. Programs on group-owned stations provided 4.19 fewer national hard news stories. Group ownership did not have a statistically significant impact on soft news coverage. Relative to stations not affiliated with the four major networks, stations with a major network affiliation generally carried more hard and soft new stories. The Fox stations had the greatest difference with unaffiliated stations, carrying 6.59 more national hard news stories. This may be because Fox stations have more stories to generate a faster pace for attracting (relatively) younger audiences. It may also relate to the fact that Fox stations do not carry a national evening news broadcast, so they may be more likely to include national hard news stories in their local broadcasts. Fox affiliates also had more national soft news stories, registering 8.77 more stories. In terms of time of day effects, programs in the afternoon or evening carried fewer national hard news stories relative to the noon broadcasts. The dinner-hour newscast (6–7 P.M.) carried significantly fewer soft news stories (6.46) relative to the noon-hour broadcasts. The dinner-hour offerings carried more stories about state/local officials, however, than the lunchtime programs. Programs that were only thirty minutes (rather than an hour) carried fewer of each story type. Programs with more days of transcripts in the sample had higher story counts. Programs in an area holding a U.S. Senate election had higher counts of officials' stories. Elections for governor or mayor, however, did not have this impact.

Within a given television market, news programs may segment so that some appeal to specific demographic groups based on age and gender. To examine this hypothesis, I use Nielsen ratings data from November 1999 to estimate for each program the percentage of a program's adult viewers that are 18–49 and the percentage that are female. This specification assumes that the actual viewers garnered by a program provide evidence on the targeted viewers and relates viewer composition to program content. Table 5.2 uses the same specifications as table 5.1 but replaces the audience demand information variables relating to

TABLE 5.2
Targeting Audiences through Local News Broadcast Content

	Hard News Story Totals	Soft News Story Totals	State and Local Officials Story Totals
Total Television Households (000)	−1.03e-3	1.53e-3***	−9.02e-4***
	(6.35e-4)	(5.82e-4)	(2.27e-4)
No. Broadcast Stations	0.14	0.66***	0.55***
	(0.21)	(0.19)	(0.08)
Broadcast Length 30 Minutes	−8.87***	−8.63***	−1.44***
	(1.01)	(0.93)	(0.36)
No. Days in Sample	0.81***	0.31***	0.19***
	(0.13)	(0.12)	(0.05)
Program Starts 4–5:30 PM	−6.82***	−0.19	−0.30
	(1.26)	(1.15)	(0.45)
Program Starts 6–7 PM	−13.53***	−4.73***	−0.03
	(1.54)	(1.41)	(0.54)
Program Starts 9–11:30 PM	−5.72***	1.97	−0.27
	(1.67)	(1.53)	(0.59)
Program Viewers (000)	1.12e-3	−4.27e-3	6.27e-3***
	(1.12e-3)	(5.04e-3)	(1.94e-3)
% Program Viewers 18–49	−0.04	−0.03	−8.03e-3
	(0.04)	(0.04)	(0.01)
% Program Viewers Female	−0.23***	0.11	−0.09***
	(0.09)	(0.08)	(0.03)
Group Owned Station	−5.59**	−1.41	−0.79
	(2.24)	(2.06)	(0.79)
No. TV Stations Held by Station Owner	0.08	0.01	0.03
	(0.06)	(0.06)	(0.02)
No. Newspapers Held by Station Owner	−0.01	−0.03*	−0.01*
	(0.02)	(0.02)	(6.36e-3)
ABC Affiliate	7.41***	1.12	1.27
	(2.58)	(2.36)	(0.91)
CBS Affiliate	7.28***	−2.11	1.12
	(2.63)	(2.41)	(0.93)
FOX Affiliate	9.19***	3.16	0.82
	(2.56)	(2.31)	(0.90)
NBC Affiliate	7.44***	−2.13	0.52
	(2.52)	(2.34)	(0.93)
Election, Governor			1.57*
			(0.93)
Election, Senator			8.39***
			(1.03)
Election, Mayor			0.03
			(0.29)
Adjusted R^2	0.29	0.34	0.21

Note: Standard errors in parentheses. *** = statistically significant at the .01 level; ** = significant at the .05 level; * = significant at the .10 level. Each specification also included an intercept term. Totals are for November 1999 broadcasts of 695 local news programs.

magazine circulation with Nielsen ratings information. The results indicate that programs targeting female viewers are less likely to cover national hard news stories and state/local official stories. This is consistent with the evidence in chapter 3 indicating that female viewers express lower interest in government and public affairs coverage. An increase in one percentage point in a program audience's female viewing percentage results in .23 fewer national hard news stories and .09 fewer state and local officials stories. The age composition of the program did not have a statistically significant impact on hard or soft news coverage. Programs with larger viewerships did cover state/local officials more.[10]

Table 5.3 offers more detailed evidence on covering local officials. The table reports logit results where the dependent variable is whether a program carried any stories during November 1999 about the state's governor, its U.S. Senators, or the mayors in the relevant television market. As the circulation for *Time* increased in a market, stations were more likely to carry stories about U.S. Senators from the state and stories about local mayors. The higher the *People* magazine circulation, the lower the probability that a program would cover the relevant senators or mayors in a market. Programs with a higher female percentage of viewers were less likely to cover governors or mayors. Female audience composition had no impact on Senate coverage. Overall, programs with larger audiences were more likely to cover local U.S. senators. Group-owned stations did not differ from others in their coverage of governors or mayors, but group-owned stations were less likely to cover U.S. Senators in their local news programs. Note, however, that as the number of stations owned by the parent company grew the likelihood that the program would contain news about U.S. Senators or the local mayors increased.

While news directors may favor soft news stories in markets where viewers are strongly interested in entertainment or celebrity stories, a station's network affiliation may influence which particular stars, shows, or movies are discussed on local television news programs. Stations may talk about stars that appear on their network to reinforce demand for the entertainment programs shown on the local station. News directors may also include stories about network stars since the network may supply ready-made stories about the programs for easy inclusion in local news shows.[11] Table 5.4 examines how coverage of specific topics from the soft news sample varied by network affiliation. The table reports the percentage of programs on stations with a given network's affiliation that had at least one story about the person or product in the column headings. The results clearly indicate that local stations insert stories about their network's stars or programs during their news programs. During November 1999, the program *Who Wants to Be a Millionaire?* attracted significant media coverage as a cultural phenomenon. The popular ABC quiz show was mentioned in 80.2% of the local news programs on ABC network affiliates. This contrasts with zero mentions on the news programs of NBC affiliates. Regis Philbin, the quiz program's host, rated mentions on 33.5% of ABC affiliate news programs,

TABLE 5.3
Determinants of Local News Broadcast Coverage of State and Local Affairs

Variable	Coefficient (Standard Error)					
	Governors	U.S. Senators	Mayors	Governors	U.S. Senators	Mayors
Intercept	-0.98	-4.75***	-4.51***	1.60	-0.48	0.97
	(1.24)	(1.48)	(1.31)	(1.57)	(1.73)	(1.58)
Total Television Households (000)	-7.5e-4***	-3.5e-4*	-1.6e-4	-5.9e-4***	-3.8e-4**	-3.0e-5
	(1.67e-4)	(2.06e-4)	(1.74e-4)	(1.47e-4)	(1.63e-4)	(1.59e-4)
No. Broadcast Stations	0.24***	0.02	0.12**	0.18***	0.02	0.10
	(0.06)	(0.06)	(0.06)	(0.05)	(0.05)	(0.05)
Broadcast Length 30 Minutes	-0.22	0.04	-0.24	-0.20	-0.22	-0.39
	(0.23)	(0.25)	(0.25)	(0.23)	(0.24)	(0.24)
No. Days in Sample	0.11***	-3.40e-3	0.09***	0.10***	0.02	0.10***
	(0.03)	(0.03)	(0.03)	(0.03)	(0.03)	(0.03)
Program Starts 4–5:30 P.M.	0.12	-0.03	0.54**	-0.17	-0.54*	-0.02
	(0.25)	(0.28)	(0.25)	(0.28)	(0.31)	(0.28)
Program Starts 6–7 P.M.	-0.18	0.39	0.76***	-0.62*	-0.24	-0.10
	(0.27)	(0.30)	(0.28)	(0.34)	(0.36)	(0.35)
Program Starts 9–11:30 P.M.	0.04	0.04	0.36	-0.45	-0.74*	-0.49
	(0.28)	(0.31)	(0.28)	(0.37)	(0.41)	(0.38)
Time Circulation, %	-0.36*	0.96***	0.93***			
	(0.19)	(0.21)	(0.22)			
People Circulation, %	0.17	-0.34*	-0.52***			
	(0.19)	(0.20)	(0.20)			
Modern Maturity Circulation, %	-0.03	-0.07***	-0.03			
	(0.02)	(0.03)	(0.02)			
Playboy Circulation, %	-0.09	0.69***	0.16			
	(0.24)	(0.27)	(0.26)			

	(1)	(2)	(3)	(4)	(5)
Program Viewers (000)	0.22		1.52e-3	5.21e-3***	1.11e-3
	(0.51)		(1.25e-3)	(1.37e-3)	(1.41e-3)
% Program Viewers 18–49	5.07e-3		-0.22	1.24	1.09
	(0.01)		(0.92)	(1.02)	(0.94)
% Program Viewers Female	-2.37e-3		-5.57***	-1.57	-7.29***
	(4.06e-3)		(1.95)	(2.17)	(2.01)
Group Owned Station	-1.06**	-0.39	-0.37	-0.99**	-0.71
	(0.52)	(0.49)	(0.52)	(0.50)	(0.50)
No. TV Stations Held by Station Owner	0.03*	0.04***	9.30e-3	0.02	0.04***
	(0.02)	(0.02)	(0.01)	(0.02)	(0.01)
No. Newspapers Held by Station Owner	-0.01**	-5.57e-3	-2.82e-3	-0.01**	-7.15e-3*
	(4.99e-3)	(4.25e-3)	(3.94e-3)	(4.88e-3)	(4.06e-3)
ABC Affiliate	0.29	0.79	0.45	0.80	1.78***
	(0.55)	(0.51)	(0.58)	(0.68)	(0.58)
CBS Affiliate	-0.10	0.63	0.19	0.89	1.76***
	(0.54)	(0.50)	(0.59)	(0.69)	(0.60)
FOX Affiliate	-0.62	1.07*	-0.35	0.65	1.55***
	(0.59)	(0.57)	(0.57)	(0.68)	(0.59)
NBC Affiliate	0.11	0.60	0.24	0.54	1.45**
	(0.54)	(0.50)	(0.57)	(0.67)	(0.57)
Election, Governor	-0.26		0.17		
	(0.64)		(0.61)		
Election, U.S. Senator	16.82	16.82		16.97	
	(752.6)	(752.6)		(738.6)	
Election, Mayor		-0.03			-0.05
		(0.19)			(0.18)
Log Likelihood	-404.8	-391.9	-427.0	-379.8	-403.8

Note: Dependent variable in logit analysis equals 1 if program covered the state's governor or U.S. Senators or the mayors within the DMA in November 1999 programming. *** = statistically significant at the .01 level; ** = significant at the .05 level; * = significant at the .10 level. Sample contained 672 local news programs.

versus 1% of CBS affiliate news programs in the sample. The Fox network introduced a quiz show called *Greed* that was modeled after ABC's successful program. The program gained mentions on 37.9% of Fox news programs versus zero for CBS or NBC affiliates.

Promotion of a particular episode of a program during a sweeps period is also evident in the data. During November 1999 the Fox program *Ally McBeal* contained a lesbian kiss scene, a story line covered in the popular press.[12] Among Fox affiliates, 34.7% of the news programs contained stories about *Ally McBeal* versus 2.5% for CBS affiliates. In November 1999 Barbara Walters scored the journalistic coup of landing an interview with Monica Lewinsky, the intern involved in a sex scandal with President Clinton. Though for a time she was featured nightly on news programs, by 1999 coverage of Lewinsky had faded. In order to promote her book, Lewinsky granted Barbara Walters an interview on ABC. On the ABC affiliates, 17.6% of programs mentioned Monica Lewinsky during the month versus 4.0% on CBS affiliates. Ricky Martin had a music special on CBS during the month. While 29.2% of programs on CBS affiliates mentioned Ricky Martin, high percentages of programs on ABC (28.6%) and Fox (27.4%) also discussed the Latin pop star.

When *Toy Story 2* was released in November 1999 the movie received wide coverage across all networks. The film was produced by Disney, the parent company of ABC. Among news programs on ABC affiliates, 37.9% mentioned *Toy Story* during the month versus 30.7% for CBS and 28.9% on NBC. Fox affiliates, which aim for a younger demographic audience, actually had the highest percentage of programs mentioning the movie, 44.2%. In terms of talking about the stars of this animated movie, Fox affiliate news programs referred to Tom Hanks so frequently that 41.1% carried at least one reference to him.

TABLE 5.4
Impact of Network Affiliation on Local News Broadcast Coverage of Soft News Stories

Program's Station Affiliation	*Percentage of Programs Covering during November 1999*								
	Tim Allen	*Greed*	*Tom Hanks*	*Monica Lewinsky*	*Ricky Martin*	*Ally McBeal*	*Regis Philbin*	*Toy Story*	*Who Wants to Be a Millionaire?*
ABC Affiliate (N = 182)	13.2	1.7	19.2	17.6	28.6	5.0	33.5	37.9	80.2
CBS Affiliate (N = 199)	5.0	0.0	13.6	4.0	29.2	2.5	1.0	30.7	2.5
Fox Affiliate (N = 95)	23.2	37.9	41.1	6.3	27.4	34.7	6.3	44.2	3.2
NBC Affiliate (N = 204)	7.8	0.0	23.0	5.9	15.7	3.9	0.5	28.9	0.0

Hanks also had at least one production deal with the Fox parent company at this time. Tim Allen was mentioned on 23.2% of the programs on Fox affiliates; he too had a production deal with Fox. News programs on ABC, which once showed his program *Home Improvement*, mentioned Allen at the next-highest rate (13.2%). This compares to references of 5.0% on CBS affiliates and 7.8% on NBC. Overall, table 5.4 provides strong evidence that local news programs promote the stars and shows of their networks and some indication that the amount of movie coverage is related to the ownership interests of the parent company of the network.

Local Newspapers

A different economic calculus drives the content decisions of newspaper editors than the process that governs actions of local television news directors. Local television news programs sell audiences to advertisers, which means that viewers who bring few returns in the advertising marketplace have little influence in content decisions. Newspapers sell readers to advertisers too, but they also gain revenues from subscriptions so that readers with less value to advertisers may still matter in a financial sense. A news director in a local market may worry about competition from three or more competing news broadcasts and entertainment fare on cable channels. Many newspaper editors make content decisions in towns with only one local newspaper.[13] While a station may thus try to segment the market and carve out a niche, the newspaper can appeal to a broader portion of the city's population. The technology of information transmission limits television news programs to one story at a time, so that news directors have to balance the relative interests of different viewers in any particular topic. Newspapers bundle stories into a portfolio and leave readers free to choose the stories they consume, which allows papers to cover a greater variety of stories in a single edition. To explore how audience demand and the real-world incidence of problems affect the content decisions of local newspapers, I examine in this section the content of the sixty-eight daily papers in the top fifty cities in the United States whose texts are collected in Lexis.[14]

In table 5.5 I examine how newspapers chose to cover the ninety-six soft news stories in November 1999 previously analyzed in the local television news models. For each newspaper I searched the file in Lexis containing the text of the November 1999 articles from the paper. Two dependent variables were calculated, the total number of stories dealing with these ninety-six soft news topics published in the paper during November 1999 and the percentage of the ninety-six celebrities/entertainment products that received at least one story in the paper. The market variables are defined by the same geographic boundaries as in the television analysis, that is, the top fifty television markets. Since a local television market may encompass more than one city, this means that the vari-

TABLE 5.5
Soft News Coverage by Local Newspapers

Variable	Number of Soft News Stories	% of Soft News Topics Covered
Total Television Households (000)	4.82e-3	−1.39e-3
	(0.02)	(2.14e-3)
No. Daily Newspapers	−8.48	−0.91
	(7.11)	(0.89)
Total Lexis Articles, Nov. 99	0.07***	7.71e-3***
	(7.81e-3)	(9.83e-4)
Time Circulation, %	15.93	6.20
	(33.73)	(4.24)
People Circulation, %	19.82	2.07
	(27.82)	(3.50)
Modern Maturity Circulation, %	−5.08	−0.34
	(3.51)	(0.44)
Playboy Circulation, %	−50.64	−4.47
	(42.43)	(5.34)
Group-Owned Paper	45.34	7.17
	(38.99)	(4.91)
No. Daily Papers Held by Owner	0.64	0.26**
	(0.86)	(0.11)
Adjusted R^2	0.64	0.55
No. Papers	68	68

Note: Standard errors in parentheses. *** = statistically significant at the .01 level; ** = significant at the .05 level; * = significant at the .10 level. Each specification also included an intercept term.

ables, such as the number of daily newspapers in the area, may refer to the number of newspapers in a cluster of cities. The results indicate that soft news coverage is not influenced by audience-demand variables. Circulation percentages for *Time* magazine and for *People* magazine did not have a statistically significant impact on soft news content decisions (unlike the results in the local television news analysis). The total number of stories cataloged in Lexis from the newspaper in November 1999 did increase the number of stories and the percentage of soft news figures covered, which may indicate that as newspaper size expands soft news stories are more likely to be included. Whether the paper was controlled by a group owner did not influence the coverage of soft news. As the number of papers controlled by the parent company grew, however, the percentage of soft news figures covered increased.

Coverage of hard news topics in local newspapers appears more responsive to audience demand. The incidence of a problem in a city also influences coverage, if the problem is one likely to be of interest to a paper's readers. To explore how variations in the nature of policy problems across cities affect coverage in local newspapers, I first assembled quantitative information on how cities vary in terms of policy outcomes that are quantifiable. I found statistical measures across the largest cities in the United States for variables relating to topics such as poverty, health, and the environment.[15] In table 5.6 I explore how a paper's coverage varies with audience interest and the incidence of the policy problem in the city. The dependent variable in the analysis is the number of articles in the paper dealing with the policy problem over a given time period, where the time period is defined by the time covered by the real-world incidence variable. For example, in the first column I model the total number of stories using the term "poverty" that appeared in a paper as a function of audience-demand variables, market-structure variables, and the amount of family-assistance payments provided by the federal government in the city. I use the later variable as an indicator of poverty in the city.

The results in table 5.6 suggest that editors add hard news stories depending on audience interest in the topic. As the percentage of residents subscribing to *Time* magazine increased, papers were more likely to add stories about poverty, Medicaid, soft money political contributions, and campaign finance reform. As *People* magazine subscription percentages increased, editors were less likely to cover Medicaid. Since survey data indicate that younger readers are more interested in entertainment news, this is consistent with editors downplaying Medicaid if there is less audience interest in the topic. The higher the circulation for *Modern Maturity*, a proxy for the interests of older readers, the less coverage of poverty, computers (consistent with their appeal to the young), AIDS, and HIV.[16] Areas with higher *Playboy* subscriptions had fewer discussions of food stamps and Medicaid in their newspapers. Not surprisingly, the larger the number of stories in a newspaper during the sample period the greater the number of stories about each particular policy area.

The real-world incidence of a problem in a city influences its coverage, yet the effect may depend on whether the problem is of interest to likely readers of a paper. Newspaper readers are unlikely to be on welfare or food stamps. The real-world incidence of poverty and food stamps is actually negatively correlated with newspaper coverage. The higher the level of family assistance payments or food stamp payments in a city, the lower the number of stories about poverty or food stamps in the paper. The level of public medical assistance payments in a city had no statistical impact on the number of stories about Medicaid in the paper. For stories of broader interest to likely readers, however, the greater the real-world effects of a policy in a city the more likely the paper was to cover it. Cities with more computer programmers had more stories about computers during 1998. Interest in campaigns and campaign finance is likely to be higher in areas with more political contributions. Table 5.6 indicates that as the amount of presidential campaign contributions grew in a city, a newspa-

TABLE 5.6
Hard News Coverage by Local Newspapers

Variable	Poverty (1998)	Food Stamps (1998)	Medicaid (1998)	Computers (1998)	Soft Money (1999)	Campaign Finance Reform (1999)	AIDS (7/98–6/99)	HIV (7/98–6/99)	EPA (6–8/99)
				Total Stories Using Term					
Intercept	183.84	75.45***	192.79**	−173.37	−0.63	−12.15	44.40	49.80	−758.72*
	(182.69)	(23.96)	(84.29)	(797.40)	(31.51)	(49.70)	(154.75)	(96.42)	(448.06)
Total Television Households (000)	0.08*	0.02***	−4.25e-3	−0.02	−0.02***	−0.02***	−0.06**	−0.04***	2.07e-3
	(0.05)	(7.23e-3)	(0.02)	(0.09)	(4.80e-3)	(7.56e-3)	(0.02)	(0.02)	(3.41e-3)
No. Daily Newspapers	−13.68*	−0.92	−3.99	−49.60	−1.28	−2.27	−1.25	3.05	0.82
	(8.04)	(1.12)	(3.82)	(34.40)	(1.43)	(2.26)	(7.37)	(4.59)	(1.41)
Total Lexis Articles in Sample Period	8.07e-3***	1.03e-3***	2.41e-3***	0.05***	6.73e-4***	1.44e-3***	6.84e-3***	4.24e-3***	9.97e-4***
	(7.50e-4)	(9.89e-5)	(3.52e-4)	(3.33e-3)	(1.26e-4)	(1.99e-4)	(6.10e-4)	(3.80e-4)	(1.26e-4)
Time Circulation, %	87.04**	−7.84	35.37*	228.12	17.53**	25.35**	50.07	15.56	9.08
	(37.43)	(4.90)	(17.98)	(172.21)	(7.27)	(11.47)	(36.51)	(22.75)	(6.55)
People Circulation, %	−17.02	−1.67	−29.35**	−2.80	−8.63	−10.15	−13.95	−0.14	−5.94
	(30.50)	(4.03)	(14.26)	(137.52)	(5.62)	(8.86)	(29.19)	(18.19)	(5.67)
Modern Maturity Circulation, %	−20.78***	0.79	0.68	−59.36***	−0.32	−0.90	−6.37*	−3.77*	0.08
	(4.01)	(0.52)	(1.83)	(17.32)	(0.68)	(1.06)	(3.47)	(2.16)	(0.69)
Playboy Circulation, %	−38.59	−12.21*	−49.74*	94.17	−7.03	−5.44	−23.93	−11.24	15.41
	(48.74)	(6.50)	(25.25)	(207.34)	(8.14)	(12.84)	(41.47)	(25.84)	(10.50)
Group Owned Paper	91.95**	−7.20	13.98	252.67	3.65	−7.03	90.41**	41.74*	−11.35
	(44.18)	(5.81)	(20.67)	(193.28)	(7.47)	(11.78)	(36.83)	(22.95)	(7.97)
No. of Daily Papers Held by Owner	0.34	0.08	0.42	1.44	0.12	0.29	0.04	0.07	0.47**
	(0.95)	(0.12)	(0.44)	(4.38)	(0.16)	(0.26)	(0.80)	(0.50)	(0.18)

	(1)	(2)	(3)	(4)	(5)	(6)	(7)	(8)
DMA City Missing Indicator	−150.79 (134.19)	61.94*** (17.70)	−158.96** (61.53)	203.59 (347.50)			−5.05 (42.67)	−0.44 (26.59)
Family Assistance (000$)	−3.06e-4*** (1.15e-4)							
Food Stamps (000$)		−1.61e-4*** (4.39e-5)						
Public Assistance Medical Care (000$)			−1.61e-5 (1.31e-5)					
Computer Programmer Employment				0.02** (0.01)				
Presidential Campaign Contributions ($)					1.01e-5*** (2.30e-6)	1.44e-3*** (1.94e-4)		
Cumulative AIDS Cases							6.43e-3** (2.52e-3)	4.19e-3*** (1.57e-3)
Good Air Pollutant Index Days								7.52 (4.76)
Moderate Air Pollutant Index								7.54 (4.77)
Unhealthful Air Pollutant Index Days								8.86* (4.80)
Very Unhealthful Air Pollutant Index Days								−3.67 (13.36)
Adjusted R^2	0.74	0.72	0.57	0.87	0.55	0.61	0.74	0.49
Number of Papers	68	68	68	67	68	67	68	68

Note: *** = statistically significant at the .01 level; ** = significant at the .05 level; * = significant at the .10 level.

per editor included more stories about soft money contributions and campaign finance reform. The higher the cumulative number of AIDS cases in a city, the more stories about AIDS or HIV included in a paper. The larger the number of unhealthful air pollutant index days in an area, the more stories about the Environmental Protection Agency (EPA) were included in a paper.

Market structure had some limited impacts on the coverage analyzed in table 5.6. The number of daily newspapers in a market did not have a statistically significant impact on story counts, except for a negative impact on the number of stories about poverty. Group ownership had a positive impact on the number of stories devoted to poverty, AIDS, and HIV. This may indicate that papers that are part of a chain were able to share stories and gain additional coverage at little cost on these topics. As the number of papers owned by a parent company grew, a paper was more likely to include stories about the EPA. Larger chains again may facilitate the sharing of hard news stories across papers.[17]

Table 5.7 explores how crime coverage relates to audience demand, market structure, and real-world incidence of crime. In this table I use U.S. Department of Justice (1999a, 1999b) statistics on the number of murders, assaults, and rapes in the city and on the percentage of white arrestees testing positive for drugs as indicators of the nature of crime and drug use in an area.[18] The results indicate that crime coverage in newspapers is driven more by audience interests than the level of crime in a city. In areas with higher interest in hard news, as reflected in higher-circulation percentages for *Time* magazine, editors are more likely to include stories about rape or drugs. As the subscription percentage for *Modern Maturity* increases, newspapers include fewer stories about murder and shootings. As the young male audience in a city increases, denoted by increasing *Playboy* subscriptions, editors were more likely to include stories about the two Columbine high school shooters, Eric Harris and Dylan Klebold. The real-world incidence of crime did not have an impact on coverage overall. The number of murders in a city did not have a statistically significant impact on the number of stories about murder or the Columbine shooters. The number of stories about rape or drugs were not related to the number of rapes or incidence of drug use in a city. Stories about shooting actually declined slightly as the number of assaults increased in a city. Group ownership and the number of daily newspapers in the city had no impact on crime coverage.

Newspapers may vary not only in their decisions about whether to cover a particular hard news story; they may also differ in the tone they use to cover a specific topic or event.[19] Chapter 2 develops the argument that political independence in newspaper coverage may be profitable because it allows the assemblage of a large audience to sell to advertisers. In the current era of objective news coverage, newspapers do not identify themselves with a particular party or faction. Some papers do, however, continue the practice of making editorial endorsements in campaigns. The endorsement of a Republican presidential candidate on the editorial page could arise from numerous motives: a desire of a paper's owner to influence readers to vote Republican; an attempt by editors to gain favor with Republican readers; or a move by a paper's editors (as distinct from its owners) to use the paper to influence voters. Regardless of why a paper chooses a particular candidate, the question arises of whether this endorsement is reflected in the manner in which the news department covers the race in question.

In table 5.8 I explore whether a paper's editorial endorsement is reflected in the tone of candidate coverage. I chose two events likely to be covered by newspapers in 2000, the convention acceptance speeches of George W. Bush and Al Gore. For each paper's coverage I ran the articles through the DICTION software, which provides summary indicators of five different dimensions of coverage: certainty, optimism, activity, realism, and commonality. This process yielded 390 segments of coverage of at least 250 words for the Bush speech and 365 segments of coverage of the Gore speech. These segments came from the twenty-eight papers in the top fifty cities for which I was able to ascertain that they endorsed Bush, Gore, or no candidate.[20] The results in table 5.8 indicate that there were not statistically significant differences in the mean DICTION coverage dimensions of the Gore convention speech related to the editorial positions of the newspapers in the sample. Whether the tone of coverage is compared for pro-Bush versus pro-Gore, neutral versus pro-Bush, or neutral versus pro-Gore, newspapers did not differ in the language they used to describe and convey Gore's acceptance speech. There were only slight differences in how types of papers treated the Bush acceptance speech. The papers that endorsed Bush were slightly more likely to use active words to describe his speech than the papers that endorsed Gore. Those outlets that endorsed Gore, however, used slightly more optimistic language in covering the Bush speech than those that eventually endorsed the Republican presidential candidates. Overall these results indicate that the editorial positions of newspapers do not influence the tone of coverage used to describe major campaign events.

Conclusions

While local television news programs and newspapers are often overshadowed by national news organizations in discussions of the media, these local outlets in aggregate capture a larger share of viewers and readers. More than half (55.8%) of survey respondents report that they regularly watch local television news, compared to 29.9% for the national network evening news programs.[21] A high number of adults (62.5%) report that they regularly read a daily newspaper, compared to 12.5% that say they read the national news magazines. This chapter shows that local news outlets are able to tailor their coverage to the tastes of their targeted readers and viewers. For local television news directors, the public's interests appear to define stations' definitions of broadcasting in

TABLE 5.7
Crime Coverage by Local Newspapers

Variable	Total Stories Using Term					
	Murder	Shooting	Rape	Drugs	Eric Harris	Dylan Klebold
Intercept	104.44	407.49	74.56	1269.03	−182.43**	−171.05**
	(398.59)	(442.43)	(114.96)	(819.74)	(71.54)	(68.08)
Total Television Households (000)	0.01	0.14	6.31e-3	−0.06	−3.13e-3	−3.80e-3
	(0.06)	(0.09)	(0.02)	(0.06)	(9.87e-3)	(9.39e-3)
No. Daily Newspapers	−13.33	−26.35	−2.67	−34.07	0.67	1.20
	(18.20)	(19.95)	(4.57)	(31.94)	(3.26)	(0.41)
Total Lexis Articles in Sample Period	0.02***	0.02***	3.74e-3***	0.03***	9.48e-4***	9.03e-4***
	(1.66e-3)	(1.81e-3)	(4.62e-4)	(2.65e-3)	(2.98e-4)	(2.84e-4)
Time Circulation, %	101.73	−20.22	43.93*	297.38**	7.32	5.05
	(79.56)	(94.45)	(22.71)	(129.09)	(14.27)	(13.58)
People Circulation, %	−9.25	72.07	−20.32	102.89	1.96	3.00
	(70.41)	(79.02)	(18.68)	(121.98)	(12.63)	(12.02)
Modern Maturity Circulation, %	−20.95**	−22.56*	−3.37	−8.51	−0.82	−0.75
	(10.18)	(11.48)	(2.70)	(23.73)	(1.83)	(1.74)

	(1)	(2)	(3)	(4)	(5)	(6)
Playboy Circulation, %	−39.09	−1.28	−23.91	−513.05***	51.51***	48.65***
	(99.61)	(111.18)	(26.46)	(160.70)	(17.87)	(17.00)
Group-Owned Paper	89.94	31.37	−24.33	24.94	11.21	10.09
	(94.15)	(105.60)	(25.59)	(163.80)	(16.89)	(16.07)
No. of Daily Papers Held by Owner	2.17	3.02	1.10*	3.54	0.34	0.32
	(2.43)	(2.70)	(0.63)	(4.19)	(0.44)	(0.41)
DMA City Missing Indicator	42.00	52.30	−6.10	−61.11	−15.95	−14.16
	(94.60)	(105.75)	(25.59)	(174.64)	(16.97)	(16.14)
Murders	−0.07				−0.09	−0.08
	(0.69)				(0.12)	(0.12)
Assaults		−0.03*				
		(0.02)				
Rapes			−0.05			
			(0.11)			
White Arrestees Using Drugs, %				−1.14		
				(9.50)		
Adjust R^2	0.75	0.78	0.60	0.87	0.19	0.19
No. Papers	63	62	60	33	63	63

Note: Standard errors in parentheses. *** = statistically significant at the .01 level; ** = significant at the .05 level; * = significant at the .10 level. Sample period for each regression was January through June, 1999, except for drugs (where the sample period was 1998).

TABLE 5.8
Local Newspaper Coverage of 2000 Convention Speeches

DICTION Dimension	Bush Convention Speech				Gore Convention Speech			
	All Papers Mean	Difference of Means			All Papers Mean	Difference of Means		
		Pro Bush–Pro Gore	Neutral–Pro Bush	Neutral–Pro Gore		Pro Bush–Pro Gore	Neutral–Pro Bush	Neutral–Pro Gore
Certainty	46.5	0.3	−0.4	−0.1	45.9	0.1	−0.3	−0.2
Optimism	50.4	−0.7**	0.4	−0.2	50.4	−0.2	0.0	−0.2
Activity	52.2	0.5**	−0.3	0.2	51.6	−0.2	−0.2	−0.5
Realism	48.1	−0.3	0.1	−0.2	48.2	−0.3	0.2	−0.1
Commonality	49.9	0.1	0.3	0.3	50.0	0.1	−0.1	−0.1
Number of Segments First Paper Category	390	124	74	74	365	90	88	88
Number of Segments Second Paper Category	192	192	124	192	187	187	90	187

Note: *** = statistically significant at the .01 level; ** = significant at the .05 level; * = significant at the .10 level. Papers are categorized by their editorial endorsements in the 2000 presidential election.

the public interest. The higher the subscriptions for *People* magazine in the market, the greater the number of soft news stories about celebrities and entertainment products in local news programs. The greater the penetration of *Time* magazine in a market, the more hard news stories about national and international events are included in local television news programs. Economic forces outside the local market also influence the local television news programs. Stations are more likely to feature in their news programs the stars and shows of the network they are affiliated with, a form of promotion that benefits the local station and the national network. If a station is part of a larger group of stations controlled by a single company, its programs are less likely to cover national hard news events or stories about the area's U.S. senators.

Local newspapers operate under a different set of market conditions. Their bundling of stories into a portfolio of sections allows readers to choose which information to sample. This means that editors can add stories without considering whether all consumers will be interested. The results here indicate that local newspapers still do take tastes into account when making some content decisions. The number of soft news stories is not driven by the level of interest in entertainment or celebrity news. Hard news coverage of stories such as poverty, Medicaid, and campaign finance reform does increase as the percentage of *Time* subscribers grows. Coverage of issues also grows if the local incidence of a problem affects a newspaper's likely readers. Coverage of computers, campaign finance reform, or the EPA was higher in areas with larger computer employment, more local donations to presidential campaigns, or worse air pollution. Group ownership had impacts on newspapers too. Papers controlled by group owners covered a higher percentage of the soft news topics examined in the sample. These papers also included more stories about hard news topics such as poverty and AIDS. The news content of daily papers is not responsive to partisan pressures. Papers covered the Bush convention speech in similar tones regardless of the papers' later editorial endorsements in the race; the same held true for coverage of the Gore convention speech. This is not surprising given that objective coverage allows a newspaper to attract readers of many political allegiances, whose attention can then be sold to advertisers who value larger audiences.

These results provide a snapshot of how economics affect media content decisions across U.S. cities. Chapter 6 offers a view of how content has changed across time due to the changing economic fortunes of a particular media institution, the national network evening news programs.

Chapter 6

The Changing Nature of the Network Evening News Programs

IN 1969, the daily debates among network news executives and reporters about what stories to include in the evening news broadcasts centered around which domestic politics and foreign policy stories to cover. Each television network was part of a media company. For each of the three networks, the founder or early leader was still involved and was identified with the organization's operations. Network news operations were expected to generate prestige, part of which reflected back on the owners and broadcasters. The Federal Communications Commission (FCC) routinely examined the number of hours of public affairs programming stations provided when they had their licenses renewed. A reputation for covering public affairs well in the news provided added security when licenses were up for renewal. If viewers did not enjoy the hard news stories provided in the evening news programs, they had few other options on the dial. The average television household received seven channels. At the dinner hour more than one-third of all television households watched the network evening news. The stories they saw were news to most viewers. National news programs were not on earlier in the afternoon, and local news programs lacked the technology and time to cover national events on their own. Decision makers on network news programs felt a responsibility to provide viewers with information they needed as citizens. The large audience share and focus on politics attracted significant scrutiny for the programs, which were a frequent target of criticism from the White House.[1]

In 2000, the daily debates in network story conferences centered around whether to include domestic political stories or softer news items about health and entertainment topics. Foreign coverage was not often on the agenda, except in cases of military action. Each network was part of a publicly traded conglomerate. Network news operations were expected by corporate managers and Wall Street analysts to generate profits. The FCC no longer scrutinized public affairs coverage and license renewals were virtually assured. Television households received an average of sixty-three channels. Viewers at the dinner hour could watch sitcoms, entertainment news, sports news, and news on PBS. The three major network news programs combined only captured 23% of all television households. Viewers often came to the network news programs with a sense already of the day's headline stories, after watching news on cable channels or local television programs containing stories and footage from around the nation. Network decision makers felt pressure to gain ratings, which translated into a competition to discover and serve viewers' interests. Anchors and reporters were promoted as celebrities. Political criticisms of news coverage focused more on the content of cable news programs, though press critics faulted the network evening news shows for an increasing shift to soft news stories.

This chapter examines how content on the network evening news broadcasts has changed as the incentives for broadcasters have changed. The analysis consists of two parts, a history of the network news programs as seen through press accounts and media memoirs and a statistical breakdown of hard news and soft news coverage on the programs for the thirty-year period from 1969 through 1998. The results show how changes in demand and supply factors led to reduced coverage of hard news topics. The five Ws help highlight the differences in news decisions across time. Network news executives became more focused on who cared about particular stories and the value of viewers to advertisers. The focus on what stories generated viewer interests became particularly important as competition from multiple channels increased. Though the advent of cable television lowered the ratings for network news, the programs were able to attract higher advertising rates per thousand viewers. This in part reflected the premium advertisers placed on attracting a relatively large audience in a world where viewers were spread across a dial. When and why particular types of information became profitable also changed. As the founders of the networks disappeared from ownership control, as the FCC partially deregulated television, and as networks became part of conglomerates that were not first and foremost media companies, the focus on generating profits from news increased.

The consumption of the network evening news programs in millions of households and impact of the shows on national politics have made the newscasts the topic of thousands of newspaper articles and multiple broadcast memoirs. Two themes—lessening and lowering—appear in journalists' reflections on the nightly news broadcasts over the past thirty years. Reporters write about the declines in hard news stories offered, the share of viewers attracted, a sense of public interest responsibilities in the newsroom, and the independence of news judgment from commercial pressures. Competition changes the nature of broadcasts significantly. Press critics and business reporters note the promotion of the programs as products, the development of anchors and reporters into celebrities, and the explicit positioning of the programs in viewers' minds. The attempts of a network newscast, trailing in the ratings, to reposition itself—by changing the blend of domestic/foreign stories, using shorter or longer stories, and focusing more or less on human interest stories—are frequently recounted in newspaper columns that track the programs. Though these accounts are often written as if a Golden Age of network news coverage had existed and passed, most of the stories fail to note that as the network news content changed the total hours available of public affairs broadcasting was growing and the diversity in news types was also increasing.[2]

To measure trends in coverage of hard and soft news stories by the network evening news programs, I need ways to track these different news types. Each year *People* magazine develops its list of the "25 Most Intriguing People." The *Harvard Law Review* publishes its compilation of the term's major Supreme Court cases. *Congressional Quarterly (CQ)* summarizes the key votes that occurred in the House of Representatives and Senate. The Americans for Democratic Action select a set of votes to measure the liberalism of candidates, while the American Conservative Union tallies the key conservative votes in Congress. In this chapter I use *People*'s people to represent soft news topics, and the law review cases, *CQ* key votes, and interest group ratings to define hard news topics. I use the Vanderbilt Television News Archive to determine whether the network evening news programs covered these particular celebrities, court cases, and congressional votes over the thirty-year period 1969–98. Overall, the results indicate growing coverage on the networks of soft news personalities (e.g., entertainers, sports figures). The percentage of important Supreme Court cases covered on the network evening news programs remained relatively constant over time. The percentage of *CQ* votes in the Senate and House that generated stories on these broadcasts declined over time. A large decrease in the coverage of votes deemed important by liberal and conservative lobbying groups is also evident. The analysis indicates that network news decisions about covering hard and soft news topics were influenced both by the partial deregulation of television and the increasing competition from cable channels.

An Economic History in Newspapers and Memoirs

Changes in the operation of the network evening news programs make news and generate memoirs. Media reporters write frequently about the performance of network anchors and reporters, who in turn produce their own books about the fate of broadcast news. The attention devoted to network news programs makes their history a now familiar tale. From the 1970s through the 1990s, change was a constant theme in evening news coverage. The owners of each broadcast network changed. ABC was purchased by Capital Cities in 1986 and became part of Disney in 1996, CBS became part of Westinghouse in 1995 and Viacom in 2000, and General Electric purchased NBC (as part of RCA) in 1986. The identities and number of anchors changed over time. ABC, for example, tried three anchors (Peter Jennings, Frank Reynolds, Max Robinson) in 1978, two anchors (Harry Reasoner and Barbara Walters) in 1976, and one anchor (Jennings, 1983–) in its nightly news broadcasts. The program dominant in the Nielsen ratings varied, with Chet Huntley and David Brinkley giving way to Walter Cronkite, then Dan Rather, followed by Jennings, who was surpassed by Tom Brokaw. Broadcast producers experimented with different styles by altering the number of stories covered, the length of sound bites, and the focus on hard or soft news. The expansion of viewing options starting in the 1980s brought a further predictable change, the decline nearly every year in the total ratings for the three network evening news broadcasts.

The spatial competition model presented in chapter 1 offers a way to understand the operation of the evening news programs as a changing function of ownership goals, product differentiation decisions, audience demands for information, and the costs of assembling stories. When the ownership of the networks shifted to conglomerates without a history of journalism involvement, managers in news divisions became more focused on profit maximization. Producers sought to create viewer expectations about program content by emphasizing the anchors as celebrities, creating segments with titles within the broadcasts (e.g., "Person of the Week" or "The Fleecing of America"), and picking a consistent mix of hard and soft news stories. Music, graphics, short sound bites, and anchors standing to deliver the news became part of the stylistic devices used to attract viewers. Audience demand led to changes in program form and content. As viewers became more likely to be familiar with breaking stories from local news or cable programs, the networks shifted from a headline service to a news product providing context for hard news and feature stories. The value of particular marginal viewers to advertisers drove programs to target some stories to female viewers and younger viewers (defined in the world of broadcast news as those less than fifty years old). The increasing prices for ads led to an expansion of ad time that shrunk the amount of time devoted to news. The ratings race became a battle that was written about weekly in the newspapers. The networks tracked ratings by the minute during broadcasts, which provided immediate feedback on how different stories fared with the audience. Cutting costs became another way to increase profits. The shutdown of network bureaus abroad reflected the lower priority accorded foreign news and revealed how cost considerations changed the scope of stories covered. This section uses newspaper accounts and memoirs to explore how these economic changes affected the nightly news.

Throughout the 1960s and into the 1970s, network news division goals could be described as delivery of public service and generation of prestige. At least three factors help explain why the network news divisions concentrated on creating high quality programs that contained a large amount of public affairs content. The founders or early leaders of each network were still active in company affairs and could gain personal satisfaction from the provision of quality news programs. The prestige generated by the news divisions also provided regulatory protection, for it allowed the networks to point to public service programming when their station licenses and those of their affiliates came up for renewal at the FCC. In this sense, high quality news could be seen as the "price" that networks paid for their licenses. The networks enjoyed a highly profitable oligopoly at this time, since there were few viewing alternatives. This meant that licenses were extremely valuable. The oligopoly structure also lowered the cost of putting on programming that may not have been of greatest interest to viewers since, if each network did this during the dinner hour, households had few other viewing options to pursue.

The expectation of quality and the financial protection provided by prestige were well understood within the networks. James Aubrey, the president of CBS television from 1959 to 1965, told the head of the news division, "They say to me, 'Take your soiled little hands, get the ratings, and make as much money as you can.' They say to you, 'Take your lily-white hands, do your best, go the high road, and bring up prestige.'"[3] Arthur Taylor, president of CBS from 1972–76, described the willingness of the network to sacrifice profits in news provision this way: "Making money from news was thought to be a very bad idea. The thinking was if you are a broadcaster and charged with performing a public service, it was a good idea to be able to tell the FCC, 'Well, I do make all this money, but on the other hand, I have to be able to support our big loss leader, the news division.' And if your big loss leader, to which you are making large, financial contributions to serve the public, is making money, it doesn't look like you're doing all that much of a public service, does it?"[4]

The prestige of providing serious journalism on television helped develop the reputation of the companies for quality and provided them with protection from government action. Describing the actions of CBS chairman William Paley, *CBS Evening News* executive producer Tom Bettag recalled: "There was a time when Paley was asked before the stockholders, 'How dare you lose six million dollars a year on news?' And Paley said, 'Because I like what that six million dollars buys me.' It bought him respectability. It bought him the ability to go before Congress and every time he got beat up on *The Beverly Hillbillies* he'd say, 'Yeah, but I take a loss every year on Walter Cronkite. I do that as a public service.' It gave the corporation a sheen and a cachet."[5]

Freed from concerns about profit maximization, those involved in producing the network evening news programs could focus on what they believed people needed to know. CBS News President Richard Salant described the process of making news decisions this way in a 1974 speech to affiliates: "It is a harsh but inevitable fact that news judgments just must be unilateral, can't be shared, can't be delegated outside the news organization, and can't be put to a committee vote. Sound journalism does not permit substituting a head count for news judgment. In fact, the whole business of journalism is a great deal more than, and is inconsistent with, providing only those stories which most people want to hear, giving those stories the treatment most agreeable to a majority of the people."[6] In a 1976 memo included as a preface to the guidelines, *CBS News Standards*, Salant noted: "To the extent that radio and television are mass media of entertainment, it is entirely proper to give most of the people what most of them want most of the time. But we in broadcast journalism cannot, should not, and will not base our judgments on what we think viewers and listeners are 'most interested' in, or hinge our news judgment and our news treatment on our guesses as to what news the people want to hear or see ... the judgments must be professional news judgments—nothing more, nothing less."[7]

The transition to ownership by nonmedia companies, deregulation by the FCC, and competition from cable outlets changed the incentives faced by the network news organizations.[8] Losses were no longer seen as an element of prestige. The success of news magazines demonstrated how some types of news products could earn substantial revenues. Describing the changed atmosphere, Dan Rather noted that for the president of CBS News in 1981 (Bill Leonard), "What he cared about was the integrity of what we were doing covering the news." In contrast, in 2000 at CBS News "the driving force every day" was "delivering the profit." In an extended interview with Downie and Kaiser (2002), Rather noted that when profits replace integrity as the focus: "It's inevitable that a lot is going to go out of your organization ... and a lot is going to go out of yourself. And that's what has happened to television journalism as a whole, and it's what's happened here.... Once we begin to see ourselves as more of a business and less a public service, the decline in quality is accelerated."[9]

Frustrations with the profit focus were especially prevalent among older network journalists, in part because they retained a view of news as a profession and because they remembered how news judgments operated when revenues were not a guiding concern.

The spatial competition model assumes that a firm chooses where to locate its product along some continuum of variety or quality. For the network evening news, the mix of hard and soft news regularly selected by producers partly defines the programs. Hard news stories typically involve public affairs, government action, or international relations stories. Soft news may center on celebrities, entertainment news, or tabloid crimes. The hard/soft distinction also enters into how political stories are covered, with decisions made about whether to cover a story from Washington, D.C. or to relate how an issue affects the lives of particular individuals. Starting in the early 1980s television reviewers began to bemoan the decline of political news from Washington, D.C. on the evening news. The changes in product mix were consciously made by the program producers. As the head of the CBS news division, Van Gordon Sauter, put it: "We moved the broadcast out of Washington. We emphasized stories from across the country, where we could tell national stories through human experience and human perceptions more than through statements of bureaucrats and politicians. We tried to find the theme stories that responded to what the aspirations and apprehensions of the American people were. We emphasized story telling, both verbally and visually."[10] CBS anchor Dan Rather described the emphasis on human stories this way: "Van keeps saying we need stories that reach out and touch people.... Moments. Every broadcast needs moments.... When somebody watches something and feels it, smells it and knows it.... If a broadcast does not have at least two or three of those moments, it does not have it."[11]

In relating how decisions were made about the treatment of hard and soft stories, Rather related how the "back fence" principle helped decide whether to lead a program with the birth of a royal baby, the Falklands dispute, or events in the Middle East: "The back-fence principle is, well, you imagine two neighbor ladies leaning over a back fence at the end of the day and one is asking the other what happened today and you figure out which of your stories they'd most want to know about. Well, you have to say today it's going to be what happened with the princess—did she have her baby."[12]

The move to de-emphasize hard news sparked controversy even as it was implemented. Former CBS News president Richard Salant said of Sauter's "Moments" strategy: "The whole purpose of the news is not to capture the moment but to explain. And you don't ignore it if you don't have a picture. He said that he went for the emotion, he went for the gut. News, to me, is information that goes to the head and not to the gut."[13] The focus on political issues as told through individuals' stories overlapped with federal government cuts in domestic spending advocated by President Reagan. Describing how his network covered the budget debate, correspondent Fred Graham noted, "The *CBS Evening News* responded with a torrent of pathetic victims of these cutbacks, thus giving the impression that the network was on an anti-Reagan crusade, when it was actually only attempting to wring as many heart-wrenching moments as it could out of the affected farmers, steelworkers, and welfare families."[14] When Roger Mudd was dropped in 1983 as a coanchor from Washington, D.C. for the *NBC Nightly News*, he complained that "I think it's important for people to see the government operating, have public officials held accountable for what they're doing. It's valuable, it's necessary, it's mandatory. There's a built in anti-Washington bias among network management. They think most Washington news is 'inside' and boring. I think it's the most important news city in the world."[15] Mudd noted that the networks were offering "less and less substance, more and more Kilauea volcanoes and Diana Ross concerts."

By 2000 the network evening news programs were positioned to avoid the extremes of the hard/soft continuum, avoiding a focus on public affairs stories from Washington or foreign news and avoiding a focus on entertainment news or tabloid stories. Contrasting how *ABC World News Tonight* had changed since the 1980s, Peter Jennings noted that "there's much greater demand for personal news ... about health and personal finance" and said that they "try to do something on business every day." NBC anchor Tom Brokaw said of evening news coverage that "more and more of it is in the medical and scientific field." CBS anchor Dan Rather indicated that in the struggle to cover what is important and of interest, his program sometimes tilted so that there was "more celebrity news in the broadcast than I would like to have." Rather summarized the state of network news this way: "Now it's popular to say in television journalism.... What we need is a rich mix.... It's going to be entertainment and news all in a kind of bouillabaisse, and we do a lot of stuff that is pretty far over the line in the direction of entertainment, and we will mix in enough news that we will still call it a newscast. That's my definition of a rich mix."[16]

Evidence that the evening news program staff view their product locations along a hard/soft continuum, as conscious choices continuously reassessed, comes from the language they use. As one NBC news staffer put it, "There are always cycles in this business. Individual correspondents are in favor, then out of favor. The broadcast gets softer, then harder, then softer, then harder.... What there is is a more heightened vigilance against inside-the-Beltway stuff, process stuff."[17]

Despite the experimentation with a soft news focus in the early 1980s, in 1986 Dan Rather was signaling his broadcast's product mix by declaring, "We were hard news yesterday, we're hard news today, and we'll be hard news tomorrow."[18] After the *CBS Evening News* fell into third place in the ratings in 1991, press coverage indicated there "was debate within the network about whether CBS should go even more 'hard news' in its approach or try to add softer features to appeal to viewers."[19] A new executive producer, Erik Sorenson, backed away from a hard news approach at CBS in 1992, indicating, "I think there's been an absolute Washington bias on the part of the network newscasts.... Los Angeles is the second biggest city in the U.S., and Hollywood is very influential in our culture. Routinely reporting on everything that Congress does—just because it did it—is irrelevant, and I think the mood of the public in this presidential campaign bears me out on this. Pocketbook and health-care issues aren't trivial pieces just because some guys in Congress haven't been talking about them."[20]

In the late 1990s *NBC Nightly News* had a reputation for carrying more soft news, which led Dan Rather to describe the broadcast as "news lite."[21] Anchor Tom Brokaw replied, in reference to the CBS news fixation with hurricanes, "Whenever there is the first hint of a counterclockwise symbol on a weather map in the fall that a hurricane might hit hard, 'Mr. Hard News' is down there wrapped around a lamppost somewhere." Rather then noted: "They called me 'Hard News Dan' as derision; they meant it as a taunt.... But I'll take that. Of the three newscasts, it's very clear that we try the hardest to avoid confusing news and entertainment."

The sniping among the network anchors reflects another aspect of the spatial competition model, that firms choose their product mix relative to the location of others. Network executives will often explain how their news strategies relate to the product decisions of their competitors.[22] During an attempt in 1992 by CBS to shift its balance of stories away from Washington, the executive producer of *NBC Nightly News* Steve Friedman noted:

> CBS has gone to a more popular broadcast with stories on money and health and "news you can use" rather than its traditional emphasis as the "broadcast of record".... They got a tremendous boost from the (Winter) Olympics, and that's when they made their move. I'm not going to knock them for their strategy—it's similar to what I did when I came here. But I'm not here to be in third place, and they've given us an oppor-

tunity. Our research shows that people in these times want hard news, and that's the direction we're going to go in. We think the upcoming Summer Olympics will give us a boost in the ratings and an opportunity to showcase our newscast this summer.[23]

Assessing the ratings gains made by CBS in 1992, the network's research chief David Poltrack concluded: "What's significant about these numbers is that CBS has cut in half the distance between itself and ABC, while NBC showed no net gain, despite the increase in viewing during the Los Angeles riots.... The Olympics brought us sampling from baby-boomer viewers, who apparently liked the new look of the show and found the health and economics segments relevant to their lives. We have made gains in younger viewers for the newscast, which traditionally has skewed older than ABC or NBC." Dan Rather described the new decision rules about product mix (i.e., story selection) this way: "There has been a mandate here to make the broadcast more contemporary and more relevant and to no longer give special weight to stories from New York and Washington.... We're doing more lifestyle features, the way that newspapers are doing more lifestyle stories on their front pages. We're still committed to foreign news, although all of us are doing less of it today than we did fifteen years ago."

In 2001 the evening news programs were still seeking to differentiate themselves. Referring to the increase in news sources available, the executive producer of the *CBS Evening News*, Jim Murphy, noted that "to survive in the coming climate you need a distinct image and a distinct editorial line."[24] He defined the niche for the CBS broadcast as "innovative reporting, really good international reporting, complicated, interesting issues like the energy crisis in California." CBS also attracted attention during this time period for what it did not cover, including the initial refusal to cover the story of missing intern Chandra Levy and the decision not to report during the 2000 election rumors that George W. Bush had used drugs. The executive producer of *ABC World News Tonight* Paul Slavin defined his broadcast in 2001 in relative terms: "We tend to do fewer features than NBC. They're very much into storytelling. That's terrific, and sometimes it works great. Sometimes it keeps you from delivering as much news as you need to deliver."[25] He noted that relative to CBS, ABC "tended to be more modern in some respects.... We deliver more different sorts of information within the program than they do." Slavin credited the rise in the ratings for the ABC news broadcast to changes made to increase hard news coverage, foreign news stories, and analysis. He described this repositioning as playing to the strengths of anchor Peter Jennings, admitting, "In the past they were trying to push Peter into being more NBC-like—softer features, more domestic stories about feelings. I don't want to denigrate that. It's just not Peter."

A challenge in creating viewer expectations about the content of a news product is that much of the information presented will by definition be new to the consumer. The network evening news shows draw on at least three program elements to generate familiar and predictable information delivery: celebrity anchors and reporters; the branding and promoting of stories; and consistent style elements such as music, graphics, and editing techniques. Commenting on the drawing power of anchors, CBS correspondent Richard Threlkeld noted, "Research has shown that the reason people watch is because of personality. It's not a coincidence that the anchors' names are there on the show. Those personalities are crucial."[26] Analyzing how these personalities meshed with audiences, media critic Edwin Diamond described the anchors as offering thee distinct images: "The iconographic Dan, of course, is country and western, appealing to an older, idealized America of the imagination. Peter is urban, projecting an image with which a more youthful market can identify. Tom positions himself somewhere in between, in the middle, as an avatar of suburban values."[27] Correspondents also play a role in establishing viewer expectations through their frequent appearances. Assessing how ABC News president Roone Arledge shaped news programming, Marc Gunther observes, "Arledge expected his correspondents to be able to grab people's attention too. As he built his 'A-Team,' a group of regulars who could become known and trusted by the viewers, he was not just looking for good reporters—he was casting a show. He wanted his top correspondents to have a distinctive presence, one that would pique interest and inspire confidence among viewers."[28]

Having the anchor on camera more became a way to capitalize on a familiar face. As a 1992 internal memo at *NBC Nightly News* put it, "The show is moving away from the networks' standard anchor-and-two-minute tape, anchor-and-two-minute tape monotony. You will be seeing more of Tom Brokaw.... The format of the show is becoming fixed. Our goal is to make it standard enough so the viewer knows what to expect and when, yet flexible enough to give the producers room to best display the news of the day."[29]

Branding stories became another way for the networks to signal to viewers what they can expect from a broadcast. Each network has created longer segments within the evening news programs that carry a particular name (e.g., "American Agenda" on ABC, "Eye on America" on CBS, "Daily Difference" or "America Close-Up" on NBC), are produced in advance, and appear on predictable days or places within the broadcast. When ABC in 1986 began its "Person of the Week" segment on Fridays, the practice of profiling individuals within the evening news format attracted attention and criticism. Alex Jones described the innovation this way:

> Ongoing criticism from the older generation of television broadcasters and others charges that the nightly news shows have de-emphasized substantive news in favor of "softer" items that are mainly crowd-pleasing and designed to raise ratings. For instance, ABC recently installed "person of the week," a long segment at the end of each Friday's broadcast. Roone Arledge, president of ABC News, says it was created in large part to attract younger viewers, who frequently skip the Friday news in favor of other weekend pursuits. The people profiled have ranged from Speaker of the House Thomas P. (Tip) O'Neill to the pianist Vladimir Horowitz. While Mr. Arledge defends the creation as newsworthy, others have labeled it something else. "You're talk-

ing *People* magazine more than you're talking news," sniffs Thomas H. Wyman, chairman and chief executive officer of CBS.[30]

The use of regular segments on predictable topics allows the evening news broadcasts to promote stories to appear on future broadcasts and create an expectation about types of stories viewers will see. ABC decided to focus on problems and solutions in the United States in a consistently marketed segment called "American Agenda." Explaining the reasoning behind these branded stories, an ABC producer noted, "The ABC philosophy on news is called 'appointment viewing.' 'American Agenda' provides the opportunity to promote a piece in advance so viewers will feel they have an appointment to see it. The future is going to be newsmagazine shows in prime time that the viewers will also have an appointment to see. Especially the key demographic groups, such as women aged nineteen to thirty-nine whom advertisers love. It's no accident that 'American Agenda' concentrates on family, education, health—things that particularly appeal to women."[31]

The focus of "American Agenda" on solutions resulted in a perception by some that the program was biased. Peter Jennings noted in 1993, "Liberals are just historically more activist than conservatives; conservatives prefer the status quo. And so you could argue, in that purely technical way, that the American Agenda therefore had a fairly liberal—I'm not going to use the word 'bias,' because you'll print it—had a liberal bent because it was solution-oriented."[32]

Elements of style—music, graphics, and editing—are another way that the evening news broadcasts can create product identities. Under Roone Arledge, ABC News used new technology to transform the look of the evening news broadcast. ABC in 1978 bought the first Quantel machine, which "could take a picture, shrink it, expand it, and move it around the screen."[33] The ABC broadcast also began to use Chyrons, which "generated brightly colored maps, charts, graphs, and illustrations and imposed text over pictures. A red slash, like the one on the cover of *Time* magazine, was superimposed on stories, in an effort to give ABC's newscast a distinctive identity."[34] *World News Tonight* also began to use music, starting the program with a fanfare written especially for ABC. These innovations were eventually copied by NBC and CBS. Each network began to shorten its sound bites, so even in longer stories there were many short quotations. The networks backed away from short stories that simply consisted of the anchor reading a brief headline and a few sentences about an event. Reflecting in 2000 how the ABC broadcast stories of 1983 would be updated to reflect style changes, Peter Jennings noted: "Production capabilities in the main have much greater potential, so the technology of production, the graphics . . . the ability to do maps and things . . . has much greater capacity today than it did then. . . . We would strive to put more sound in them, we would strive to put more effect in them, because I think increasingly . . . we are mindful of . . . the variety of competitive universes in which we operate. . . . Competition for the viewer's attention has become greater."[35]

The style changes generated criticism similar to the (simultaneous) shifts in content. As ABC experimented by opening the program by four content boxes promoting stories in the broadcast, an ABC producer noted that the use of technology "got out of control.... All we were doing was watching things squeeze and zoom and bounce and turn and spin and freeze."[36] Richard Salant, the former president of CBS News, declared, "I don't like music at the beginning, at the end and in the midst of network evening news broadcasts. It's a matter of principle: The music is a fiction, a part of entertainment and not of journalism."[37] Reflecting on the editing in his stories for CBS in the 1980s, Fred Graham said it was the "era of the three-second sound bite, too quick to be boring, or, frequently, intelligible. Out of curiosity, I went back into my scripts ... and calculated that the average time of a sound bite in my pieces was nine seconds. That meant that some were so short as to defy understanding."[38] For those who rejected the style changes in the network evening news programs, public television offered for many years a contrasting product in the form of *The MacNeil/Lehrer NewsHour*. Explaining the design of the program, coanchor Jim Lehrer noted in 1992: "Nothing should be noticed or absorbed except the information. Nothing else should be memorable. There is no such thing as a pretty slide, a zippy piece of music, a trendy shirt, a dynamic set, a tough question, or anything else, if it deflects even a blink of attention from the information. Those few seconds while the viewer admires or retches over the gaudy green tie or the red-white-and-blue-flashing map of the drought belt can destroy the whole point of the exercise, the transmitting of information."[39]

While the changes in product content and style on the network evening news often generated criticisms, many involved in the industry viewed the overall product quality as improving over time. News programs in the Cronkite era were often video headline services, with the anchor reading a number of short stories and with correspondents given a short amount of time to cover events. Van Gordon Sauter described Washington D.C. stories on the *CBS Evening News* in the 1970s in this way: "[Y]ou'd make your minute-fifteen piece that was almost exclusively a picture of somebody sitting at a table, a picture of other people sitting at an opposing table, somebody at table one talks, somebody at table two talks, and then one of your correspondents stands in front of an important-looking building telling you what you just heard and what it might mean. The quintessential *Evening News* piece was that."[40]

Producers in the 1980s stressed that their new approaches brought the broadcasts outside of Washington, expanded the topics covered on the news, and used technology to attract viewer attention. When the evening news programs were criticized for the brevity of sound bites in their coverage of the 1988 elections relative to soundbite length in 1968, *CBS Evening News* producer Tom Bettag noted:

> I don't think the past was that good. I think there is a glorification of '68. One of the problems in '68 was that is was the "just-the-facts-ma'am" wire services reporting....
> I would attribute the [longer sound bites] to the idea that they were trying to fill up

a broadcast. The problem at that time was how to fill up a half-hour broadcast.... It just laid out what the politicians said. It was a broadcast dominated by reports from beat correspondents in and around Washington. So much of the agenda was just filling it up with Washington stuff. You could let sound bites run for two minutes because it helped fill out the broadcast.[41]

Bettag contended that the broadcasts of the 1980s compressed more information into the programs because "people's ability to receive visual information has speeded up."[42] Assessing the relative quality of the network evening news in 1986 (the midpoint of the years examined in this chapter), *Los Angeles Times* media reporter David Shaw concluded: "Many stories on the evening newscasts today provide more explanation, detail and perspective than they did 10 or 20 years ago. The stories are fewer but longer; they often are accompanied by one or two analytical stories on the same subject; they more often come from cities other than Washington; they are illustrated and explained by better, clearer, more sophisticated charts, graphs and other visual aids—and, thanks to satellite transmissions, they are accompanied by pictures that are more immediate than ever before."[43]

If news executives are concerned about profits, the spatial model predicts they will focus particular attention on viewers valued by advertisers, will measure success in part by ratings, and will respond to changes in viewer information demands by changing the news delivered. Newspaper coverage of the evening news programs and journalists' memoirs confirm these three predictions. Stories about the network news in the 1970s had executives measuring the progress of their newscasts with specific demographic groups. Noting in 1977 that the audience for the *ABC Evening News*, anchored by Barbara Walters and Harry Reasoner, had increased 16% in a year, ABC News president William Sheehan said, "More importantly, two thirds of audience gain is among young adults between 18 and 49."[44] Discussing the market reaction to the pairing of Dan Rather and Connie Chung as coanchors on the *CBS Evening News*, CBS executive David Poltrack in 1993 analyzed audience changes by age group: "We have lost some 55-and-older viewers who may be put off by the faster pace and dynamics of having dual anchors, but we have made some gains among adults 35 to 54 years old."[45] Dan Rather described the difference between the attention given to ratings when he became anchor in 1981 to the focus given in 2000: "[When I started] we looked at the ratings probably every week, but I'm not even sure every week. We tended to want to see a trend line [over] three or four or five weeks.... Now the ratings are looked at overnight, and looked at every day."[46] Rather and Jennings noted that in 2000 the networks had minute-by-minute ratings that allowed producers to determine what stories caused viewers to shift. The ratings even allowed the networks to determine when individuals in particular demographic groups changed the channel.[47]

The focus on younger viewers and women, both groups highly valued by advertisers, changed the content of the network evening news. A *New York Times* article in 1992 about the changes wrought by *CBS Evening News* executive producer Erik Sorenson concluded that "Sorenson ... acknowledged that traditional political coverage and foreign-news stories are less prominent on his newscast than when he took over the then-third-ranked newscast. 'I think younger viewers are more interested in the environment, health care and pocketbook issues that are relevant to their lives,' Sorenson said."[48]

Another analyst of the network evening news battles in the early 1990s noticed: "In an attempt to close the gap with ABC, the *CBS Evening News* began to air so-called user-friendly segments, such as the 'Health Watch' or the 'Money Crunch,' in order to label news developments that ordinarily might not make the broadcast. The former category was heavily oriented toward items (such as breast cancer) deemed to be of particular interest to female viewers. The latter was used to label any spot news development that seemed to have impact on viewers' pocketbooks."[49]

A network evening news program's attempts to attract marginal viewers resemble a politician's attempts to gather marginal voters. Just as a candidate may offer issue combinations to build support among the undecided, the network evening news programs tried to find combinations of stories and approaches that would appeal to valuable viewers who might prefer other viewing options. When Roger Ailes was a political advisor, he noted the similarity between his job and that of the network news producers:

> We're all worried about the arithmetic. They're worried about their ratings; I'm worried about the number of voters that are going to vote for my guy. ... They're trying to make their newscast the most exciting and visual and the least wordy and thoughtful. If they can do that they may get the highest ratings. There's nothing wrong with that, just admit it. Just say, "Folks, we're in show business and these candidates are in show business. You are the audience, and everybody is trying to get to you and entertain you. We'll give you whatever you want, because we're all in the business of selling." The thing that I object to is these journalists running around saying that Roger Ailes is doing something different from what they're doing. We're all in the same business.[50]

Candidates often garner criticism from their base because of moderate positions chosen to attract the undecided. The results from chapter 3 indicate that the marginal viewers sought by the nightly news programs (e.g., younger or female consumers) tend to have less interest in hard news topics. This runs the risk of alienating the base of older consumers who do appreciate coverage of public affairs topics. Looking at the willingness of the news programs to reduce international coverage, correspondent Garrick Utley notes that this strategy "amounts to an editorial downsizing, a narrowing of focus that gives viewers who are searching for a greater exposure to the world even less reason to watch the programs. It is a slippery slope that leads not only to smaller audiences but also to reduced relevance in the broadcast industry and in society."[51]

The networks measured success by ratings because ultimately their business involved selling viewers to advertisers. Press accounts of the competition between the network evening news programs frequently remarked on the commercial value of the ratings. In 1983, an account in the *New York Times*, entitled "The Great Chase in Network News," estimated that a rating point translated into $25 million in annual advertising revenue and noted that the two point rating advantage of the *CBS Evening News* meant $50 million in extra income.[52] By the late 1980s, analysts were noting that even though ABC's *World News Tonight* did not have the highest ratings among total households it "had higher commercial rates than its rivals because its viewers are younger and thus more desirable to advertisers."[53] In November 1999 the ratings lead by *NBC Nightly News* translated into an average price for a thirty-second ad on the evening news programs of $54,200 on NBC, $45,000 for ABC, and $36,600 for CBS.[54] The increased focus on profits on the programs led to an expansion of advertising and promotion and shrinking of news time. When Downie and Kaiser compared a 1981 *CBS Evening News* broadcast with a 2000 version, the time allotted to news coverage on the half-hour program had dropped from 23:20 minutes to 18:20.[55] In the 2000 broadcast, over ten minutes were devoted to commercials and eighty seconds within the program were consumed by teasers, story previews meant to retain viewers across the commercial breaks.

While the time used for news coverage within the programs was growing shorter, the length of some stories in the news broadcasts was growing longer in response to technological changes. The ability of local stations to use satellite footage to cover breaking national and international stories and the growth of news coverage on cable reduced viewer demand for network evening newscasts as video headline services. Writing in 1986, Alex Jones observed:

> Change wrought by technology—particularly readily available satellite transmission—is another of the principal pressures the anchors and their programs face. Local stations now have the ability to cover national and international news, and this has placed them in competition for the first time with the network news shows. There is also new pressure from competing organizations such as Ted Turner's Cable News Network and potential competition from the fourth commercial broadcast network Rupert Murdoch is attempting to assemble. As a result, all three networks are struggling to redefine their shows to make them somehow unique.[56]

NBC News president Lawrence Grossman described in 1985 how the consumption of news earlier in the day was changing the focus of the networks: "We start with the assumption now that a good part of the country knows the headlines by the time they get to Rather or Brokaw or Jennings at 7 P.M. Therefore, now our job is to provide context, perspective, and history."[57] Since many viewers knew the day's headlines, the networks tried providing longer stories. Some of these provided background on the headlines, some focused on topics out of the headlines that were related to "news you can use" categories like health or finance, and some were feature stories on human interest or celebrities. Assessing the pressures in 1991 to provide a different type of information than found on local news or CNN, the executive producer of *CBS Evening News* (Erik Sorenson) declared, "We can have all the same footage of Lech Walesa shaking hands with President Bush. But poverty, education, health care, insurance, banks—these are big stories that local stations won't touch. They're too complicated, they're too hard, and they don't usually have news 'pegs' until the problem explodes. We need to do enterprise reporting, stories that we identify as trends."[58] Comparing the headline approach on CBS under Walter Cronkite to the 1991 *CBS Evening News*, a CBS News official said, "We [under Cronkite] did a minute fifteen on the State Department, a minute fifteen on the White House, a minute fifteen on the Pentagon, a minute fifteen on the hearing on the Hill.... [Now] we spend longer periods of time on social issues, consumer issues and health issues, issues that are important to the viewer.... We're trying to get away from doing the routine hearings."[59]

The popularity of entertainment programming also affected the news product. As viewing options expanded with channel growth and the spread of cable, network newscasts were competing for attention with game shows, situation comedies, and tabloid news programs. Network evening newscasts varied in their responses, at times deciding that soft news and celebrity stories would capture viewers and at other times deciding that a recommitment to hard news was the best way to differentiate their products. Describing the uncertainty about how to capture fleeing viewers, one correspondent noted in 1991, "I don't think any of the networks have figured out how to make the evening newscasts work so that people are going to want to watch them at 6:30 rather than 'Family Feud.'"[60] The profitability of game shows also shifted when the network evening news programs were shown on stations, as evidenced by changes made by New York City stations. WABC shifted *World News Tonight* to 6:30 in 1986 so it could show *Jeopardy* at 7 P.M. when more people are watching television. In 1988 WCBS moved *CBS Evening News* to 6:30 P.M. to make way for *Win, Lose, or Draw*. WNBC moved the *NBC Nightly News* to 6:30 P.M. so it could air the syndicated program *Love Connection* at 7 P.M. CBS News president Howard Stringer noted "as the competition gets fiercer out there, not only is the competition directly against the evening news stronger, the affiliates move the evening news into less dominant positions.... As the [network] evening news gets moved from 7 P.M. to 6:30 to 6 and to 5:30 P.M., in some instances, the viewing levels go down. So it's really kind of a victim of the whole ratings wars at all levels of television."[61] ABC had a positive spillover from one programming genre, talk shows. Industry analysts credited part of the ratings success of *World News Tonight* to viewers who watched *Oprah* on many ABC affiliates and then stayed with the local news and network evening news.[62]

Cost reductions offered the networks another way to generate profits in their news divisions. In 1985 alone CBS News made headlines by cutting its news staff by 10% and ABC News reduced its work force by laying off 3%.[63] Some foreign bureaus were closed, domestic bureaus shut down, and beat reporters eliminated.[64] Fewer resources translated into stories not covered or told with footage provided from other sources. Describing the pressures to produce the news with less, CBS News president Howard Stringer said in 1986, "The dreadful dilemma is that we want to cover the news as effectively and comprehensively as before, but ... you feel the hot breath of debtor's prison."[65] To save money the networks pooled coverage efforts. One example was the creation for the 1990 elections of Voter Research and Surveys, a consortium formed by the networks and CNN to survey voters and create projections on election day. The networks estimated $9 million in savings for each network over four years, from the centralization of voter projections. Yet as one expert warned in 1990, "Anyone should be concerned if there's only one source of information. No matter how well planned surveys are, there's always sampling error, poorly written questions and just simply calculation errors."[66] This foreshadowed the problems with election data provided by the Voter News Service, the joint venture created by the networks and other news organizations, in the 2000 presidential elections.

The fate of foreign coverage on the network evening news programs captures well the focus on profits, cost cutting, and viewer interests. After the budget cuts at CBS in the mid-1980s, Richard Cohen (the *Evening News* producer who directed international coverage) said, "It is inevitable, and it is already here, that we are going to cover less news.... We have fewer people, less resources, fewer options, which are spread thinner. We're not going to go to the places that we used to go. We'll do fewer discretionary stories. We had a piece on the rising Arab fundamentalism movement; those are the analytical stories that really separate us from other news organizations. But we're so busy covering our ass on hard news, we have fewer and fewer people to send places to get those kinds of stories."[67]

Reflecting in 2000 on how CBS covered the civil war in El Salvador in 1981, Dan Rather observed, "we wanted at least two correspondents assigned there with at least two camera crews and at least two producers.... The key point is that nobody said, 'Well it costs too much and we can't afford that.' ... Those decisions were made on the basis of, Is it important? Is it interesting?... That's changed quite a bit."[68] Peter Jennings in 2000 too noted how the networks now factored costs into decisions about foreign coverage, saying, "When we send a reporter into the field today it has to be costed out before the reporter travels.... In other words, if we want to send a reporter to Libya, our accounting department wants to know in advance how much is it going to cost."[69] Detailing the reasons behind the drop in foreign coverage, Thomas Rosenstiel reported in 1994:

> Yes, perhaps CBS "did better work" overseas in many places of the world 20 years ago, said Lane Venardos, vice president of hard news and special events for CBS News. "But the issue is nobody can afford to do that in this day and age. So it doesn't do any good to talk about what might have been. It is a new age." What's more, surveys consistently

reveal that the public doesn't care as much about foreign news. So while the networks have good people abroad, executives limit foreign news on their broadcasts. "There is a feeling that certainly exists at CBS that the State Department and the process of diplomacy is not a good TV story," says CBS correspondent David Martin.[70]

These press accounts and journalists' memoirs offer one way to chart the changes in network evening news programs brought about by changes in ownership, viewer demand, and technology. The following section uses more quantitative measures to analyze how coverage of hard and soft news on the network evening news programs changed over the past thirty years.

Tracking Trends from 1969 through 1998

The editors of *People* know people. In particular, these editors know which celebrities and personalities will generate subscriptions and grocery check-out purchases from readers in search of diversion. In this section I analyze changes over time in network coverage of the individuals chosen annually by *People* magazine as the year's 25 Most Intriguing People. I use this as a way to measure whether the evening news broadcasts are covering soft news topics.[71] Critics often contend that a focus on soft news crowds out the provision of information voters need to know about politics. Controversy surrounds the amount of information voters actually need, since they effectively delegate many policy decisions to legislators, judges, and executive branch officials. For those whose work is policymaking, however, there is a need to know the details of bills and court cases. Viewed in terms of Downs's four information demands discussed in chapter 1, those working in and around government have a producer demand for information, since this information can help with their production activities. In this section I use information from outlets and organizations involved in policymaking to measure network news coverage of hard news topics. I use *Harvard Law Review*'s annual roundup of Supreme Court cases, *Congressional Quarterly*'s assessment of the year's key Senate and House votes, and interest group legislative scorecards from the left (i.e., Americans for Democratic Action) and right (i.e., American Conservative Union) to see how networks may have changed over time in the ways they cover government.

The results in table 6.1 provide some evidence that the network evening news broadcasts are covering more soft news topics. *People* magazine began publishing a yearly list of the 25 Most Intriguing People in 1974. For each year I took the individuals on the annual list and searched the Vanderbilt Television News Archive, which contains an abstract of each story on the network evening newscasts starting in 1969. Though *People*'s list contained a large number of movie stars and entertainers, the magazine also focused on famous politicians. To use the magazine as an indicator for soft news coverage, I divided the sam-

TABLE 6.1
Coverage of *People*'s Most Intriguing People by Network, 1974–1998

	% of People Covered			
	ABC	CBS	NBC	All Networks
Full Sample				
(N = 571)				
1974–78	49.6	47.0	48.7	58.3
1979–83	50.9	50.0	50.0	62.3
1984–88	57.4	53.9	52.2	64.3
1989–93	49.6	53.1	60.2	66.4
1994–98	52.6	54.4	51.8	59.6
Soft News Personalities				
(N = 339)				
1974–78	28.3	26.4	30.2	39.6
1979–83	42.6	39.3	36.1	50.8
1984–88	50.0	45.8	43.0	59.7
1989–93	40.8	44.7	51.3	57.9
1994–98	46.8	46.8	45.5	51.9
Not Soft News Personalities				
(N = 232)				
1974–78	67.7	64.5	64.5	74.2
1979–83	60.4	66.0	66.0	75.5
1984–88	69.8	67.4	67.4	72.1
1989–93	67.6	70.3	78.4	83.8
1994–98	64.9	70.3	64.9	75.7

ple into two subsets. Soft news personalities included television stars, movie actors, sports figures, persons involved in famous crimes, and royalty. Categories of Intriguing People who are not soft news personalities included business leaders and political figures.[72] For the full sample of 571 personalities, network coverage as measured by the percentage of *People* people mentioned in a news broadcast appears to soften only slightly over time. In the period 1974 to 1978, 58.3% of the individuals on the *People* magazine list were mentioned in network news stories during the year they were featured in *People*. The figure is 59.6% for the years 1994–98.[73]

Once the sample is divided into soft news personalities and other personalities, a different pattern emerges. In the years 1974–78, 39.6% of the soft news celebrities in *People* were covered in network news stories. By the years 1994–98 this figure was 51.9%. For the individual networks the coverage of soft news celebrities in *People* was similar within most time periods.[74] From 1974 to 1978, the percentage of soft news figures covered was 28.3% for ABC, 26.4% for CBS, and 30.2% for NBC. Coverage on each network grew over time. For the

1994–98 period, the percentage of soft news figures covered was 46.8% for ABC, 46.8% for CBS, and 45.5% for NBC. Table 6.1 shows that coverage of the "harder" news personalities from *People* is higher in each time period than coverage for the lighter figures. From 1974 to 1978, 74.2% of the non-soft news personalities had at least one story on the network news. In the period 1994–98, 75.7% of these non-soft news figures garnered coverage. Within each time period, the networks had similar percentages for their coverage of "hard news" Intriguing People. The results suggest that for individuals defined by *People* as of interest, networks are more likely to cover those with hard news associations. Over time, however, the networks have also grown more likely to include stories in the evening broadcasts about soft news celebrities.

Table 6.2 examines network coverage of the Supreme Court by analyzing the percentage of cases discussed on the broadcasts when they were decided. For the set of cases identified annually in the *Harvard Law Review* review of the

TABLE 6.2
Coverage of Supreme Court's Key Cases, 1969–1998

	% of Cases Covered			
	ABC	*CBS*	*NBC*	*All Networks*
Full Sample				
(N = 831)				
1969–73	37.8	43.6	38.5	52.6
1974–78	40.1	42.6	37.0	48.1
1979–83	46.1	56.6	46.1	63.8
1984–88	37.7	54.9	39.3	59.0
1989–93	46.7	41.8	32.8	54.9
1994–98	45.3	41.0	31.6	53.0
Constitutional Law Cases				
(N = 528)				
1969–73	48.6	55.0	47.7	65.8
1974–78	48.1	49.0	41.3	54.8
1979–83	51.0	63.3	52.0	72.4
1984–88	44.2	64.9	48.0	68.8
1989–93	51.3	45.9	37.8	59.5
1994–98	56.3	48.4	39.1	60.9
Not Constitutional Law Cases				
(N = 303)				
1969–73	11.1	15.6	15.6	20.0
1974–78	25.9	31.0	29.3	36.2
1979–83	37.0	44.4	35.2	48.1
1984–88	26.7	37.8	24.4	42.2
1989–93	39.6	35.4	25.0	47.9
1994–98	32.1	32.1	22.6	43.4

Supreme Court's decisions, I searched the Vanderbilt archives for coverage of the case on the day, and day after, the decision was handed down.[75] The results show that within any given time period the networks were much more likely to cover constitutional law cases decided by the Court than nonconstitutional law cases. In the interval 1969–73, 65.8% of the court cases involving constitutional issues were covered by the networks versus 20.0% of the other cases. The coverage of constitutional law cases has remained relatively high over time. From 1994 to 1998, 60.9% of constitutional law cases generated at least one story upon announcement by the court. For the sample as a whole, 52.6% of cases were covered from 1969 to 1973 and 53.0% were covered from 1994 to 1998.

These general patterns miss the differences across networks in how they choose to cover the court. From 1984 to 1988, CBS covered 54.9% of the Supreme court decisions versus 37.7% for ABC. In the period 1989–93 it was ABC that had the highest percentage of cases covered (46.7%) and NBC which had the lowest (32.8%). From 1994 to 1998, ABC again covered the largest percentage of the cases (45.3%), while NBC covered 31.6%. These differences among networks are consistent with the newspaper accounts during these time periods, which alternatively identified first CBS and then ABC as having a harder news focus. NBC was singled out in press coverage for slighting public affairs stories and favoring human interest topics, which may translate into the relatively lower coverage of major Supreme Court cases on the network's evening news broadcasts.

Table 6.3 examines the percentage of key votes identified by *Congressional Quarterly* that were covered on the evening news broadcasts on the day or day after the legislative action.[76] Most key votes in most years have been covered by at least one of the network evening news programs. Yet coverage has declined significantly over time. From 1969 to 1973, 81.6% of the major congressional votes were mentioned on at least one of the network evening newscasts. In the period 1994–98 that percentage dropped to 61.9%. Senate votes attract more attention than those in the House. From 1994 to 1998, 65.8% of the Senate votes generated a network news story versus 58.4% of the House actions. Individual viewers do not watch "the networks"; they tend to watch a specific network. Viewed from that perspective, about half of the votes in Congress in recent years were covered on each network. For the most recent interval, 60% of Senate votes were mentioned on CBS, 52.9% on NBC, and 50.0% on ABC. The reputation of CBS as the "Tiffany network," the quality purveyor of hard news, is reflected in the data. In each five-year interval for Senate votes, CBS had the highest coverage percentage. The changes within this network reflect the decline overall in hard news, with coverage of Senate votes on CBS declining from 81.1% (1969–73) to 60.0% (1994–98). The position of NBC as the lowest provider of hard news is evident in House coverage in the 1994–98 era. While CBS did stories on 49.4% of key House votes, NBC covered only 37.7% of these congressional actions.

TABLE 6.3

Coverage of *Congressional Quarterly*'s Key Votes, 1969–1998

	% of Congressional Quarterly Votes Covered			
	ABC	*CBS*	*NBC*	*All Networks*
Full Sample (N = 913)				
1969–73	67.2	75.2	61.0	81.6
1974–78	57.9	60.4	52.8	69.2
1979–83	46.8	53.8	48.7	62.8
1984–88	40.4	46.4	37.1	50.3
1989–93	40.3	45.3	42.1	51.6
1994–98	47.6	54.4	44.9	61.9
Senate (N = 451)				
1969–73	70.3	81.1	63.5	86.5
1974–78	60.8	70.9	55.7	77.2
1979–83	45.5	49.3	45.4	58.4
1984–88	38.9	47.2	36.1	51.4
1989–93	45.6	48.1	41.8	54.4
1994–98	50.0	60.0	52.9	65.8
House (N = 462)				
1969–73	63.6	68.7	58.2	76.1
1974–78	55.0	50.0	50.0	61.3
1979–83	48.1	58.2	51.9	67.1
1984–88	41.8	45.6	38.0	49.4
1989–93	35.0	42.5	42.5	48.8
1994–98	45.5	49.4	37.7	58.4

Lobbying groups in search of voters and networks in search of viewers must both contend with limited public interests in politics. Many interest groups attempt to summarize their evaluations of incumbents in Congress through a single measure, a legislative scorecard that indicates the percentage of time a legislator has voted in favor of a particular position. The scorecard vote number becomes an easy way to convey to voters, lobbyists, and candidates how a particular interest group views an incumbent. For each Congress, the Americans for Democratic Action identifies a set of votes, designates the liberal position on each measure, and calculates the percentage of times (i.e., the ADA rating) a legislator voted in favor of the ADA's position.[77] The American Conservative Union (ACU) similarly calculates the percentage of time a legislator voted the conservative position on a set of key measures. In table 6.4, I use coverage of the ADA and ACU key Senate votes on the day, or day after, the votes to measure how network treatment of liberal and conservative legislative issues has changed over time.

TABLE 6.4
Coverage of Interest Group Key Votes, 1969–1998

	% of Interest Group Votes Covered			
	ABC	CBS	NBC	All Networks
Full Sample (N = 1,203)				
1969–73	49.3	55.3	50.7	63.8
1974–78	46.6	59.3	40.7	64.7
1979–83	32.8	43.4	41.9	55.1
1984–88	36.1	38.5	30.2	46.8
1989–93	30.8	28.9	33.2	44.1
1994–98	29.6	34.7	26.4	44.0
Americans for Democratic Action Votes (N = 606)				
1969–73	51.8	58.9	52.7	67.9
1974–78	54.1	64.3	46.9	70.4
1979–83	35.7	49.0	45.9	60.2
1984–88	36.0	38.0	26.0	46.0
1989–93	28.6	31.6	35.7	46.9
1994–98	31.0	35.0	24.0	43.0
American Conservative Union Votes (N = 597)				
1969–73	42.5	45.0	45.0	52.5
1974–78	40.7	55.3	35.8	60.2
1979–83	30.0	38.0	38.0	50.0
1984–88	36.2	39.0	34.3	47.6
1989–93	32.7	26.5	31.0	41.6
1994–98	28.4	34.5	28.4	44.8

Votes that define liberalism and conservatism for interest groups have consistently attracted less network attention than the key votes defined by *Congressional Quarterly*. Table 6.4 shows that from 1969 to 1973, 63.8% of interest group Senate votes were mentioned in at least one evening news broadcast versus 86.5% for the Senate key votes tracked by *CQ*. During the years 1994–98 both these hard news measures had declined, with the networks covering 44.0% of the interest group votes and 65.8% of the *CQ* measures. For the first three time intervals, network coverage of liberal votes is much greater than coverage of conservative measures. From 1969 to 1973, networks covered 67.9% of votes in the ADA legislative scorecard. The measures used in the ACU indicator only generated stories 52.5% of the time. In the period 1979–83, the evening news programs covered 60.2% of ADA votes versus 50.0% of ACU actions. In the later time intervals, however, coverage of liberal and conservative votes was nearly equal. In the 1994–98 time period, networks did stories on 43.0% of ADA votes and 44.8% for ACU measures.

The patterns for individual network coverage in table 6.4 show that for each time period CBS covered the highest percentage of liberal votes. From 1969 to 1973, CBS did stories on 58.9% of the ADA measures versus 51.8% for ABC. From 1994 to 1998, CBS covered 35.0% of ADA votes versus NBC's figure of 24.0%. CBS was also the leader in terms of covering conservative votes, covering 34.5% of ACU votes (1994–98) versus 28.4% for NBC. The hard news focus of CBS relative to the other networks may mean that it covers issues of interest to liberals and to conservatives. The soft news focus for NBC in the 1994–98 period is evident in low coverage of ADA and ACU votes. For each network liberal votes were more likely to get coverage than conservative ones for the first three intervals. At CBS, the 58.9% coverage of ADA votes (1969–73) contrasts with a 45.0% figure for ACU measures. In that time period, ABC (51.8% ADA versus 42.5% ACU) and NBC (52.7% ADA versus 45.0% ACU) were also more likely to cover the votes that went into liberalism scores. In the later years the networks treated liberal versus conservative votes more evenly. For the years 1994 to 1998, each network covered the interest groups in similar numbers (ABC 31.0% ADA versus 28.4% ACU, CBS 35.0% versus 34.5%, and NBC 24.0% versus 28.4%).

Table 6.5 offers another way to track changes in hard and soft news coverage on the networks over time. The table reports the mean number of stories and average number of seconds devoted to particular celebrities, court cases, and votes that were covered on the network broadcasts. For the soft news celebrities, defined as Intriguing People by *People*, the mean number of stories about each celebrity and mean airtime devoted to coverage over the course of the year doubled on each network. For CBS, a soft news celebrity generated 11.4 stories on average in the year they were featured in *People* (1974–78). This translated into an average of 1,382 seconds of news stories. By the years 1994–98, each soft news figure garnered an average of 23.4 stories and 3,036 seconds of airtime.[78] Among the three networks, NBC had the highest average number of stories about the *People* celebrities (25.6 per person) and the highest mean coverage length (3,238 seconds). The doubling of stories and airtime also held for the *People* figures who were not in soft news fields. For NBC, coverage of these non-soft *People* notables jumped from a mean of 12.5 stories (1974–78) to 24.0 stories (1994–98). The mean airtime devoted on NBC to someone in this *People* category went from 1,490 seconds to 2,817 seconds.

Though coverage of hard news topics has declined over time on the evening news, table 6.5 shows that for hard news topics that make it into the broadcast there is actually more time devoted to the story in later years. This is consistent with the shift by the networks in providing longer stories with more context and background for the policy issues that do get covered. For the Supreme Court cases covered on a network evening news program, there is generally one story on the day, or day after, the decision. For ABC, the mean number of sto-

TABLE 6.5
Space and Time Devoted on Network Television to Stories Covered

	ABC		CBS		NBC	
	Mean Number of Stories	*Mean Coverage Length (seconds)*	*Mean Number of Stories*	*Mean Coverage Length (seconds)*	*Mean Number of Stories*	*Mean Coverage Length (seconds)*
People, Soft News Personalities						
1974–78	9.9	1,274.7	11.4	1,382.1	9.9	1,254.4
1994–98	17.2	2,140.6	23.4	3,036.1	25.6	3,238.0
People, Not Soft News Personalities						
1974–78	11.6	1,311.4	13.3	1,528.0	12.5	1,490.4
1994–98	21.7	2,809.6	25.6	2,705.4	24.0	2,817.1
Supreme Court Key Cases						
1969–73	1.2	102.9	1.1	89.8	1.2	81.3
1994–98	1.0	140.8	1.1	96.7	1.1	124.2
Congressional Quarterly Key Votes						
1969–73	1.3	116.9	1.3	116.2	1.2	106.7
1994–98	1.3	211.2	1.3	168.1	1.2	207.0
Interest Group Key Votes						
1969–73	1.4	130.9	1.3	116.3	1.3	115.9
1994–98	1.2	146.6	1.3	139.7	1.1	90.3

ries for cases covered was 1.2 (1969–73) and 1.0 (1994–98). The mean coverage length, however, increased from 102.9 seconds (1969–73) to 140.8 seconds (1994–98). Similar increases in mean coverage length are evident for CBS (89.8 to 96.7 seconds) and NBC (81.3 to 124.2). For *CQ* votes covered on the broadcasts, the mean number of stories was identical in the periods 1969–73 and 1994–98 (i.e., 1.3 for ABC, 1.3 for CBS, and 1.2 for NBC). On each network the total time devoted to votes that got coverage on the day, or day after, they occurred increased over time. The mean coverage length of covered *CQ* votes went from 116.9 to 211.2 for ABC, 116.2 to 168.1 on CBS, and 106.7 to 207.0

on NBC. For interest group votes the mean number of stories dropped slightly over time. For ABC and CBS the mean coverage times increased from the years 1969–73 to 1994–98. On NBC, however, the mean time declined from 115.9 seconds to 90.3 seconds. Overall these figures indicate that if a network did do a story on a vote or decision, the program devoted more time to a key legislative vote than a key Supreme Court decision.

Media critics and journalists offer many competing hypotheses about the increasing presence of soft news and declining coverage of hard news topics on the evening news. Table 6.6 analyzes factors that explain network decision making over time. For each network I developed a model to predict whether a particular topic would be covered on that network's news program. The model was run for each network with four samples: coverage of *People* personalities; Supreme Court cases; *Congressional Quarterly* votes; and the interest group scorecard votes. Each equation contained the percentage of households receiving cable in the given year, to test whether more competition from cable drove the networks to forsake hard news. A variable is included to determine whether overall decision making changed after television was partially deregulated in 1984.[79] An indicator was included for presidential election years, on the theory that coverage of campaigns can crowd out different types of news. The pressure on networks to reduce costs is reflected in a variable defined as the percentage of stories about the network news in Lexis that mention the word "cost" or "cut." Factors specific to each sample (e.g., whether the person was a soft news personality or not) were also included in the models.[80]

Table 6.6 reports the change in the probability a topic was covered on the network brought about by a change in each factor in the coverage models. Consider first the determinants of decision making about covering *People* people. The results indicate that for the sample of 571 Intriguing People from 1974 through 1998, competition from cable television did not have a statistically significant impact on whether a network did a story on the person. Overall, individuals in the soft news categories had a lower probability of being covered than the "non-soft" news figures; probability of coverage for a soft news figure was .24 to .27 lower than for the "harder" news Intriguing People. Deregulation did have a statistically significant impact on the coverage of *People* figures. The figures covered in *People* magazine had a .21 to .24 higher probability of getting on the network evening news broadcasts in the deregulated era (e.g., in the era when the FCC stopped closely scrutinizing public affairs coverage).

For network coverage of the Supreme Court, cable competition and deregulation were not statistically significant predictors of the decision whether to cover a key Supreme Court case. On CBS, cases were more likely to be covered in election years and in years where stories were circulating about costs in CBS news coverage. The later effect may mean that as the network cut costs it used more Supreme Court stories, which may have been relatively cheaper to produce if they involved a regular court reporter. The factor with a statistically

TABLE 6.6
Determinants of Network Story Coverage

| | Change in Probability of Coverage | | | | | |
| | People (N = 571) | | | Supreme Court Key Cases (N = 831) | | |
Variable	ABC	CBS	NBC	ABC	CBS	NBC
(Mean +1)% Households with Cable vs. Mean %	−3.61e-3	−2.04e-3	−2.88e-3	2.97e-3	−1.53e-3	−1.72e-3
TV Deregulated vs. Not Deregulated	0.20*	0.21*	0.24*	−0.04	0.04	0.07
Election Year vs. Not Election Year	−0.03	−0.02	−0.07	0.06	0.08*	0.07
(Mean +1)% Lexis Network Stories about Cost vs. Mean %	7.07e-3	−0.02	−0.02	−9.90e-3	0.03***	−6.30e-3
Soft News Personality vs. Not Soft News Personality	−0.24***	−0.27***	−0.27***			
Constitutional Law Case vs. Not Constitutional Law Case				0.21***	0.22***	0.19***

| | Congressional Quarterly Key Votes (N = 912) | | | Interest Group Key Votes (N = 1,203) | | |
	ABC	CBS	NBC	ABC	CBS	NBC
(Mean +1)% Households with Cable vs. Mean %	−2.93e-3	−3.25e-3	−9.39e-4	−4.76e-3***	−4.58e-3**	1.26e-3
TV Deregulated vs. Not Deregulated	−0.02	0.03	−0.06	0.09	3.0e-3	−0.17**
Election Year vs. Not Election Year	−0.10**	−0.09**	−0.06	−0.10***	−0.14***	−0.11***
(Mean +1)% Lexis Network Stories about Cost vs. Mean %	−9.20e-3	−0.02**	−0.01	0.01	−7.41e-4	−3.64e-3
Bill Passed vs. Bill Not Passed	0.15***	0.13***	0.10***	−0.01	−0.02	0.03
Issue Domestic vs. Not Domestic Issue	0.01	0.04	0.03	0.02	0.04	−0.05*
Senate vs. House	0.04	0.08**	0.03			
ADA Key Vote vs. ACU Key Vote				0.04	0.05*	0.04

Note: Change in probability = probability of coverage with first characteristic—probability with second characteristic, with other variables in logit analysis set to their means. *** = statistically significant at the .01 level; ** = significant at the .05 level; * = significant at the .10 level.

significant impact in all three networks was whether a case involved an issue of constitutional law. Those key cases that did involve constitutional issues had a higher probability of being covered (ranging from .19 at NBC to .22 at CBS).

Cable competition and deregulation did not have a statistically significant impact on whether the key congressional votes tracked by *CQ* were covered on the nightly news. On CBS and ABC congressional votes were crowded out during presidential elections. In those election years, the probability a *CQ* vote was covered was about .10 lower. Bills that passed were deemed much more newsworthy by each network. Those *CQ* votes that resulted in legislation passing had a .15 higher probability of coverage on ABC, .13 on CBS, and .10 on NBC. Whether the bill dealt with domestic or foreign issues did not have a statistically significant impact on whether the networks did a story around the vote. For CBS, votes in the Senate had a .08 higher probability of coverage compared to votes in the House. CBS was less likely to do a story about votes in years in which there was attention focused on cutting costs in the network.

The impact of economics is more readily visible in decisions about which interest groups votes to cover. For ABC and CBS, higher cable competition translated into a reduced probability that a vote in the ADA or ACU scorecard would be covered on the evening news. For NBC, the probability of interest group coverage dropped dramatically (by .17) in the years when television was deregulated. For each network, the election years brought less attention for the votes tracked by the interest groups. The probability of coverage was lower by .14 for CBS in election years, .11 lower for NBC, and .10 lower for ABC. Domestic issues were less likely (.05 lower probability) to generate coverage on NBC. CBS treated the interest group votes differently. Votes of interest to the ADA had a .05 higher probability of coverage than votes in the ACU scorecard.

Table 6.7 offers another way to examine the determinants of network news coverage. For a set of words associated with soft news topics, I counted each year the number of stories in the Vanderbilt Television News Archives that had a particular word in a story abstract. The number of stories in each year from 1969 to 1999 is modeled as a function of the percentage of television households with cable, an indicator for whether television is deregulated (i.e., 1984 or later), and a control for whether the year features a presidential election. I did the same analyses for words associated with hard news stories (education, GAO (Government Accounting Office), Medicaid, NATO, technology). For the soft news words (actor, baseball, cancer, crime, movie, sex), the networks increased the number of stories about these topics as competition with cable grew. The same phenomenon is true, however, for the hard news stories. As the percentage of cable households increased, stories about topics such as education or technology grew.

Networks' reactions to the deregulation of television differed markedly for hard and soft news coverage. There was no statistically significant impact of deregulation on the number of soft news stories tracked in table 6.7. For the hard news topics, however, coverage of each hard news story was much lower

TABLE 6.7
Coverage of Soft and Hard News Topics, 1969–1999

| | Number of Network News Stories About | | | | | |
	Actor	Baseball	Cancer	Crime	Movie	Sex
Television Households	0.77**	1.50**	1.77*	2.78*	0.68*	1.30*
with Cable, %	(6.09)	(0.73)	(0.93)	(1.56)	(0.39)	(0.67)
Television Deregulated	−4.45	13.54	−39.39	−51.35	−15.71	−28.89
(1984+)	(13.08)	(32.37)	(41.17)	(69.24)	(17.42)	(29.93)
Presidential Election Year	4.37	−5.09	−10.90	−14.52	1.14	13.48
	(5.98)	(14.80)	(18.81)	(31.65)	(7.96)	(13.68)
Adjusted R^2	0.53	0.57	0.16	0.17	0.11	0.17

	Education	GAO	Medicaid	NATO	Technology
Television Households	3.63***	0.44*	0.39*	4.12***	2.52***
with Cable, %	(0.88)	(0.22)	(0.22)	(1.47)	(0.59)
Television Deregulated	−88.55**	−17.96*	−18.51*	−125.32*	−57.33**
(1984+)	(39.22)	(9.70)	(9.72)	(65.46)	(26.14)
Presidential Election Year	11.46	3.56	2.78	−27.00	−5.05
	(17.93)	(4.43)	(4.44)	(29.92)	(11.95)
Adjusted R^2	0.51	0.04	0.02	0.24	0.56

Note: N = 31. Standard errors in parentheses. *** = statistically significant at the .01 level; ** = significant at the .05 level; * = significant at the .10 level. Each specification also included an intercept term.

in the years when television was deregulated. The variable 1984+ is meant to capture the impact of a changed regulatory environment, one in which the FCC has signaled to stations that public affairs content will not be measured and license renewal will be nearly automatic. The deregulated period is also one of cost cutting, change in company ownership, and increased competition from cable channels. To the extent that competition is measured by households with cable and cost cutting is partly a reaction to this competition, the deregulation variable indicates that weakening expectations about public service requirements reduced hard news coverage. For the set of topics examined here, whether a year was a presidential election year had no statistically significant impact on story counts.

Conclusions

Chapter 3 offered a snapshot of the network evening news market in 2000 that underscored how economics affects decision making on these programs. Survey data reveal that the majority of network news viewers are fifty years old or older. A high percentage of the marginal viewers, those who watch only some-times, are female or young (i.e., 18–34). Young female viewers are particularly valued by advertisers, who hope to influence their purchasing decisions. These marginal viewers are less interested in politics, which means that networks try-ing to attract them will de-emphasize hard news stories such as the daily polit-ical battles on Capitol Hill. Interests in particular political issues vary by age and gender. Young females are more likely to say that gun control or education, for example, should be national priorities. The results indicate that when the evening news broadcasts do cover politics, they are more likely to devote time to stories about political issues deemed important by their marginal viewers, particularly the young and female.

This chapter shows how economics can be used to chart the changes in the network evening news broadcasts over a thirty-year period. The five Ws of the spatial model predict how the content offered on the evening news will re-spond to changes in ownership goals, audience demand, and technology. Press accounts and journalists' memoirs stress how news decisions on these broad-casts were shaped by strategies of product location. The programs went to great lengths to promote their anchors, brand their stories, and position their shows relative to other sources of news and entertainment. The statistical analysis confirms the observations made by press critics and reporters that changes in the news brought more soft news tales and fewer stories about votes on major congressional legislation. The final chapter assesses the impact on public affairs of media content such as the network broadcasts.

Chapter 7

News on the Net

THE INTERNET reconfigures space and time. Geographic space shrinks. Readers can access local papers from around the world, while companies can aggregate interested consumers across many different communities. Product space expands. No longer constrained by shelf space on newsstands or the costs of print, individuals and organizations can offer their take on events to millions by starting a website. Instant communication contracts the time news organizations have to do research before publishing and expands the demand for more news now. The changes in technology make novelty a constant, with the distribution of data over the Internet dubbed the "New New Thing" and the type of information conveyed called the "New News."[1] Though the form of information delivery on the Internet is new, this chapter shows that familiar theories explain how information markets function on the World Wide Web.

The economic fundamentals of information on the Internet are clear. The large fixed costs of production (e.g., printing presses, television studio equipment) disappear, as do the fixed costs of a delivery system and the marginal costs of paper and ink. Network effects become more important, since the value you derive from a site may depend on how many users it has and how these users contribute to its operation. Despite these changes in production and delivery, many of the properties of information delivered via newspapers or television also apply to the Internet. Content creation can still involve the fixed costs of investigating a story and learning what has transpired over the course of an hour or a day. Attention from consumers remains scarce.[2] With the large number of outlets contending for attention, the costs of becoming noticed and remembered remain important for Internet sites. Information on the Web retains the properties of a public good: one viewer's consumption does not prevent another from logging onto a website, and once information has been provided it is hard (in an age of emails, links, and attachments) to prevent another from consuming without paying for it. News on the Web is still an experience good; to know the good is to consume the good. This means brand names and reputations will be important as signals about the potential content of sites.

How these economic factors will interact to influence the provision of news remains an open question as the Internet evolves. Many of the theories about information on the World Wide Web take the form of bets or warnings about the likely paths of evolution.[3] Organizing these ideas and concerns around the five Ws shows again how the provision of news on the Internet raises questions that are common across media technologies.

Who cares about a particular piece of information? The large fixed costs of production and delivery have traditionally limited the number of papers or channels that can profitably survive in a local or national market. The disappearance of these costs on the Internet have led some to envision a world where a news source on the Internet becomes the "Daily Me," a collection of stories tailored to the interests of each person. This glosses over the fixed costs of content creation. Even if transmission on the Web is costless, it will still matter how many "Me's" are interested enough in a topic to justify the creation of a story about it by a news agency. It is true that once stories are created, the technology of the Internet makes it easy to rearrange and bundle these stories for an individual based on his or her interests. The drop in fixed costs will also mean that more varieties of information outlets will appear on the Internet. These niche sites mean consumers may get closer to their ideal bundle of information than if they had to consume a mass appeal product. Two potential drawbacks are that the implied fragmentation of the market may reduce common experiences and lead to the polarization of views among groups.[4] The division of the audience into smaller groups may also reduce the revenues available to each outlet to produce a high quality product. This would mean that the topics covered were closer to the interests of consumers but the depth of coverage might be limited by the number of viewers.

What are they willing to pay to find it, or what are others willing to pay to reach them? An early analysis of intellectual property in the digital age proclaimed, "Information wants to be free."[5] While consumers may in the short run prefer a price of zero for information, in the long run the question arises of how free information would get produced. The search for revenue from information leads back to two familiar income sources, advertising and subscription. The use of advertising reintroduces the importance of who cares about particular pieces of information, since advertisers vary in their willingness to pay for particular demographic groups. News sites on the Web often require registration so that they can describe the zip code, age, and gender of their users to advertisers. The question of how much consumers are willing to pay for information on the Web leads back to the four types of information demand identified by Downs (1957). Consumers may be willing to pay for information related to entertainment demands, consumer purchases, or business decisions. For data that would help in making voting decisions, the logic of free riding implies that most will not express a demand for civics information and policy details. Note that these considerations of revenue may play less of a role on sites where content is created by consumers. If people get utility from self-expression on the Web, then content creation costs are reduced. If the ratings of information by others helps a viewer sort and screen data, again the need for revenues to cover editors and managers may be reduced.

Where can media outlets or advertisers reach these people? The Internet in part changes the meaning and importance of "where" a consumer is. The ability of a website to draw viewers from across the globe expands the varieties of news products available to a viewer. While fixed costs may limit the varieties of newspapers or channels available in a given area, a consumer with interests relatively rare in a particular locality may find the desired information combination in cyberspace. The low fixed costs of website operation and potential for aggregating like-minded individuals from many different areas or countries implies great variety in news provision on the Internet. The prospect of niche outlets can also raise the specter of reduced common experiences and increased group polarization. If specialized sites do not expose consumers to opposite or unexpected views, learning or tolerance may be reduced.

Where the consumption of others takes them on the Net also influences the options available to a particular user. Internet sites are subject to network effects. The value of a site to an individual may grow as more people use the site. More users can increase content variety when sites are interactive, improve content targeting where the decisions of others provide information on likely tastes for stories, and provide more basis for discussion of common viewing experiences. A greater number of users for a site can translate into better quality and better recognition, which in turn reinforces greater use of the site. Where others have been on the Internet also matters in information cascades. When individuals use the choices of others as a short cut to reduce the costs of making their own decisions, then the Internet can give rise to cascades. News sites without significant reporting resources can contribute to cascades by simply repeating rumors or stories without independent investigation. Individuals can also propagate stories on the Net simply by repeating the statements of others.[6]

When is it profitable to provide the information? Though the technology of the Internet reduces delivery costs, creating content for a site can create significant costs. Traditional media firms, however, already pay the costs of hiring reporters and investing resources in developing stories for their newspapers, programs, or magazines. For these companies, putting stories they have already generated for other media on the Web gives them another way to earn revenues. This means that news on the Web may involve repackaging rather than original reporting. Established media companies also have an advantage in brand name recognition. Faced with limited time, viewers may forgo the costs of searching out new sites and rely on the reputation of established companies as a short cut to finding reliable news on the Web.

The existence of news sites on the Web does not imply profitability. In the late 1990s investors were willing to make large wagers on the potential profitability of many different types of Internet sites, including those providing news and public affairs information. Analysts predicted that Internet markets would behave like winner-take-all markets, which meant that gaining market share early on would translate into survival and then dominance down the road. The willingness to invest in sites promising political information took on the air of a speculative bubble. Investors believed the sites would generate revenue because other investors believed the sites would prosper. When the bubble burst for Internet companies, news and politics sites deflated as quickly as counterparts providing other services.[7] Sites with original political content do remain on the Web, but they may survive on the support of patrons, foundations, parties, or interest groups.[8]

Two traditional sources of revenue, subscription and advertising, have brought mixed success to Internet information sites. The *Wall Street Journal* has garnered more than 450,000 paid subscribers by charging annual online access fees of $29 for its newspaper subscribers and $59 for those who do not subscribe to the paper edition. Despite the large number of online subscriptions, the site has failed to make money (except for one month) over the course of five years. Companies charging consumers for pornographic content on the Web earned an estimated $1 billion in revenues in 2000. Sites devoted to covering politics, society, or the media have generally failed in their attempts to sign up paying subscribers.[9] Though banner ads and pop-up displays attest to the willingness of advertisers to pay for the attention of Internet users, expenditures on Internet ads by companies with major advertising budgets remain minuscule. Firms apportioning advertising dollars across direct mail, television, newspapers, radio, and the Internet have many opportunities to reach consumers in larger numbers than those currently offered by most Internet sites.[10]

Why is this profitable? The Internet is often seen as a communications medium best left unregulated by the government. Yet the functioning of information markets on the Web already relies on property rights established by laws and interpreted by regulators and judges. The ease of copying and accessibility of the Web have created disputes about how intellectual property rights should be defined and enforced on the Internet. Should sites allow individuals to post full copies of news stories from other outlets for discussion? Does a story pulled by a company from its electronic archive constitute a new publication that should generate additional revenues for its freelance author? Does the streaming of continuously updated scores from sporting events constitute an infringement on broadcast rights purchased by another media company? These are the types of disputes which have generated court cases about how information is transmitted in the Internet era.[11] Some analysts believe that much information should be defined as in the public domain, a move that would reduce the costs to consumers of accessing information. Others stress the need to protect the rights of producers in order to maintain long-term incentives for creating content. Disputes between consumers and producers about copying and conveying content on the Web will continue to affect how information is consumed and what types of information provision will be profitable.

This chapter does not try to predict the future of news on the Internet. Instead, I have taken snapshots of the Internet in 1999 and 2000 in order to examine questions about who uses the Web for news, how expression is concentrated or dispersed online, and what types of ideas fare well in information markets on the Internet. I use four different types of information: 1) survey data from the Pew Center; 2) information on the popularity online of the top one hundred daily papers in the United States; 3) measures of the relative incidence of authors, campaign contributions, and websites across a random sample of five hundred zip codes; and 4) statistics on Web searches for and advertiser support for soft news, hard news, and consumer or producer information. The results in general show that access to the Web is broader than for other forms of expression. Use of the Internet is correlated with income, but this correlation is lower than that for other forms of political expression. Concentration of attention is higher for the Internet than some other forms of expression, consistent with the impacts of network effects, brand names, and aggregation of interests across many localities. The relative demand expressed for information on the Web shows patterns familiar from other media. Soft news and "news you can use" often generate more interest than hard news. Differences in information preferences by age and gender also appear in the types of news viewers seek on the Internet.

News Online and Online Newspapers

If information were to be had for the asking, what questions would you seek to answer? Would the data relate to daily life (What will the weather be like tomorrow?) and its diversions (Did my team win last night?)? Would the news relate more to society (Will a Patients' Bill of Rights pass?) or to the world (Does a recent study provide evidence of global warming?)? The Internet offers information on all of these questions, with most sites offering their data for free. Yet viewers still face the opportunity costs of attention. Time spent consuming one type of information is time that cannot be spent on another task. This means the relative interest of viewers still plays a large role in the types of news demanded by news consumers on the Internet. Given the choice between the mundane and the momentous, individuals on the Net will prefer news they can use in their daily life to reports about significant political policies and questions. Survey data from the Pew Research Center for the People and the Press (2000b) confirms that the hierarchy of news interests evident in Internet news consumption is similar to the patterns found in print and broadcast news consumption.

In the Pew survey on media consumption conducted in 2000, Internet use was significantly influenced by age and gender.[12] Table 7.1 shows that over 70% of males and females 18–34 went online to access the Internet, Web, or email. Among males 50+, only 39.9% went online. Women 50+ had the lowest rate of Internet use, just 27.8%. Of those who are online, men are much more likely to go online for news (a pattern similar to the greater use of newspapers by men than women). Among online users 18–34, 55.0% of women went online for news at least one to two times per week versus 70.0% of men. For those women online, a similar percentage in each age group went online for news. The same is true for men. In the online community, 70.0% of males 18–34 went searching for news online at least one to two days per week versus 67.2% of males 50+.

When they are online consuming news, men and women explore topics in a fashion predicted by Downs's theories of information used for consumption, production, entertainment, and voting. News one can use in everyday life tops the interests of online consumers. Table 7.1 indicates that among nine categories of online news, for women news about science and health has the highest

TABLE 7.1
Internet News Consumption

		% of Column Respondents					
	Total	Females 18–34	Females 35–49	Females 50+	Males 18–34	Males 35–49	Males 50+
Go online to access the Internet, web, or email	54.0	71.0	62.8	27.8	71.6	58.5	39.9
Of those that go online . . .							
Go online daily to get news	27.0	21.2	21.3	20.9	29.6	34.0	36.6
Go online at least 1–2 days per week to get news	60.7	55.0	51.0	51.4	70.0	67.7	67.2
Of those that go online for news, go online for . . .							
Political News	39.2	37.9	28.9	33.3	42.1	48.7	42.7
Sports News	42.2	31.0	22.5	25.8	68.1	51.9	46.0
International News	45.0	41.7	33.3	40.7	55.5	52.4	42.7
Science and Health News	63.2	65.8	66.9	70.6	59.8	58.3	60.0
Technology News	58.7	42.6	46.5	49.5	71.5	72.2	71.0
Weather News	66.0	63.7	63.9	63.4	65.2	72.5	67.4
Entertainment	43.6	57.2	40.6	34.9	53.6	34.5	26.5
Local News	36.7	41.3	37.3	36.3	37.6	36.3	27.4
Business News	52.5	38.0	45.5	46.5	54.6	65.3	70.8

percentage of users. Among females 18–34, 65.8% go online for science and health news. For women 50+ the figure is 70.6%. This mirrors the strong interest in health news by women documented in chapter 3. Among males 18–34 the top category of online news is technology news, which attracts 71.5% of online news consumers in that demographic. Technology news is also first among males 50+ (71.0% go online for this) and second among males 35–49 (72.2%). The strong preference for technology news among those online is not surprising, given that going online involves some interaction with technology. A popular category with many demographic groups among those going online for news is the weather. The percentage of online news consumers seeking out this information ranges from 72.5% for males 35–49 to 63.4% among females 50+. In contrast, political news ranks near the bottom for each demographic group. Political news ranks eighth out of nine for all female demographics, seventh among males 35–49 or 50+, and eighth among males 18–34.

Many of the gender and age differences in news interests in print and broadcast audiences are also evident among online news consumers. Women are more interested in entertainment news than are men. Among female online news consumers, entertainment news was the third most popular category among women 18–34 (57.2% of online news consumers viewing this category). Among males consuming news online, entertainment news ranked last among those 35–49 (34.5%) and 50+ (26.5%). Interest in entertainment news within each gender was highest among those 18–34 and lowest among those 50+. Sports news ranked last in use among women online. For males 18–34 this was the second most popular category, with 68.1% going online for this type of news. Within every age group men were much more likely to consume sports information online than women. Among those 35–49 who go online for news, 51.9% of males went online for sports news versus 22.5% of women.

Business news was consumed in higher percentages in each age group among men than among women. For males 50+ consuming online business news ranked second among news categories, with 70.8% consuming this category online. For females 18–34 consuming news online, this category of news ranked seventh (38%). In each age group online, men were much more interested in political news than women were. For those 35–49, 28.9% of female online users sought out political news versus 48.7% of men. International news ranked higher in five of the six demographic groups than political news. Among those 18–34 or 35–49, men reported consuming international news online in higher proportions than woman. Among those 50+ this gender gap declines, with 42.7% of male online news consumers viewing international news versus 40.7% of women.

Though topics that Internet news consumers pursue are similar to those of print and broadcast consumers, the concentration of attention on the Internet is greater than in print markets. Prior to the evolution of the Internet, the relevant market for most local newspapers was local. The costs of physical

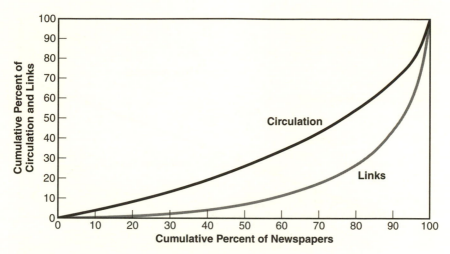

FIGURE 7.1. Relative concentration of circulation and links.

distribution, remote printing, and content creation meant most papers were consumed locally. There were newspapers that had national distribution, including *USA Today, Wall Street Journal,* and *New York Times.* With the arrival of the Internet, however, consumers were free to search the Net and sample the offerings of papers without being limited by geography. If readers in a small or medium city in the United States did not find their interests served by a local paper, they could easily read the *New York Times* (or the *Washington Times*) on line. To investigate how this freedom affected consumption of news sites on the Internet, I examined how popular local newspapers fared on the Internet. I started with the one hundred largest newspapers measured by 1999 circulation, according to a list compiled by *Editor and Publisher.* I then entered the Web addresses of these newspapers into an Internet site that tracks how frequently other websites link to a particular address. For each newspaper I developed a link count, which I treat as a measure of relative popularity on the Internet.

For the top one hundred newspapers in the United States, figure 7.1 traces out the cumulative percentage of newspapers that account for a cumulative percentage of circulation and links. The figure shows clearly that attention on the web is much more highly concentrated than the circulation of printed papers. The top five newspapers (*Wall Street Journal, USA Today, New York Times, Los Angeles Times, Washington Post*) accounted for 21.5% of the total circulation of the one hundred newspapers analyzed. The top five newspaper websites in the sample (*USA Today, New York Times, Detroit News, Washington Post, Seattle Times*) accounted for 41.4% of the total links generated by the top one

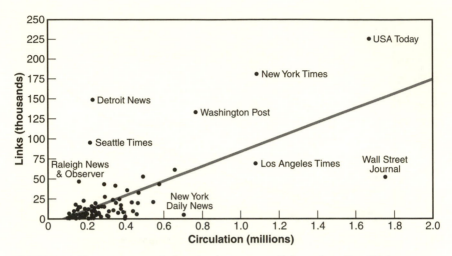

FIGURE 7.2. Newspaper popularity: circulation versus links and predicted links.

hundred newspapers.[13] Many theories predict that attention on the Web should be more concentrated than attention in the print world. If the value of a website to a consumer increases with the use of others (e.g., through interactive features, polls, or better targeting of content by papers), then network effects will multiply the advantages of sites that get used early on. The variety of choices on the Internet enhances the advantages of brands established in the physical world. Internet users may go to *USA Today* or the *New York Times* in the virtual world because they already recognize their names and reputations as newspapers. The use of links can operate like an information cascade, with Internet users spreading a link through emails to friends who post the link again on their sites.

Figure 7.2 shows the early winners among newspapers on the web. The solid line represents the number of links for a newspaper website predicted by its circulation. Three of the top five newspapers in circulation fare extremely well in terms of links: *USA Today, New York Times,* and *Washington Post.* Their success shows that advantages in the physical world can be magnified on the Web through network and brand names effects. The link count for the *Wall Street Journal* vastly understates its relative popularity on the web for a simple reason—the *Journal* charges for access to most of its Internet content. This means that individuals are less likely to propagate links to *Journal* content, since accessing the information requires a subscription. Two of the outliers with greater than expected links are *Seattle Times* and *Raleigh News and Observer.* Both of these are published in areas with a high concentration of high-tech and Internet businesses, so it is not surprising that their readers/viewers are likely to spread links via the Internet.

Space and Speech

Speech on the Internet is cheap but not free. Talking with a friend about politics in the home or office involves opportunity costs, such as the time taken to develop your political views and the energy used to express them. Conveying your ideas on the Internet involves time spent learning, composing, and typing. Use of the Internet may also involve fixed costs such as paying for space on a server or subscribing to a company that provides online access. These fees are still relatively small when compared to the costs of buying advertising space in a newspaper to convey your views or purchasing advertising time on television. Opening a full-fledged outlet on the Internet may involve up-front costs for servers and continuous costs for Web page design and content creation, but these still pale in comparison to the costs of setting up a newspaper or buying a radio or television station. For all of these reasons, conveying ideas on the Internet should be cheaper than in print or broadcast. The drop in costs should make Internet speech more accessible than other forms of communication.

Measuring and tracking political speech and expression at the individual level can be difficult, in part because of privacy concerns. More information, however, is available on expression aggregated at the zip code level. In this section I use the zip code as my unit of observation to study how use of the Internet compares to two other forms of speech. I start with a random sample of five hundred zip codes. To measure the use of the Internet, I entered each zip code and its state abbreviation into the search engine www.google.com. I counted the number of Web pages associated with a zip code as evidence of Internet expression. I also did a search using the zip code, its state abbreviation, and the term "news" to capture more directly Internet use related to the market for news. I used the Gale Contemporary Authors database to track another form of speech, publishing by authors. By searching this database of authors I was able to determine the number of authors who list a particular zip code in their contact information. Finally, I used the website www.opensecrets.org to develop a third indicator of speech, the amount of political contributions emanating from a zip code.[14] The Supreme Court in the 1976 decision *Buckley v. Valeo* recognized the relationship between political campaign contributions and expenditures and political expression. I used the contributions database to measure for the residents of each zip code the total political contributions to federal races in 1996 and 2000 (through July 1, 2000), including donations to the presidential campaigns of George W. Bush and Al Gore.

Table 7.2 shows that individuals from more communities participate in Internet speech than other forms of expression and that expression on the Internet is less geographically concentrated. The top five zip codes account for 6.4% of population and 18.7% of Web pages using the word "news" and a zip code in the sample. Authors and political contributions are much more highly concentrated. The top five zip codes contain nearly a third (31.3%) of all authors in

TABLE 7.2
Measures of Expression by Zip Code (N = 500)

	Gini Coefficient	Cumulative % in Top 5 Zip Codes	# Zip Codes with Non-zero/ Non-missing Data	Mean	Maximum
Total Households, 1999	.63	5.8	500	3,763	24,967
Total Population, 1999	.63	6.4	500	9,973	81,047
Web Pages with Zip Code	.73	16.2	486	616	12,600
Web Pages with Zip Code and "News"	.76	18.7	482	129	4,258
Authors	.89	31.3	156	2	69
Political Contributions, 1996 ($)	.86	29.3	374	28,793	1,277,944
Political Contributions, 2000 ($)	.87	31.3	345	25,588	1,184,049
Contributions to George Bush, 2000 ($)	.91	37.7	175	3,001	264,179
Contributions to Al Gore, 2000 ($)	.94	39.6	95	1,001	65,250

the random sample of five hundred zip codes. The five zip codes with the heaviest donations accounted for 31.3% of political contributions to federal candidates in 2000, 37.7% of contributions to the George W. Bush campaign, and 39.6% of donations to the Al Gore campaign. The broader access to expression via the Internet is evident from the number of zip codes that had some expression recorded on the Internet. In the sample of five hundred zip codes, 486 turned up on Web pages and 482 turned up on at least one Web page with the term "news." In contrast, 156 zip codes had authors living in them according to the writers' database. While 345 out of five hundred zip codes registered some contributions in the 2000 federal elections data, only ninety-five had positive contributions to Al Gore's campaign. George W. Bush's campaign had broader support, generating contributions in 175 of the zip codes.

The Gini coefficient represents another way to convey the relative concentration of expression. The calculation is meant to represent the degree of inequality in the distribution of a variable, with 0 representing equality of distribution and 1 representing total inequality of distribution. The higher the value the greater the inequality of distribution.[15] By this measure, total households and total population in the sample of five hundred zip codes had a Gini coefficient value of .63. The Gini for Web pages was .73, and for Web pages with the term "news" was .76. Authors and contributions were much more concentrated. Authors had a Gini coefficient of .89, compared to .91 for Bush contributions and .94 for Gore contributions. A final way to see the greater disparities across zip codes in authors and contributions is to compare mean values of expression with maximums. For the zip code sample, the mean number Web page listings for a zip code was 616 and the maximum was 12,600. For authors the mean number living in a zip code was 2 and the maximum was 69. While the mean number of political contributions to 2000 federal political campaigns in a zip code was $25,588, the maximum value for a zip code was $1,184,049. The ratio of maximum to mean values was thus 20.5 for Web pages, 34.5 for authors, and 46.3 for political contributions.

Expression on the Web is related in predictable ways to the demographics of zip code areas. Table 7.3 shows that Web page mentions of a zip code are positively correlated with zip population (.42 correlation). Authors and contributions are also positively correlated with population, though the relationship is less strong than for Web page counts. Median age is not correlated with author counts or contributions. Mentions of a zip code on Web pages and on pages with the term "news" are negatively correlated with median age. This is consistent with the Pew survey data showing that younger adults are more likely to log onto the Internet. Household income is positively correlated with Web pages mentions (.25), authors (.30), and political contributions in 2000 (.35), although the strength of the relationship is smaller for Internet expression than for other forms of speech. The forms of expression are correlated with one another, so that zip codes higher in one form are likely to be higher in another. Author counts and contributions are more closely related to each other than Web page counts, again suggesting that expression on the Web is more accessible and dispersed. Political contributions in 2000 are correlated .45 with Web pages listing the term "news" and .63 with author counts. Contribution patterns remain relatively fixed over time, with contributions in 2000 having a correlation of .95 with contributions in 1996. The presidential contributions in 2000 indicate that author counts are more highly correlated with Gore contributions (.65) than Bush (.42). Note that zip codes participating in one party's fund-raising are likely to be contributing to the other party too. In 2000, contributions to Bush had a .76 correlation with contributions to Gore at the zip code level.

Table 7.4 shows that at the zip code level that population size and median household income drive the magnitude of Web expression. The larger the population in a zip code, the more Web pages that refer to the area and the greater the number of sites that refer to the zip code and the news. The higher the median household income, the larger the number of websites that refer to a zip code. Median age and percent black population do not have a statistically significant impact on these measures of Web expression. Overall, the analysis of speech at the zip code level shows that the Internet offers greater access to more areas than some other forms of expression, that this expression is less

TABLE 7.3
Correlations among Demographic Factors and Expression at the Zip Code Level (N = 500)

	Web Pages with Zip Code	Web Pages with Zip Code and "News"	Authors	Political Contributions, 1996 ($)	Political Contributions, 2000 ($)	Contributions to George Bush, 2000 ($)	Contributions to Al Gore, 2000 ($)
Total Population	.42***	.35***	.33***	.29***	.27***	.18***	.20***
Median Age	−.07*	−.10**	.00	.06	.05	.05	.07
Median Household Income ($)	.25***	.22***	.30***	.35***	.36***	.31***	.37***
% Black Population	.06	.08*	.07	.00	.00	−.02	.01
Web Pages with Zip Code and "News"	.87***						
Authors	.43***	.44***					
Political Contributions, 1996 ($)	.46***	.49***	.63***				
Political Contributions, 2000 ($)	.44***	.45***	.63***	.95***			
Contributions to George Bush, 2000 ($)	.30***	.28***	.42***	.83***	.85***		
Contributions to Al Gore, 2000 ($)	.38***	.39***	.65***	.87***	.87***	.76***	

Note: *** = statistically significant at the .01 level, ** = statistically significant at the .05 level, * = statistically significant at the .10 level.

TABLE 7.4
Determinants of Web Expression at Zip Code Level

	(1) Web Pages with Zip Code	(2) Web Pages with Zip Code and "News"
Total Population	0.04***	7.08e-3***
	(4.34e-3)	(1.10e-3)
Median Age	1.42	−1.83
	(11.06)	(2.79)
Median Household Income ($)	0.01***	2.76e-3***
	(3.92e-3)	(9.90e-4)
% Black Population	1.62	0.79
	(3.77)	(0.95)
Adjusted R^2	0.19	0.13
Number of Zip Codes	486	486

Note: Each specification includes an intercept. Standard errors are in parentheses. *** = statistically significant at the .01 level, ** = statistically significant at the .05 level, * = statistically significant at the .10 level.

concentrated than authorship or political contributions, and that expression on the Internet is positively correlated with income but that this relationship is less strong than for other forms of speech.

Ideas on the Internet

Though the marketplace of ideas meets continuously on the Internet, the concept of an intellectual marketplace is only a metaphor unless one uses economic theory and data to explore its operation. The work of Anthony Downs (1957) provides a structure to examine the demand side of the market. According to Downs, people seek information to facilitate consumption decisions, improve business decisions, engage in entertainment, and make political choices. The first three types of demand lead people to seek out data, for if they do not make the effort to get the information they miss out on many of its benefits. The logic of collective action implies that most people will remain rationally ignorant about the details of politics and policy. Even if a policy might affect a person's livelihood deeply, the small probability that a person has of affecting an election, a legislator's vote, or a regulator's decision means that most individuals will not seek out data to improve their political decisions. This implies that individuals on the Net will search for information that helps them buy products, make work decisions, or entertains. The relative search for politically important and relevant information should remain small.

Exploring how these four types of information demands operate on the Net requires definitions and samples. In this section I use four sources to define information markets on the Net as they existed in May 2000. Hard news, the mix of current events reporting that emphasizes politics and government, is the type of civic information Downs predicts people will not seek out. To define hard news topics of interest in May 2000, I used the transcripts of the *News-Hour with Jim Lehrer.* At the end of this weekday evening news broadcast on PBS, the anchor provides a summary of the day's two or three top news stories. Collecting these for May 2000 yielded a sample of fifty-four different news topics. Soft news fits Downs's definition of information sought solely for entertainment, the pure pleasure of knowing. I used the people, programs, and topics that surfaced on the front page of the *USA Today* Life section in May 2000 as my guide to soft news topics. This resulted in 123 celebrities, shows, and topics in my sample of soft news products. The GoTo website (www.goto.com) organizes searches by categories that capture consumer and producer questions: computing; education and career; finance; health; homelife; reference; shopping; travel. Using the search categories as examples of consumer or producer information yields a sample of ninety-six terms. The most popular search terms on the Internet are defined by many different sites. I chose the Lycos Top 50 as my source for popular search terms. This weekly list of the top fifty search terms on Lycos (www.lycos.com) yielded a total of sixty-four terms for May 2000.

For my snapshot of the Internet, in May 2000, I thus use four different types of information. The stories from the *Lehrer* program represent hard news topics. The people, groups, and entertainment products described on the *USA Today* Life section (front page) define soft news. The GoTo queries represent consumer and producer information demands. The Lycos data represent the most popular search terms on the Internet. Comparing how these different types of information fare in Internet markets requires rough measures of demand, supply, and pricing. To capture the relative demand for a piece of information, I used a function on the GoTo website that reported how many searches in the previous month had used the term on that search engine.[16] For each term in my four categories of information I used this function to find out how many searches had been done using the term. To measure the relative supply of the information, I used www.google.com. I entered each term in Google, which yielded a count of the number of Web pages cataloged by that engine that use the term.

To measure financial support for an idea on the Web, I used the GoTo website. GoTo allows advertisers to bid to support a search term. The advertiser with the highest bid is the first link that appears when the results of a search are reported from GoTo. The next highest bid gets the second listing in a search result on GoTo. When the list of sponsoring sites is exhausted GoTo then lists Web pages that use the term but have not paid an advertising fee. Since GoTo needs to provide advertisers with information on how much search terms are selling for, the engine lists the price paid for the link when results are reported from the search engine. Entering each of the terms in my sample into GoTo thus allowed me to explore the relative support by advertisers for different types of information on the Web. For each term I calculated the total advertisers for the term (i.e., number of links where sponsors paid for a listing in search results), the total of the advertiser bids in cents, the average advertiser bid, and the maximum of the advertiser bids (i.e., the price paid to be the top listing in a search term result).

Table 7.5 bears out the predictions that when people search for information on the Internet, they search for things that are entertaining or personally useful rather than information related to broader social or political decisions. The mean number of searches for soft news terms (11,522) was twice that for hard news topics (4,295) in May 2000. The mean number of queries (81,822) for information used in consumer or business decisions was nearly twenty times the mean for hard news topics. The differences in audience interest and value to the searcher of the information sought translate into different advertiser support for ideas on the Internet. For hard news topics, the mean number of total advertisers willing to pay to appear in search responses was 6.2. This contrasts with means of 17.4 total advertisers for soft news topics, 36.4 advertisers for the popular terms on Lycos, and 94.4 for the consumer and business related terms defined by GoTo. Adding the bids for each term provides one way to characterize the relative advertiser support for different types of ideas. For hard news topics, the mean value of the total advertiser bids to support a term was 36.9¢. For soft news topics this figure was 93.9¢, and for Lycos terms the figure was 369.8¢. The total advertiser bids for the GoTo terms was 1,901.8¢. The average and maximum bid patterns tell a similar tale. Hard news average bids had a mean of 2.5¢, versus 3.5¢ for soft news and 16.2¢ for GoTo terms. Companies that paid the maximum bid for a term earned the first spot in search term listings. The means of the maximum bid for each term were 8.0¢ for hard news, 13.0¢ for soft news, and 121.6¢ for GoTo terms.

Hard news information did dominate soft news and Lycos information on one dimension, the average number of Web pages with a search term. This at first appears counterintuitive, since it suggests that websites are more likely to offer information that is less sought after. Yet hard news topics are often covered by websites operated by entities that are not making decisions based on advertising. Government, academic, lobbying, and nonprofit websites may provide data that relate to hard news topics even though there would be little return in an economic marketplace for the information. These sites may offer data aimed at influencing votes or impressions rather than individual purchase decisions. Hard news topics had a mean of 390,467 websites using the hard news term. This is higher than the mean for soft news (174,629) and for Lycos terms (353,607). The GoTo terms have the highest number of mean websites using a term (1,092,596).

TABLE 7.5
The Market for Ideas on the Internet by Topic Area, May 2000

	Hard News Mean	Soft News Mean	Lycos Mean	GoTo Mean
Total Searches for Term	4,295	11,522	50,505	81,822
Number of Web Pages with Term	390,467	174,629	353,607	1,092,596
Total Advertisers for Term	6.2	17.4	36.4	94.4
Total of Advertiser Bids (Cents)	36.9	93.9	369.8	1,901.8
Average Advertiser Bid (Cents)	2.5	3.5	5.8	16.2
Max Advertiser Bid (Cents)	8.0	13.0	31.6	121.6
Ratio of Searches/Web Sites	0.01	0.11	0.95	0.10
N	54	123	64	96

Difference of Means

	Hard News-Soft News	Hard News-Lycos	Hard News-GoTo	Soft News-Lycos	Soft News-GoTo	Lycos-GoTo
Total Searches for Term	−7,227**	−46,210***	−77,527***	−38,983***	−70,300***	−31,317*
Number of Web Pages with Term	215,838***	36,860	−702,129***	−178,987***	−917,967***	−738,989***
Total Advertisers for Term	−11.2***	−30.3***	−88.2***	−19.0***	−77.0***	−57.9***
Total of Advertiser Bids (Cents)	−57.0***	−332.8***	−1,864.9***	−275.8***	−1,807.9***	−1,532.1***
Average Advertiser Bid (Cents)	−0.9**	−3.2***	−13.7***	−2.3***	−12.7***	−10.4***
Max Advertiser Bid (Cents)	−4.9**	−23.6***	−113.5***	−18.7***	−108.6***	−89.9***
Ratio of Searches/Web Sites	−0.10***	−0.94	−0.08**	−0.84	−0.01	−0.86

Note: *** = statistically significant at the .01 level, ** = statistically significant at the .05 level, * = statistically significant at the .10 level.

Dividing the number of searches for a term by the number of sites using the term puts the demand and supply sides of the Internet together in one measure. The mean ratio of searches to websites for hard news topics is .01, which means that there was one query about the topic for every one hundred sites with information about it. The ratio is ten times greater for soft news stories (.11) and for GoTo topics (.10). For these terms, there was approximately one query about a person or topic for every ten websites using the term. The Lycos lists track search terms that are particularly popular in a given month, so it is not surprising that the mean ratio for these terms is .95. For every query about the term there was about one website using the term available. Overall, the figures in table 7.5 show that individuals search out entertaining or personally useful information more often than they look for hard news stories. Advertisers are more willing to support soft news or data used for consumer and business decisions. There are more websites that offer information related to hard news topics than soft news, in part because government and nonprofits may offer data that are not heavily demanded. Lack of discussion of hard news topics is not due to lack of supply. The ratio of searches to sites shows how audiences are much more likely to seek out data that entertain or help in purchasing decisions than information that aids in voting or other civic decisions.

Assessments of the operation of the Internet offer conflicting tales about the concentration and dispersion of attention. One strand of research emphasizes the concentration of viewership encouraged by network effects, media concentration, and information cascades. Another strand points out the diversity of expression and creation of niche markets on the Internet made possible by the low fixed costs of entry and the agglomeration of people with specialized interests across the Internet. Table 7.6 offers evidence on the relative concentration of attention to ideas, by calculating Gini coefficients for different categories of information. In terms of the questions that people ask on the Internet in search engines, soft news stories have the highest concentration of attention (measured by a Gini coefficient of .81). Searches for hard news topics (.74 coefficient) and consumer or business information (.71) are less concentrated. The supply of information is much more dispersed for information relating to purchasing decisions than for other types of data. The Gini coefficient for the number of Web pages using a term takes on a value of .35 for the GoTo terms. This contrasts with .54 for the Lycos terms and .56 for hard news topics. Soft news items had the highest concentration of offerings, with a coefficient of .64. For hard news, soft news, and GoTo information the pattern holds that audience demand for information is more concentrated than the supply of information by websites. For each of these categories of information, searches are more concentrated (i.e., have a higher Gini coefficient) than websites offering a particular type of information.

While table 7.5 shows that hard news topics attracted fewer advertisers and lower total or average bids, table 7.6 indicates that the advertising that hard

TABLE 7.6

The Relative Concentration of Attention to Ideas on the Internet by Topic Area,
May 2000

	Gini Coefficients by Sample			
	Hard News	Soft News	Lycos	GoTo
Total Searches for Term	0.74	0.81	0.48	0.71
Number of Web Pages with Term	0.56	0.64	0.54	0.35
Total Advertisers for Term	0.66	0.55	0.63	0.47
Total of Advertiser Bids (Cents)	0.78	0.68	0.79	0.60

news does manage to attract is more concentrated than the support provided for other types of information. The Gini coefficient for the total advertisers supporting a term is .66 for hard news, compared to .55 for soft news and .47 for GoTo. The total advertiser bids are also more concentrated among the hard news terms. The Gini coefficient for total advertiser bids was .78 for hard news stories, versus .68 for soft news topics and .60 for GoTo. These results indicate that overall soft news or information that helps consumers and producers make decisions enjoy greater advertising support than information that aids in social or political decisions. The willingness of advertisers to sponsor links for hard news is less robust than for soft news, whether the measure used is total advertisers, average bids, or dispersion of support across topics within a news category.

Table 7.7 examines the markets for different types of information by looking at the top five terms for each of the measures of Internet activity. For total searches conducted using a specific term, the top item in the soft news category was pop star Britney Spears (who generated 357,818 searches in May 2000 on GoTo). The top item in the Lycos sample was Pokemon, the trading card cartoon figures favored by children (387,147). The GoTo term with the largest number of searches was computers (736,113), which is not surprising given that the searches were done by people using computers. The top five stories in the soft news category predictably relate to entertainment (e.g., a singer, band, movie). The top five hard news stories include terms that individuals might use in business or consumer searches, such as "Cuba" or "computer virus." Those searching for "Social Security" may be more interested in pursuing payments than debating policy. The Lycos top five tend toward the interests of young consumers (e.g., trading cards, two singers, and tattoos); the exception might be "flowers," which was a popular term in the weeks surrounding Mother's Day. The GoTo terms related to consumer or business decisions, including those involving computers, travel, health, software, and Web hosting. Note that the top five searches in the GoTo category are at least twenty times greater than the corresponding figures for hard news stories. "Computer virus" earned the fifth

TABLE 7.7
Relative Popularity of Terms on the Internet, May 2000

	Soft News	Hard News	Lycos	GoTo
		Top 5 Terms by Sample		
Total Searches				
1.	Britney Spears (357,818)	Social Security (31,557)	Pokemon (387,147)	Computers (736,113)
2.	EBAY (117,214)	Memorial Day (18,549)	Britney Spears (357,818)	Travel (671,149)
3.	Napster (100,785)	Cuba (18,039)	Flowers (185,820)	Health (434,322)
4.	Oasis (76,791)	Crime (16,322)	Tattoos (154,760)	Software (434,321)
5.	*Gladiator* (49,941)	Computer Virus (14,877)	Eminem (104,582)	Web Hosting (426,597)
Number of Web Pages				
1.	*X Files* (1,689,999)	May Day (3,180,000)	Golf (1,556,999)	Family (2,920,000)
2.	*South Park* (1,190,000)	Crime (1,150,000)	The Big Game (1,440,000)	News (2,439,991)
3.	*Party of Five* (1,069,995)	President Clinton (979,997)	Las Vegas (1,260,000)	History (2,370,000)
4.	Prince (1,060,000)	Social Security (967,993)	*South Park* (1,190,000)	Books (2,339,999)
5.	James Brown (985,000)	Supreme Court (818,000)	Flowers (1,180,000)	Computers (2,309,998)
Total Advertisers				
1.	*Star Wars* (113)	Cuba (40)	Flowers (238)	Books (242)
2.	Britney Spears (90)	Computer Virus/Crime (27)	Golf (237)	Gifts/Health/ Marketing/ Shopping/ Software/ Wedding (240)
3.	Vitamin C (80)		Baseball (154)	
4.	N Sync (64)	George W. Bush/ Social Security (23)	Mother's Day (129)	
5.	*Harry Potter* (57)		*Star Wars* (113)	

TABLE 7.7 *Continued*

	Top 5 Terms by Sample			
	Soft News	Hard News	Lycos	GoTo
Total of Advertiser Bids (Cents)				
1.	Vitamin C (831)	Crime (369)	Flowers (4,402)	Web Hosting (13,262)
2.	Star Wars (718)	Cuba (290)	Golf (3,867)	Gifts (12,306)
3.	Britney Spears (664)	Computer Virus (233)	Baseball (2,175)	Marketing (8,058)
4.	Harry Potter (531)	Social Security (163)	Pokemon (1,370)	Website Design (7,544)
5.	N Sync (525)	George W. Bush (107)	Mother's Day (1,298)	Shopping (6,851)
Average Bid (Cents)				
1.	Vitamin C (10.39)	Crime (13.67)	Flowers (18.50)	Web Hosting (55.96)
2.	Metallica (9.50)	Computer Virus (8.63)	Golf (16.32)	Gifts (51.28)
3.	Harry Potter (9.32)	China Trade (7.42)	Baseball (14.12)	Debt (48.80)
4.	N Sync (8.20)	Cuba (7.25)	Las Vegas (14.09)	Health Insurance (41.17)
5.	Faith Hill (8.10)	Korean War (7.13)	Pokemon (13.70)	Home Finance (40.26)
Maximum Bids (Cents)				
1.	Vitamin C (79)	Social Security (64)	Flowers (215)	Web Hosting (590)
2.	Metallica (68)	Crime (61)	Golf (205)	Small Business (554)
3.	Britney Spears (51)	Computer Virus (41)	Baseball (121)	Insurance (436)
4.	Star Wars (48)	Cuba (33)	Mother's Day (117)	Marketing (433)
5.	Ricky Martin (43)	Supreme Court (21)	Backstreet Boys (87)	Debt (415)

Note: Counts of dimension ranked are in parentheses (e.g., Social Security (31,557) in the total searches ranking indicates there were 31,557 searches for that term).

place on the hard news list with 14,877 searches, while Web hosting garnered the fifth place in the GoTo set with 426,597 searches.

On the supply side, the top items in hard news are generally smaller than for other categories (with the exception of May Day, which garnered 3,180,000 mentions on Web pages). The top sites in soft news relate to television shows and music performers. Web pages referring to the cartoon program *South Park* (1,190,000) outnumber those that discuss crime (1,150,000). References to the teen soap opera *Party of Five* (1,069,995) are more frequent than to President Clinton (979,997). The soft news figure with the fifth highest count of Web page references (James Brown, 985,000 sites) generates more citations than the fifth item in the hard news category (Supreme Court, 818,000 sites). The figures for soft news, hard news, and Lycos terms are generally much smaller than the top terms in the GoTo section (family, news, history, books, and computers).

The desire of advertisers to support terms used by those making purchase decisions is evident in the top five terms for total advertisers or bids. The GoTo terms that attracted the most advertisers were "books" (242 advertisers willing to pay for links), and "gifts," "health," "marketing," "shopping," "software," and "wedding" (each of which had 240 advertisers). The terms that attracted the most advertisers in soft news related to movies (*Star Wars*, 113 advertisers), music (Britney Spears, 90; N Sync, 64), books (*Harry Potter*, 57), and health (Vitamin C, 80).[17] The advertisers sponsoring hard news topics were more likely to be companies trying to sell products related to these topics rather than interest groups or parties trying to influence opinions or votes. The hard news topic with the most advertisers was Cuba. The forty sponsored links generally were from companies selling travel packages to Cuba or books about Cuba. The links for Social Security related to service companies offering to help a person obtain benefits or detective agencies offering to trace individuals via social security numbers. Links to the hard news topics were often related to the purchase of products rather than the discussion of public policies.

Advertisers on GoTo pay their bid price when someone clicks through to their sites after viewing the results of a GoTo search. The prices companies are willing to pay to be associated with different terms on this search engine reveal how strong the returns are for providing entertaining or personally useful information compared to the returns for providing analysis of hard news. Table 7.7 offers three ways to analyze prices paid by Internet advertisers. If one sums the total ad prices from sponsored links for each term, the top terms for total potential ad revenue are similar to the rankings for total number of advertisers. The soft news term "Vitamin C" had a total of 831¢ in advertising bids, compared to 369¢ for the top hard news, crime. The support for the top Lycos search term was 4,402¢ for "flowers." The advertising totals for the GoTo terms swamp all these figures, with 13,262 for "web hosting," 12,306 for "gifts," 8,058 for "marketing," 7,544 for "website design," and 6,851 for "shopping." The potential to influence a purchasing decision on the Web elicits large total bids for information helpful to consumer and producer decisions. This pattern is also evident in the average bids. The average bids for the top terms in each category were 55.96¢ for "web hosting" (GoTo), 18.50 for "flowers" (Lycos), 13.67 for "crime" (hard news), and 10.39 for "Vitamin C" (soft news). The sponsors for the "crime" term were primarily lawyers seeking clients and companies selling protection services, which yielded a higher average price than that paid by companies selling Vitamin C. For the second through fifth terms, the soft news average prices are higher than those for hard news (e.g., the heavy metal band Metallica had an average bid of 9.50 versus 8.63 for the hard news topic computer virus). The prospect of influencing purchasing decisions generated relatively high average bids in the GoTo category, yielding 51.28 for "gifts," 48.80 for "debt," 41.17 for "health insurance," and 40.26 for "home finance."

The GoTo site instructions for advertisers estimate that the top listing in a search term receives three times more clicks by viewers than the fifth term. The maximum prices listed in table 7.7 reflect the bid paid to be listed first in the search term list. The disparities in advertiser support across information categories are again apparent using this measure. "Web hosting" was the top term in the GoTo category of producer and consumer information, with a maximum bid of 590¢. This compares to top maximums of 215 for "flowers," 64 for "social security," and 79 for "Vitamin C." At the fifth spot the dominance of personally useful information in attracting advertiser support is still clear. The GoTo term "debt" attracted a high bid of 415¢, versus 87 for the "Backstreet Boys" (Lycos), 43 for "Ricky Martin" (soft news), and 21 for the "Supreme Court" (hard news).

Advertisers value attention that can be translated into sales. Table 7.8 shows that the attention of those seeking out information related to consumer and producer choices generates the highest bidding activity from advertisers. Advertisers' total bids, average bids, and maximum bids all increase with total searches for a term. Advertisers are willing to pay more for clicks for popular terms. The transaction costs of assembling audiences may play a role here. It may be cheaper for a company to pay a higher price to generate traffic with a few terms than to try and assemble traffic through small click throughs from less popular (and cheaper) terms. Total bids and maximum bids, controlling for other factors, increase as the number of Web pages mentioning a term grows. This may indicate that with many sites talking about a topic, companies are more willing to spend to generate traffic for their particular sites. The indicator variables in the equation measure whether there is a special impact on prices for a category of information relative to the hard news terms. In the total bids equation, only the GoTo indicator variable is statistically significant. The coefficient indicates that relative to a hard news topic, a topic relating to consumer/producer decisions would generate a bid total that was 1,012¢ higher. In the average bid equation, Lycos terms generate higher bids (by 2.27¢) and GoTo terms receive higher bids (by 11.42¢). Even after one con-

TABLE 7.8
Advertisers' Willingness to Pay to Support Search Terms (cents), May 2000

	(1) Total of Advertiser Bids	(2) Average Bid	(3) Maximum Bid
Total Searches for Term	7.29e-3***	1.62e-5***	2.20e-4***
	(8.82e-4)	(4.58e-6)	(4.95e-5)
Number of Web Pages	3.26e-4**	1.24e-6	2.18e-5***
with Term	(1.48e-4)	(7.71e-7)	(8.34e-6)
Soft News Term	28.63	0.73	4.27
	(178.83)	(0.93)	(10.04)
Lycos Term	−52.39	2.27**	10.65
	(199.31)	(1.04)	(11.19)
GoTo Term	1012.11***	11.42***	78.29***
	(220.70)	(1.15)	(12.40)
Adjusted R^2	0.44	0.49	0.40
Number of Terms	318	318	318
Mean of Bid Term	672.63	7.47	47.73

Note: Dependent variable in the OLS regression in 1 is (in cents) the total amount of advertiser bids, in 2 the average bid, and in 3 the maximum bid. Each specification also included an intercept. Standard errors are in parentheses. *** = statistically significant at the .01 level, ** = statistically significant at the .05 level, * = statistically significant at the .10 level.

trols in the maximum bid equation for audience demand (measured by total searches) and supply side factors (represented by the number of Web pages using a term), the GoTo terms generate a higher maximum bid (by 78.29¢) relative to hard news topics. In each equation the soft news term was not statistically significant, indicating that once one controls for the magnitude of traffic or interest related to a topic that whether it is a hard or soft news term does not affect the willingness of advertisers to bid for a link. Overall, these results show the strong advertiser support for information related to consumer and purchasing decisions and the relatively weaker advertising support provided for hard news topics.

Conclusions

What will news markets look like when information is costly to create but nearly costless to disseminate? The Internet offers many possible answers to that question. Current guesses about the development of news on the World Wide Web often emphasize the change on the supply side brought about by technology and ignore the demand side composed of people's interests in different types of news. The results in this chapter confirm that the low costs of information distribution on the Net make it possible for more voices to be heard through this medium. At the zip code level, expression is more dispersed on the Internet than the relative concentration of authors or political contributions. Topics in hard news are discussed on a greater number of Web pages than topics in soft news or consumer/producer information. In terms of information demanded by individuals, however, the dominance of entertaining and personally useful information predicted by Downs does hold true on the Internet. People are much more likely to search the Net for information about entertainment figures than political issues. Decisions about purchasing a consumer item or making a business purchase attract more attention (and advertiser support) than voting decisions.

In a world of many outlets and scarce attention, consumers on the Internet are likely to go with familiar media brands. The analysis here shows that online use of newspapers is much more concentrated, as measured by links, than newspaper circulation. The pressures to stand out in a world of many viewing options extends beyond company brand names to the use of individual brand names to attract attention. In print and broadcast markets, the personal fame of anchors, reporters, pundits, and columnists may draw consumers to a particular media outlet. The following chapter explores the extent to which journalists are becoming part of the products marketed as news.

Chapter **8**

Journalists as Goods

To LEARN what's new in the world, you have to start with what's old. This is the paradox that explains why journalists are increasingly becoming part of the news goods they deliver. In a world of multiplying news outlets, journalists can be the familiar faces or trusted sources that draw consumers to a program or publication. News products are experience goods, which means that you need to use the good to judge its attributes. Once you investigate and examine a news product, however, you have in effect consumed it. In trying to attract your attention to their version of the day's events, firms use many types of signals to convey what their products will contain. Headlines in print and promotions for upcoming stories alert the consumer to content. Lettering, graphics, music, and sets convey different approaches to the news. The association of the delivery of the news with a particular anchor or reporter is another way for companies to signal what the news product will contain. Though you may not yet know the day's events, the personalities of Peter Jennings, Larry King, Barbara Walters, Geraldo Rivera, Mike Wallace, or Chris Matthews create for some consumers an image of the type of news they will experience. Though news involves learning about the unfamiliar, the familiarity of readers or viewers with specific journalists becomes a way for news outlets to create expectations about their content.

News products have always been experience goods, which means that companies have always sought ways to signal to potential customers what today's version of events will look like in their papers or programs. The pressure for journalists to become part of the news product, however, is increasing as the number of news outlets is expanding. In a world of four broadcast television channels, a consumer can easily switch among viewing options to sample content. In a world where channels can number in the hundreds, sampling becomes more time consuming.[1] If viewers recognize and enjoy watching a particular journalist on television, they may be more likely to watch a given channel because of this familiarity. The personalities of those who present the information become shortcuts for viewers to find their news niche. This chapter examines three areas for evidence on how journalists have become part of the product in news: the salary rewards in network evening news programs; the speaking fees generated by journalists; and the type of language used by pundits who cover politics across different media.

Though network anchors deliver the news, they are rewarded in the marketplace for delivering viewers to advertisers. The salary patterns for network evening news anchors suggest that the value attached to the personal ability of these stars to deliver viewers increased markedly during the 1990s. The pay trends at first appear counterintuitive. The share of television viewers who watch the evening news has declined dramatically from 72% in 1980 to 44% in 2000.[2] In terms of viewing households for one of the network evening news programs, an average of 9,790,000 watched in 1975 versus 8,146,000 in 1999.[3] Yet the real dollar amounts paid for ads on the shows and the cost per thousand viewing households reached actually increased during this time period. Expressed in 1999 dollars, advertisers paid $3.93 to reach one thousand households in 1975 and $5.78 in 1999. Though the absolute size of the network evening news audience has shrunk with the increased viewing options available on cable, ratings for network programs overall have declined. Between 1985 and 1997, the share of the viewing audience watching network stations in prime time declined from 74% to 57%. Network news still attracts a relatively large program audience, which advertisers value since it means lower transaction costs in getting a viewer and less duplication of effort to reach a give audience size. So even though the absolute number of households tuned to a network evening news program has declined, advertisers are now willing to pay more per thousand viewers reached. This may reflect higher ad rates overall, and a premium attached to reaching a relatively larger audience in an era marked by highly fractured viewing.

Though expansion of viewing options and diminishment of audience sizes may raise the value of advertising on the network news, it may also raise the value of network anchors. When consumers have many more choices, the value of a known commodity can increase. Network anchors become a way for channels to create a brand image in viewers' minds. If anchors become more important in drawing viewers to programs, this may translate into higher returns for anchors in salary negotiations. The pattern in salaries from 1970 to 1999 confirms this story. The amount in salary that an anchor received for attracting a thousand viewing households increased from a range of 13¢ to 31¢ (1999$) in 1976 to a range of 86¢ to $1.07 in 1999. Another way to view this is to look at the ratio of the anchor's salary to the ad price on the evening news programs. In 1976 anchors such as Walter Cronkite and John Chancellor were paid the equivalent of 28 ads per year, while in 1999 this had grown to 149 ads for Dan Rather and Tom Brokaw. The marked increase in the amount paid per viewing household, salary expressed in ad revenues, and the absolute magnitude of the salary took place in the 1990s. This was a time of declining absolute audiences, but rising importance of anchors in attracting viewers. The increased value placed on anchors is consistent with these personalities playing a growing role in attracting viewers in a multichannel universe.

The widespread exposure of journalists made famous by the reach of their programs or publications transforms some into celebrities.[4] The star quality associated with well-known television reporters and some print journalists translates into a demand for speeches. I find in analyzing rates for journalists listed with a leading speakers' bureau that the mean speaking fee for reporters is higher than for the former politicians that they once covered. The magnitude of the speaking fee received by a journalist is highly correlated with the "buzz" about the reporter in the popular press, which I measure by references in major papers or magazines. The lure of speaking fees carries an opportunity cost, since time spent giving an address is time not spent working to gather news or learn new skills. The content of a journalist's on-the-job output may also change because of its effect on speaking fees. Some pundits report that quick outrage and cutting talk on a television program translates into stronger demand for outside speaking engagements.[5] Ironically, media employers may encourage the building of personal celebrity brand names by reporters because this can attract more viewers to a program. This encouragement can take the form of payments to print reporters by their employers to appear on television, of requests from television executives for journalists to get into the gossip columns, and of advice from management that relates to cosmetic appearances rather than content construction.

Political pundits are a subset of journalists with strong incentives to develop brand names for delivering different combinations of entertainment, insight, and ideology. To study how pundits differ, I used DICTION to analyze the language used by set of fifty-six political pundits during twelve weeks in 1999. The results reveal that the language of politics differs across media. Given the same subset of possible events and ideas to talk about, those appearing on television were more likely to focus on human interest elements, use simplified language, and make self-references than those writing in print outlets. Journalists who appear in two media adopt the conventions of the particular outlet type when discussing events. For a set of eight journalists, I was able to examine the difference between the journalist's words on television and the words used in print. Each journalist was generally more focused on entertainment values and less likely to focus on abstract terms or analyze group actions on television than in print. The combination of audience demands served by television and the technology of information delivery creates incentives for individual journalists to approach politics differently in print than in broadcast.

Language also differed by ideology in the sample. Pundits such as Mary McGory and Mark Shields are often identified as liberal commentators in press coverage. Robert Novak and George Will are frequently referred to as conservative. I find that when you compare the language of liberals versus that of conservatives, liberals are more likely to use language emphasizing groups and use language containing positive or optimistic words. Conservatives are more likely to use terms that stress distinctions among individuals and terms that convey ambivalence and negative tones. This in part may be due to the positions associated with the different ideologies. Research on political campaign advertising indicates that Republicans may be more successful with negative ads since the critical ads resonate with criticisms of government action.[6] For pundits attempting to establish themselves as products in the market for analysis, at least two constraints are clear from these data. Those who appear on television need to use language that is simple and entertaining. Those who try to establish themselves as conservatives need to use negative language. Even though pundits are seen in the market as individuals, the method of reaching audiences and the need to use shorthand or ideological language to convey ideas imposes constraints on what they can say about political people and events.

Marshall McLuhan famously observed in 1964 that "the medium is the message."[7] The results in this chapter confirm that the medium still influences the message. Information about politics provided on television tends to be less focused on abstract ideas or on groups than that conveyed in print. For the set of pundits who appear both on television and in print, they change the language they use depending on the medium. In an era of increasing news outlets, however, it can also be said that the messenger becomes part of the medium. The individuals who provide news become part of the product. Their familiar presence helps create expectations of what the news product will be like, and their reputations become product brand names. The transformation of a person into a product generates large rewards for journalists who are widely known and allows some reporters to reap returns normally associated with celebrities. The need to build a product brand name may also influence the way a journalist expresses ideas and the worldview the journalist adopts in covering politics and government.

Network News Salaries

Evening network news programs have always been identified by their anchors. In 1970 a viewer could choose among Walter Cronkite, Chet Huntley and David Brinkley, or Howard K. Smith and Harry Reasoner. In 2001 a viewer could select Dan Rather, Tom Brokaw, or Peter Jennings. Top billing of anchors has always translated into star-like salaries for these journalists. Salary patterns for network anchors over time suggest that these personalities are increasingly important in attracting and retaining viewers. Even though the average audience of a network evening news program has declined by millions, the relatively large audience still watching represents an attractive advertising target; the recognition value of anchors in a world of multiplying channels has translated into higher returns in salary.

To examine the pay of famous broadcasters, I searched for reports of network news salaries in popular press accounts or in journalism memoirs. For the years 1970 through 1999, I found sixty-three reports about the pay being earned by a specific individual in network news operations. Figure 8.1 shows

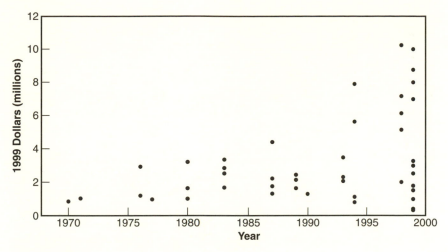

FIGURE 8.1. Real network news salaries.

that pay has increased substantially over time. In 1970 Harry Reasoner, the ABC evening news co anchor, earned the equivalent of $859,000 in 1999 dollars per year. In 1999 the network anchor salaries were $8,750,000 for Peter Jennings and $7,000,000 each for Tom Brokaw and Dan Rather. The large number of observations for 1999 in figure 8.1 arise from an article on journalists' salaries in *Brill's Content* (1999). This shows the wide distribution of pay on network news in 1999, ranging from $300,000 for NBC reporter David Bloom to $10,000,000 for news magazine anchor/talk show host Barbara Walters. Figure 8.2 reports the salary figures for the network evening news anchors. Here again the upward trend in salaries is evident, with the largest increase coming in the later years.

Figure 8.3 traces the size of the average audience tuned to a network evening news program over time. In 1975 a network evening news program attracted on average 9,790,000 households. By 1999 this figure had dropped to 8,146,000. The real cost (1999$) of a thirty-second ad on the network news program increased over this time period from $38,400 in 1975 to $47,100 in 1999. The rising ad price and declining audience indicates that over time companies have been willing to pay more to reach a given number of evening news viewers. Figure 8.4 shows that in 1975 advertisers paid $3.93 per one thousand viewing households watching the network evening news. By 1999 this had grown to $5.78 per thousand viewing households. The increase in this price may reflect many factors, such as a general increase in advertising prices and a change in the nature of households watching network news.[8] In an era of fractionalized viewing, the large audience still attracted to the network evening news may also make advertisers willing to buy time on those programs. Buying

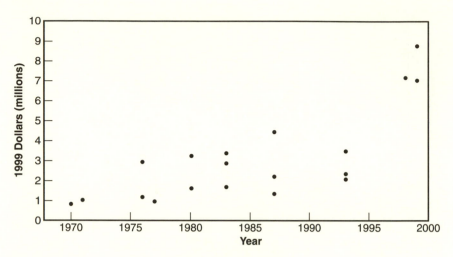

FIGURE 8.2. Real network evening news anchor salaries.

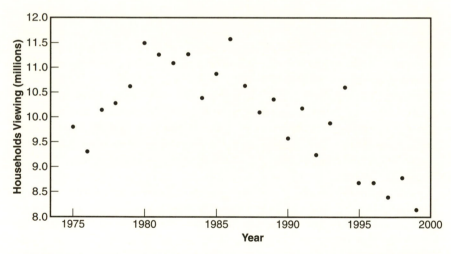

FIGURE 8.3. Average households viewing network television early evening news program.

larger audiences carries many advantages, including lower transaction costs and reduced probability of duplicating the purchase of the same viewer across multiple programs.

In an era of shrinking network audiences, network news anchors have actually become more valuable because of their name recognition and ability to draw viewers. With the proliferation of channels, the personalities of the anchors became a way for channels to differentiate themselves in viewers' minds.

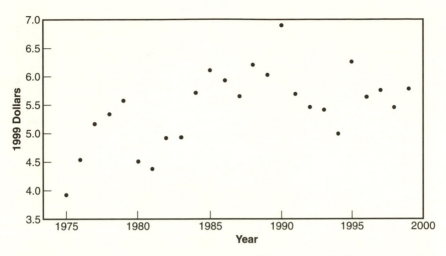

FIGURE 8.4. Real cost per thousand homes viewing network television early evening news.

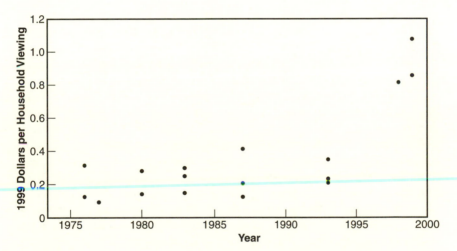

FIGURE 8.5. Real network evening news anchor salary per household viewing.

The increased role of anchors in drawing viewers translates into higher absolute salary figures. The rise in competition among channels may also lead to an increase in salaries, since companies may offer higher rewards to retain their marquee players. Figure 8.5 shows how the amount anchors are paid per household viewing has increased over time. Dividing an anchor's salary by the average viewership for a network news program yields this measure of what the journalist gets per year for attracting a household to watch regularly. In 1976 the salary

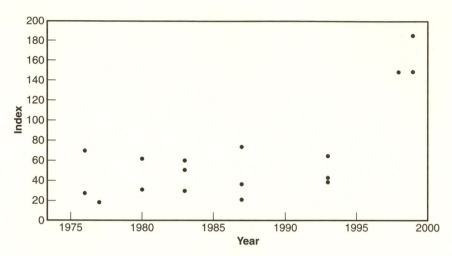

FIGURE 8.6. Network evening news anchor salary per cost per thirty seconds.

per viewing household ranged from 13¢ for Cronkite, Chancellor, and Reasoner to 31¢ for Walters.[9] In 1999 this figure had grown to $1.07 for Jennings and 86¢ for Brokaw and Rather.

Another way to see the increasing returns for news anchors is to divide the anchor's salary by the average cost of an ad on the network news program. Figure 8.6 shows that this figure increased over time, with a dramatic jump in the late 1990s. In 1976 Cronkite, Chancellor, and Reasoner were paid the equivalent of revenues from twenty-eight ads and Walters earned the equivalent of sixty-nine ads. By 1999 Brokaw and Rather were paid with the equivalent of 149 ad revenues, while Jennings earned the equivalent of 186 ads. The largest jump in network anchor salaries—measured in terms of ads, price per viewing household, and absolute dollar figures—came in the later 1990s. This was a time of shrinking network audiences, including the audiences for network evening news programs. As the number of channels expanded and network audiences eroded, the value of anchors as brand names grew. This led to greater returns for the anchors in terms of salary. Yet it also increased the pressure for anchors to become celebrities, a general trend evident in many broadcast and some print outlets.

Journalists as Entertainers

One of the advantages of journalists' wide exposure is the creation of a demand for more personal audiences. Media personalities, politicians, and authors often can command large speaking fees to appear at meetings and conventions.

The speaking fee is spread across many listeners, who may derive added enjoyment from hearing famous individuals deliver their familiar views in person. To study the size of the speaking fees available to reporters, I examined the fees for speakers provided by a company called Leading Authorities. The firm listed 127 speakers in April 2000 willing to discuss politics and the media for hire, and provided a range of speaking fees for ninety-six of these speakers. Among the fifty-two media figures with fees listed in the Leading Authorities data, the price for a speech ranged from a low of $5,000 for many print journalists to a high of $75,000 for controversial radio host Dr. Laura Schlessinger. The fees for broadcast television personalities were often among the highest, including those of Bryant Gumbel ($50,000), Andrea Mitchell ($30,000), and Irving R. Levine ($30,000). The average speaking fee for the fifty-two media personalities in the sample was $14,800. The average salary for the twenty-one politicians whose speaking fees were listed with Leading Authorities was $10,200.[10] In terms of celebrity value, journalists command higher average speaking fees than the politicians they cover. Part of this may stem from the ability of journalists to give speeches while they are still at the height of their recognition. Politicians often wait until they are out of office before joining the speakers' circuit, so their celebrity value may have declined by the time they start giving speeches.

The demand for journalists as speakers relates directly to the "buzz" in popular culture about their work. To measure the degree that particular media personalities are discussed or appear in the media, I did a search for each person's name in three Lexis news files: one containing the text of current news stories in print and broadcast, one containing the text of major newspapers, and one containing the text of magazines.[11] I found that speaker fees for media personalities in 2000 were strongly correlated with the number of times they were mentioned or appeared in these files in 1999. The speech fee for journalists was correlated .42 (statistically significant at .01 level) with mentions in the major papers, .31 (.05 level) for references in current news, and .25 (.10 level) for appearances in magazine coverage. The speaking fees for politicians were not correlated in a statistically significant manner (e.g., .10 level) with references to them in any of the three Lexis files.

Individuals who produce ideas often do not earn a full return from consumption of their work, since ideas often become public goods freely consumed without payment by others. Speaking fees represent one way for these individuals, including journalists, to capitalize on the fame they have earned in providing information to the public.[12] The restriction of the audience to a small paying audience allows the reporter to earn more while providing listeners the feeling of being in touch with fame and in the know about current events.

The downside of journalists being marketed as personalities is evident but hard to measure. In terms of opportunity costs, hours spent speaking before conventions and traveling to meetings are hours not spent covering the news.

The media outlet that employs the journalist may encourage the development of a reporter's brand name, since this in turn may attract additional readers and viewers. David Westin, as president of ABC News, encouraged journalists in his network to get mentioned in the gossip columns more often, a recognition that buzz about a reporter can help build a show's audience.[13] Print outlets such as *Newsweek* and *Time* actually encourage their reporters to appear on television to generate an audience for their printed work.[14] The fame associated with appearances on television may also help journalists gain access to politicians and other sources.[15] The emphasis on building broadcast reporters into performers has been well documented and includes attempts to counsel reporters on clothes, hairstyles, and demeanor.[16] The rewards that journalists reap for developing an entertaining style may be high. The degree these rewards influence what reporters say, not simply the way that they say it, requires a more detailed analysis of how individual journalists convey ideas about politics.

Pundits and Political Language

Political pundits may establish reputations for many skills: providing the context of political events; predicting the future of an issue or politician; describing the process of elections and governing in an entertaining manner. Personality is part of a pundit's brand image. The expectations about objectivity are often relaxed for pundits. Readers and viewers expect to hear pundits give their personal opinions about what will happen or should happen in politics. Even though their product is personal expression, market forces shape these expressions in at least two ways. The medium of expression leads pundits to change their language depending on whether their thoughts are expressed in print, on television, or through radio.[17] For commentators associated with a specific worldview, the expectations associated with the ideology may lead these journalists to use a particular language. Though pundits are free to express their opinions, the language they use will depend on what medium they choose and what ideology they espouse.

To study the expression of pundits, I started with the sample of journalists listed in *Slate* as political pundits.[18] For those individuals who registered 100 or more references in Lexis for 1999, I downloaded their writings and broadcast transcripts for a random week of each month in 1999. For articles that appeared in newspapers or magazines I used the full text that they authored. For appearances on television or radio I edited the transcript so that I only examined their spoken words (e.g., I edited out the words of other commentators or guests). This yielded a sample of fifty-six pundits, who generated 3,225 segments of between four hundred and five hundred words over the twelve weeks examined in 1999. I ran these segments through the software program DICTION (described in chapter 4), to explore how political expression varies by medium and political position.

Table 8.1 shows that the language used by political pundits differs across media for almost all the dimensions measured by DICTION. These differences are rooted in audience demand, costs of production, and technology. The relative use of types of words when pundits express themselves in print versus their speech on television reflects the market for analysis in these two media. Print reporters write for a more educated audience. The bundling of different types of stories in newspapers and the ability of readers to select the news they consume means that pundits can write in abstract terms and focus on topics of interest to only a fraction of a paper's consumers. They have the ability to invest in story research and the space to provide details and context. Pundits on television face incentives to adopt the conventions of the medium. Entertainment is emphasized over education in audience demand. Time for expression is limited, so details and context are sacrificed. An emphasis on human interest, focus on movement, and use of stories about individuals rather than broad social forces keep audiences tuned to programs.[19]

The analysis of pundit language in print versus television makes clear these differences. Pundits in print use a greater variety of words and choose longer words, consistent with an appeal to a more educated audience than viewers of the television programs that feature pundits. In their writing, pundits are more likely to use abstract terms. This allows more use of inspiring language (e.g., words relating to abstract virtues) and terms relating to collectives (e.g., social groups or geographic entities). The ability of print journalists to write about groups rather than simply focus on individual stories is reflected in higher dimension counts based on centrality (institutions and core values), cooperation (interactions across groups), rapport (attitude similarities), diversity, exclusion, and liberation. The freedom to invest in research and provide details in print are reflected in greater use of numeric language, a focus on the past (which provides context), and a higher ratio of adjectives to verbs (measured in the embellishment score).[20]

Entertainment values are evident in the dimensions where pundits use types of words more frequently on television than in print. Journalists are more likely to use self-references (e.g., first-person terms such as "I," "me," "mine") on television. This is consistent with a human interest focus and with the journalist becoming a large part of the product on television. The language of human interest (e.g., personal pronouns, family references) is used more frequently on television than in print. Terms of praise, blame, and satisfaction that often accompany dramatic stories are used more on television. A focus on immediacy and action translates into higher counts for present concerns, motion, communication, and temporal awareness. The difficulty of generating and providing details and context on television surfaces in the certainty expressed in opinions. Television is higher in both extremes of belief. Pundits are more likely to use leveling language that ignores differences and conveys assurance (e.g., "everybody," "always") and language relating to tenacity (e.g., "will," "shall," "must"). This is part of the need to summarize and simplify. Yet television pundits also are more

TABLE 8.1
Pundit Language by Medium

DICTION Dimension	Print Mean	TV Mean	Radio Mean	Difference of Means		
				Print-TV	Radio-TV	Print-Radio
Certainty						
Tenacity	27.0	39.7	33.7	−12.7***	−6.0***	−6.7***
Leveling	6.0	6.7	6.5	−0.7***	−0.3	−0.4
Collectives	8.8	7.1	9.2	1.7***	2.1***	−0.4
Insistence	29.9	35.4	39.8	−5.5***	4.4	−9.9***
Numerical Terms	10.8	6.3	5.8	4.5***	−0.5	5.0***
Ambivalence	14.9	20.4	17.2	−5.5***	−3.2***	−2.3***
Self-Reference	3.2	8.0	1.7	−4.8***	−6.3***	1.5***
Variety	0.6	0.5	0.5	0.1***	0.02***	0.04***
Optimism						
Praise	4.5	5.1	3.6	−0.6***	−1.5***	0.9***
Satisfaction	2.9	3.4	2.1	−0.5***	−1.3***	0.9***
Inspiration	3.4	2.1	2.6	1.2***	0.5**	0.8***
Blame	2.1	2.3	1.7	−0.2***	−0.6***	0.4***
Hardship	5.1	3.6	3.9	1.5***	0.3	1.2***
Denial	6.0	8.2	6.4	−2.1***	−1.8***	−0.3
Activity						
Aggression	5.3	4.4	7.0	0.9***	2.6***	−1.6***
Accomplishment	10.2	7.1	9.7	3.0***	2.6***	0.4
Communication	11.9	12.9	13.0	−1.1***	0.1	−1.2*
Motion	2.6	5.0	3.2	−2.4***	−1.8***	−0.7***
Cognitive Terms	7.6	10.3	7.3	−2.7***	−3.0***	0.4
Passivity	4.0	4.0	4.5	0.0	0.5*	0.5**
Embellishment	0.6	0.5	0.4	0.02**	−0.1***	0.1***
Realism						
Familiarity	125.9	125.6	131.3	0.4	5.7***	−5.4***
Spatial Awareness	7.8	8.3	11.7	−0.5***	3.3***	−3.8***
Temporal Awareness	15.7	16.3	15.9	−0.6***	−0.3	−0.2
Present Concern	9.6	12.3	10.2	−2.7***	−2.1***	−0.6
Human Interest	22.9	28.4	20.7	−5.5***	−7.7***	2.2**
Concreteness	24.4	22.6	27.5	1.8***	4.9***	−3.1***
Past Concern	3.8	3.7	3.8	0.1*	0.1	0.0
Complexity	4.8	4.5	4.7	0.3***	0.2***	0.1***
Commonality						
Centrality	3.6	2.2	2.9	1.4***	0.8***	0.5***
Cooperation	3.9	3.0	4.1	0.9***	1.1***	−0.2
Rapport	2.0	1.6	2.1	0.4***	0.6***	−0.2
Diversity	1.9	1.4	1.9	0.5***	0.4**	0.1
Exclusion	2.1	1.5	2.4	0.6***	0.9***	−0.3
Liberation	1.9	1.4	1.5	0.5***	0.1	0.4***

TABLE 8.1 *Continued*

DICTION Dimension	Print Mean	TV Mean	Radio Mean	Difference of Means		
				Print-TV	Radio-TV	Print-Radio
Summary Scores						
Certainty	45.8	48.1	48.6	−2.3***	0.5*	−2.7***
Optimism	49.1	48.8	48.7	0.3***	−0.1	0.4*
Activity	51.6	51.9	52.6	−0.3***	0.7***	−1.1***
Realism	47.8	49.9	49.3	−2.1***	−0.5***	−1.5***
Commonality	49.5	49.4	49.6	0.1*	0.1	0.0
Number of Total Segments	1378	1745	102			

Note: *** = statistically significant at the .01 level; ** = significant at the .05 level; * = significant at the .10 level.

likely to use shorthand phrases related to ambivalence. Without the ability to go into detailed explanations, pundits on television are more likely to use words such as "allegedly," "perhaps," "guess," and "suppose." The need to present a simplified view is also captured in the higher insistence measure, which reflects the repetition of frequently used terms in a discussion.

The summary scores calculated by DICTION combine the word counts from the different dimensions listed in table 8.1 into five indices. These summary measures confirm that the language used by political pundits differs by medium in ways consistent with the market for expression. Relative to print, television provides more entertainment, conveys activity more easily through pictures, and relies on simplified languages and images. This translates into higher scores on television for realism (e.g., a focus on people's everyday lives), activity (e.g., movement), and certainty.[21] Pundits in print, who serve a more educated and narrow audience, can use abstract terms and analyze group behavior. This translates into higher scores for optimism (e.g., language endorsing a group or concept) and for commonality (e.g., language relating to values in a group).

Three of the fifty-six pundits had transcripts for radio appearances: Tom Gjelten, Mara Liasson, and Cokie Roberts. Since these radio transcripts came from National Public Radio, the comparisons in table 8.1 using language on radio should be thought of as reflecting public radio rather than commercial talk radio. The results in table 8.1 show that the differences between language on radio and television are similar to those between print and television. The dimensions that pundits score higher on in print relative to television are generally those they score higher on in radio relative to television. Many of the differences between print and television are also reflected in comparisons between print and radio.

The pressure on pundits to use different language in different media are evident in table 8.2. Eight of the journalists in the sample generated a sufficient number of content segments in both print and television to allow a

TABLE 8.2
Differences across Media by Individual Pundit

DICTION Dimension	Print Mean-TV Mean								Radio Mean-TV Mean	
	Fred Barnes	Ronald Brownstein	Tucker Carlson	Paul Gigot	Al Hunt	Howard Kurtz	Robert Novak	George Will	Mara Liasson	Cokie Roberts
Certainty										
Tenacity	-16.1***	-16.6***	-18.9***	-19.3***	-15.6***	0.1	-21.9***	-18.3***	-20.0***	-0.4
Leveling	-1.2*	-1.2*	-1.5*	0.1	-0.1	-1.0*	-1.8**	0.0	-2.9***	1.8*
Collectives	3.5***	1.6*	3.2***	2.4***	3.2***	-0.6	6.1***	0.5	5.8***	-0.7
Insistence	-3.6	21.2***	5.1	7.0	-1.5	-19.5***	13.5*	0.4	37.9***	-6.1
Numerical Terms	5.9***	5.1***	4.6***	2.9***	4.5**	2.8**	4.5**	6.7***	1.2*	-2.5***
Ambivalence	-7.6***	-9.1***	-10.8***	-8.1***	-10.0***	-3.5***	-7.1***	-8.8***	-11.8***	0.2
Self-Reference	-7.0***	-4.7***	-16.6***	-10.8***	-12.9***	0.5	-11.1***	-5.4***	-10.8***	-2.3***
Variety	4.8***	0.1***	0.1***	0.1***	0.1***	0.04***	0.1***	0.1***	0.05***	0.0
Optimism										
Praise	1.1***	-0.5	-2.2**	-0.5	-0.3	-0.7	-2.9***	-0.6	-3.3***	0.5
Satisfaction	0.4	0.0	0.5	-1.4**	0.4	-0.6	-1.0**	1.1*	-0.2	-2.3***
Inspiration	1.4**	1.5*	0.6	0.1	2.9***	1.2***	0.2	1.7***	1.6***	0.6
Blame	-1.6***	0.3	-2.7***	-1.2***	-0.1	0.4	-1.1*	0.1	-1.4***	0.4
Hardship	0.5	2.7***	0.3	2.4**	-0.5	0.6	1.1	-1.6**	1.0*	1.0
Denial	-4.7***	-1.3**	-5.6***	-4.8	-4.3***	0.9	-4.3***	-0.9***	-5.6***	0.6
Activity										
Aggression	0.9	2.5***	0.4	2.0*	0.5	0.1	3.3***	0.5	3.1***	1.1
Accomplishment	5.4***	3.4***	3.5***	1.2	3.7***	0.9	5.6***	1.1	4.8***	1.1
Communication	1.7	2.7**	-0.2	-0.7	-4.6***	5.2***	-5.1***	-4.9***	2.5**	-1.6
Motion	-3.0***	-3.1***	-1.2*	-2.3***	-1.5***	-0.7*	-2.4***	-3.1***	-3.8***	0.2
Cognitive Terms	-4.0***	-2.1*	-10.2***	-7.3***	-7.3***	0.5	-4.2***	-3.2***	-8.2***	0.2
Passivity	0.5	1.9***	0.9	1.1*	-0.5	-0.3	1.5***	-0.1	0.9*	0.3
Embellishment	-0.1*	0.1**	-0.2***	0.0	0.1	0.1	-0.1*	0.1	-0.2***	0.0

Realism										
Familiarity	5.3**	−15.0***	9.8***	−10.5***	11.5***	−10.8***	0.1	−1.6	12.6***	8.8***
Spatial Awareness	−0.6	0.6	−1.1	−1.2	1.8	−1.3*	1.9**	−0.3	1.6	−1.0
Temporal Awareness	−1.0	2.8*	4.8***	4.6***	−0.4	−3.4***	0.2	0.3	4.2***	−3.7***
Present Concern	−3.1***	−4.7***	−2.3**	−1.6	−1.3	−2.4***	−3.8***	−4.3***	−5.5***	0.0
Human Interest	−8.5***	−6.5***	−4.5**	−8.3***	−11.5***	3.8*	−17.5***	−8.3***	−12.2***	−1.6
Concreteness	5.2***	7.1***	6.9***	5.5***	10.0***	−1.7	11.2***	1.5	18.0***	1.8
Past Concern	1.3**	−0.7	0.8	−2.0***	−0.9	0.1	0.0	−0.8	0.4	0.2
Complexity	0.4***	0.5***	0.4***	0.5***	0.6***	0.2***	0.7***	0.5***	0.5***	0.0
Commonality										
Centrality	1.9***	−0.3	2.0***	0.6	1.9***	−0.7**	1.6***	1.4**	0.6**	0.0
Cooperation	−0.1*	1.8***	1.4**	2.4**	2.1**	−0.2	2.8***	1.0**	2.2***	−0.2
Rapport	0.5	1.5***	0.8*	0.3	0.1	0.6***	0.5*	0.6	0.7*	0.0
Diversity	0.1	−0.7	−1.1**	−0.3	0.6	−0.3	0.4	0.6*	−0.1	0.6
Exclusion	0.9**	1.3***	1.1***	1.1**	1.9**	0.4	2.1***	0.7*	1.3***	0.0
Liberation	0.8**	1.0***	0.9*	0.7	1.0**	0.4	−0.2	0.3	−0.3	0.1
Summary Scores										
Certainty	−1.8***	−2.2***	−0.1**	−2.4***	−0.3	−1.5***	−1.9***	−2.2***	0.5	1.0*
Optimism	1.1**	−0.2	2.3***	0.7	1.9***	−0.8**	0.3	1.5***	1.2***	−1.1*
Activity	0.6	−0.5	1.9***	0.6	0.1	0.7*	−0.2	−1.8***	1.6***	0.0
Realism	−2.5***	−2.6***	−0.6	−1.3**	−0.6	−2.4***	−2.7***	−2.8***	0.0	0.0
Commonality	0.3	0.5	1.1**	0.3	0.0	−0.1	0.4	0.2	0.7*	−0.4
Number of Print Segments	27	77	21	18	24	95	18	54		
Number of TV Segments	67	19	38	26	20	36	100	20	63	46
Number of Radio Segments									30	15

Note. *** = statistically significant at the .01 level; ** = significant at the .05 level; * = significant at the .10 level.

comparison of an individual's expression across media. Two of the journalists generated enough content in radio and television to allow individual comparisons there. These results indicate that each pundit chose different ways to describe politics depending on whether the product was written or spoken. Given the same set of events to talk about and the same set of personal opinions to offer, a pundit chose different language depending on the avenue of expression. The patterns for each individual are similar to the broader differences analyzed between expression in print versus television.[22]

Consider the case of George Will, who writes a syndicated column and appears as a commentator on ABC News programming. In print, George Will uses a greater variety of terms and longer words than on television. When composing for a print audience, Will uses more abstract terms such those relating to inspiration and uses more numeric terms. He writes about groups rather than individuals, reflecting a greater focus on core values and institutions (as measured by centrality), diversity, and exclusion. In television appearances, Will changes expression to comply with the greater demands for entertainment. He uses more human interest language. He makes more self-references. He simplifies and summarizes (higher tenacity), and at the same time hedges his bets through qualifications (higher ambivalence). His statements on television focus more on the present and emphasize motion. In terms of the summary measures calculated by DICTION, George Will's changes between print and television embody the different market imperatives of the two media. On television Will offers opinions that are marked by greater activity, realism, and certainty. In print he is more likely to use abstract terms relating to groups and their actions. Though George Will has developed a brand name for expression, he changes the delivery of his product to suit the audience demands and cost constraints of the medium.

Developing a brand name for a particular type of political analysis can be restrictive for a pundit. Creating an expectation in a consumer's mind for a particular take on world events can involve placing your opinion within a given spectrum of views. For example, if you wish to be classified as a conservative pundit there may be modes of expression associated with a conservative ideology. To examine whether pundits with a brand name for liberalism or conservatism have distinct ways of expressing their views, I first needed to classify the sample of fifty-six pundits according to ideology. For each pundit I searched the current news file in Lexis for a reference to the person's name within two words of liberal and within two words of conservative. I used this as a proxy for the market reputation of the pundit, since the search captured the different ways that writers were referred to as "liberal columnist" or "conservative commentator." Commentators with ten or more references as a liberal or conservative were classified by that ideology, while those who did not meet this reference requirement were labeled as moderates. Using this definition, I classified Fred Barnes, Tucker Carlson, Paul Gigot, Charles Krauthammer, William Kristol, Mary Matalin, Robert Novak, William Safire, Tony Snow, and George Will as conservatives. Liberal pundits were Richard Cohen, Maureen Dowd, Bob Herbert, Al Hunt, Molly Ivins, Mary McGory, Bill Press, and Mark Shields. All other pundits were labeled as moderates.[23]

Table 8.3 shows that there are differences in the language that liberal and conservative pundits use and that these differences may relate to the substance of these ideologies. If each ideology is reduced to a few points, one may associate conservatism with an emphasis on individual action and a skepticism about government and the prospects for change in human nature. Liberalism emphasizes group activities or rights and denotes an optimism about the power of government and the permeability of human nature.[24] If one uses DICTION to compare the writings and speech of pundits with liberal versus conservative brand names, the results in table 8.3 show that the political positions associated with these pundits are reflected in their use of particular vocabularies. Conservatives are more likely to use phrases that reflect ambivalence/uncertainty or involve denial and negative expressions. They are more likely to use words that emphasize distinctions among individuals (reflected in the diversity measure). Liberals are more likely to use words that reflect an emphasis on groups (as seen in the higher collectives measure). The higher score on the rapport indicator, which measures similarities in attitudes among groups, is also typical of the emphasis on groups. The language of liberal pundits is more positive, as seen in higher scores for praise and accomplishment. In the summary measures, liberals score higher than conservatives on the optimism scale and the commonality scale.

When the sample of expressions is divided up by ideology and medium, a slightly different pattern emerges. There are more statistically significant differences in expression between liberals and conservatives on television than between liberals and conservatives in print. The demand for entertainment and suppression of detail and context on television can give rise to conversations based on shortcuts and extremes. In television, the expected ideological differences appear clearly between liberals and conservatives. Conservatives are ambivalent, insistent, and emphasize the distinctions among individuals. Liberals use language that is positive and stresses groups. Overall, liberals on television are more optimistic and score higher on the commonality scale (which relates to group values) than conservatives.

In print there are fewer differences between liberal and conservative pundits. Those that appear are less easily associated with the ideological content of the expression. This may reflect less pressure in print for pundits to adopt easily recognized and categorized positions, which are the mainstay of political conversations on television. If one looks across television and print, there are not many differences between liberals and conservatives that hold for both media. Within each medium, conservatives do have higher scores on the variety of language employed (which indicates an avoidance of overstatement) and on the use of familiar terms. Liberals are more likely to use self-references, use words reflecting praise, and speak about tangible or material concerns.

TABLE 8.3
Pundit Language by Ideology

	Difference of Means				
DICTION *Dimension*	*Conservative-* *Liberal*	*Moderate-* *Liberal*	*Moderate-* *Conservative*	*Print:* *Conservative-* *Liberal*	*TV:* *Conservative-* *Liberal*
Certainty					
Tenacity	3.3***	−0.5	−3.8***	−3.0***	3.9***
Leveling	−0.3	0.1	0.4***	−0.3	−0.4
Collectives	−0.6**	0.1	0.7***	−0.2	−0.4
Insistence	−4.5***	1.1	5.6***	2.0	−15.4***
Numerical Terms	−0.4	0.4	0.8***	1.7***	−1.4***
Ambivalence	1.5***	1.3***	−0.3	−1.3***	2.3***
Self-Reference	−0.3	−3.0***	−2.7***	−1.9***	−1.7***
Variety	−0.01**	−0.01**	0.0	0.01***	0.01*
Optimism					
Praise	−0.4**	−1.0***	−0.6***	−0.7***	−0.7***
Satisfaction	−0.1	−0.5***	−0.4***	−0.2	−0.2
Inspiration	−0.1	−0.1	0.0	0.1	0.1
Blame	0.0	−0.6***	−0.5***	−0.2	0.0
Hardship	−0.2	−0.4***	−0.2*	−0.2	0.3
Denial	0.7***	−1.5***	−2.2***	−0.4	0.5
Activity					
Aggression	0.2	−0.1	−0.2	1.1***	−0.3
Accomplishment	−0.9***	0.7***	1.6***	−0.5	−0.3
Communication	−0.4	0.4	0.8***	−0.4	−1.6***
Motion	0.6***	0.5***	−0.1	−0.1	0.3
Cognitive Terms	1.4***	−0.1	−1.6***	0.3	1.2***
Passivity	−0.2	−0.2*	0.0	0.1	−0.5**
Embellishment	−0.04*	−0.1***	−0.1***	−0.02	−0.1**
Realism					
Familiarity	1.9***	5.2***	3.4***	2.5**	3.3***
Spatial Awareness	−0.6**	0.3	0.9***	0.6	−1.7***
Temporal Awareness	−0.3	1.5***	1.8***	0.2	−1.0**
Present Concern	0.3	0.6***	0.3	−0.4	0.1

TABLE 8.3 *Continued*

			Difference of Means		
DICTION Dimension	Conservative-Liberal	Moderate-Liberal	Moderate-Conservative	Print: Conservative-Liberal	TV: Conservative-Liberal
Human					
Interest	−0.6	−2.4***	−1.8***	−6.5***	2.3***
Concreteness	−1.9***	−0.5	1.4***	−1.6**	−2.0***
Past Concern	−0.4***	−0.4***	0.0	−0.7***	0.0
Complexity	0.0	0.05***	0.1***	0.1***	0.0
Commonality					
Centrality	0.1	0.3***	0.2*	0.6***	0.3*
Cooperation	0.1	0.2*	0.2	0.2	0.3
Rapport	−0.4***	−0.1	0.3***	−0.1	−0.4***
Diversity	0.2**	0.2***	0.1	0.1	0.4***
Exclusion	−0.1	−0.1	0.0	0.2	0.0
Liberation	0.1	0.2**	0.0	0.3**	0.1
Summary Scores					
Certainty	0.1	0.3**	0.2*	−0.4**	−0.1
Optimism	−0.3**	0.3***	0.6***	0.0	−0.5**
Activity	0.0	0.7***	0.7***	0.0	−0.2
Realism	0.0	0.5***	0.5***	−0.7***	−0.2
Commonality	−0.3**	−0.1	0.2**	−0.1	−0.3***
Number of Segments First Ideology	667	2094	2094	237	430
Number of Segments Second Ideology	464	464	667	256	208

Note: *** = statistically significant at the .01 level; ** = significant at the .05 level; * = significant at the .10 level.

The set of pundits who are not strongly identified in the opinion market as liberals or conservatives are referred to as moderates in table 8.3. The results demonstrate that the differences between moderates and liberals, and moderates and conservatives, in expression are very similar. Pundits on either extreme of the ideology scale are more likely than moderates to score higher on measures of self-reference, embellishment, and human interest. This may indicate that pundits who seek a reputation for neutrality or fairness may avoid direct statements about their own beliefs (e.g., avoid "I," "me," "mine") and may avoid a focus on personal (e.g., human interest) stories. Moderates score higher on the complexity measure than liberals or conservatives, which may reflect a more nuanced approach than the simple and direct language used by those on the ideological extremes. In terms of the summary indicators, moderates score higher on certainty, optimism, activity, and realism than liberals or conservatives. This suggests there is a moderate approach to political punditry that is distinct from either ideological extreme. These results overall indicate that if a pundit wishes to establish a brand position for liberalism or conservatism, there are some regularities readers and viewers may expect in the language the commentator will use, especially on television. There the pressure to summarize and entertain may lead to a use of language where liberals are positive and talk about groups and conservatives are negative and focus on distinctions among individuals. These differences are much less likely to arise in print, where pundits are freer to provide details, context, and the reasoning behind their positions.

Conclusions

The increasing array of technologies that convey information ironically increase the value of a simple news conduit—the person who delivers the news. Though the absolute audiences for network evening news programs have declined with the growth of cable, the value of anchors has increased because of their ability to draw viewers confronted with many channel options. Measured in real dollars or dollars per household delivered, network anchor salaries have increased with the importance of their personalities in drawing people to programs. Journalists can also capture the returns to celebrity through rewards other than salary. The analysis here shows that journalists now often command higher speaking fees than the politicians they cover.

Political pundits are particularly known for establishing reputations for their personal take on events. The market for political news clearly affects, however, the way these pundits express their opinions. Pundits who appear both in print and broadcast alter their expression depending on the medium. When they appear on television, they are much more likely to use language conveying action, certainty, and the details of everyday life. When writing for a print outlet, they emphasize abstract terms and analyze broader group behavior. The need to use a particular language may also arise for pundits who wish to be seen as liberal or conservative. These pressures are greater in television, where the push to entertain and simplify leads liberals and conservatives to use distinct vocabularies. The pressures are less evident in print expression.

Chapter **9**

Content, Consequences, and Policy Choices

I<small>F THE</small> F<small>IRST</small> A<small>MENDMENT</small> were interpreted literally, this would be a short chapter. Though the amendment says "Congress shall make no law ... abridging the freedom of speech, or of the press," Congress makes many laws that affect the flow of media information. Consider how the property rights governing the production, distribution, and consumption of news depend upon how an image reaches your screen. For broadcast television, FCC ownership regulations limit the number of stations a company can own in a local television market, prohibit the ownership of a television (or radio) station and a major local daily paper in the same market, and restrict a firm from owning stations that reach more than 35% of the total U.S. television audience. Through its spectrum policies the FCC determines who can speak and what types of data can be transmitted over particular parts of the airways. For cable television, must-carry provisions require cable systems to carry local broadcast television signals. Merger policies affect the configuration of both broadcast and cable firms. Campaign finance laws limit the amount of political speech a group can provide through television commercials. Congress subsidizes the provision of some commercials, such as anti-drug advertisements in newspapers and television purchased by the Office of National Drug Control Policy. On the Internet, the interpretations of copyright and patent laws affect the ability of papers to make freelance articles on a political discussion website available in electronic archives, prohibit the reproduction of the full text of a newspaper article on a political discussion website without permission, and restrict the access to certain software codes that make Internet communication to date relatively easy.[1]

Judging the desirability of particular media policies involves answering a set of complicated questions. What criteria should be used to evaluate outcomes? How does economics affect media content? What are the consequences of the consumption of media content? Which policy tools can affect the provision and absorption of information? This chapter explores the degree to which economic research can provide answers to these questions.

Criteria

Broadcasters receive their spectrum licences for free in return for a promise to operate in the "public interest, convenience, and necessity."[2] In 1972, Ken Arrow won the Nobel Prize in economics in part for his proof that the public interest does not exist. By public interest, Arrow meant a function or decision rule that would take into account individuals' feelings on any set of questions and translate those preferences into a group decision that satisfied a basic set of fairness conditions. Arrow demonstrated that such a function does not exist, that any group decision process one might propose would fail to give an answer or would violate one of the fairness conditions he set up as desirable.[3] Individuals often use the term "public interest" to refer to situations where the social pie can be made larger, to describe policies where gains for consumers or voters can be realized, or to generate popular support since the phrase has a powerful symbolic appeal. The fact that FCC regulators are challenged to define and enforce a standard that technically cannot exist captures well the problems with making judgments in media policy. If the FCC tries to make explicit its conception of the public interest, it runs the risk of violating the First Amendment if its regulations are too detailed. The impossibility of defining the public interest, and the legal challenges entailed if regulators try, have left broadcasters relatively free from direct content regulations.

If the public interest does not exist, what criteria should govern media policymaking? Economists often nominate efficiency as the standard to use in comparing outcomes in media markets.[4] The notion is that policymakers should attempt to maximize the size of the social pie, where the size is determined by the willingness of individuals to pay for particular goods and services. This utilitarian philosophy is at the heart of benefit-cost analysis, which translates potential gains and losses from a policy into dollar values. At least three problems arise with equating efficiency with the public interest. Making decisions about what people are willing to pay for outcomes requires starting with a given distribution of income. If the policy question one wants answered involves deciding what income distribution is desirable, efficiency cannot serve as the definitive guideline. Critics also point out that economists often take preferences as given. If the exchange of information in the media is designed to alter preferences, however, the willingness to pay standard is problematic since it assumes a set of preferences to start with.[5]

A third problem lies in the definition of whose values count in a benefit-cost assessment of a media policy. Amartya Sen, also a Nobel laureate, identified an inevitable conflict between the value of self-determination embodied in classical liberalism and the decision-making approach based on efficiency. Sen (1970) writes about the example of a person deciding what color to paint the walls of his room. Liberalism would allow the person to make the decision based on his own preferences, while the approach based on benefit-cost analysis would add into the decision the reactions that others have knowing that an individual has chosen a particular color. Sen points out that it is impossible to be a "Paretian liberal," a liberal who believes in both individual freedom of choice and efficiency in this example. It may well be the case that the individual prefers blue, society's other members prefer crimson, and the individual's willingness to pay for a blue room is swamped by the value that other members of society place on having the room a different color. In this case, liberalism and efficiency yield different outcomes. Respect for an individual's choice yields blue, while calculation of the most efficient outcome yields crimson. If one substitutes media content for wall color, the same problem arises.[6] Using the efficiency criteria as the sole arbiter of media policy can mean the preferences of others about your media consumption may trump your own willingness to pay for particular content.

Debates about government policies dealing with news markets rarely mention efficiency. Multiple criteria are offered as guides for decision makers, including the fostering of democracy, exchange of ideas, pursuit of truth, and freedom of expression.[7] Deciding the extent to value information as an intrinsic good (appreciated in and of itself) or as an instrumental good (as a means to make a decision) adds another complication. For example, one could compare media policies dealing with the exchange of public affairs information based on the participation in politics produced by coverage, the amount of political knowledge disseminated, the number of speakers involved, the number of views expressed, the quality of viewpoints exchanged, and the truths arrived at through political debate. Each of these aspects could be analyzed from an intrinsic and an instrumental perspective. One might value political participation engendered by media exposure solely because one values participation, while another might also value this participation because of its impact on a set of social or government decisions.[8]

The economist's criteria of judging outcomes by individuals' willingness to pay could play multiple roles in media policy. One possibility is to monetize the other criteria involved in media policy through surveys. This process, called "contingent valuation," would ask individuals to place a dollar value on freedom of expression in a particular area. Economists use this method to measure existence values for environmental preservation, such as the value people place on protecting an Alaskan bay simply because they know it exists in a pristine state.[9] Individuals could be asked, for example, the value they place on preserving a particular aspect of a media market (e.g., prohibition of newspaper ownership by a local television station). A drawback of the contingent valuation approach is that individuals value, in surveys, goods that they may not routinely think about and are asked to spend hypothetical sums of money. With the exception of individuals who contribute to groups linked to free expression, such as the American Civil Liberties Union, people rarely put a price on the ideologies involved in media markets. Economics offers more guidance in estimating the costs of achieving particular goals in media policy. The willingness to pay methodology, for example, can provide policymakers with estimates of the costs of using telephone taxes to fund Internet hookups for schools. This use of efficiency can also help identify ways to achieve public interest goals at lower costs.[10]

Economics can only offer part of the answer in establishing criteria to value the outcomes of media policies. Efficiency as a standard cannot define the public interest, although as Arrow has noted there is no social decision-making method that can adequately serve to define the public interest. Media policy inevitably involves trade-offs among contending values. "Willingness to pay" can serve as one of those values, can measure in part the values associated with different criteria, and can establish the costs of achieving different goals or identify less costly ways to attain them.

Content

Reporters in journalism textbooks try to provide readers and viewers with what they need to know and try to produce stories that answer Who?, What?, When?, Where?, and Why?. Journalists in real world news markets are driven, either consciously or indirectly, to produce stories that are generated by a different set of Five Ws: Who cares about information? What are they willing to pay, or others willing to pay to reach them? Where can media outlets and advertisers reach them? When is this profitable? Why is it profitable? These economic concerns help predict media content and explain why information in news reports differs from an accounting of a day's most significant events.

A small set of economic concepts explains the particular characteristics of news products: public goods, experience goods, product differentiation, high fixed costs/low variable costs, and positive externalities. The public goods nature of information means that one reader's consumption does not preclude another's and that once the information is circulating one can consume the knowledge without paying for it. This may give rise to underproduction of some information about politics and government, since there may not be sufficient incentives for news organizations to invest heavily in the production of the information. Once a paper or program discovers and documents something, the news can be easily transmitted and consumed by readers and viewers of other outlets. To know a news product's content fully one must consume (e.g., experience) it. News firms develop ways to signal to consumers what the potential content of their goods are, so that the consumers can anticipate content without having to examine it before purchase. The development of product brand names is one way to generate consumer expectations about quality and content. The transformation of anchors and other journalists into celebrities is another way to create consumer expectations about content. If the reporter becomes part of the product consumed, a reader or viewer may know that even if events change over time the style and perspective of the familiar journalist remains relatively fixed.

News goods typically have high fixed costs/low variable costs. The resources devoted to researching a story, composing its presentation, and making the first copy for delivery can be tremendous. They may involve the fixed costs of maintaining a set of reporters and a configuration of costly production and transmission technology. The second or subsequent copies of a news good may involve relatively low costs, such as ink or paper for daily newspapers or server space for Internet sites. The high size of fixed costs limits the number of providers who can survive in a particular news market. Product differentiation allows providers to distinguish the version of the news they offer and tailor it to particular consumer interests. The types of data people desire in their role as purchasers, producers, entertainment consumers, and voters affect what information news organizations will choose to offer. Downs's theory of rational ignorance predicts that news about politics may be underprovided. Some individuals may find public affairs news entertaining or feel an obligation to stay informed to cast an informed ballot. Since an individual's vote has little chance of affecting the outcome of an election, however, people typically remain ignorant about the details of politics and do not consider the potential benefits to society if they stayed abreast of current affairs.

The spatial model described in chapter 1 shows how economic incentives can be used to predict the mix of hard and soft news products offered in a market. One would expect more soft news programs if their consumers were more highly valued by advertisers. If programmers pay less for soft news content they will be more likely to offer it. As the number of channels increases, the number of soft news programs will also rise. If the number of viewers attracted to the genre increases, more programs will be added. In equilibrium, there is no reason to expect soft news programs to have higher/lower ratings or costs. The average rating for a soft news program should go down as the number of programs offered in the genre increases. If broadcasters internalized the benefits of hard news (such as better informed voters) to society, they would be more likely to offer hard news fare.

The empirical tests presented in previous chapters show how the spatial model and other economic concepts can be used to predict content in many different settings. Chapter 2 reveals how journalistic independence emerged as a commercial product in the late nineteenth century. As economies of scale in printing grew and local and national advertisers began to pay newspapers for assembling "eyeballs," it became more profitable for some outlets to grow by covering politics in a nonpartisan fashion that attracted readers from both parties. Chapter 3 indicates that bias can reemerge in story selection for economic reasons. If network news programs are trying to attract younger women as marginal viewers, and if these viewers are particularly interested in issues often identified with the Democratic party such as education or gun control, then the networks may focus on liberal issues in an attempt to garner viewers highly valued by advertisers. The increase in soft news on the network evening news and drop in coverage of key congressional votes analyzed in chapter 6 show how cable competition, deregulation, and change in company ownership have changed the mix of stories offered in the evening news. The analysis in chapter 7 of data on the Internet shows that the predictions by Downs of strong information demand for privately valuable data remains true on the Net. Hard news topics on the Internet were less likely to be searched and generated lower advertiser support. The rise of the value of anchors as celebrities, and the impact of the medium on the print versus broadcast utterances of pundits, document the degree that journalists have become part of the news product.

A growing empirical literature has established a number of results about how economics influences actions in media markets.[11] As the number of newspaper owners declines in a local market, product differentiation increases and the total number of beat types covered in a market increases. This result suggests that increased concentration can in some markets lead to more diversity since sellers in a concentrated market may offer products aimed at attracting additional customers to the market rather than aimed at stealing customers from already offered varieties. Newspapers do appear to target content based on reader preferences, and customers in turn are likely to subscribe if the content matches their interests. Across cities, blacks are more likely to purchase a newspaper in cities with more blacks (and hence more material targeted to blacks) and less likely to purchase a paper as the number of whites increases. As penetration of the *New York Times* increases in a city, readership of the local paper among college-educated people declines and the voting rate in local elections among this demographic declines. In local television, market conditions appear to have little impact on the quantity of public affairs programming offered by a local television station. Among radio stations, informational programming expanded significantly once the FCC's Fairness Doctrine was dropped, suggesting that the requirement had had a chilling effect among stations afraid to provide controversial political programming if they might be called upon to offer opposing viewpoints. In cable markets, analysis of the structure of cable subscription prices allows one to analyze the average willingness to pay by consumers for individual cable networks such as C-SPAN or CNN. Contingent valuation surveys can also be used to estimate the willingness of consumers to pay for public broadcasting.

Economic theories of information suggest a list of problems that may arise in news markets: underconsumption of news about public affairs; inadequate investment in developing or reporting hard news; a bias in broadcasting against high-cost news programs or those that deliver information valued by a minority of viewers; the tilt toward satisfying the information demands of viewers or readers most valued by advertisers; the need to develop journalists into celebrities to build product brand names; the temptation of conduit owners to favor content they own over the offerings of other producers; the possibility that journalist herding will cause reporters to go with common wisdom rather than developing their own takes on stories; or the potential for conglomerate owners to view news provision solely through the lens of profit maximization. In some cases economic reasoning alone cannot indicate whether the market for content is working well. For copyright law cases, for example, it is hard to predict the proper balance between strong laws that encourage production and less stringent protections that favor dissemination and consumption. In other cases the direction of the market failure may be clearer, such as the under provision of hard news because of rational ignorance among viewers/voters. Quantifying the degree of problems with news markets involves many challenges. Part of the difficulty lies in estimating the impact of a lack of information. Since information is in part an instrumental good valued because it influences many types of decisions, analyzing news markets also requires an examination of how political markets work.

Consequences

The *New York Times* published a front-page article indicating the EPA administrator proposes to relax the air pollution control rules governing utilities.[12] If you read the article, what are the consequences? You may derive enjoyment from reading about the political battles involved. One way to measure this pleasure is by the opportunity cost of the time it took you to read the article. Another is to allocate a fraction of the paper's purchase price to your "purchase" of this story. Survey data could indicate ex post facto whether you did in fact enjoy the article after you'd made the decision and investment to read it. Continued consumption of the *Times*, or of articles by the *Times* correspondent, might indicate your happiness with the coverage. Others might place an existence value on simply knowing that the paper is free to publish articles about the government, that individuals quoted in the article are free to express their opinions, and that you as the reader are free to consume their ideas.

An article about pollution control could also influence policy formation. You may have read the article because you feel a duty to stay informed as a citizen and voter. You may simply enjoy reading about the politics of the environment. The knowledge in this case is simply fun, and any impact on your future voting decision is a by-product of your intrinsic desire to know what's happening. Assessing the political consequences of your consumption of the article requires a model of how politics works. To see the variety of conclusions that might arise, consider the role that information plays in three different political decision-making models: principal-agent, Condorcet jury theorem, and optimistic pluralism.[13]

In the principal-agent model, principals delegate decision-making power to agents. This frees principals to pursue other interests, allows agents to become experts in particular decisions, and raises the nagging question of whether the agents are making the decisions principals would make if they were fully in-

formed. Hidden actions and hidden information give the agents some power to
pursue their own political interests. Principals hope to constrain agents by setting up contracts to reward the decisions they prefer, by sorting and screening
when agents are initially selected to pick the "right kind" of decision makers, by
monitoring what the agents are doing, and by setting up institutional designs
such as the delegation of the same task to multiple agents to make sure they
compete to please the principals. Politics can be viewed as a series of principal-
agent relationships. Voters are principals who delegate decisions over policy to
members of Congress, the president, and the courts. Congressional members
delegate decisions to agencies, who in turn may receive oversight and instruction from the courts and the president. Difficulties arise with the principal-
agent relationship in part because there are multiple principals, for example, a
representative may receive conflicting signals from different groups of con-
stituents in a district. Agency heads may get different instructions from the
president, the House or Senate oversight committees, and the Supreme Court.
Difficulties also arise because agents can influence the ability of principals to
monitor their actions.

The ability of media information to influence policymaking depends on
how one envisions the principal-agent mechanism working. If members of
Congress are seen as relatively insulated from voter actions because of the
power of incumbency (including the power to craft campaign finance laws that
favor incumbents), provision of information about pollution control in the
New York Times would have little impact on decision making. Elites would be
seen as the relevant decision makers, and media coverage would have its greatest impact as an entertainment vehicle rather than an instrument of democracy. If there is sufficient transparency in what agents are doing, and significant
stakes involved, however, then stories about pollution control could provide
voters with data that allow them to cast informed ballots for president or Congress. Since regulators and judges are appointed by the executive branch and
influenced by the legislative branch, voters can also influence their policy decisions. Political scientists debate the amount of information needed to cast a
ballot that constrains officials. Some models rest on the assumption that voters
know the details of policy proposals, while others posit that voters can use
shortcuts and heuristics to cast an informed vote.[14]

A second model of the policy process abstracts away from many institutional
details and focuses instead on the ability of individuals in the aggregate to ar-
rive at "the truth." Formulated by Condorcet as the jury theorem, this approach
to group decision making notes that as the number of individuals involved in
decisions increases that the majority is more likely to select the better of two alternatives than any single individual is. Modern Condorcet models often assume that individuals have common preferences but different information and
trace out how the aggregation of decisions can improve on the outcome of having a single individual make the choice. In this model the newspaper article

about pollution policy will provide more information to some voters. An individual voter selected at random may not select the best pollution policy after the story appears (perhaps because she or he missed the coverage). In the aggregate, however, voters may be more likely to select the better alternative as the quality of their information improves.[15]

A final model of the political process revolves around interest groups. Under a traditional view of political debates in Congress, interest groups contend for policy advantage but no one set of interests dominates because of the operation of checks and balances.[16] Interest groups are the political actors in this model, which means that media may play a role to the extent that their coverage causes individuals to recognize group interests and mobilize. If the pollution story causes a reader to identify with a group interest (e.g., environmentalists, utility shareholders, rate payers), then media coverage can influence the activities of organizations that lobby Congress.

To see the relationship between media content and political consequences, consider the finding in chapter 3 that the network evening news programs are more likely to cover political issues of interest to a valuable set of marginal viewers, women 18–34. These viewers are relatively interested in liberal concerns such as education, gun control, and the environment. Does this bias in story selection, which is generated by profit concerns, have an impact on politics? This depends on your assessment of a number of questions. What is the impact of network news consumption on viewers? Which viewers are voters? What baseline knowledge do these voters bring to an issue? Does the focus by the networks on particular issues focus candidates on these topics? What is the relationship between candidates' talk during campaigns and their performance in office? When do voters gather the data that influence their decisions (before September? in October?)? Do the voters use shortcuts such as party identification to make their decisions, or do they look for details about policies? If the networks cover liberal issues, will these be used to hold officials accountable? Can viewers and voters see a causal chain that links real world outcomes with policy decisions? What voting rule do individuals use? Do they vote on results or on promises? Do they hold the party accountable or the person?

Current research in political science and economics offers some evidence on the consequences of media market operation.[17] Bartels and Rahn (2000) have found that the declining audience size for the network evening news translates into lower interest in political campaigns and less faith in the electoral process. The rise of cable television has allowed viewers to flee political coverage in favor of entertainment, lowering the audiences for presidential news conferences (Baum and Kernell 1999) and lowering the likelihood that politically moderate individuals will vote (Prior 2001a and b). The focus of soft news coverage on violence in foreign policy affects viewers' attitudes toward U.S. policy and raises the risks for policymakers of foreign interventions (Baum 2003). As the

New York Times captures more college-educated readers with a national edition across the country, these target readers are less likely to vote in local elections (George and Waldfogel, 2001). If voters were fully informed, electoral patterns would be significantly different. Bartels (1996b) finds that at the presidential level, incumbents garnered about five more percentage points and Democratic candidates earned two more percentage points than they would have if voters were fully informed.

The economic incentives that influence media content can have a spillover effect on politics through that coverage. The market-driven nature of reporting leads to simple rules of thumb: cover the horse race in politics; focus on the human impact of government policies; treat bad news more often than good news; and talk to your targeted audience. Each of these ways of holding viewer attention has a specific effect on political attitudes and actions. Mutz (1995) finds that the media coverage of a candidate's potential political support in presidential primaries affects campaign contributions raised. Iyengar (1991) discovers through lab experiments that viewers shown news stories that tell the story of particular poor people are more likely to attribute poverty to individual factors rather than social causes. Groeling and Kernell (1998) find some evidence that surveys that detect declines in presidential approval are more likely to be reported on the major television networks. Oberholzer-Gee and Waldfogel (2001) determine that blacks are more likely to vote in areas with higher black populations and trace this effect in part to a larger presence of black-targeted media outlets.

Prominent media effects analyzed in political science include agenda setting, framing, and priming. Agenda-setting theories focus on how media coverage can define the set of issues considered to be important by citizens and government officials. Framing refers to the impact that the way a choice or event is described in coverage can affect public reaction. Priming refers to the ability of the media to help define the events and issues used to judge politicians. Tracing out whether and how these effects combine to influence voting decisions is extremely difficult.[18] Researchers have identified many problems with equating media consumption with media effects. How can one make sure that a person received a particular media message?[19] What was the content of the media consumed? What were a person's baseline opinions before the media exposure?[20] If the media respond to real world events, the actions of politicians, and popular interests and opinions, how can one separate out the particular contribution of the media from these other influences?[21] Laboratory experiments in which viewers are shown particular combinations of television stories offer one way to isolate media effects.[22] Internet experiments with online information consumption provide another way to measure the impact of content on opinions or actions. Careful analysis of survey data, especially with data that involve the reinterview of people over time, gives researchers another way to isolate the impact of news coverage.[23]

Downs's economic theory of democracy suggests widespread, rational ignorance among citizens about the details of policy and governance. Survey research indicates that Americans are often hard pressed to identify how government operates, who holds particular offices, or what are the details of current events or policy proposals. In their analysis of public opinion data, Delli Carpini and Keeter (1996) find that knowledge about politics among Americans is relatively low, that this level of knowledge has remained generally stable over the last fifty years, and that there are some segments of the population with high levels of political knowledge and activity. Scholars in political science continue to debate, however, the implications of low levels of factual knowledge about government. Recent work has focused on the question of what knowledge is required for citizens to act competently.[24] Voters with little information may be able to vote as if they were fully informed if they are able to rely on information shortcuts or heuristics. Symbols, brand names, ideologies, and endorsements are all low-cost ways for voters to gain information that allow them to determine who stands for what in politics. Popkin (1994) describes the practical reasoning voters use as "low-information" rationality. Lupia and McCubbins (1998) investigate the conditions under which voters may be able to make reasoned choices about the agents they have endowed with decision-making power. In survey and laboratory settings Lupia (1994, 2001b and c) has explored how voters can learn through information shortcuts and crutches. Determining the implications of a given type of media coverage ultimately will depend on the outcome of current research in political science on what types of information citizens need to make informed choices.

The selection of policy criteria, examination of how content emerges from the operation of media markets, and assessment of the consequences of media information should be a necessary part of media policymaking. Even if a decision maker is able to meld together assumptions about criteria, content, and consequences, there remains the need to assess which policy tools (if any) can contribute to the outcomes desired in media and political markets.

Policy Tools

What sets media markets apart from other types of exchange is the relationship between news and democracy. Yet this link is often far from the minds of those who participate in the market for public affairs information. Owners and managers in media companies seek profits; anchors and reporters try to fashion and further careers; readers and viewers seek entertainment; and the politicians covered search for re-election. The pursuit of individual self-interest here will not add up to the best of all worlds. Readers and viewers will not calculate the broader benefits to society of becoming informed about political issues, which translates into reduced incentives for journalists and owners to cover these topics. This is a classic case of positive externalities, where many of the benefits to knowledge remain external to the decisions by voters about how much to learn about candidates and government. Economists have fashioned many tools to deal with markets characterized by positive externalities. These tools include taxes, subsidies, direct regulation, government provision of the good, and the definition of property rights aimed at encouraging individuals to consider the externalities in their decision making. Table 9.1 lists the options available to change the incentives reporters have to create hard news reports and the incentives readers and viewers have to consume news about politics and government.

A key way to increase the production of hard news stories is to lower the cost of information acquisition for reporters. Government production of statistics such as census data and economic indicators, support for research on policy outcomes, and expenditures on press offices and public relations generate the data that form the basis of news stories. The Freedom of Information Act (FOIA) provides journalists with a way to gain access to the raw materials of executive branch decision making.[25] Nonprofits can lower information costs by supporting research on policy issues and the translation of that research into terms understandable by reporters. Since the labor market for reporters will not fully reward training that helps reporters cover policy issues, foundations can also lower the costs of reporters' learning by subsidizing mid-career training and supporting short-term seminars on specific policy issues.

Direct payment for journalists who focus on hard news stories is another way to increase coverage of policy topics. Public broadcast programs, such as *The NewsHour with Jim Lehrer* on PBS or *All Things Considered* on NPR, employ reporters to cover hard news.[26] Nonprofits can employ reporters, either directly through the ownership of media outlets or indirectly through grants to commercial or PBS outlets that hire reporters to cover particular topics.[27] Families or individuals that own media companies may be willing to offer more hard news than the market demands, simply because they are willing to trade-off some profit for the satisfaction of contributing to policy debates.[28] Tax or other polices that encourage family ownership can thus increase support for hard news provision. The use of spectrum auctions to establish a government trust fund to support information provision offers another source of resources. Political parties and interest groups offer another source for the provision of information about politics, though campaign finance laws may currently restrict their fund-raising and expenditures on advertising.

Raising the psychic benefits of covering hard news could encourage reporters to cover more complex topics. Though managers may focus on profit maximization, the lack of perfect oversight may give journalists some scope to pursue stories with lower commercial but higher social payoffs. Professional groups that support the norms of traditional journalism may lead reporters to gain more satisfaction from trying to cover policy issues. Creating norms among

TABLE 9.1
Menu of Options to Increase the Production, Distribution, and Consumption of Hard News

To Change the Incentives of Reporters

Lower costs of information discovery
    Improve Freedom of Information Act electronic access to government information
    Government or nonprofit production/distribution of data

Direct payment for hard news to reporters
    Public broadcast entity hires journalist to provide in-depth coverage
    Nonprofit owns and operates outlet
    Nonprofit provides subsidy to PBS or commercial organization for hard news
    Ideological owner trades off some profit to provide public affairs news
    Digital Trust Fund establishes agency to distribute grants for hard news projects
    Payment by parties/interest groups for partisan press focused on hard news

Reduce costs of journalist education
    Subsidize mid-career education
    Provide short-term training sessions on specific issues, skills

Raise professional returns
    Create norms among journalists encouraging duty to provide information public needs
    Create norms among boards or owners to praise or reward hard news coverage

Lower costs of distribution
    Postal subsidies for publications
    Blogging software allows individuals writing about public affairs to reach Internet readers
    Internet aggregation functions allow writers to assemble those interested in hard news
    Develop access channels paid for by nonprofits or parties

Create demand through regulation
    Broadcast license renewal requirement that involves public affairs coverage
    Pay or play provision that allows licensees to pay others to cover hard news
    Ownership restrictions that encourage survival of multiple outlets in markets
    Information provision about media entity's public interest actions

Change property rights impediments
    Keep Fairness Doctrine dormant
    Remove cross-ownership restrictions
    Remove must-carry provisions
    Enforce antitrust laws

Copyright
    Encourage information resources left in public domain, to lower production costs
    Favor definitions that direct resources to original authors of works

Excludable goods
    Foster side payments for excludable goods such as books, speech

TABLE 9.1 *Continued*

To Change the Incentives of Consumers

Change preferences:
  Civic education to increase demand for public affairs reporting
  Stress duty to be informed
  Gift exchange/tip jar for reporting

Subsidize hard news consumption:
  Internet access fee pricing, broadband access policies
  Cable rate regulation

Embed hard news in entertainment:
  National Drug Office subsidies for antidrug plots in entertainment programming
  Collaboration between foundations and Hollywood to stress pro-social themes
  Intellectual product placement

Encourage partisan political discourse:
  Remove campaign finance restrictions on contributions or advertising expenditures
  Allow corporate free speech
  Engage parties and interest groups in creation of new programming channels

Facilitate individual involvement with reporting
  Allow individuals to post copies of reporting to discuss/criticize
  Filtering/data mining mechanisms that match reader interests with media content

Direct contracting by individuals for reporting
  Support for journalism as philanthropy

---

board members or owners that emphasize the public responsibility of media companies may lead them to be more willing to trade off some profits for prestige. Media companies may also be able to support the coverage of hard news by allowing their reporters to offer more "excludable" goods away from their jobs. Speeches and book projects, for example, could allow hard news reporters to gain returns that they might not earn directly through their salaries.

  Lowering the cost of distribution of public affairs information can also increase attention paid to politics. The postal service could charge reduced rates for the distribution of periodicals and newspapers. Politicians are guaranteed the lowest comparable rate for their campaign commercials on television. Public access channels are negotiated into the cable service agreements by communities as part of the "price" of doing business in an area. The potential for new local digital channels may offer parties and interest groups the chance to set up their own media outlets, although again campaign finance laws might need revision to permit the development of a partisan press. On the Internet, blogging software that allows individuals to express their views readily to wide audiences offers a way for experts and citizens to help frame public debates.[29] The aggregation functions performed by the Internet give writers a chance to assemble the attention of those interested in policy topics. Even if writers do not earn a monetary return, the satisfactions of self-expression and virtual conversation may lead to an expansion of hard news analysis by those who are not full-time journalists.

Some favor direct government policies to stimulate demand for public affairs reporting. Prior to the 1980s the FCC's broadcast license requirements encouraged at least a minimal amount of public affairs coverage, though the efficacy of these requirements in changing the incentives of for-profit operators is open to debate. Proposals have been made to adopt pay-or-play provisions in which broadcasters would have to either provide public interest programming or pay another entity to do this.[30] Some proponents of the FCC rules restricting media ownership view one benefit of these rules as the survival of multiple outlets in a local market covering government and politics as a benefit.[31] Information provision programs about the degree that broadcasters are meeting their public interest obligations are another policy tool designed to encourage the distribution of information with positive spillovers.[32]

Another set of analysts views removing FCC policies as a stimulus to public affairs coverage. The Fairness Doctrine once required that broadcast outlets offer equal time to policy proponents who disagreed with specific broadcast political content. Empirical analysis by Hazlett and Sosa (1997) suggests that this policy had a chilling effect, since broadcasters avoided discussing politics for fear of engendering a demand for time by outsiders. Once the Fairness Doctrine was removed, radio stations were much more willing to offer programming that discussed public affairs. The current "must-carry" provisions that require cable operators to carry marginally successful broadcast outlets appears to favor the survival of home-shopping channels over broader circulation of public affairs channels such as C-SPAN. The prohibition of newspaper and television cross-ownership in local markets may actually hinder the survival of marginal outlets and hence lower the provision of public affairs coverage in a city.

Antitrust policy offers an additional way to affect the distribution of news. Media mergers generate concerns about how the concentration of ownership affects the diversity of viewpoints expressed, the ability of individuals to gain access through the media, and the opportunity for a relatively small number of firms to control a wide array of outlets in local and national media markets. In analyzing content across local markets in chapter 5, I found that group-owned television stations carried fewer hard news stories, network affiliates did more stories in their local news programs about the network's entertainment programming, and that papers owned by chains covered a higher percentage of soft news topics. Using antitrust laws to address issues of content selection might prove difficult, since current antitrust theories generally focus on price and quantity rather than product variety, diversity, or positive externalities.[33] Antitrust policy could be used more readily to address issues that arise in vertical integration. For example, concerns about the incentives that conduit owners

have to favor the content they own may lead regulators to make special requirements in media merger approvals for the treatment of news channels.[34]

Lenient interpretations of copyright laws allow reporters to build on the
work of others, without paying those who discovered particular facts or first
noticed trends in ideas.[35] Expanding the information treated as in the public
domain increases the likelihood that journalists' work will be copied, distributed, and consumed. A countervailing consideration, however, is the need to
provide some degree of copyright protection for hard news reporting, so media
outlets will earn sufficient returns to hire journalists to write about government and politics.

Even when interesting hard news stories are produced and distributed, there
are no guarantees that they will be consumed. The logic of rational ignorance
predicts that many viewers will not choose to learn about politics and government, a logic confirmed every day by the relatively low audience for *The
NewsHour with Jim Lehrer* on PBS. Consumption of news about government
might be stimulated by attempts to change perceptions about the duties and
rewards of citizenship. This could take the form of advertising that encourages
staying informed. Politicians and others can encourage a norm of citizenship
by emphasizing the need for individuals to learn about politics and government.[36] Since enjoyment of news consumption may depend in part on past
consumption, starting efforts to encourage news consumption early in childhood education may set individuals on a path of future learning. The idea that
news consumers have responsibilities as citizens could also lead them to support hard news through donations to public broadcasting, or contributions
("tips") at favored websites.

Aside from time spent reading or watching, the marginal cost of consuming
news on the Internet or cable television is often zero. Yet the monthly fixed fee
that consumers pay for overall services does deter some from subscribing to cable or connecting to broadband Internet services. If regulatory and antitrust
policies can keep these prices from rising above competitive levels, a side benefit may be increased access to public affairs coverage by individuals who would
choose to join a subscription media service if the price were lower. The positive
externalities gained from consuming political coverage are arguments for subsidizing access to the Internet or cable, though the difficulty of determining
whether consumers actually use the services to follow hard news and of assessing the actual benefits to society make setting the subsidy extremely difficult.

Another way to reach consumers is to embed discussion of hard news topics
within or around entertainment programming. The government provides subsidies in the form of advertising purchases for commercials that discuss drug
abuse. Commercial television networks have also gained credit for producing
entertainment series that discuss drug use. The National Science Foundation
subsidizes the production of educational programming for children, such as
Bill Nye the Science Guy. The encouragement provided to broadcast television

stations for offering educational programming to children in exchange for their broadcast licenses can be viewed as a "price" that these outlets pay for their spectrum rights.[37] Foundations already recognize the benefits of using entertainment programs to reach audiences with messages about topics such as drunk driving and health care. Nonprofits will often work with producers of prime-time programs to provide information that may have prosocial spillovers, such as discussion of a particular health treatment on a medical program. Down the road, intellectual product placements may even be considered, where producers include discussion of particular issues or topics in exchange for financial contributions or in exchange for the provision of free advice and help in programming.

Political parties and interest groups have the incentive to offer information that attracts the attention of potential voters. Campaign finance laws currently restrict the amounts of money raised by, and types of speech used by, parties and interest groups.[38] If these restrictions were removed, more political speech could reach consumers through the form of advertisements. The opening up of additional digital broadcast channels, and convergence of programming with the Internet, may even offer the opportunity for the development of a renewed partisan press. Corporations also desire to reach individuals with political messages, in part because of firms' involvement with policy debates and in part because company positions affect the brand images of consumer products. Court decisions that curb corporate speech may have the unintended effect of diminishing the variety of opinions available to readers and viewers interested in the interplay between the public and private sectors.[39]

If the political becomes personal, then individuals may follow politics because they find information that involves them entertaining. Websites that allow individuals to post comments and discuss hard news tap into the satisfaction people gain from self-expression. Copyright restrictions that make it difficult for a site to incorporate the text of hard news stories or even links to these stories discourage participation in public affairs. Innovations on the Internet that mine and filter data about reader interests allow better matching of individuals' preferences with stories. The technology employed by Amazon.com to alert readers to books in which they might be interested, for example, could allow consumers to find stories enjoyed by people with similar interests. The ability of news sites to tailor offerings to a viewer, and the development by Google of a news site edited in effect by data on the attention of other readers, are examples of how technology can make it easier to match interests with content.[40] Websites in 2000 matched voter opinions with candidate stands and allowed voters to calculate potential tax benefits from candidate policy proposals. If the media can personalize the outcomes of policy debates through such interactive elements, then hard news topics may gain more attention.

Individual philanthropy offers another way for an individual consumer to become engaged with media content. Some foundations aggregate large gifts solicited specifically to support investigative reporting or coverage of particular topics.[41] Donors gain the satisfaction of knowing that reporting only takes place because of their support. For millionaires or billionaires, ownership of a media outlet offers an avenue to influence policy debate. The support may come in the form of a willingness to fund an outlet unlikely ever to earn a profit or a willingness to accept positive but less than maximum financial returns.

Assessing the return on investments in media market policies is extremely difficult.[42] Trying to improve public decision making through improving reporting can be a long-term prospect. Is it more effective to change attitudes about health exams through a public information campaign, or is money better spent on creation of a community health clinic? Is information provision best aimed at reaching readers of general publications, or can information provision work when the data are used mostly in technical debates and policy research consumed on Capitol Hill? How can media policies go wrong, so that interventions aimed at improving political decision making are steered toward particular partisan ends? These are the types of questions that should be answered when media policies are proposed and examined.

Decisions and Analysis

To see how far economic reasoning can take one in evaluating efforts to influence media markets, consider the following hypothetical decision. Assume that you are a foundation officer with a $50 million program budget and a desire to influence individual and policy choices about health care by stimulating the production and consumption of news about health.[43] There are a variety of endeavors you could fund that would lower the costs of reporters. You could fund a research study and produce an accessible summary for reporters. The Henry J. Kaiser Family Foundation and the Pew Charitable Trust frequently fund studies that are widely covered by the press. You could commission a poll whose results were shared with news organizations, who treat the opinion information as newly discovered data. The Pew Research Center for the People and the Press regularly conducts surveys that generate press coverage. You might even partner with a news organization to conduct the study, which could lower the quantity of coverage in other outlets but raise the depth of coverage in the partnering organization. The Kaiser Family Foundation has funded surveys through the Washington Post/Kaiser/Harvard University Survey Project and the National Public Radio/Kaiser Family Foundation/Kennedy School of Government Survey Project. The nonprofit could pay for the development of a health database made available online, with the hope that reporters will use the data and that individuals will use the database to investigate their own interests. The Trust for America's Health website (www.health-track.org) provides researchers and reporters with easy access to data on cancer and disease clusters by local area. The

Environmental Working Group's website (www.ewg.org) allows individuals to calculate how close their homes are to proposed travel routes for radioactive waste shipments to Nevada, an interaction that makes policy personal. The non-profit might also pay for journalism midcareer education, either short-term conferences designed to teach the basics of health care policy or a longer term sabbatical study meant to allow a reporter to develop significant expertise. The Foundation for American Communications provides training seminars for print and broadcast journalists on many economic topics. The Kaiser Family Foundation funds year-long fellowships for journalists to study health topics and provides short-term funding for reporters to pursue specific story topics.

Nonprofits may also choose to become more directly involved in the provision of broadcast programming. The Kaiser Foundation Program on the Entertainment Media and Public Health gives writers and producers of entertainment programming information on health care issues and diseases. The Kaiser Foundation provided the staff of the NBC medical drama *ER* with information about emergency contraception for an episode that included discussion of date rape, an episode which reached thirty-four million viewers. Kaiser also partnered with the Johns Hopkins School of Public Health and a Baltimore television station to produce news segments on topics covered by *ER*, which were provided free to NBC affiliates and often shown as part of local news programming. During the debate in 1994 over the Clinton health care plan, the Robert Wood Johnson Foundation gave NBC $3.5 million to underwrite and promote a two-hour special entitled "To Your Health."[44] NBC retained control over the content of the program. Kaiser provides funding for a reporting unit on *The NewsHour with Jim Lehrer*, which allows the PBS program to provide more in-depth coverage of the issue. Foundations may also choose to sponsor advertising on commercial programming, as the Kaiser Family Foundation and California Wellness Foundation did during the health care debate in 1994.

A foundation executive might want to foster discussion of a portfolio of issues, not simply health care. In that case funding options might focus on encouragement of the general provision, distribution, and consumption of hard news. One option is for the nonprofit to purchase or run a news outlet. *Harper's Magazine* is run as a nonprofit foundation; the *St. Petersburg Times* is also controlled by a nonprofit foundation, the Poynter Institute. The foundation might focus on the creation of norms that focus on the responsibility of owners and managers to care about the impact of media properties on democracy. The Aspen Institute runs roundtable discussions that focus on these topics.[45] Efforts to encourage family or personal owners to pursue civic as well as corporate goals could help properties still influenced by individual owners. The Project for Excellence in Journalism attempts to support journalists who view reporting as a profession and take their roles seriously as participants in democracy.[46] Foundation contributions to PBS help further the provision of hard news. Foundation efforts might also support the creation of a government entity that provides direct subsidies for information creation and distribution. The Digital Promise Project, led by Lawrence Grossman and Newton Minow and supported by a range of foundations, calls upon the government to use funds generated by spectrum auctions to develop digital projects related to social and political needs. The project would result in the creation of an agency akin to the National Science Foundation that would provide venture capital funds to promote learning and enhance knowledge through the use of new telecommunication and information technologies.[47]

How might a foundation project manager decide to allocate the $50 million budget across these funding choices? If the manager cares about the provision of information as an intrinsic good, the simple creation of information about a topic such as health care would be one outcome to measure. Many individuals are interested in media markets, however, because of the instrumental role that information plays in influencing public and private decisions. To get at the relative efficacy of the funding opportunities, the project manager could track the creation of stories, the exposure of particular demographic groups to the media product, and changes in public opinion. Short-term and long-term changes in consumer action could be monitored, such as the change in doctor visits relating to a particular medical procedure among *ER* viewers who saw the episode about the topic. In terms of political action, changes in individuals' propensity to vote, political opinions, or candidate selection can be tracked through surveys. Ultimately, changes in political debates and policy choices could be monitored and related back to media consumption and public opinion.

Tracing out the impact of knowledge on policy outcomes involves a long causal chain.[48] There are many factors that might lead the media to have little or no impact on a particular policy. Journalists might not know enough to cover a topic, because private and public actors were trying to cover up their activities. This might describe the relative lack of critical coverage of the energy company Enron during the time that the company was using limited partnerships to hide the true state of business operations from investors. Even if facts were known, reporters might not perceive any reader or viewer interest. This applies to lack of coverage of fighting or famine in Africa on major broadcast news outlets. Readers or viewers might choose not to consume a particular media outlet covering hard news, or might choose not to read a story or listen closely when a topic is covered. Even if a news story is consumed, it might not change a reader's opinion because of prior experiences or other information the person has. Opinions might change, but a viewer might operate on the logic of collective action and decide not to vote or participate in politics. Even if the reader or viewer becomes a voter, he or she might not be a swing voter for the candidate and thus might be ignored in policy calculations. The person might be in the group of voters targeted by a candidate, but the representative in turn might not be a swing voter in Congress. This might be the case if a vote were going to be lopsided and the representative's decision had no impact on the bill's final passage. Even if the chain of causation were perfectly clear, and one could match media inputs with policy outcomes, the challenge would remain about how to monetize or evaluate the change in policy.

The difficulties of assessing probabilities and values here do not mean that analysis cannot rank the different ways to influence hard news provision about a particular topic. One could select exposure count as a variable to track and then estimate the number of exposures generated by a particular funding option. Video Monitoring Services tracks the content of local news programs in many markets, and Nielsen Media Research compiles estimates of viewers for each local news program. These types of data allowed Kaiser to estimate that the "Following *ER*" news segments it helped support reached 1.7 million local news viewers each week.[49] One can also use surveys, lab experiments, and focus groups to estimate how information has an impact on opinion. The Kaiser Family Foundation conducted surveys before, immediately after, and two months after the *ER* program on date rape to see the impact of information about emergency contraception on health care knowledge among *ER* viewers.[50] One could even establish a system to capture the relative value of different types of media impressions. When the networks wanted to reduce the number of advertisements they had contracted to show for the Office of National Drug Control Policy, they developed an arrangement with the office so that antidrug messages in entertainment programs would be allowed to "count" for antidrug commercials.[51] White House drug policy officials read the scripts and then determined based on the quantity of discussion, message, and length of program involved the number of commercials the networks would not have to run if they used a particular script.

If one took exposure as a way to measure the relative efficacy of attempts to promote consumption of policy information, economics could help a nonprofit manager choose among funding options. Thinking about which viewers, readers, and voters the effort would want to reach would lead to a consideration of the particular demographic groups consuming a given media product. Recognizing the dominant role that entertainment incentives have in the consumption of information might lead the foundation to fund polls on a topic, since these may be likely to generate "news" of interest to readers. The battle for attention and importance of brand names might lead a foundation to partner with a well-recognized media outlet. The foundation would also want to test the impact of information provided through focus groups, lab settings, and surveys.

A full benefit-cost assessment of a foundation decision to fund the provision of health care news would be unwieldy and unlikely. The transaction costs of making such a study can be significant. The government's own guidelines on benefit-cost analysis, for example, do not generally require a large-scale regulatory impact assessment for a proposed regulation unless it would have at least a $100 million impact on the economy. Nonprofits view resources spent on evaluation as resources not spent in production. The desire to avoid scrutiny of mistakes also means there is not a well-established literature on the track record of nonprofit expenditures. Yet as this example demonstrates, intermediate indicators and economic reasoning can help one make bets about the relative desirability of different interventions in media markets. If one wishes to further citizen learning through improved media coverage, remembering that you must "reach before you teach" (that is, you need to attract attention) and measuring your success in reaching particular sets of readers and viewers are imperfect but helpful guides in assessing the desirability of different media policies.

If information costs were lower and our knowledge of media effects better, one could make a rough calculation of the benefits and costs involved in trying to change media content. Table 9.2 presents a template for the categories of effects to consider. Assume that an analyst is trying to evaluate the impact of an intervention aimed at changing policymaking by changing media coverage of a particular topic I. Such interventions might include a nonprofit funding a new study or a new government regulation affecting media ownership. Benefit-cost analysis provides a way to examine the desirability of adopting a particular ap-

TABLE 9.2
Assessing the Benefits and Costs of Changing Media Content about Politics

---

Costs of new information on topic I:
    Generation of data, analysis, ideas
    Creation of media content by journalists
    Distribution of content
    Opportunity costs (i.e., time) of readers/viewers

Benefits of new information on topic I:

$$\sum_{I,J} \text{Private benefits}_{I,J} + \text{Policy benefits}_I \text{ where}$$

Private benefits$_{I,J}$ are:
(# exposed to content)$_{I,J}$ × (probability consume/exposure)$_{I,J}$ × \$$_{I,J}$ entertainment, duty

Policy benefits$_I$ are:
Probability of policy I change $f\left(\sum_{I,J}$ (# exposed to content)$_{I,J}$ × (probability

consume/exposed)$_{I,J}$ × (probability change opinion/consumed)$_{I,J}$ × (probability change actions/change opinion)$_{I,J}\right)$ × \$ policy change I

Costs of I policy change:
(Probability of policy I change) × (resource costs of I policy change)

Net benefits of changing media content I are:

$$\sum_{I,J} \text{Private benefits}_{I,J} + \text{Policy benefits}_I - \text{Costs of new information on topic } I - \text{Costs}$$

of I policy change

---

proach by assessing overall the net impact on society of the intervention. Phrased another way, Does the size of the social pie (as measured in dollars) grow after one takes into account both the costs of an endeavor and its benefits? The costs of new information about topic I are readily identified and may include the resources involved in generating new data or studies, the time spent by journalists to write about the topic, the additional costs of distribution of the coverage, and the opportunity costs of time spent by readers and viewers to consume the information. Salaries, travel expenses, and data purchases factor into the calculation of how much research studies or reporters' inquiries cost. For consumers the value of their time spent reading or viewing offers evidence on the costs of information consumption.

In most benefit-cost calculations, benefits are harder to assess than costs. This is true in part because the areas where benefit-cost analyses are employed are often those involving market failures of positive or negative externalities, so that an analyst must assess the value of things that escape full accounting in the market. This pattern holds true for media benefit-cost calculations. There are private benefits considered by readers and viewers in their consumption of media coverage. For the sake of simplicity, assume that one can break down media audiences into different demographic categories and that within these categories individuals react in similar ways to economic and political choices. Calculating the private benefits to media coverage produced by a policy intervention involves estimating the number of individuals in demographic group J exposed to content about topic I. Not all those who see a program or read a paper will consume a particular story, so table 9.2 includes a probability that one consumes a story given exposure to the media outlet. A person in demographic group J may enjoy consuming a story about topic I for several reasons. For political news, some individuals will find the coverage entertaining. They gain utility from following a political story in and of itself; the simple knowledge of the facts brings happiness. Additionally, some may gain utility from following news of government because they feel a duty as a citizen to stay informed. Analysis of consumer expenditure surveys and evidence from contingent valuation studies could provide estimates of the dollar values individuals associate with knowing the details of politics and policymaking.

News of politics can also be instrumental, since knowledge about policy can help a citizen make decisions about votes, contributions, and other political actions. Capturing the benefits arising from policy changes involves more detailed calculations. To estimate the impact of media coverage about topic I, one would calculate the number of individuals in demographic group J exposed to the coverage, the probability that a person exposed consumed the report, the probability that the consumed report changed the opinion of the individual, and the probability that the changed opinion resulted in a changed action by the individual (such as a changed vote). Since benefit-cost analysis examines how an intervention changes the status quo, the focus here is on changes in perceptions and decisions. If new information on topic I generates media coverage but does not change opinions, then there is no effect on public decision making. Assume that one can assess the connection between content, coverage, and opinions to derive an estimate of the number of votes changed among a demographic group. This parallels in part the decisions that political campaigns make in choosing where to run ads to influence votes. Once one has the change in votes, you still need a model of politics to determine how the actions of demographic group J change policymaking. This model of politics would translate a change in actions such as votes into a probability that policy in area I changes. If one can determine the change in policy that results from changed votes, there still remains the play within the play—the calculation of the dollar values placed on the benefits and costs of the policy change itself. For those demographic groups whose actions influence policy, the change in political actions can result in estimated changes in policy that are monetized by another round of benefit-cost analysis. This would include assessing the likely costs involved in the policy change.

Table 9.3 adds further complications to this story. Some are common twists involved in standard benefit-cost analyses. If costs and benefits occur in the future, the dollar figures must be discounted to reflect the net present value of the actions involved. Advertisers and media planners often assume that individuals within a demographic group are similar, as do political strategists. Yet the responses to information assumed may vary within a demographic group, across demographic groups, across issues, and across time. There may be threshold effects, so that a given repetition of coverage may be necessary to trigger a change in opinion. The calculation of how coverage is consumed may need to be altered as coverage spreads from a given media outlet and is repeated. Analyses often assume that an intervention proceeds as planned. But sophisticated analyses will reflect the likelihood of unintended consequences. These may include the provision of inaccurate information by the media or misunderstanding of a message by consumers. Crowding out can also occur, so that consumption about topic I leads to less consumption about another topic, which can affect policy on the neglected area. Policy analysis may also assume that interventions affect media coverage. Yet the link between intention and outcome should be examined to make sure that the envisioned actions are compatible with the incentives of readers, reporters, and editors. Simply providing reporters with information, for example, does not mean they will have the incentive to incorporate the information into their reporting.

Assessment of the benefits and costs of trying to change media content involves other challenging questions. In environmental policy, individuals often have existence values they place on knowing that a pristine forest exists and a bequest motive to pass on the forest to future generations. Some individuals have similar existence and bequest motives about the operation of media and democracy. This means that individuals will have preferences about the proper roles played by government, the media, nonprofits, and citizens. These prefer-

TABLE 9.3
Additional Factors in Media Benefit-Cost Analysis

Discounting the future—in what time periods are costs incurred or benefits realized?

How is coverage amplified through the spreading of stories across outlets?

Are there threshold effects, e.g., a number of times an idea is consumed before an opinion changes?

Unintended consequences:
- Is the wrong information provided?
- Do individuals derive an inaccurate or incorrect message?
- Is there information crowding out, so that increased exposure to or consumption of topic I precludes attention to another topic?
- Is the intervention aimed at changing content incentive compatible, e.g., do media markets work so that content is changed?

How does anticipation of changes in media coverage affect policy decisions?

What existence values or bequest motives do people have over the roles played by government, the media, nonprofits, and citizens? How can those be monetized (e.g., contingent valuation)?

How do parameters vary by issue? By demographic group? Over time?

In assessing the value of a changed policy, what model predicts policy choice? How are benefits and costs of the policy monetized?

Sensitivity analysis—need to use different estimates of parameter values to create different scenarios that may arise.

What should be the decision rule used—maximize expected value? Minimize worst outcome?

---

ences can be independent of the impact of a policy intervention on coverage; they simply may relate to the value individuals place on freedom of expression. If one could translate media coverage into a policy change, the challenge remains to then monetize the value of this policy change. In essence this requires a second benefit-cost analysis of the policy affected, for example, of the change in health policy brought about by additional media coverage of health issues. The calculations in table 9.2 appear to imply there is a single value for each of the parameters involved, for example, there is "a" probability that consumption of information about topic I leads to opinion change among individuals in demographic group J. This probability itself has a distribution, with some individuals having a high likelihood of changing their opinion and others having a low probability of opinion change. Sensitivity analysis is one way to reflect the variabilities and uncertainties involved here. This would entail varying the values used in the calculations in table 9.2 so that a range of scenarios is presented. Once the math is done and scenario results calculated, the analyst still must select a decision rule to judge the outcomes. Should one compare the expected value of different media interventions and select the one with the highest net benefit? Or should one select the intervention that minimizes the worst outcome that might arise?

In a world where information was costless, one could make the calculations in table 9.2. You could determine how to spend a given budget on media interventions by looking across a set of topics, assessing how policies change with reactions to changes in media policies, and spending the funds to yield the highest expected benefits. Yet we do not live in a world where information is costless. Much of the analysis of this book, for example, discusses how information costs drive decisions in media markets. In this world of incomplete and costly information, the best approach to media policy may involve assessments that acknowledge assumptions made in the analysis and accept imperfect indicators of outcomes. This means that analysts will disagree over the desirability of particular policies in part because they disagree over models of how markets work, assessments of how individuals respond to information, and beliefs about how government operates. The utility of the benefit-cost framework, however, is that it sets up questions that expose whether analysts disagree because of different assessments of probabilities or preferences.

The variability and uncertainty described in tables 9.2 and 9.3 should make one hesitant to claim to know the optimal set of media policies. At the same time, decisions about how to deal with potential market failures in the media require action in the face of uncertainty. A decision to wait for more research implicitly favors the status quo. When I examine the operation of media markets, I am struck by the lack of interest in politics, the focus on profits by media outlets, and the potential for mistakes in government efforts to engage in direct content regulation.[52] These assessments lead me to favor four broad classes of policy reforms to influence the market for news. The first is a focus on efforts that reduce the cost of information about how government operates. The Freedom of Information Act and provision of electronic data by the government all lower the costs to reporters of covering the news. In a world of weak demand for news about government, shifting the costs of news collection and analysis downward is one way to expand coverage of government. A second avenue lies in the expanded provision of information by nonprofits. This may include funding of research studies, subsidizing of media research on particular topics, support for journalists' education, and outright ownership and operation of media outlets. Critics of nonprofit support for information provision as biased miss a key point—information provision is generally driven by some desire to influence decisions. Advertisers seek consumers, politicians seek voters, and nonprofits seek minds to change. Nearly all information provision involves some measure of self-interest on the part of the sponsor.

A third way to improve news coverage is to stress the development of professional norms among journalists. While it is true that media markets focus on profits, within media companies there exists some slack between the interests of owners, managers, and reporters. Journalists have some leeway to provide stories that are not profit-maximizing but do provide broad social returns. This is because it is costly for owners and managers to monitor constantly whether reporters are paying sufficient attention to reader interests and production costs.[53] The difficulties in monitoring make it possible for reporters at the margin to cover hard news. Journalists' organizations, such as the Committee of Concerned Journalists and nonprofits such as the Poynter Institute and the Pew Center for Civic Journalism, can encourage the development of norms that lead editors and reporters to provide readers with the information they need to function as citizens.

A fourth set of policies relates to the government's definition of property rights. As indicated earlier, economics does not provide precise answers to questions about the exact definition of intellectual property rights. Long periods of copyright protection, for example, can increase incentives for the production of works but decrease the efficient circulation and consumption of ideas once they have been produced. The development of the Internet and its rapid circulation of ideas has raised many challenges to intellectual property. One set of advocates favors restricting the sphere of the public domain, a movement that would privatize more types of information to provide greater incentives for production. Another set of advocates points out the potential restrictions on the development of new ideas and conversations if individuals are discouraged from consuming particular intellectual products by prices set above marginal costs. Considerations of the market for news and public affairs should add another argument in favor of the preservation of the public domain. Since consuming news about government involves benefits not factored into individuals' consumption calculus, efforts to lower the costs of consumption by granting less stringent copyright protection may increase the consumption of political news.

A final question of property rights revolves around the auctioning of the spectrum. The Digital Promise Project, headed by Lawrence Grossman and Newton Minow, argues that proceeds from spectrum auctions should be placed in a trust. Funds would be dispersed by an agency akin to the National Science Foundation or National Institutes of Health, with the monies being awarded in open competition for grants. The funds would serve as venture capital for projects that enhance the creation and transmission of knowledge. Proponents note that the Congressional Budget Office estimated spectrum auctions would raise $18 billion over the course of several years.[54] Placing a bet with funds of this magnitude does involve substantial risk. One possibility to overcoming uncertainty about the program is to run a trial project. The interest alone on the spectrum fees would yield hundreds of millions of dollars in one year, which would be enough to provide an initial round for funding for the trust. Running the trust on a trial basis would allow proponents to demonstrate the type of ideas that are waiting to be funded. Analysis of these pilot projects could then demonstrate whether the social returns to investment from the auction funds would be higher in supporting information provision or in direct expenditures on other government services.

Conclusions

At the first Hackers Conference in 1984, Stewart Brand (author of *The Whole Earth Catalog*) famously declared, "Information wants to be free."[55] This artfully conveys several truths described in the theory of public goods, namely that my consumption of an idea does not preclude your consumption of it and you can often consume an idea without having to pay for its generation. Yet if you are trying to understand the operation of information markets, in particular the market for news, you should focus on the private interests individuals have in the production and consumption of information.

Debates about the media often start with the premise that journalists try their best to answer a simple set of questions: Who? What? Where? When? and Why? In this book I have tried to establish that a different set of five Ws helps explain the content of news. Owners and managers may consider these questions explicitly. Reporters and anchors may not always consciously think about these, but if their actions do not conform to the logic of these questions then they run the risk of losing ratings, raises, or even their jobs. Readers and viewers remain (rationally) ignorant about these questions, unless they find reading books such as this entertaining. If one wants to comprehend the rise of nonpartisan reporting, the decline of hard news reporting, or the transformation of reporters into celebrities, I believe the spatial model embodied in the five Ws helps you determine what type of news will be produced in a market. Those who produce and distribute the news will ask themselves the following questions: Who cares about information? What are they willing to pay, or others willing to pay to reach them? Where can media outlets and advertisers reach them? When is this profitable? Why is it profitable?

There are limitations to the ability of economics to provide criteria to judge the outcomes of media markets or predict the consequences of information consumption. Values that are not easily monetized are involved in assessing the impact of reporting on democracy. Trying to estimate with confidence the impact on group decision making of changes in media operations is difficult. Economics does, however, provide a way to understand the forces that govern the production and distribution of news goods. If one is willing to assert a set of criteria and assume a given goal, the policy tools provided by economics offer a way to influence outcomes in media markets. The imprecision and uncertainty involved, combined with the First Amendment, may make government action less likely in this policy area. This should not prevent nonprofits, however, from trying to remedy market failures here by producing their own information, lowering the costs to journalists of covering issues, and trying to facilitate the distribution of data directly to readers and viewers. This should also not prevent individuals from taking their own steps to combat rational ignorance. If you believe that an informed citizenry is important in the functioning of democracy, the means to act on this are only a click away. Discussions of media policy often take place on a plane of high abstraction. Yet outcomes in media markets are really only the aggregation of millions of decisions by individuals about what to read and consume.

Notes

Introduction

1. For a discussion of the Fowler quotations and the FCC's public interest doctrine, see Hamilton 1996. Ahrens 2001 profiles FCC chairman Michael Powell.

Chapter 1
Economic Theories of News

1. The impact of the market on news content is a frequent theme in analyses of the media industry, memoirs of reporters, and narratives that describe the history of journalism. Works that stress the effect of financial incentives on the production and distribution of the news include: Powers 1977, Jensen 1979, Fishman 1988, Picard, Winter, McCombs, and Lacy 1988, Lacy, Atwater, and Qin 1989, Cook, Gomery, and Lichty 1992, Lacy and Bernstein 1992, Kurtz 1993, 2000, Neuman 1993, Underwood 1993, Baker 1994a, Branscomb 1994, Kimball 1994, McManus 1994, Squires 1994, Grossman 1995, Fallows 1996, Hamilton and Krimsky 1996, Radio and Television News Directors Foundation 1996, Schudson 1996, Bagdikian 1997, Herman and McChesney 1997, MacNeil 1997, Parker 1997, Hamill 1998, Krajicek 1998, Reeves 1998, Bollier 1999, Frankel 1999, Janeway 1999, Zaller 1999a, and Kerbel 2000. Memoirs of journalists or books that describe a particular media outlet also provide descriptions of how economics alters content. These include Broder 1987, Donaldson 1987, McCabe 1987, Lehrer 1992, Burns 1993, Corry 1993, Diamond 1993, Goldberg and Goldberg 1995, Tifft and Jones 1999, and Utley 2000. Journalism or communication histories that focus on the impact of the market on news and information distribution include Shaw 1967, 1981, Knights 1968, Garbade and Silber 1978, Schudson 1978, DuBoff 1980, 1983, 1984a, b, Schiller 1981, Brooker-Gross 1983, Nord 1986, 1988, Shmanske 1986, Blanchard 1987, Nerone 1987, Stensaas 1987, Goldstein 1989, Rutenbeck 1990a,b, 1991, 1995, Baldasty 1992, 1999, Kaplan 1993, 1995, Blondheim 1994, Smulyan 1994, Bates 1995, Adams 1996, Neiva 1996, Mindich 1998, and Littlewood 2000.

2. I derive this definition from Shapiro and Varian (1999, p. 3), who observe, "essentially anything that can be digitized—encoded as a stream of bits—is information. For our purposes, baseball scores, books, databases, magazines, movies, music, stock quotes, and web pages are all information goods." Their book, *Information Rules: A Strategic Guide to the Network Economy* (1999) outlines economic theories of information, many of which apply to news markets. DeLong and Froomkin (2000) provide an overview of the application of microeconomics to analysis of the Internet and developing markets for information.

3. In his classic *Deciding What's News: A Study of CBS Evening News, NBC Nightly News, Newsweek, and Time*, Herbert J. Gans (1980, p. 80) wrote, "I view news as information which is transmitted from sources to audiences, with journalists—who are both employees of bureaucratic commercial organizations and members of a profession—

summarizing, refining, and altering what becomes available to them from sources in order to make the information suitable for their audiences." In *News from Nowhere*, Edward J. Epstein (1973, p. 30) found that

> "the correspondents I interviewed almost all defined 'news' in terms of time. 'News is what is new in the world since our last broadcast' or 'News is what has happened today' or 'News is change' are typical of the definitions given by newsmen. When pressed, virtually all the correspondents related 'news' either to the time element or change in a situation; what distinguished 'news' from other forms of knowledge, such as history, was its 'immediacy.'"

4. Carlton and Perloff (1990, p. 596) provide definitions and examples of search versus experience goods. See also Nelson 1970, 1974.

5. Caves and Williamson (1985) investigate how one can measure product differentiation. They point out that the concept rests on two conditions (p. 113): "First, buyers must recognize that goods ('brands') belonging to a product class are close substitutes for one another but face only relatively poor substitutes with goods outside the class. At the same time, these brands must be sufficiently imperfect substitutes that each seller perceives his brand to face a downward-sloping demand curve." In the market for news this would mean that consumers have expectations that particular news outlets will offer different varieties of news, e.g., *People* will focus on entertainment figures and *The Wall Street Journal* will provide business data. If news goods were "all the same" then a producer would face a flat demand curve. If the firm tried to raise the price it would lose all consumers since they would flee to a perfect substitute. The fact that news goods are perceived to be different among consumers means that a firm faces a downward sloping demand. An increase in price reduces the numbers of buyers for a firm's good but does not result in zero customers. Png and Reitman (1995) explore what factors influence whether or not a product will be marketed with brand names.

6. There is substantial literature on the economics of newspaper publishing. See Rosse 1967, 1970, 1978, Rosse, Owen, and Dertouzos 1975, Udell 1978, Norton and Norton 1986, Thompson 1988, Picard, Winter, McCombs, and Lacy 1988, Lacy 1989, 1992, Busterna 1991, Lacy and Fico 1991, Demers 1996, Picard 1997, 1998, Chaudhri 1998, Demers 1999, Genesove 1999, George and Waldfogel 2000, and Cranberg, Bezanson, and Soloski 2001.

7. For a discussion of the economics of "superstars," see Rosen 1981, Hamlen 1991, Hausman and Leonard 1997, and Borghans and Groot 1998.

8. Simon (1978) points out that attention is a scarce resource in that individuals have limited time and processing capacity to deal with information. Aigrain (1997) and Goldhaber (1997) discuss the implications of attention economics in the development of the Internet.

9. The impact of information on consumption and production decisions will depend on how individuals interpret the information and how many individuals possess it. For empirical evidence on the effect of information in purchase and production decisions, see Price, Feick, and Higie 1987; Slovin, Sushka, and Polonchek 1992, Ippolito and Mathios 1995, Kandel and Zilberfarb 1999; Milyo and Waldfogel 1999, and Chwe 2001. For evidence on the impact of informed citizens on local public goods, see Lowery, Lyons, and DeHoog 1995, Teske, Schneider, Mintrom, and Best 1993, 1995, and Schneider, Teske, Marschall, and Roch 1998.

10. Robert J. Shiller (2000) stresses that information used for business decisions may be affected by entertainment demands, so that media content aimed at investors may differ from that expected if individuals were only concerned about making rational investment decisions. He notes (p. 95):

> The role of the news media in the stock market is not, as commonly believed, simply as a convenient tool for investors who are reacting directly to the economically significant news itself. The media actively shape public attention and categories of thought, and they create the environment within which the stock market events we see are played out.... The news media are fundamental propagators of speculative price movements through their efforts to make news interesting to their audience. They sometimes strive to enhance such interest by attaching news stories to stock price movements that the public has already observed, thereby enhancing the salience of these movements and focusing greater attention on them.

11. See Downs 1957, pp. 240–59. Noll (1993) discusses how Downsian theories relate to the impact of political advertising.

12. Downs concluded (1957, p. 259) that "[i]n general, it is irrational to be politically well-informed because the low returns from data simply do not justify their cost in time and other scarce resources." Political scientists and economists now refer to this as the "rational ignorance" hypothesis. Green and Shapiro (1994) argue that the notion of rational ignorance is frequently cited but rarely tested in political science. See Hamilton (1996) for a discussion of private incentives to gain information about politics and the implications for media policies. For discussions of the relationships between public ignorance and the media, see Anderson 1998, Friedman 1998, Hoffman 1998, and Somin 1998.

13. See Drinkard 2001.

14. Commenting on the presence of some informed voters in a world of rational ignorance, Morris Fiorina observes (1990, p. 335), "voters are irrational—not because they have so little information, but because they have so much!" Delli Carpini and Keeter (1996) provide extensive data on what types of information citizens have about politics.

15. The rational ignorance theory focuses on the lack of news demanded by an individual. Many questions also exist about how people process the information they are exposed to. Posner (1998) explores the role symbols play in political reasoning. Rabin and Schrag (1999) describe the cognitive biases that cause individuals to misinterpret new information. For other analyses of how individuals sort through information to make assessments, see Caplan 2000, Mullainathan 2000, and Caplan 2002. The anti-smoking ads funded by tobacco company settlements illustrate the impact of framing on decision making. Tugend (2002) indicates that anti-smoking advocates believed that simple statements about health effects would not deter teenagers from smoking, so ads were designed to deter teenage smoking by portraying the tobacco companies as manipulative.

16. Summarizing a survey about news interests in 2002, a Pew Research Center study (p. 1) concluded that "the public's news habits have been largely unaffected by the Sept. 11 attacks and subsequent war on terrorism. Reported levels of reading, watching and listening to the news are not markedly different than in the spring of 2000. At best, a slightly larger percentage of the public is expressing general interest in international and national news, but there is no evidence its appetite for international news extends much beyond terrorism and the Middle East."

17. Stigler (1961) provides a classic account of search costs and information provi-

sion. Akerlof (1970) describes how uncertainty about quality can affect the types of goods offered in a market.

18. Justman (1994), Davis (1997), and Netz and Taylor (1998) discuss the difficulties associated with testing spatial models and provide examples of empirical assessments of firm location decisions. Endersby and Ognianova (1997) find that in a spatial model of political ideology the survey respondents place major media figures as near the center of the political preferences held by the general public.

19. The presentation and descriptions of the programming model of public affairs content is almost identical to the model of violent programming in Hamilton (1998, pp. 33–39). The main difference is that public affairs content involves positive externalities for society while violent television content generates negative externalities. Owen and Wildman (1992) provide the best review of the development of models of television programming, including those by Steiner (1952), Beebe (1977), Spence and Owen (1977), Wildman and Owen (1985), Noam (1987), Wildman and Lee (1989), Waterman (1992a), and Spitzer (1991). Additional works that focus in part on empirical assessments of television industry outcomes include Noll, Peck, and McGowan 1973, Owen, Beebe, and Manning 1974, Owen 1975, 1999, Levin 1980, Fournier 1985, 1986, Noam 1991, Waterman and Grant 1991, Waterman 1992b, 1996, Powers 1993, Wildman and Robinson 1995, Shachar and Anand 1996, 1998, Shachar and Emerson 1996, Waterman and Weiss 1996, 1997, Crawford 1997a,b, Emmons and Prager 1997, Hazlett 1997, Hazlett and Spitzer 1997, Ise and Perloff 1997, Papandrea 1997, Webster and Phalen 1997, Bae 1999, Chipty and Snyder 1999, Goettler 1999, Goettler and Shachar 1999, 2000, Kennedy 1999, Anand and Shachar 2000, and Anderson and Coate 2000. Relevant works on radio broadcasting models include Rogers and Woodbury 1996, Berry and Waldfogel 1999a,b,c, and Waldfogel 1999. Many of these media models focus on questions of the impact of market structure on program diversity and social welfare. Spitzer (1997) uses a spatial model in the manner of Hotelling (1929) to examine explicitly the market for violent television programming and the potential impacts of the V-chip on that market. What distinguishes the model developed in Hamilton 1998 that I modify here is the combination of assumptions that viewers fall within discrete viewing groups, that advertisers may value these viewers differently, that costs of programming vary by genre, and that externalities arise from consumption. This combination of assumptions yields testable hypotheses about the market for public affairs programming.

20. In studying the content of national broadcast network news programs from 1972 to 1987, Scott and Gobetz (1992) found a slight increase in the amount of "soft news" content in these programs over time. They define (p. 408) soft news as stories focusing on "a human interest topic, feature, or non-policy issue." In studying the content of newspapers, nightly national news programs, and news magazines from 1977 to 1997, the Committee of Concerned Journalists (1998, p. 1) found that "there has been a shift toward lifestyle, celebrity, entertainment and celebrity crime/scandal in the news and away from government and foreign affairs. But infotainment still comes nowhere near dominating the traditional news package. There is an even more pervasive shift toward featurized and people-oriented approach to the news, away from traditional straight news accounts. This tends to make the news more thematic and make the journalist more a story teller and mediator than a reporter." Marvin Kalb (1998) uses coverage of the Lewinsky scandal to examine how changes in technology and the economics of the

news industry have given rise to a "new news." Patterson (2000) details the rise of soft news coverage across different types of national and local media outlets.

21. This description of how economic considerations determine the types of news offered can be formalized in the following manner. Consider the market for news programming at a particular time of day. Let X_l be the number of viewers (in thousands) who prefer news with low public affairs content, X_m be the number that watch shows with moderate levels of public affairs content, and X_h be the number who watch news programs with high public affairs content. Viewers in each group are assumed to watch their preferred type of news programming only (e.g., high public affairs viewers select programs to view only among shows that carry high levels of news about politics and government). The values, in terms of dollars-per-thousand viewers, placed by advertisers on viewers of particular programs are denoted by P_l, P_m, and P_h (e.g., advertisers will pay P_h for one thousand viewers of a program with high public affairs content). The costs of programming will vary with the type of news offered. The cost to a programmer is C_l for a program with low public affairs content, C_m for moderate content, and C_h for high public affairs content. The additional cost to a programmer of providing the show to an additional customer is zero, so a channel's cost is assumed to equal what it pays for programming. The combination of technology (e.g., spectrum scarcity, cable capacity) and property rights (e.g., FCC licenses, local cable regulation) yields a total of N independent competitors in this market. Each channel is viewed as an independent firm trying to maximize its profits. The number of channels that choose to offer shows with low, moderate, or high levels of public affairs content will be defined as N_l, N_m, and N_h. Channels offering a particular type of programming are assumed to face identical costs and to split the number of viewers for that "genre" equally. The profits for a channel offering a news show with moderate levels of public affairs coverage, for example, are thus defined as $P_m{}^*(X_m/N_m) - C_m$.

In equilibrium, the profits of channels across the three types of news programming will be equal. If they were not, then a channel would have an incentive to switch programming into the news genre with the higher profits. Thus we know in equilibrium that

$$P_l^*(X_l/N_l) - C_l = P_m{}^*(X_m/N_m) - C_m = P_h{}^*(X_h/N_h) - C_h \text{ and } N_l + N_m + N_h = N.$$

With these conditions holding true, we can explore how changes in the exogenous variables in the market $(P_l, P_m, P_h, X_l, X_m, X_h, C_l, C_m, C_h, N)$ affect the number of channels offering particular types of news programming (N_l, N_m, N_h). Soft news refers to programs with low levels of public affairs content (N_l) and hard news refers to shows with high levels of public affairs stories (N_h).

22. The model of public affairs programming makes the same simplifying assumptions as Hamilton (1998):

> A. Programming is portrayed in terms of a single dimension, the amount of public affairs content contained in the news program. Particular viewers are assumed to watch only a given type of programming, rather than choosing among different genres. For spatial models in which a given viewer may consume many different types of programming (depending on the location of programming alternatives), see Noam 1987 and Spitzer 1997. One difficulty with spatial models is that results are highly sensitive to assumptions made about the shape of the distribution of viewer preferences and number of competitors.

B. Advertising values are taken as determined outside the interactions of the television market. That is, the value placed by advertisers on particular viewers is assumed to emerge from a larger market for advertising across different media. For discussion of models of advertising purchases, see Rust 1986. Baker 1994a details how advertising values may influence the content of the print media.

C. The costs of programming are assumed to be given, so that if a channel wants to show a news program with low public affairs content it faces a set cost of C_l for the show. Channels competing for viewers within a genre are all assumed to offer shows with the same costs and to split viewers evenly. The number of viewers attracted to a given show is not assumed to vary with the (production) cost of the program.

D. An equilibrium where profits are equal across all three programming genres may, depending in part on the value of N, imply fractional values for the number of channels that choose to program within a given genre such as N_l. One can think of the channel divided up into fractions as providing part of its programming in each of these genres (which also entails assumptions about the programming costs faced by this fractional channel).

23. The model generates another prediction about ratings: *In equilibrium, there is no reason to expect soft news programs to have higher or lower ratings or costs.* Much of the attention focused on soft news programming considers this genre unique in terms of ratings and costs. Consider, however, the relationships among costs, ratings, and advertiser values that hold in equilibrium. Since profits are the same across the programming niches, one knows that $P_m{}^*(X_m/N_m) - C_m = P_l{}^*(X_l/N_l) - C_l$, or

$$P_m{}^*(X_m/N_m) - P_l{}^*(X_l/N_l) = C_m - C_l.$$

Rearranging the terms in this manner underscores that in equilibrium it is the values that advertisers place on viewers, the number of viewers in a given market niche, the number of competitors, and the costs of programming that help determine the relationships one would predict among costs and ratings. If the difference on the left-hand side of the equation is positive, then one will predict that soft news programming is cheaper for programmers to purchase than shows with moderate levels of public affairs information (i.e., $C_m > C_l$). If the left-hand side were negative, then one would predict that programming with low levels of public affairs content is more costly than shows with moderate public affairs content.

One can also derive different predictions about the ratings of soft news programs. Many predictions of the relationships between soft news and viewership focus on the overall ratings for a show—that is, the percentage of total television households watching a particular program. Broadcasters focus, however, on the viewing of particular demographic groups (e.g., women 18–34, men 18–49). The model predicts that the relationship between the number of people watching a show with moderate levels of public affairs content (X_m/N_m) and the number of viewers watching a soft news programs (X_l/N_l) will depend on both the values that advertisers place on these viewing groups (P_m for each thousand viewers of the moderate programming and P_l for each thousand viewers of the soft news programming). Assume, for example, that $P_l = P_m$ (i.e., advertisers valued these two groups equally). This would mean $X_m/N_m - X_l/N_l = (C_m - C_l)/P_l$. One would then expect in equilibrium that the number of viewers for a program with moderate levels of public affairs information would be higher than a show with low levels if the costs of moderate programming were higher than the costs of soft news programming (i.e., $C_m - C_l$). If soft news programming were more expensive, then one would predict more viewers for a program with low public affairs content

24. One could express the value of these externalities by a benefit to society E per thousand viewers multiplied by the number of thousands of viewers of the program. E would reflect the dollar value of the improved government decisions flowing from more informed voters. Then in equilibrium the market equations become

$$P_l{}^*(X_l/N_l) - C_l = P_m{}^*(X_m/N_m) - C_m = P_h{}^*(X_h/N_h) - C_h + E^*(X_h/N_h)$$
$$\text{and } N_l + N_m + N_h = N.$$

25. Economic models point out many ways that the quality and variety of goods offered in a market may diverge from the socially optimal ideal. Spence (1975) notes that if the marginal customer values quality less than the average consumer, a firm with market power will set quality too low from society's perspective because it focuses on the marginal customer's valuation of quality. Spence (1976) establishes that in markets where fixed costs are important, prices charged by firms may not capture enough of the social benefits of products to make the offering of particular varieties profitable. There will thus arise instances where varieties that have a net positive benefit to society will not be offered by firms since they cannot cover the fixed costs of production. Mankiw and Whinston (1986) note that when the goods offered across firms are the same (e.g., homogeneous), there may be too many firms entering the market if production involves fixed costs. This arises because a firm weighing entry will consider the sales "stolen" from incumbent firms in making the decision to enter, while from society's perspective these sales do not represent an additional value to society.

26. This example is derived from the analysis of software application bundling in Shapiro and Varian, 1999, p. 75.

27. DeVany and Walls (1996) discuss how the spread of information about movie preferences among potential viewers affects the likely success of a film and influences the type of contracts signed by movie theaters.

28. For discussions of how individuals with limited information may look to the decisions of others to gain information, see Bikhchandani, Hirshleifer, and Welch 1992, 1998, and Banerjee 1993. Studies of "herd behavior" in financial markets, where investors follow in part the actions of previous investors, include Froot, Scharfstein, and Stein 1992, and Avery and Zemsky 1998. Related work on the influence of noise traders (defined by DeLong, Shleifer, Summers, and Waldmann [1990, p. 706] as those who "falsely believe that they have special information about the future price behavior of the risky asset") includes Bhushan, Brown, and Mello 1997, Dow and Gorton 1997, and Greene and Smart 1999. Shiller and Pound (1989) explore how important contagion of interest is among investors.

29. Graham (1999) examines herding by analysts offering investment advice. Kennedy (1999) examines herding in the introduction of programs by broadcast television networks.

30. The presentation of the Steiner model here draws upon the formulation in Owen and Wildman, 1992, pp. 65–70.

31. Owen and Wildman (1992) analyze the implications for social welfare of competitive versus monopoly markets in advertiser-supported and pay television. They point out (p. 100) that in advertiser-supported television, competitive duplication will be less

of a problem if viewer preferences are relatively evenly split across programming types since this reduces the returns to duplicating programs. If the number of channels is relatively large, programs appealing to a small proportion of viewers may still be profitable to offer in a competitive market as long as there are enough viewers to generate revenues to pay for program production/distribution costs. The impact of competition versus monopoly on programming outcomes is left open as a matter of theory. Owen and Wildman (p. 148) conclude, "From a social welfare perspective, there is no unambiguous ranking of alternative ways to organize a television industry."

32. Demsetz and Lehn (1985) explore how the concentration of ownership in a firm, e.g., the percentage of a firm's shares owned by the top five and top twenty shareholders in a company, varies across industries. They find that ownership of media firms is more highly concentrated than in other firms and that this is due to greater concentration of ownership interests in media firms among families and individual investors. They link this pattern to the ability of families or individuals that own media firms to exercise some control over the type of product produced and the personal satisfaction that this opportunity can afford, noting that "believing that one is systematically influencing public opinion plausibly provides utility to some owners even if profit is reduced from levels otherwise achievable" (p. 1162).

33. Baker (1994b) reviews the evidence of the impact of chain ownership on newspapers. Chan-Olmsted (1997) discusses the implications of competition among firms owning multiple channels of content distribution. Compaine and Gomery (2000), McChesney (2000), and Miller (2002) examine concentration of media ownership. The Commission on Freedom of the Press (1947) analyzed the implications of media ownership in the 1940s.

34. For research on the origins and perceptions of media bias, see Hackett 1984, Niven 1999, Rouner, Slater, and Buddenbaum 1999, Bovitz, Druckman, and Lupia 2000, Sutter 2001, 2002a–c, and Mullainathan and Shleifer 2002. Snider and Page (1997) discuss media bias in the coverage of the Telecommunications Act of 1996, which gave television broadcasters free use of additional broadcast spectrum rights.

35. Local television stations, for example, may have contracts with the major broadcast networks or CNN to purchase footage for inclusion in their local news programs.

36. The option to repeat a story across different parts of a day's programming can also increase the amount invested in the original development of the story. If increased budgets for program production translate into increased viewers or a higher willingness to pay for cable viewers, then the existence of a second or third source of revenue from repeating a program will translate into higher original budgets. Note that incentives to repeat a story will be higher for outlets with lower initial audiences, since they face a lower probability of losing viewers who have already seen a program. One would thus expect cable channels to be more likely to reuse footage in news stories across the day than network broadcast channels. For a discussion of budgets and program audiences and episode repetitions in entertainment programming, see Owen and Wildman, 1992.

37. Kovach and Rosenstiel (1999) use coverage of the Lewinsky scandal to examine the pressures on print and broadcast outlets to rush information into circulation. Sabato, Stencel, and Lichter (2000) assess how the media cover political scandals.

38. See Owen and Wildman 1992, and Hamilton 1998 (pp. 46–50) for discussions of biases in television programming that is supported by advertising.

39. Coase (1974) compares the market for goods with the market for ideas and dis-

cusses how government policies treat these two markets differently. For the use of economics to explain the diffusion of economic ideas, see Colander and Coats 1989.

40. For discussions of the impact of the media on U.S. politics, see Neuman 1986, Iyengar and Kinder 1987, Bartels 1988, 1993, 1996a, Entman 1989, Ferejohn and Kuklinski 1990, Iyengar 1991, Sabato 1991, Dearing and Rogers 1992, Jamieson 1992, 2000, Neuman, Just, and Crigler 1992, Page and Shapiro 1992, Zaller 1992, 1997, Patterson 1993, Rosenstiel 1993, Bennett and Paletz 1994, Hart 1994, 2000, Kerbel 1994, Popkin 1994, Lichter and Noyes 1995, Bennett 1996, Alvarez 1997, Cappella and Jamieson 1997, Cook 1998, Task Force on Campaign Reform 1998, Paletz 1999, Farnsworth and Lichter 2002, and Jamieson and Waldman 2003. For examinations of how media affect the exchange of ideas in society, see Postman 1985, Bourdieu 1998, Postman and Powers 1992, Adatto 1993, Kuran 1995, Cowen 1998, 2000, Elster 1998, Comstock and Scharrer 1999, and Scheuer 1999.

41. Lupia and McCubbins (1998) model the interactions between citizens with limited political information and those who possess delegated decision-making powers in democracy. Baker (1997, 1998) explores how incentives affect the information citizens possess and the implications of the distribution of information for different models of democracy. Hoyer, Hadenius, and Weibull (1975) look at the political economy aspects of the media across countries.

42. Entman and Wildman (1992), Geller (1998), Noll and Price (1998), and Wildman (1998) demonstrate how economic ideas can be integrated into media policies. Hundt (2000) describes the political difficulties associated with making communications policies at the Federal Communications Commission.

43. Fowler and Brenner 1982, p. 210.

Chapter 2
A Market for Press Independence

1. There is no canonical definition of "objective reporting." Mindich (1998) defines objective reporting by a series of traits: detachment and nonpartisanship; a use of the "inverted pyramid" style of reporting where the most important data comes in the first paragraph; an emphasis on the collection and use of facts; and a sense of balance in coverage. He notes that all these elements were present in newspaper reporting by the 1890s. Schudson (1978, p. 5) defines objectivity in part as "the belief that one can and should separate facts from values" and marks the prevalence of this view among journalists after World War I. Stensaas (1987, p. 53) classifies a newspaper account as objective "if it contains only verifiable assertions, does not make claims to significance, and avoids statements of prediction, value, advocacy, or inductive generalizations without clear attribution to source." Using this definition to categorize a sample of stories in six daily newspapers, he finds that objective reporting was not widespread 1865–74, was common 1905–14, and had become the norm 1925–34. This chapter uses the term "objectivity" at times in discussion of press independence, since nonpartisan coverage is a strong element of objective reporting. During the period 1870–1900, however, reporters did not use the term to refer to their coverage. Discussions focused on newspaper "independence."

2. The term "independent" is used to refer to the political affiliation label newspapers applied to themselves during this time period. In this sense it is a brand location that

distinguished some papers from other daily newspapers that labeled themselves as Republican or Democratic.

3. There is a large literature in journalism history on the origins of nonpartisan papers. Schudson (1978) provides a detailed social history of the development of the independent press. Baldasty (1992) examines how business practices of newspapers in the nineteenth century influenced the presentation of news. Rutenbeck (1990a, 1990b, 1991, 1995) and Kaplan (1993, 1995) examine the interaction between economic and political factors in the growth of independent papers.

4. For a description of financial support provided by parties and the government to the partisan press, see Smith 1977 and Baldasty 1992.

5. Lee (1937) provides data on newsprint costs over time. In current dollars, the price of newsprint per pound dropped from 12.3 cents in 1870 to 1.8 cents in 1900. If the figure for 1870 is converted into 1900 dollars, the price decline was from 8.1 cents in 1870 to 1.8 cents in 1900.

6. Figures on federal government budget expenditures for this time period are available in U.S. Bureau of the Census (1997). Though nominal government expenditures were decreasing during part of this time period, real expenditures (e.g., expenditures expressed in 1900 dollars) were generally increasing throughout the time period.

7. The literature on newspaper markets stresses the impact of economies of scale, product differentiation, and the interaction of subscription revenues and advertising revenues on a firm's decision about what price to charge for the paper. Litman (1988) notes that a local newspaper market could be characterized by monopoly, oligopoly, or monopolistic competition depending on the number of papers in the area and discusses the likely origins and attributes of each of these outcomes.

8. Hudson 1873, p. 433.

9. See Schudson 1978 for a description of the penny press and its detractors.

10. Bleyer 1927, p. 213.

11. Ibid., p. 218. Greeley, the editor of the *New York Tribune*, was the presidential nominee of both the Liberal Republican Party and the Democratic Party in 1872. His unsuccessful race that year generated much editorial debate over the degree that papers should be independent or partisan. See Rutenbeck 1990a and Summers 1994.

12. Mott 1950, p. 412.

13. Bleyer 1927, p. 267.

14. Hudson 1873, p. 676.

15. Kaplan 1993, p. 88.

16. Rutenbeck 1990b, p. 168.

17. Baldasty 1999, p. 139.

18. Baldasty 1992, p. 130.

19. Beniger 1986, pp. 272–86.

20. Hudson 1873, p. 418.

21. Hazel 1989, p. 61.

22. Bleyer 1918, p. 3.

23. Bleyer 1918, p. 81.

24. Essary 1927, p. 28.

25. Watson 1936, p. 37.

26. Baker 1994a, p. 15. Baker describes in detail the many impacts of advertising on press incentives and coverage.

27. Hower 1949, p. 589–90. For a discussion of which brands were advertised nationwide during this period, see Presbrey 1929.

28. Baldasty 1992, p. 121. In this section I draw heavily on Baldasty's work *The Commercialization of News in the Nineteenth Century*, which is an excellent history of the influence of economic factors on the evolution of daily newspapers.

29. Ibid., p. 59.

30. Ibid., p. 79.

31. N. W. Ayer and Son 1880, p. 465.

32. Ibid., p. 494.

33. Ibid., p. 535.

34. Ibid., p. 477. The ad on that page for the *Cincinnati Gazette, Chicago Times, St. Louis Republican,* and *Louisville Courier-Journal* noted, "Contract advertising in them, per thousand actual circulation, averages about a half a cent a line in the weekly editions, and from a third to a fourth of a cent per line in the daily editions, each insertion."

35. Ibid., p. 610.

36. Each of the fifty most populous cities in the United States contained at least one political daily newspaper, with the exceptions in 1870 of Cambridge, Charlestown, and Lynn, Mass., in 1880 of Cambridge, and in 1890 and 1900 of Allegheny, Pa.

37. Some cities contained daily newspapers devoted to information targeted at particular industries, such as financial newspapers. Political papers, those that carried the general news of the day, accounted for an increasingly large fraction of the total daily newspapers in the top fifty cities. The analysis in this chapter focuses solely on the political daily newspapers. These political newspapers accounted for 178 of 249 daily papers in the largest cities in 1870, 251 of 291 total dailies in 1880, 315 of 359 total dailies in 1890, and 321 of 373 total dailies in 1900.

Unless otherwise noted, the use of the term "daily papers" in the text refers to newspapers that covered general current events, i.e., the political daily papers. Note that the total daily circulation for political papers is the sum of the daily circulations of papers, rather than the total number of papers consumed across a year (which would involve multiplying the daily circulations by the number of publishing days).

38. In addition to differentiation based on political affiliation, newspapers also established market niches based on when during the day they were published and what language they used. In 1870, 52% of the newspapers were published as morning papers, while by 1900 the majority of papers (55%) were published in the evening. In 1900, 66% of the independent outlets were published as evening papers. The overlap of evening publication and independent brand location is not surprising. Mott (1950, 447) notes that evening papers garnered significant street sales, were often carried home, and were read by women, a prime target of department store advertisers. Language is another way that papers were differentiated. In 1870, 21% percent of the daily political newspapers analyzed here were published in a foreign language, a figure that grew to 28% in 1900. Many of these were newspapers published in German.

39. The circulation per person figure for each city category is derived by calculating for each city the total circulation of the political dailies, dividing this number for each city by the city's population, and then taking the average of these figures for cities in the size category. Since the data do not exist to link readers with specific newspapers, an increase in the number of papers per person in a city could represent more people reading papers or the same number of people in the city reading multiple daily newspapers. The

historical evidence indicates that at least some of the increase in the papers per resident calculation is due to the spread of newspaper reading among a larger fraction of the population. Baldasty (1999) describes how E. W. Scripps chose to start newspapers in cities where he believed independent newspapers aimed at laborers would attract new readers, i.e., people not currently reading the higher-priced partisan press.

40. The HHI reported for newspapers in these periods would still rank these markets as concentrated, relative to other product markets. The antitrust guidelines announced in 1992 by the U.S. Justice Department establish three ranges for market HHI. The Department considers markets with an HHI of less than .1 to be unconcentrated, with an HHI between .1 and .18 to be moderately concentrated, and with an index value greater than .18 to be concentrated. By this calculation, in 1900 only one local political newspaper market was in the unconcentrated range (New York) and six were in the moderately concentrated zone. See U.S. Department of Justice and Federal Trade Commission 1997.

41. The comparison between a city's characteristics and a paper's affiliation choice often assumes that a paper is choosing a political brand position in the given year examined. In one sense this is true, since papers did have the continuous option to select their political brand locations and some papers did change their affiliation across the time period examined. In addition, since many of the papers analyzed were recently established, the city characteristics examined in a census year would correspond to the factors considered when the brand location was chosen. For papers established many years prior to the time period examined, however, there might be costs associated with changing a brand location quickly so that the outlet's political affiliation would be different than one its owners might chose if the paper were a new entrant facing a given set of city demographics.

42. The city population and demographic data analyzed here come from Interuniversity Consortium for Political and Social Research 1992; note that the population percentages reported are for the counties in which the cities were located. The voting data come from Clubb, Fanigan, and Zingale 1986 and represent the percentages of votes cast in the counties for candidates in the presidential elections of 1868, 1880, 1888, and 1900. The information on paper characteristics comes from assembling individual paper data from the 1880, 1890, and 1900 editions of N. W. Ayer and Son's *American Newspaper Annual* and George P. Rowell's *American Newspaper Directory* for 1870. Circulation is an estimate of the daily circulation for a paper. I multiplied the paper's dimensions and page numbers to derive a paper size. The subscription rate per 100 square inches is derived by dividing the annual subscription rate by the size of the paper; this figure thus represents the annual amount paid per daily 100 square inches. The daily subscription base multiplied by the annual rate yields the total subscription revenue figure. Dividing the total subscription revenue by the paper size gives a subscription revenue per square inch figure. For the 1880 advertising data, I divide the advertising rate by the circulation to get the cost per thousand readers. This number represents the cost of reaching 1,000 subscribers to a paper (per month).

43. Unless otherwise noted, the dollar figures reported in the chapter are expressed in current year figures. The time period 1870 to 1900 was a time of deflation in consumer prices. If the dollar values in table 2.3 are expressed in constant dollars (e.g., 1900 dollars), the drop over time in subscription prices is still evident. For Independent newspapers the annual subscription rate (1900 dollars) went from $5.39 in 1870 to $4.41 in

1900. The subscription rate per 100 daily inches of newspaper was 14¢ in both 1870 and 1900. See table 2.4 for paper financial characteristics expressed in 1900 dollars.

44. For each year I estimated a logistic regression with the dependent variable = 1 if the paper was in the top 20% of circulation and with independent variables of city size (in thousands), an indicator variable = 1 for independent papers, and an indicator variable = 1 if the paper was a foreign language publication. I took the coefficients from this model, used mean values of the variables to estimate probabilities, and then altered the values of the independent variables as indicated in table 2.7 to estimate the effect of different factors on a paper's likelihood of achieving large scale circulation.

45. See North 1884.

46. See United States Congress 1870, 1880, 1890, and 1900.

47. These models were logistic regressions with the dependent variable based on whether the paper had at least one congressional correspondent and the independent variables consisting of city size, newspaper circulation, foreign language publication, and independent affiliation.

Chapter 3
News Audiences

1. For discussion of the types of information audiences express demand for, and for conceptions of the public interest (e.g., the "wants" versus "need" debate), see Fowler and Brenner 1982, Rainey 1993, Baker 1997, 1998, and Sunstein 2000.

2. See Hamilton 1998, p. 53 for a discussion of the value advertisers place on reaching younger and female consumers. Media accounts of the success of reality-based programs such as *Survivor* (Carter and Fass 2000, Mink 2000, Whitehouse 2000) and *Temptation Island* (Bruinius 2001) stress the use of these shows to attract 18–34 viewers because of the prices advertisers are willing to pay to reach young adults. Stories about the WB (Warner Brothers) network targeting female viewers (Mason 2001, Werts 2001) and the programming of women's basketball and soccer on television (Heath 2001) also note the high value advertisers place on reaching female consumers. Goettler (1999) analyzes how audience demographics affect advertising rates on network television programs. Dee (2002) challenges the advertising industry's targeting of 18 to 34-year-old consumers.

3. Spence 1975.

4. Endersby and Ognianova (1997) explicitly use a spatial model of ideology to examine the relative placement of television news anchors, politicians, and political parties in the perceptions of survey respondents. They find that journalists are perceived to be located near the ideological center in their model. Bovitz, Druckman, and Lupia (2002) explore the conditions under which reporters or media owners would try to use news reporting to affect public opinion and how effective they could be. D'Alessio and Allen (2000) find, in a meta-analysis of fifty-nine quantitative studies of media coverage of presidential elections, no significant biases in newspaper or newsmagazine coverage and small but insubstantial biases in television network news coverage.

5. Page and Shapiro (1992) evaluate fifty years of survey data to demonstrate the "rationality" of policy preferences expressed in opinion surveys. They find that expressed opinions are relatively stable over time, and that when opinions change the movements are consistent with world events and economic or social changes. Popkin (1994) examines how voters can reason about candidates and parties with low levels of information.

Bartels (1996b) finds votes in presidential elections diverge in significant ways from re-sults expected if voters had been fully informed about candidates. Kuklinski et al. (2000) explore the political impact of misinformation, which they define as confidently held inaccurate factual beliefs.

6. The Pew Research Center for the People and the Press conducts frequent surveys (available at www.people-press.org) on media issues. The Pew 1999 survey on political ideology was conducted July–September 1999 with a sample size of 3,973 adult respon-dents. The Pew 2000a survey about media bias was conducted in January 2000 with a sample size of 1,091 adults. The Pew 2000b survey on media consumption was con-ducted in April-May 2000 with a sample size of 3,142. Each survey contains sample weights based on census data that are designed to adjust the survey results to be repre-sentative of the U.S. population. Unless noted otherwise I use these sample weights in the analysis in this chapter. I thank the Pew Research Center for making the survey data available to researchers via its website.

7. Zaller (2000) discusses the difficulties associated with determining actual exposure to particular media outlets from survey questions since some respondents appear to overstate their media consumption. Price and Zaller (1993) note that the political infor-mation respondents have is the best indicator of media exposure.

8. National Television Violence Study (1998) examines the prevalence of visual de-pictions of violence and discussions of violent acts in nonfictional television program-ming. Police programs contain frequent depictions of violence, while some talk shows often feature "talk" about violence. The high interest in crime news, found in the Pew surveys of audience members for these programs, is consistent with the interest in vio-lent expression demonstrated by watching *Cops* or *Jerry Springer*.

9. In a chi-square test of whether the interest in a particular news type was independ-ent of demographic group in table 3.3, I rejected the hypothesis of independence at the .01 level for each news type except culture and the arts. I conducted similar chi-square tests of the independence of row responses to column categories and rejected the inde-pendence hypothesis at the .01 level for tables 3.4, 3.5, 3.6 and 3.7 (except for Fox News Cable Channel and MSNBC), 3.8 (except sports, religion, entertainment, and culture/ arts), 3.11 (except strong economy and minimum wage), 3.13, 3.14, 3.15, 3.18, 3.19, 3.20 (except for voting with ESPN, *Entertainment Tonight* and *Access Hollywood*, talk shows such as *Rosie O'Donnell* and *Oprah*, *The National Enquirer*, *Sun*, and *Star*, and maga-zines such as *The Atlantic Monthly*, *Harper's*, and *The New Yorker*; following the 2000 presidential election and daytime talk shows such as *Ricki Lake* and *Jerry Springer*, day-time talk programs such as *Rosie O'Donnell* and *Oprah*, and *The National Enquirer*, *Sun*, and *Star*; and identification of Alan Greenspan and the morning network programs, ESPN, documentary channels, and personality magazines such as *People*), 3.21 (except crime and marginal voters, following Elian Gonzales and marginal viewers of CNN, and crime and marginal NPR listeners), and 3.23.

10. Aldrich, Sullivan, and Borgida (1989) present evidence that, despite the low levels of interest in international affairs often expressed in survey data, candidates in presi-dential elections through 1984 were able to use foreign policy issues to appeal to voters.

11. For examinations of how knowledge about politics varies across demographic groups, across time, and by media exposure, see Zaller 1992, Delli Carpini and Keeter 1996, Jennings 1996,

12. The Pew survey data may understate the degree that the network news audience is

concentrated among older or female viewers. For November 1999 Nielsen ratings data, I summed the audience data for the ABC, CBS, and NBC evening news programs. For the 30.3 million adults in the weekday evening news audience, I found that 59.5% were age 55 or higher and that 57.7% were female. By age category, the percentage audience accounted for by a demographic group was 10.1% 18–34, 30.9% 18–49, 38.1% 25–54, 49.1% 35–64, and 59.5% 55+. The audience composition across household income categories was 12.3% $30,000–39,999, 19.3% $40,000–59,999, 9.0% $60,000–74,999, and 20.2% $75,000+. In terms of education by head of household, 53.1% had no college and 22.3% had 4+ years of college. See Nielsen 2000b.

13. Abstracts of stories on the evening news, the length of each story, and records of what commercials aired during the news programs are available at tvnews. vanderbilt.edu from the Vanderbilt Television News Archive.

14. The questions about issue priority were asked in a survey (Pew 2000a) conducted from January 12–16, 2000. Story and time counts were calculated for January through December 2000. I treat the early January survey data as a proxy for the expectations that news directors had about public opinion when they made decisions in 2000 about what issues to cover. One can make the argument that the opinions held by different demographic groups are in part a product of the network news coverage from earlier periods (e.g., 1999). In this case the pattern of causation would be network coverage influencing opinion, rather than opinion influencing the course of network coverage. The ability of the news media to influence the priority assigned to different issues by the public is called agenda-setting. For an overview of agenda-setting research, see Rogers and Dearing 1988. Paletz (1999) provides a succinct summary of this and other media effects on public opinion.

15. Petrocik (1996) explores how issue ownership affects presidential elections and describes how parties and candidates may have reputations among parts of the electorate for better handling of particular issues.

16. Pew 2000a used a six-point ideology scale, while Pew 2000b used a five-point ideology scale. For each survey, I conducted difference of means tests comparing the audience mean ideology of the shows at each extreme of the ideology spectrum with each other and with values for programs at the median ideology value of the program audiences. For Pew 2000a (i.e., data in table 3.16), I rejected the no difference hypothesis at the .10 level or better for religious radio programs versus late-night shows such as those hosted by Jay Leno or David Letterman, and for late-night programs versus cable news networks or versus national network news programs. I could not reject the hypothesis of no difference for late-night programs versus National Public Radio (NPR), or religious radio programs versus cable news networks, national network news programs, or NPR. For Pew 2000b (i.e., data in table 3.17) I could reject the no difference hypothesis for Fox News Cable Channel versus magazines such as *The Atlantic Monthly*, *Harper's*, or *The New Yorker*. I could also reject the no difference hypothesis when each of these endpoints of the ideological spectrum was compared with the daily newspaper, network morning shows, or *The National Enquirer*, *Sun*, and *Star* (except that I could not reject this hypothesis when the mean for the Fox News Cable Channel was compared with the mean for *The National Enquirer*, *Sun*, and *Star*).

17. Prior (2001a,b) explores how the expansion of choices in viewing can reduce political knowledge for some individuals. He notes that the expanded number of viewing options provided by cable television allows those seeking news to get more political in-

formation and those seeking entertainment to find programs with little or no information about public affairs. The diversity of cable programs can thus lead to a widening of the gap between those who follow politics closely and those who do not. Baum and Kernell (1999) find that the viewing opportunities provided by cable television have reduced the television audience for presidential appearances.

18. Elian Gonzales was the child rescued off the coast Florida after a boat he was traveling on with his mother from Cuba sank. His stay in Miami with relatives and eventual return to Cuba with his father attracted widespread media attention.

19. George and Waldfogel (2000) stress how the likelihood that a product an individual prefers will be provided in a market depends on the number of consumers with similar preferences and the size of fixed costs of production.

Chapter 4
Information Programs on Network Television

1. One television critic (see de Moraes 1999b, p. c7) described the November 1999 content of NBC's *World's Most Amazing Videos* in the following terms: "On Monday there'll be one featuring firefighters at a fireworks factory, a motorcycle racer who slams into a wall, and horses colliding at a rodeo. Then, for your enjoyment, on the final Saturday of the sweeps, *Amazing Video* offers footage of a guy being flipped off his crashing boat and onto a nearby island, a gasoline tanker truck that explodes into a fireball, and a matador being gored by a raging bull." In summarizing the shows to watch and avoid during the November 1999 sweeps, another television critic noted (see Zurawik 1999 p. 1E): "Must miss: *When Good Pets Go Bad 2*. This "reality" special showing out-of-control animals in the attack mode is one of the most vile programs network television has ever done." Though viewers 18–34 watched these two programs in large numbers, they were less likely to view *60 Minutes*. Among females 18–34 *60 Minutes* ranked 22nd out of 96 informational programs, while among males 18–34 the program ranked 14th.

2. See Nielsen Media Research 2000a. The programs included shows from ABC, CBS, Fox, NBC, PAX, and UPN. The viewing audience figures and commercial price reported for a program are averages since a given program might have many telecasts during a sweeps period. The audience figures for *NBC Nightly News*, for example, are averages based on 19 telecasts. Other program data will represent figures for just one telecast, since the episode may be a special. Note that networks have the option of marking an episode of a regularly scheduled program as a special. The large number of specials accounts for many of the 96 programs listed as informational in Nielsen Media Research 2000a. Ratings data by demographic group came from Nielsen Media Research 2000b.

3. Scott and Gobetz (1992) found that from 1972 through 1987 the coverage of soft news stories (e.g., human interest stories, features, or nonpolicy issues) on the network evening news programs grew over time but remained a relatively small part of the broadcasts. A study by the Committee of Concerned Journalists (1998) found that in 1997 over half of the stories on prime time broadcast network news magazines focused on personal stories, lifestyles, "news you can use," and celebrities. See Patterson (2000) for an analysis of the impact of soft news coverage.

4. See Hart 2000, especially pp. 245–51. The description of DICTION here draws heavily on Hart 2000 and the documentation for the program, Hart 1997. Patterson (2000) uses DICTION to trace the growth over time of soft news coverage in the media.

Loomis and Meyer (2000) use the program to examine executives' messages in the annual reports of media companies.

5. The twenty-seven programs in the initial sample included the morning news programs (*Early Show, Good Morning, America, Today Show*), evening news programs (*ABC World News Tonight, CBS Evening News, NBC Nightly News*), news magazines (*Dateline, 48 Hours, 60 Minutes, 60 Minutes II, 20/20*), and Sunday public affairs programs (*Face the Nation, Meet the Press, This Week, Fox News Sunday*). Additional programs included *Sunday Morning, Sunday Today, Early Today, Later Today, CBS Morning News, Nightline, Saturday Today, Saturday Early Show*, and *ABC World News This Morning*. Though transcripts were collected for *ABC World News Now* programs shown at 2 A.M., 2:30 A.M., and 3 A.M., they were dropped from the final sample. If a text segment is less than five hundred words, DICTION will project the relative word count for each dimension. Text segments of less than four hundred words were also dropped from the final sample.

6. The focus on language use across programs omits many factors that influence how a person consumes and is affected by a broadcast news program, particularly the visual and audio elements associated with a television image. For an excellent review of how television influences learning about politics, see Graber 2001. Gunter (1987) explores how the presentation of news on television affects the way viewers process and store information presented in the news.

7. Strate, Ford, and Jankowski (1994) explore differences between women and men in the types of media used to follow politics. Parker and Deane (1997) find differences in the types of news stories that women and men follow very closely. A higher percentage of men than women report that they follow very closely stories about the military, business, scandals in politics, international relations, and sports. Women are more likely to follow stories about disasters and Supreme Court rulings (which include decisions about abortion).

8. On the incentives to target a program toward a broad versus a narrow audience, see Waterman 1992b, and Chae and Flores 1998. Bae (1999) explores product segmentation within a genre of cable programming, the shows on all-news national cable channels (i.e., CNN, MSNBC, and the Fox News Channel).

9. The mean of the dependent variable in table 4.4 was 41.12, which translates into an average price of $41,120 for a thirty-second ad.

10. See Nielsen Media Research 2000b, p. 83.

Chapter 5
What Is News on Local Television Stations and in Local Newspapers

1. Shapiro and Varian (1999) discuss the implications of information bundling. George and Waldfogel (2000) describe how the presence of demographic groups with different media preferences affects product positioning in newspaper markets. Beam (1998) examines the impact of "market-orientation" on a newspaper's decision-making process. Baker (1994a) analyzes how advertising affects news coverage by changing the trade-offs newspapers make in considering content, advertising revenues, and subscription fees.

2. Survey data indicate that readership of a daily newspaper increases with age, household income, and education. In a 1999 survey, the percentage of those reading a daily newspaper was 42% for those 18–24 versus 72% for 65+, 49% for those with

household incomes less than $40,000 versus 68% for those $75,000+, and 39% for those who did not graduate from high school versus 64% for those with a college degree. See Scripps Treasure Coast Publishing (2001).

3. Researchers vary in how they use the terms "hard" and "soft" news. Scott and Gobetz (1992) define soft news stories on network evening news programs as those that involve human interest topics, features, or nonpolicy issues and find that this news was a small but slightly increasing part of network evening news over time. Patterson (2000, p. 3) defines hard news as "coverage of breaking events involving top leaders, major issues, or significant disruptions in the routines of daily life, such as earthquake or airline disaster." He finds that soft news accounts for an increasing proportion of stories in the media and that the emphasis on soft news coverage contributes to declining interest in the news. The Committee of Concerned Journalists (1998, p. 2) finds that:

> The news media are dividing into market-based niches, with a result that a citizen's perception of society can vary greatly depending on the source of news. Prime time network news magazines ... have all but abandoned covering traditional topics such as government, social welfare, education and economics in favor of lifestyle and news-you-can-use. News magazines which once concentrated heavily on coverage of ideas have moved heavily toward celebrity. Newspapers continue to cover government, foreign policy and domestic policy as a staple. The network news has become a hybrid of all the others.

4. In *Channeling Violence: The Economic Market for Violent Television Programming* (1998), I devote a chapter to analyzing how market forces influence the decisions made by local news directors about how to cover crime. I find that across markets, crime coverage depends on audience interests and that within markets stations often segment into high-crime and low-crime stations. High-crime stations are more likely to cover the details of crimes, are faster paced, use more visuals, and are less likely to provide coverage of trials or discuss crime statistics. Fox and Van Sickel (2001) explore patterns of crime coverage in national media outlets. McManus (1994) and Kerbel (2000) analyze how audience interests and other market factors influence local news decisions. Bernstein, Lacy, Cassara, and Lau (1990) examine how station size affects attention to local versus national/world events, while Harmon (1989) explores how market size affects local news content. Napoli (2001) explores the impact of market conditions on the amount of public affairs programming in local television markets.

5. The Committee of Concerned Journalists (1998) found that coverage in news magazines such as *Time* and *Newsweek* has over time tended to focus less on ideas and more on consumer, health, and celebrity entertainment news. On the spectrum of mass circulation magazines, however, I believe *Time* contains more hard news than magazines that focus on entertainment. Information on circulation by television market comes from Nielsen 1999. Note that *Modern Maturity* is provided to AARP members age 56 or older as part of their membership benefits.

6. The median ages for network viewers in prime time for the 1999/2000 television season were 43.4 ABC, 52.4 CBS, 45.2 NBC, 35.2 Fox, 32.8 UPN, and 28.7 WB (see Downey 2001). Reviewing the 10 P.M. news broadcast of Fox affiliate XETV in San Diego, a television critic noted, "XETV embraces 'the Fox attitude,' a network slogan that refers to prime-time programming such as *The Simpsons, The X-Files, Ally McBeal,* and *Dark Angel.* Pando [the news director] defined the attitude as 'edgy, fearless, and intelligent'" (see Turegano 2001, p. F1). Boemer (1987) examines the impact of the ratings of preceding shows on ratings for local late-evening news broadcasts.

7. Data on television markets comes from Nielsen 1999. Information on station ownership was assembled from Warren Publishing 1999. Nielsen 2000c contains program-level ratings for the local news broadcasts in the sample.

8. Though *People* magazine focuses on entertainment/celebrity news, the evidence in chapter 6 indicates that famous government officials also generate coverage in the magazine. This may indicate some interest in *People* readers in hard news topics. Note that a one percentage point increase in *Time* circulation has a larger impact on hard news coverage than a one percentage point increase in *People* circulation. The means of the dependent variables in table 5.1 are 17.2 for hard news story totals, 12.8 for soft news, and 4.2 for state and local officials.

9. See table 3.3 for data on the relative interests in different news topics of males and females.

10. In extensive empirical analyses of local television news content from 1998 through 2001, the Project for Excellence in Journalism (1998, 1999, 2000, 2001) determined that higher-quality reporting in local television news does bring higher ratings. This research project over four years examined 189 stations and found that outlets with the best coverage quality (i.e., the A-grade stations) had the highest percentage of stations rising in the Nielsen ratings.

11. To promote discussion of health issues, the Kaiser Foundation has funded the distribution of health news segments to NBC affiliates that are designed to run in the late-night local news programs after the entertainment drama *ER*. These "Following *ER*" segments are provided to stations so that they can "run with or without credit to the two nonprofits generating the report" (see Edmonds 2001, p. 2). Biddle (1996) and Owen and Vancheri (2001) describe how networks will often invite local newscasters to interview the stars of network programs and provide story ideas that tie-in with entertainment programming shown during sweeps. In a chi square test of whether coverage of a particular soft news topic was independent of station affiliation, I rejected the hypothesis of independence at the .01 level for each of the stories in the table except *Toy Story*.

12. De Moraes (1999a) notes that the kiss episode drew the largest audience to date (17 million viewers) for the *Ally McBeal* program.

13. George and Waldfogel (2001) find that in some markets local newspapers respond to the penetration of the *New York Times* in their area. They find (p. 15), "Local news coverage is positively related to *New York Times* penetration while national and international coverage is negatively related to *Times* penetration, suggesting that newspapers competing with the *Times* are more likely to emphasize topics not covered by the *Times* and de-emphasize topics extensively covered by the national paper." George (2001) finds that as concentration increases in local newspaper markets product differentiation and variety increase. Roberts, Kunkel, and Layton (2001) explore how market forces affect the relationships between newspapers and readers.

14. To provide comparisons between the television and newspaper analyses, I use the same geographic areas in both sets of analyses—the top fifty television markets in the United States in 1999. This definition means that a given market may be comprised of more than one city (e.g., the fifth-largest market by number of television households is the San Francisco/Oakland/San Jose market). Nielsen refers to the local television markets as Designated Market Areas (DMAs). If data are missing for one of the cities in a DMA I note this through an indicator variable in the analysis. Market-level data come from Nielsen 1999. Editor and Publisher 1999 contains information on paper ownership. The number of newspapers in the market comes from Spot Quotations and Data

1999. I assembled the sample of papers by checking whether Lexis contained transcripts for each local daily paper listed in Nielsen 1999 as one of the top four papers by circulation in each of the top fifty markets. This yielded a sample of seventy-five local daily papers. Missing data in the regression analysis reduce the number of papers analyzed to sixty-eight daily newspapers.

15. City-level data used in tables 5.6 and 5.7 are from the following sources: transfer payment figures from U.S. Department of Commerce 2000, computer employment estimates from U.S. Department of Labor 2000, 1999 contributions to presidential campaigns from Center for Responsive Politics 2000, AIDS data from U.S. Department of Health and Human Services 1999, data on air pollution from U.S. Environmental Protection Agency 2000, violent crime data from U.S. Department of Justice 1999a, and information on drug use from U.S. Department of Justice 1999b.

16. Table 3.10 indicates, for example, that males 50+ rank dealing with problems of the poor as a lower relative priority than males 18–34.

17. Picard, Winter, McCombs, and Lacy (1988) discuss the impact of ownership on newspaper operation. Looking at the content of the *Louisville Courier-Journal* after it shifted from independent ownership to control by the Gannett newspaper chain, Coulson and Hansen (1995, p. 205) found that under Gannett the newspaper "substantially increased the size of its news hole, but the average length of stories dropped, hard news coverage declined, and the number of wire-written stories exceeded staff-written stories."

18. Artwick and Gordon (1998) explore crime coverage in newspapers.

19. Examining newspaper coverage of the 1992 presidential election, Dalton, Beck and Huckfeldt (1998) and Dalton, Beck, Huckfeldt, and Koetzle (1998) find that news coverage of the candidates in the papers is independent of editorial endorsements of the candidates. In a meta-analysis of media bias in presidential elections, D'Alessio and Allen (2000) define three types of bias: gatekeeping (selection of story topics), coverage bias (relative amounts of coverage), and statement bias (favorability of coverage). They find overall no significant biases in newspaper coverage. Kahn and Kenney (2002) find that in Senate races a newspaper's coverage of candidates is affected by the paper's endorsement decision. Bovitz, Druckman, and Lupia (2002) examine the conditions under which news organizations could influence public opinion to support a specific ideology. Demsetz (1989) describes the potential for newspaper owners to influence the public through their papers as an amenity that comes with ownership.

20. In the sample there were thirteen pro-Gore papers, eleven pro-Bush papers, and four neutral papers. The newspapers included in the sample were those daily papers in the top fifty television markets (plus the *USA Today*) that had article texts in Lexis and whose editorial endorsements I could determine.

21. See table 3.7 analysis of Pew (2000b) survey data on media consumption.

Chapter 6
The Changing Nature of the Network Evening News Programs

1. In 1969 the founders or early leaders of each network still served as the chairman of the board: William S. Paley (CBS); David Sarnoff (RCA, which owned NBC); and Leonard Goldenson (ABC). For an overview of the networks that focuses on the 1980s, see Auletta 1992. Data on channels per television household come from Media Dynamics (2001, p. 22), which indicates that averages were 7.1 for 1970 and 63.4 for 2000. Bar-

tels and Rahn (2000) report that the sum of the Nielsen ratings for the three network evening news programs was close to 36 in 1970–71 and 23 in 1999–2000. For the text of Vice President Spiro Agnew's speech attacking network television news on November 13, 1969, see Keogh 1972.

2. Survey data in the 1990s indicated a sharp drop in those who reported that they were regular viewers of the three network nightly new programs. In May 1993, 60% of adults surveyed said they were regular viewers, while 6% reported they never viewed the network evening newscasts. In April and May 2000, only 30% said they were regular viewers and 25% reported they never viewed (Media Dynamics 2001, p. 214). At the same time, the proliferation of viewing options translated into higher consumption overall of television news. In terms of weekly consumption of newscasts and prime-time news magazines, adults in television households averaged 133 minutes per week in the early 1970s versus 349 minutes per week in the late 1990s (Media Dynamics 2000, p. 244).

3. Matusow 1983, p. 84.

4. Ibid., p. 156.

5. Goldberg and Goldberg 1995, p. 103.

6. Matusow 1983, p. 162. Polling data from 1974 indicate that news anchors John Chancellor, Howard K. Smith, and Water Cronkite were perceived by the public to be "near the center" in a spatial model of ideology. See Endersby and Ognianova 1997.

7. McCabe 1987, p. 166.

8. The ownership of the network news organizations by nonmedia companies also raised questions about how the parent companies would be covered. Andrew Heyward, president of CBS News, insisted in 1996 that, "I know it sounds like boilerplate, but I can't imagine a scenario where we would be embarking on a story on nuclear power and someone from Westinghouse said, 'Don't do that.' It's an outlandish proposition." See Marks 1996, p. 1. Yet Larry Grossman, the former president of NBC News, noted, "It's not really a simple thing of: 'You print what I like or you're fired.' It's an environment that's set up, a corporate environment where people with odd views are not encouraged and tend not to be hired."

9. Downie and Kaiser 2002, p. 127. See this work for an excellent discussion of the network evening news programs.

10. McCabe 1987, p. 27.

11. Boyer 1988a, p. 139. "Moments" journalism became increasingly controversial. After CBS aired stories looking at the human impact of President Reagan's policies, columnist George Will wrote, "[I]f journalism becomes a quest for 'moments,' the point of which is to provoke emotions, then journalism becomes avowedly manipulative. The pursuit of such 'moments' involves editorial judgments that are problematic and, at bottom, political. They are judgments about the emotions that viewers should have, and how to cause viewers to have them." See Boyer 1988a, p. 142. For evidence from laboratory experiments on how the framing of news issues by using individuals' stories affects viewers' political opinions, see Iyengar 1991.

12. Ibid., p. 140.

13. Ibid., p. 145.

14. Flickinger 1993, p. 155.

15. Shales 1983, p. A1.

16. All quotations in this paragraph come from Downie and Kaiser 2002, chapter 5, which examines in detail changes in coverage on the network evening news programs.

17. Kimball 1994, p. 43.

18. Boyer 1988a, p. 335.

19. Hall 1991, p. F1.

20. Hall 1992, p. F1.

21. Aucoin 1998, p. D1. The three quotations about the Brokaw/Rather exchanges come from this article.

22. Though the broadcasts try to differentiate themselves, there are stories that each tries to cover because the others will be covering the stories. As vice president of ABC News, Bob Murphy, put it in 1990, "We end up chasing our tails sometimes because we think the others might be chasing down a story, and it doesn't pan out.... We spend a lot of time on what we call 'protective coverage,' staking out places because everybody else is staking them out. There's a pack mentality that develops that you have to control." See Bernstein 1990, p. F1.

23. Hall 1992, p. F1, the source of all quotations in this paragraph.

24. Clarke 2001, p. 5.

25. Shister 2001, source for all Slavin quotations. The analysis of Andrew Tyndall, who produces a newsletter tracking the network news programs, suggests that NBC's reputation for less hard news coverage in the 1990s accurately reflects its product positioning. Hall (1997, p. F1) reports: "According to Tyndall's count, ABC devoted 631 minutes in 1996 to the presidential election campaign, compared to 679 on CBS and 577 on NBC. In terms of stories filed from overseas bureaus, NBC had 327 minutes in 1996, with ABC logging 577 and CBS 592. To date, NBC has devoted 1,020 minutes to the O. J. Simpson story, versus 693 on ABC and 967 on CBS."

26. Goldberg and Goldberg 1995, p. 75.

27. Diamond 1991, p. 39. Chapter 8 analyzes journalists as goods in news markets. In 2000 ABC News hired actor Leonardo DiCaprio to conduct an interview about the environment with President Clinton, a progression toward celebrities as news makers. This prompted an ABC news worker to send a letter to the *Washington Post*, noting "you don't have to be a journalist to be called one on television. The trusted, recognizable TV faces that feed us our daily ration of news are nothing more than multimillion-dollar-a-year celebrity presenters.... The kind of journalism practiced here seems to be less about the loftier goals of civic duty and public responsibility, but about providing the right vehicle to show off the Talent" (see Kovach and Rosenstiel 2001, p. 171).

28. Gunther 1994, p. 123. Examining network evening news coverage of presidential campaigns from 1968–88, Steele and Barnhurst (1996) find "a significant shift toward expressing opinions and judgments of campaign events" by network journalists. They note (p. 203) that the more frequent expressions of opinions and judgments may be related to the need to develop correspondents as "news personalities," used to develop the "sort of brand loyalty that built ratings."

29. Kimball 1994, p. 41.

30. Jones 1986, p. 6–12.

31. Kimball 1994, p. 21. Kerbel (2000, p. 112) provides a lighter description of how NBC's branded segment operates: "One of the most reliable places to turn for outrage is an NBC feature called 'The Fleecing of America,' which runs regularly on Tom's newscast. It emphasizes ways we're being ripped off, generally through government waste and other boondoggles. The name itself points us to outrage. America is being fleeced. It's offensive."

"It's nice to have a reliable place to turn for outrage stories. Actual news events will have an ebb and flow, sometimes generating a lot of outrageous news and sometimes producing very little. But with the availability of a regular feature like 'The Fleecing of America,' we know we can always look forward to a steady supply of outrage no matter what's happening in the news itself."

32. Bianco 1993, p. D1. Jennings predicted that with solutions—to certain problems dealing with social welfare or the family—coming more frequently from conservative intellectuals, that the focus on solutions would be less likely to be perceived as tilting toward a particular ideology.

33. Gunther 1994, p. 121. This book provides an excellent analysis of the evolution of ABC News under Roone Arledge.

34. Ibid., p. 122.

35. Downie and Kaiser 2002, p. 121. In his interview with Downie and Kaiser, Dan Rather indicated (p. 111) that when he reviewed a CBS broadcast from 1981 with them that he was amazed by "the number of brief news items—eight in all, each of ten to fifty seconds in length—that he simply read facing the camera, without fancy graphics or any other diversion. This, said Rather, would never happen today."

36. Gunther 1994, p. 123.

37. Salant 1988, p. 6-1. Another technology made the use of "fiction" even more prominent. On the *CBS Evening News*, images were digitally inserted into the picture so that viewers saw a billboard advertising the CBS News in Times Square when Dan Rather was broadcasting there on New Year's Eve in 1999. In reality, the billboard ad was not there. See Kuczynski 2000, p. A1.

38. Flickinger 1993, p. 301. Shachtman (1995) discusses the use of language over time on the *CBS Evening News*. Analyzing the first broadcast by Walter Cronkite in 1963, he finds that the vocabulary used was that of a "well-prepared high school graduate" and probably contained nine thousand to ten thousand words (p. 122). In Cronkite's last anchor broadcast, in 1981, the working vocabulary of the program had dropped to about seventy-five hundred words. Shachtman finds the language used in a 1993 *CBS Evening News* broadcast to be close to the vocabulary of a seventh-grader. He indicates that the newscast's language has dropped in variety to the point that it is starting to resemble the language of fiction rather than the language of newspapers, magazines, or nonfiction books.

39. Lehrer 1992, p. 231.

40. Boyer 1988a, p. 135.

41. Adatto 1993, p. 65.

42. Ibid., p. 65. Another way to view the information constraints on broadcasters is to calculate the number of words on the evening news programs. Downie and Kaiser (2002, p. 65) note, "The *New York Times* and the *Washington Post* each contain roughly 100,000 words a day—about as many as this book. A typical NBC Nightly News broadcast contains 3,600 words."

43. Shaw 1986a, p. 1.

44. Carmody 1977, p. B1.

45. Hall 1993, p. F1.

46. Downie and Kaiser 2002, p. 135. David Westin, president of ABC News, described the need to focus on the numbers this way: "If you don't care about the size of your audience, you're not in the news business. You're writing a diary." See Auletta 2001, p. 60.

47. Downie and Kaiser 2002, p. 135. The focus on audience demographics is also readily apparent on the morning news programs and prime-time news magazines. Peter McCabe, a senior producer at CBS, who in 1985 started working on *CBS Morning News*, described this exchange with news executive Howard Stringer: "I already knew that within the first hour of the broadcast the number of men watching declined precipitously. So usually, after the middle of the second half hour, by which time we had done the serious stuff, the broadcast would be watered down. The 7:45 segment was considered a kind of pivot because at this point the men went out the door en masse. 'But by eight-thirty,' Stringer explained, 'the number of men watching is even more minuscule than we thought. So it's important to persuade the ladies to stay tuned rather than switch to the others'" (see McCabe 1987, p. 87). Bernard Goldberg asserts that news magazines were less likely to include stories about people who were not their target demographic: "The line I heard over and over again at CBS News and from several sources at NBC was, 'They're not our audience. They don't watch us.' There was a feeling that if the characters were black or Hispanic or lower class, 'our [CBS News] audience' wouldn't be able to identify with them or care about their problems, because CBS news viewers are mostly older white people who live away from the big cities" (see Goldberg 2002, p. 154).

48. Hall 1992, p. F1. News executives also selected program participants in part based on their ability to pull in particular demographics. Downie and Kaiser (2002, p. 233) relate the following story about personnel decisions on Fox: "Heather Nauert had only her blond, youthful good looks and a sincere desire to become a television star when she joined the world of talkers on the Fox News Channel.... 'When I first saw her I thought Heather was our demographic, that she could bring in younger people,' Fox News executive producer Bill Shine said. 'When you have a pundit who is young, and knows what they're talking about, they exude more energy.... If you've got a debate show, you want that energy.'"

49. Kimball 1994, p. 47.

50. Adatto 1993, p. 87. Consistent with this statement that media advisors and news producers have similar tasks, Ailes later went on to work as a news executive, eventually becoming the chairman and chief executive officer of Fox News. In evaluating the political impact of the declining ratings for network news, Bartels and Rahn (2000, cover page) find: "Americans' interest in political campaigns and faith in the electoral process have declined as a result of decreasing exposure to network television news but increased as a result of increasing exposure to political advertising. Conversely, trust in government and positive evaluations of the presidential candidates have increased as a result of declining exposure to network news but declined as a result of increasing exposure to political ads."

51. Utley 2000, p. 232. In his analysis of the growth of soft news across media, Patterson (2000) notes (p. 2) that "the trend toward soft news has contributed to declining interest in the news."

52. Smith 1983, p. C21.

53. Gay 1989, p. 5.

54. See Nielsen 2000a, p. 74. The November 1999 average household audience for each program was 8,409,000 for NBC, 8,026,000 for ABC, and 7,259,000 for CBS. To see the value of scandal in terms of advertising sales, consider the thirty-second commercial price on the special *20/20* episode in 1999 that featured an interview by Barbara Walters

with Monica Lewinsky. Ad prices were estimated to sell for between $300,000 and $500,000 on the program, with ABC asking a top rate of $800,000 (which was five times the regular *20/20* ad price) for some slots. See Mifflin and Elliott 1999.

55. Downie and Kaiser 2002, p. 113. Flickinger (1993, p. 171) notes that total advertising on the *CBS Evening News* grew from 112 minutes in November 1980 to 172 minutes in November 1990. Comstock and Scharrer (1999, p. 26) find that on the networks overall the average number of commercial minutes per hour grew from 10.94 in 1982 to 11.61 in 1987. The percentage of fifteen-second commercials grew from 10.1% in 1985 to 29.5% in 1997 (when 67.1% were thirty-second ads and 1.5% were 1 minute).

56. Jones 1986, p. 6–12.

57. Rosenstiel 1985, p. 1. As vice president of NBC News, Timothy Russert estimated in 1986 that approximately 70% of the network news viewers had already seen a local news program before they watched the network evening news. See Jones 1986.

58. Hall 1991, p. F1.

59. Kurtz 1991, p. D1. While some critics welcomed segments that provided background on issues, others noted the loss of coverage for some breaking news topics as the story count dropped and the use of segments to provide features similar to those in news magazines increased. Describing the longer stories in 1985, Rosenstiel noted (p. 1): "Nightly news programs today contain about 25% fewer stories than they did in 1980, averaging fewer than 15 stories a night, according to research done by Michael Robinson, director of the Media Analysis Project at George Washington University. Many of the stories, on average, are longer. And most nights, Robinson said, the networks have adapted something akin to 'a one-story-a-day format,' in which one issue is identified as primary and much of the broadcast involves background pieces, features, and analysis on that issue."

60. Kurtz 1991, p. D1.

61. Sharbutt 1987, p. 6-1. For discussions of the New York City station changes, see Goldman 1988, Boyer 1988b, and Carter 1991.

62. Gerard 1989.

63. Rosenstiel 1985, p. 1.

64. Rosenstiel (1994, p. A14) noted, "CBS today has only four foreign bureaus, down from close to 20 in its heyday. NBC now has nine, and ABC 13. In 1993, CBS even stopped having a full-time State Department correspondent. Network executives acknowledge that they no longer attempt to systematically cover trends, events and politics of the major capitals of the world."

65. Shaw 1986, p. 1.

66. Berke 1990, p. B1. Criticism of election night television coverage for the 2000 presidential race in part focused on the operation of the polling models used by Voter News Service. See Wakin 2001.

67. Boyer 1988, p. 327.

68. Downie and Kaiser 2002, p. 113.

69. Ibid., p. 121.

70. Rosenstiel 1994, p. A14. Commenting in 1997 on the lack of foreign news coverage, Walter Cronkite said, "The 21-minute newshole they have is totally inadequate in the first place.... That's one of the sins of using any of that 21 minutes for 'Your Health and Mine' and that kind of junk. We don't have enough time to keep up with all the running stories in the world and even in our own country" (see Endrst 1997, p. A1).

71. Studies of network news consistently find an increase in soft news content over time. Defining soft news stories as those that "focus on a human interest topic, feature or nonpolicy issue," Scott and Gobetz (1992) find that from 1972–87 the amount of time on the network evening news devoted to these stories increased but remained only a "small part of the newscast." They note (p. 411), "In the early 1970s average seconds per broadcast devoted to soft news for all three networks ranged from 59 seconds to 73 seconds compared with nearly 90 seconds in 1987." Examining the content of network news in 1977, 1987, and 1997, the Committee of Concerned Journalists (1998) determined that the evening news programs had become a "hybrid," that mixed elements of prime-time news magazines such as consumer and health stories with traditional public affairs topics such as foreign policy. They noted that scandal coverage increased from less than 1% of stories in 1977 to 15% in 1997 and that human interest and quality of life coverage grew from 8% of stories to 16% in 1997. Thomas Patterson (2000) found that the probability a viewer would encounter a soft news story on the network evening news grew steadily from 1994 to 1998.

72. The twenty-five years of Intriguing People yielded a total of 629 possible people to analyze. Some were dropped from the analysis because they were historical figures (e.g., Mozart), fictitious (e.g., Max Headroom, Bart Simpson), or were not an individual (e.g., Mount Saint Helens). Presidents, Vice Presidents, and First Ladies were not included in the analysis since the *People* personalities are being used to chart trends in soft news coverage on network news, and these figures are clearly hard news personalities. Approximately 9% of the entries were thus dropped, yielding a set of 571 entries to examine. I refer to this as the full sample, and then divide it further into soft new personalities (i.e., entertainers, crime personalities, sports figures, and royalty) and those who are not soft news personalities. The soft news personalities accounted for 59% of the 571 people analyzed. To see the type of individuals selected yearly by the magazine, consider the 1998 Most Intriguing People: the American People, Judy Blume, James Brolin, Hillary Clinton, Katie Couric, Cameron Diaz, Leonardo DiCaprio, Matt Drudge, Calista Flockhart, Michael J. Fox, Edward Fugger, John Glenn, Alan Greenspan, Geri Halliwell, Lauryn Hill, David Kaczynski, Joan Kroc, Emeril Lagasse, Camryn Manheim, Mark McGwire, Chris Rock, Adam Sandler, Kenneth Starr, Oprah Winfrey, and the World War II Soldier. All but the American People, Hillary Clinton, and the Worl War II Soldier were included in the sample of 571 figures to analyze. The Vanderbilt Television News Archive (http://tvnews.vanderbilt.edu) provides summaries of network news program stories, which I searched to determine coverage in a given year of each *People* personality.

73. For tables 6.1 through 6.4, the question arises whether differences in coverage are statistically significant across time. One can view the story topics examined as the complete universe of topics rather than a sample, in which case statistical significance is not a factor. For example, the analysis of *CQ* votes captures all the *CQ* votes within a given five-year period, so coverage percentages represent a full accounting of whether *CQ* votes were covered on the day or day after a vote happened. One could also view coverage of *CQ* votes as a way to sample hard news stories, where the magazine's key votes are used as a sample to test theories about political news. In that case tests of statistical significance would be in order. For table 6.1, twelve chi-square tests were conducted. For the full *People* sample, the soft news personalities, and the not soft news personalities, a chi-square test of whether coverage percentage was inde-

pendent of the five-year time intervals was calculated for ABC, CBS, NBS, and all three networks. I could not reject at the .10 level the independence hypothesis for any of these tests. For table 6.2 I could reject the independence hypothesis at the .05 level for coverage on CBS for the full sample, coverage of constitutional law cases on CBS at the .10 level, and coverage of nonconstitutional cases for ABC (.05), CBS (.10), and the three networks (.10). For the *CQ* votes in table 6.3, I could reject the hypothesis that coverage was independent of time interval for all twelve chi-square tests at the .10 level or better. For the interest group votes in table 6.4, I reject at the .01 level the hypothesis that coverage is independent of time interval for the full sample for each network and all three networks together. The same holds true for the ADA sample. For the ACU sample I can reject the independence hypothesis for CBS (.01) and all networks combined (.10).

74. For tables 6.1 through 6.4, the question can also be asked of whether coverage within a given time period is independent of network. For each of the three samples in table 6.1, I cannot reject at the .10 level the hypothesis that coverage is independent of network within a given time interval. For table 6.2 I can reject the hypothesis at the .05 level for the full sample and constitutional law sample for 1984–88 and for the full sample at the .10 level for 1989–93 and 1994–98. For table 6.3 I can reject the hypothesis that coverage is independent of network for the 1969–73 interval for the full sample (.05) and the Senate (.1). For table 6.4, I can reject the independence hypothesis for the 1974–78 interval for the full sample (.01), ADA (.05), and ACU (.01) and for the 1979–83 period for the full sample (.10).

75. Each year the *Harvard Law Review* contains an article analyzing the previous Supreme Court term. I use the table of cases from that article to generate the set of cases to test network coverage of Supreme Court decisions over time. Cases decided in a given term (e.g., 1998 term) may actually have been announced in the following year (1999). The intervals in table 6.2 refer to term years. For the regression analysis in table 6.6, data used for independent variables relate to the actual year the decision was handed down. For a discussion of the difficulties with identifying salient Supreme Court cases and the drawbacks of using the *Harvard Law Review*, see Epstein and Segal 2000. Slotnick and Segal (1998) examine in detail network coverage of Supreme Court decisions from the 1989 and 1994 terms.

76. Each year *Congressional Quarterly* selects what it calls the "key votes" in the House and Senate. The magazine indicates that votes are selected based on whether they involve significant controversy, presidential or political power struggles, or issues that have a major impact on people. For 1998, the *CQ* key votes in the Senate involved a cloning ban, campaign finance, IMF funding, NATO expansion, skilled worker visas, tobacco legislation, education savings accounts, same-sex military training, overseas economic sanctions, partial birth abortion, and omnibus appropriations.

77. Describing its selection of Senate votes used to calculate ADA ratings in 2001, the organization's website (ADA 2002) noted: "The votes selected cover a full spectrum of domestic, foreign, economic, military, environmental and social issues. We tried to select votes which display sharp liberal/conservative contrasts. In many instances we have chosen procedural votes: amendments, motions to table, or votes on rules for debate. Often these votes reveal true attitudes frequently obscured in the final votes." The ACU website (ACU 2002) described its selection of votes in this way: "The ACU scorecard integrates votes on economic and budget matters, social and cultural issues, defense and

foreign policy concerns, and institutional reform issues to create a balanced picture of an individual Member of Congress' ideological predisposition." The willingness of the interest groups to use procedural votes (as distinct from final votes on a bill) in their scorecards may be one reason that their votes are less likely to receive network coverage than those listed by *CQ*.

78. For table 6.5 a difference of means t-test was calculated for each network for each sample (soft news personalities, not soft news personalities, Supreme Court cases, *CQ* votes, and interest group votes) to determine whether there was a statistically significant difference in mean number of stories or coverage length between the first time interval and the last time period. For ABC the only statistically significant differences were for number of Supreme Court case stories (.17 difference, .05 level), number of interest group vote stories (.20 higher in the 1969–73 period, .10 level), and coverage length of *CQ* votes (94.3 seconds higher in the 1994–98 interval, .01 level). For CBS, the only statistically significant difference was *CQ* coverage length. The 51.8 second difference between mean coverage length in the years 1969–73 (116.2) and 1994–98 (168.1) was significant at the .05 level. For NBC, the statistically significant differences were Supreme Court case coverage length (42.9 seconds higher in later period, .05 level), *CQ* mean coverage time (100.2 seconds higher in the years 1994–98 versus 1969–73, .01 level), and mean number of interest group stories (.20 stories more in earlier period, .05 level).

79. On June 27, 1984 the FCC issued a unanimous decision that removed the requirement that television stations had to broadcast a minimum amount of news and local programming and removed the requirement that stations provide the FCC with detailed information (i.e., programming logs) on their broadcast content. The FCC's previous rules had required commercial television stations to use a minimum of 5% of their time for news and public affairs programming and a minimum of 5% for local programming. The president of the National Association of Broadcasters praised the ruling as a "welcome and logical next step down the road of broadcast deregulation" (Burnham 1984, p. C1). Commenting on the changes in public affairs requirements, former CBS producer Fred W. Friendly predicted, "I think a lot of stations will do absolutely nothing if they don't have to be held accountable" (Berger 1984, C1). Though I use 1984 as an indicator for the year of television deregulation, several caveats should be noted. Restrictions on the ownership of television stations, such as the rule that limited the number of stations a company could own, meant that some aspects of the television industry remained regulated. In addition, the moves toward deregulation took place at the same time when cable competition was increasing and ownership of the networks was changing. I try to control for this in part by including in some specifications the percentage of households with cable and the percentage of stories that focused on network news costs. It still remains difficult to isolate the impact of deregulation alone through the use of the deregulation indicator variable.

80. Data on the percentage of households with cable came from Television Bureau of Advertising (http://www.tvb.org). To create the cost variable, the Lexis major newspaper file was searched for each network for articles that mentioned the network news (e.g., CBS News). Another search was done for articles mentioning the network's news within fifty words of "cost" or "employee" or "cut." The number of these articles that dealt with business aspects of the network news formed the numerator for the cost variable, with the denominator being the total articles about the network news; this ratio was multiplied by 100 to yield a percentage. For CBS News, for example, the vari-

able represents the percentage of stories about CBS News in a given year that mentioned costs or business decisions surrounding budget cuts or changes in employee numbers.

Chapter 7
News on the Net

1. Michael Lewis (1999) chronicles the search for new applications of the Internet in *The New New Thing*. Marvin Kalb (1998) uses media coverage of the Monica Lewinsky scandal to outline the characteristics of the "new news," characteristics that include a lack of sourcing, rush to judgment, and operation of journalists as celebrities. For the impact on journalism of the rapid transmission of information, see Kovach and Rosenstiel (1999). Gitlin (2001) discusses the general impact on individuals of speeding up the transmission of information

2. Herbert Simon (1996) stressed the importance of the scarcity of attention in understanding information markets. Aigrain (1997) and Goldhaber (1997) examine the impact of limited attention for information on the operation of the Internet.

3. For assessments of the operation of markets on the Internet, see Bollier 1997, Smith, Bailey, and Brynjolfsson 2000, and DeLong and Froomkin 2000.

4. Sunstein (2001a,b) analyzes the potential dangers associated with the fragmentation of expression. He notes that the ability of individuals to customize their news on the Internet and seek out specialized websites may reduce the common experiences fostered by consumption of general interest media products and reduce the likelihood that individuals are exposed to new ideas or ideas they disagree with. For an early analysis of customized online news services, see Harper (1997).

5. See Barlow 1994. Boyle (1996) discusses the tensions between laws that favor the creation versus the distribution of information and criticizes much of the economic literature on information markets.

6. Shapiro and Varian (1999) provide an overview of network effects. Bikhchandani, Hirshleifer, and Welch (1998) discuss the operation of information cascades.

7. Kerber (2001) and Irwin (2000) analyze the financial difficulties faced by political websites. The website site Voter.com attracted nearly three million unique visitors in November 2000 but shut down in February 2001. The website exhausted $22 million in venture capital financing in setting up its extensive coverage of politics, yet generated less than $1 million in annual revenues. For discussions of the possible winner-take-all nature of Internet markets, see Adamic and Huberman 1999, Barabasi and Albert 1999, and Noe and Parker 2000. Barringer (2001) describes the advantages that well-known news organizations have in attracting readers on the Internet. A study by the Committee of Concerned Journalists (2000) of the 2000 presidential primaries found that the websites of traditional media outlets were more likely to offer original reporting than the popular web portal sites (e.g., Yahoo, Netscape, AOL News), which generally used wire story services for coverage. Survey data from the Pew Research Center for the People and the Press (2000c) indicate that for individuals who went online for election 2000 news that more than half reported that they most often used websites of traditional media companies (e.g., CNN or *New York Times*) rather than news sites of commercial online services or online publications or political sites. For analysis of political journalism on the Internet, see Institute for Politics, Democracy, and the Internet 2002.

8. Lupia (2001a) analyzes the operation during the 2000 presidential election of the site webwhiteandblue.org, a political information website supported by the Markle Foundation. The site hosted the first daily online exchange among the presidential candidates.

9. Piller (2000) describes the difficulties of attracting revenues for news sites. Beauprez (2000), Lane (2000), and Schwartz (2000) discuss the market online for pornography.

10. A report by Morgan Stanley Dean Witter noted in February 2001 that the six largest advertisers in the United States spent less than 1% of their advertising budgets on the Web. The firm report estimated that between 55 and 70% of spending on Web advertising came from dot.com businesses.

11. The *Los Angeles Times* and *Washington Post* sued the conservative website *Free Republic* (www.freerepublic.com) for the posting on its site copies of their articles verbatim. The site held that the postings were part of fair use of the newspaper articles; members frequently posted full texts in their discussions of media bias and the newspapers' coverage of events. A U.S. District Court judge rejected this defense and held the website liable for copyright infringement (see *Tech Law Journal* 2000). In 2001 the Supreme Court ruled that newspaper publishers had violated the copyrights of freelance authors by placing their works in electronic databases without getting their prior permission (see Greenhouse 2001). In 1997 the NBA lost a federal appeals court case in which the league tried to prohibit Motorola from transmitting continuously updated scores during the course of a game over its pager network. The court ruled that the scores were news and not protected by the NBA's copyright (see Wolinsky 1997).

12. The data on Internet use come from Pew 2000b, a survey conducted in April–May 2000 with a sample size of 3,142. Sample weights based on census data are used in table 7.1, in the same manner as in chapter 3. In a chi-square test of whether news use or interest in a particular news type was independent of demographic group in table 7.1, I rejected the hypothesis of independence at the .01 level for each news type except the weather.

13. The circulation and link counts for the newspapers mentioned here are *Wall Street Journal* 1,752,693 daily circulation and 51,400 links; *USA Today* 1,671,539 and 225,379; *New York Times* 1,086,293 and 180,808; *Los Angeles Times* 1,078,186 and 68,665; *Washington Post* 763,305 and 132,781; *Detroit News* 232,434 and 148,820; *Seattle Times* 219,698 and 95,365; and *Raleigh News and Observer* 159,156 and 46,656. Link counts came from using the search "link:[site address]" on www.altavista.com in August, 2000. Daily circulations for newspapers (using figures dated September 1999) came from *Editor and Publisher* information available at www.mediainfo.com.

14. Demographic data on the zip codes in the sample generally came from 1999 estimates available at www.demographics.caci.com. The Gale Literary Database of Contemporary Authors was searched at www.galenet.com to derive a count of the number of authors with a given zip code appearing in their biographical information. The Opensecrets website contained information on political contributions reported to the Federal Election Commission. Zip code totals for 2000 are for contributions reported through July 1, 2000 for the federal contributions totals. Presidential campaign contribution totals are for January 1, 1999 through May 31, 2000. Levit (1993) notes that in the *Buckley v. Valeo* decision the Supreme Court held that restrictions on campaign expenditures posed more dangers to freedom of expression than limitations on political contributions.

15. See Sen (1976) for a discussion and definition of the Gini coefficient. To see how

the Gini coefficient may be defined, consider the cumulative distributions in figure 7.1. Imagine a forty-five-degree line running across the table. The more unequal the distribution of circulation across papers, the greater the gap between the forty-five-degree line and the cumulative distribution curve. If each of the one hundred papers had 1% of the circulation, then the cumulative distribution line would be the same as the forty-five-degree line. The Gini coefficient is defined as the area between the forty-five degree line and the cumulative distribution line, divided by the total area under the forty-five-degree line. If there is total equality the area is 0. If all circulation were accounted for by the top paper, the ratio would be 1. The Gini coefficients for the data in figure 7.1 are .37 for circulation and .69 for links.

16. GoTo information for advertisers (see www.goto.com/d/about/advertisers) in July 2000 indicated that the site received over 150 million searches per month. The information for advertisers noted that in December 1999 the site was the eighteenth most heavily visited site on the Internet and that Media Metrix data indicated more than 10 million unique users during the month of November 1999 for the network.

17. Some of the Internet activity using the term "Vitamin C" in May 2000 may also have been related to the singer Colleen Fitzpatrick, who performed under that name.

Chapter 8
Journalists as Goods

1. In summer 2001 DirecTV, a digital satellite service, offered subscribers more than 225 channels (see www.directv.com). The average number of channels received in U.S. television households grew from twenty-eight in 1988 to forty-nine in 1997. Households clearly have favorites among these channels. The average number of channels viewed per household, where viewing is defined as "10 or more continuous minutes per channel," was twelve in 1997. See Nielsen Media Research 1998, p. 19.

2. For historical ratings and share information, see Nielsen Media Research 1998, p. 25. The estimate of a combined 44% share for 2000 viewing comes from Smith 2001.

3. Data on average households viewing network evening news programs, advertising rates, and cost per thousand viewing households used in this chapter come from Television Bureau of Advertising 2001.

4. For a comprehensive analysis of the separation between fame and merit in the marketplace, see Cowen 2000.

5. Fallows (1996) discusses the impact of journalists accepting paid speaking engagements. Germond (1999) provides a personal account of the trade-offs involved in appearing on *The McLaughlin Group*, participating in speaking engagements, and writing newspaper columns.

6. Ansolabehere and Iyengar (1995) examine the interaction between use of negative language and ideology in political advertising. They find (p. 92) that "the more Republican and conservative the electorate, the less they like governments and its politicians, and so the more effective negative advertisements are." On the ideological differences among voters, they note (p. 94):

> Identification as either an Independent or a Republican generally carries with it a strong belief in the fallibility of government. Republicans and to some extent Independents tend to oppose

new or expanded government programs; they tend to believe in private, rather than public, so-lutions to social problems. Promises of new government actions and spending, whether on jobs programs or jails, will resonate less well with these voters than messages that implicate an op-posing candidate in the failures of existing policies. The Democratic ideology, by contrast, has developed a firm faith in the necessity of government interventions to alleviate the failures of private markets and the inequities in society. Democratic voters want to hear not what has failed, but what a candidate will do to fix what ails us. Democrats generally have faith that the federal government will do the right thing; Republicans and Independents do not.

7. McLuhan 1964, p. 23.

8. To see the increase in the real amounts paid by advertisers to reach viewers, con-sider the change in cost per thousand viewing homes. For network primetime programs in 1975, the average cost per thousand viewing homes paid by advertisers was $7.41 in 1999 dollars. In 1999 this figure had grown to $13.41.

9. The salary per viewing household figure may be high for Barbara Walters because it ignores the viewers attracted to the specials she anchored. One of the reasons she earned a higher salary than other network news anchors in 1976 was her ability to draw viewers to special programming. In 1999, when Walters earned ten million dollars in salary, she was coanchor of the newsmagazine *20/20*, cohost and executive producer of the talk show *The View*, and host of *The Barbara Walters Specials*.

10. The data on speaking fees were collected from www.leadingauthorities.com. For individuals that listed a range of fees for their appearances, I used the higher fee to cal-culate the mean speaking fees. The *T* statistic for the difference of means test for fees for journalists versus politicians was 2.3 (statistically significant at the .05 level). The higher speaking fees are not surprising since reporters often garner more airtime than the politicians they cover. In studying the presidential election coverage in 2000, the Center for Media and Public Affairs (2000) found: "On an average night, reporters speak for a total of seven minutes of election news airtime on the three network evening newscasts, compared to only one minute for Al Gore and George Bush combined—just under ten seconds per night for each candidate on each network. All other sources combined for an average of one and a half minutes of airtime per night."

11. The Lexis files searched were "curnws" (current news), "mags" (magazines), and "majpap" (major papers). Note that these files can contain the text of articles or broad-cast reports by some of the journalists, as well as references to them in articles by other reporters. I treat all of these as relevant to measuring how well-known or discussed the reporters are.

12. Dyson (1998, pp. 178–201) notes that those who create intellectual content may at times give their information away for free in order to build a demand for speeches or develop a reputation that leads to consulting or other job opportunities.

13. See Helmore 2000, which notes, "Westin has, according to some reports, also urged his correspondents to develop interesting personal lives, to get themselves in the gossip columns and create more 'buzz' to bring in viewers." Mayer 2000 also chronicles the pressure on news personnel at ABC to attract viewers. After ABC News sent Leonardo DiCaprio, a film actor, to talk with President Clinton about the state of the environment, a backlash occurred within the organization. One staffer sent a letter to the *Washington Post* that said in part: "You don't have to be a journalist to be called one on television. The trusted, recognizable TV faces that feed us our daily ration of news

are nothing more than multimillion-dollar-a-year celebrity presenters.... The kind of journalism practiced here seems to be less about the loftier goals of civic duty and public responsibility, but about providing the right vehicle to show off the Talent" (see Kovach and Rosensteil 2001, p. 171).

14. See Daley 1999. The *Columbia Journalism Review* (1999, p. 45) found that *Time* paid "up to $200" to reporters and editors for appearances in the media. In general, such payments were higher for national outlets than local ones, and appearances on television were rewarded more than those on radio. *Newsweek* similarly paid reporters and editors for broadcast appearances. Appearances on television resulted in the highest payments, followed by large market radio.

15. See Auletta 2001a, p. 243.

16. Local television anchors may have terms in their contracts that forbid significant changes in appearance without station approval. When Cindy Hernandez, a evening news anchor on KOB-TV in Albuquerque, N.M., got a short haircut without informing station management, she was suspended for two days. Commenting on the reprimand, she noted, "They think it looks mean and cold, and they want newscasters who are warm and fuzzy" (see Brown 2001, p. 3). Describing the critique of her work by news consultants and management, a former television journalist in New York City related, "They came to the conclusion that my delivery was too strong and they wanted to soften me up. So they decided that I had to wear sweaters. I was barred from wearing suits or anything black" (see Jackson 2001, which also contains a defense of the emphasis on anchor appearances). Eric Braun, vice president for news at a company (Raycom Media) that controls more than thirty-five local television stations, noted that, "Anchors are really the paper and the ink you write your journalism on. The wrong cock of a head, a wrongly raised eyebrow can affect credibility. Viewers want to watch interesting people who they can like and are nice and interesting."

17. Fallows (1996, pp. 117–18) includes this description from Paul Magnusson, a journalist from *Business Week* who was coached on how to talk on television: "The guy who was coaching us kept saying the same thing over and over to different people. He'd interview us on the screen and then play back the tape. He'd say, "When I asked you this question, you gave me a long answer! You should give me a much shorter answer! If I ask you whether the budget deficit is a good thing or a bad thing, you should not say, 'Well, it stimulates the economy but it passes on a burden.' You have to say, 'It's a great idea!' Or, 'It's a terrible idea!' It doesn't matter which."

18. *Slate* (slate.msn.com) listed a set of print columnists as pundits and provided a list of television programs where pundits appear. To develop the sample of political pundits, I searched in Lexis with the name of each print columnist listed and the names of the regular commentators or guests on the television programs listed. This yielded a set of fifty-six pundits who registered one-hundred or more hits in the Lexis transcript, major papers, and magazine files in 1999. The sample includes Elizabeth Arnold, Dan Balz, Fred Barnes, Michael Barone, Richard Berke, Tony Blankley, Wolf Blitzer, Gloria Borger, David Broder, Ronald Brownstein, Margaret Carlson, Tucker Carlson, Eleanor Clift, Richard Cohen, Ceci Connolly, E. J. Dionne, Sam Donaldson, Maureen Dowd, Matt Drudge, David Gergen, Jack Germond, Paul Gigot, Tom Gjelten, Ellen Goodman, Jeff Greenfield, Bob Herbert, Brit Hume, Al Hunt, Gwen Ifill, Molly Ivins, Al Kamen, Mickey Kaus, Michael Kelly, Morton Kondracke, Charles Krauthammer, William Kristol, Howard Kurtz, Mara Liasson, Mary Matalin, Mary McGory, Robert Novak,

Lawrence O'Donnell, Thomas Oliphant, Clarence Page, David Plotz, Bill Press, Cokie Roberts, Tim Russert, William Safire, Robert Samuelson, Bob Schieffer, Mark Shields, Tony Snow, George Will, Juan Williams, and Jules Witcover. For each of these pundits the Lexis files for transcripts, major newspapers, and magazines were searched for their written or spoken words for a set of twelve weeks (one randomly selected per month) in 1999. Transcripts from *Washington Week in Review* and *The McLaughlin Group* came from the websites for the programs. The writings and transcripts of the pundits, which totaled 3,325 segments of between four hundred and five hundred words, were collected and run through the DICTION software program.

19. McManus (1994 pp. 162–63) summarized the rules of local television reporting that emerge from market dictates as

1. Seek images over ideas.... 2. Seek emotion over analysis.... Corollary A: Avoid complexity.... Corollary B: Dramatize where possible.... 3. Exaggerate, if needed, to add appeal.... 4. Avoid extensive news-gathering.

Robert MacNeil, the former coanchor of the *MacNeil/Lehrer Newshour* on PBS, noted that on most television news programs the assumptions are made "that bite-sized is best, that complexity must be avoided, that nuances are dispensable, that qualifications impede the simple message, that visual stimulation is a substitute for thought, and that verbal precision is an anachronism" (see Postman 1985, p. 105). The impact of the market on television news has been evident since the early years of network news. In 1963 when broadcast network news expanded from a fifteen-minute program to a thirty-minute program, Reuven Frank of NBC instructed reporters, "Every news story should, without any sacrifice of probity or responsibility, display the attributes of fiction, of drama. It should have structure and conflict, problem and denouement, rising action and falling action, a beginning, a middle and an end" (see Patterson 1993, p. 80).

20. Hart, the author of DICTION, uses the software to analyze differences in how print versus television outlets have covered presidential candidates over time. He finds (2000, p. 198), "These differences are important because the two media serve such different constituencies: television delivers quick, digestible bits of information to a great many people while newspapers slow their readers down, focusing on ideas rather than personalities."

21. These comparisons between the language of pundits on print versus television ignore the additional information conveyed by sound and images on television programs. For an excellent overview of how television transmits political information, see Graber 2001.

22. The results for Mara Liasson show that the differences between her expression on public radio versus television are similar to the differences between the expression of other pundits in print versus television. Fewer statistically significant differences are apparent in the expressions of Cokie Roberts on NPR versus television.

23. Tim Russert had thirteen references within two words of conservative, out of 4,703 references in the "curnws" file. I treated this as a false positive (given his prior work for Democratic Senator Patrick Moynihan and Governor Mario Cuomo) and labeled him as a moderate. While pundit ideologies are part of market reputations, politicians also may attempt to label journalists as biased for their own partisan purposes. See Domke et al. 1999 and Watts et al. 1999.

24. Political ideologies and partisan identifications are similar to brand images that

can be used by candidates to evoke specific responses from voters. On the philosophical differences between liberalism and conservatism, see Huntington 1957, and Gould and Truitt 1973. For an example of how partisan (i.e., Democratic and Republican) stereotypes affect the reactions of voters to candidates, see Rahn 1993. Roemer (1994) explores how parties can use ideologies (e.g., theories of how the economy operates) as well as issue positions to attract voters. Jacoby (1991) explores the interaction between ideology and citizen attitudes about particular issues. Hart (2000) finds there are distinct differences in the language used by Democratic and Republican presidential candidates that are evident from the 1940s through the 1990s.

Chapter 9
Content, Consequences, and Policy Choices

1. Greenhouse (2001) describes the Supreme Court ruling that held newspaper and magazine publishers were violating copyright law by making the articles of freelance writers available via electronic archives without the writers' permission. Miller (1999) reports on a U.S. District Court preliminary ruling that rejected the argument by the conservative website, www.freerepublic.com, that users should be able under the "fair use" doctrine to post the full text of newspaper articles in discussions without seeking copyright permission. Lessig (2001) documents how copyright and patent cases are changing the way that software codes are used to facilitate communication and commerce on the Internet.

2. The Communications Act of 1934 establishes that the FCC can grant broadcast licenses to applicants who demonstrate that their stations will broadcast in the "public interest, convenience, and necessity." Krasnow and Goodman (1998) trace the historical origin of the term and examine the many different ways it has been interpreted by the FCC over decades of implementation. Fowler and Brenner (1982) offer an interpretation of the standard under the Reagan administration when Fowler chaired the FCC, while Hundt (1996) sets forth his interpretation of the standard as FCC chairman during the debate over educational programming for children in the Clinton administration. Geller (1998) discusses public interest standards in the digital age. Aufderheide (1999) describes the treatment of public interest requirements during debate over the Telecommunications Act of 1996.

3. For an accessible description of Arrow's work on social welfare functions, see Mueller 1979.

4. Posner (1986) examines free speech issues in a benefit-cost framework. Spitzer (1998) provides an overview of the economics of free expression. For examples of how economics can be used to analyze telecommunications issues, see Owen 1975, Brennan 1983, McMillan 1994, Hausman and Sidak 1999, and Noll 2002. For an analysis of the market for public intellectuals, see Posner 2001.

5. For assessments of the contributions and limitations of economic reasoning in analyzing media policy, see Sunstein 1990, 1993, 2000a, and Entman and Wildman 1992.

6. The example that Sen (1970) develops at length does involve the consumption of ideas, specifically the consumption of D. H. Lawrence's novel *Lady Chatterly's Lover*.

7. Discussions of the criteria used to judge debates about free speech, the marketplace of ideas, and the role of media and democracy include Meiklejohn 1948, Baker 1978, Schauer 1982, Smolla 1992, Entman 1993, Fish 1994, Krattenmaker and Powe 1994,

Balkin 1995, Sullivan 1995, Baker 1997, Corn-Revere 1997, Baker 1998, Shaw 1999, Kro-toszynski and Blaiklock 2000, and Sunstein 2000. Price (1994) and Baker (2000) consider the implications of global media markets for trade in ideas. Mickiewicz (1997) examines in detail the interaction of the media, markets, and elections in Russia.

8. Norris (2000) explores the links between media consumption and political participation. The debate over FCC media ownership rules has generated extensive discussion of how to measure diversity and participation in media markets (see Consumers Union et al. 2002, and FCC Roundtable Discussion on Media Ownership Policies 2001). Entman and Rojecki (2000) offer extensive evidence on media portrayals of race in both news and entertainment programming.

9. Hanemann (1994) and Portney (1994) review the use of contingent valuation to analyze environmental outcomes.

10. Hausman (1997) examines the taxes on interstate telephone service that are used to fund the program that provides discounts on Internet access for public schools. He concludes (p. 2) that "the efficiency loss to the economy for every $1 raised to pay for the Internet access discounts is an additional $1.05 to $1.25 beyond the money raised for Internet discounts" and discusses "an alternative method by which the FCC could have raised the revenue for the Internet discounts which would have a near zero cost to the economy." Hazlett (2001) notes the high costs of FCC policies meant to foster the growth of over-the-air digital television, costs that include the purchase of new sets, changes in station equipment, and use of spectrum. He estimates that with the large expected growth in subscription television by 2004, fewer than ten million U.S. households would depend on television signals received over the air. His analysis concludes that "if something less than $3 billion is invested to move remaining over-the-air TV viewers to a 'limited basic' cable or satellite TV service, substantial social gains result," since consumers could avoid costly new sets and spectrum could be reallocated.

11. Examples of empirical assessments of news markets include Schwer and Danesh-vary 1995 (contingent valuation), Crawford 1997b (cable prices), Hazlett and Sosa 1997 (Fairness Doctrine), George and Waldfogel 2000 (product positioning in newspaper markets), 2001 (impact of New York Times on local paper markets), George 2001 (concentration of newspaper ownership), and Napoli 2001 (public affairs programming). Recent theoretical models focusing on the economics of reporting include the examination by Cox and Goldman (1994) of how economic incentives affect the accuracy of reporting, and the modeling by Bovitz, Druckman, and Lupia (2002) of how the internal organization of a media firm can affect the ability of ideological reporters, editors, or owners to have an impact on public opinion. (For an assessment of legal issues involved in accuracy and reporting, see Levi 2000.) Analyzing the impact of media ownership in a sample of ninety-seven countries, Djankov, McLiesh, Nenova, and Shleifer (2001) find that government ownership of the media has a negative impact on education and health outcomes. Besley and Prat 2001, Besley and Burgess 2001, and Besley, Burgess, and Prat 2002 examine the impact of the media on political accountability. Lott (1999) explores the incentives politicians have for government media ownership.

12. See "White House Seeks a Change in Rules on Air Pollution," by Katharine Q. Seelye, which appeared on the page A1 of the New York Times on June 14, 2002.

13. There are many models of how information affects the operation of democracy; see Hinich and Munger 1994, Bartels and Vavreck 2000, and Bennett and Entman 2001. Baker (2002) sets forth four different conceptions of democracy (elite, republican, lib-

eral pluralist, complex) and traces out the implications for media policy of the role of citizens in each type of democracy. Ferejohn and Kuklinski (1990) examine how information affects political decision making. For a general description of principal-agent relations in politics, see Kiewiet and McCubbins 1991. Wood (1988) examines the principal-agent relationships involved in the EPA's enforcement of the Clean Air Act. Hamilton (1997) examines how information available to voters may have affected congressional votes on technical amendments versus general passage of the Superfund reauthorization bill.

14. See Lupia, McCubbins, Popkin 2000.

15. For debates about the operation and implications of the Condorcet jury theorem, see Ladha 1992, Austen-Smith and Banks 1996, and McLennan 1998.

16. Eskridge (1988) describes how public choice models have supplanted the traditional "optimistic pluralism" view of politics. Lohmann (1998) describes the advantages that accrue to interest groups that are better able to monitor legislative actions. Baker (2000) details how segmented media outlets can provide content that stimulates interest and activity among different groups of citizens.

17. The spread of a new media technology often brings changes in political interactions. Stromberg (2001) indicates that, controlling for other factors, more New Deal relief funds were distributed to counties with more radio listeners. Prior (2002) finds that the incumbency advantage in the House of Representatives increased with the rise of television, and traces this to local news coverage of incumbents. Kalb (1998, 2001) describes how the Internet affected the reporting of the Monica Lewinsky scandal.

18. For evidence on agenda setting, see Watt, Mazza, and Snyder 1993, Dalton, Beck, Huckfeldt, Koetzle 1998, and Edwards and Wood 1999. Miller and Krosnick (2000) analyze the factors that influence priming. Druckman (2001a,b) shows how lab experiments can be used to test framing theories. For other evidence on how the media affect public opinion, see Entman 1989, Mutz and Soss 1997, Graber, McQuail, and Norris 1998, Mutz 1998, Watts, Domke, Shah, and Fan 1999, Eveland and Scheufele 2000, Graber 2000, Mutz and Martin 2001, and Prior 2003. Ansolabehere, Behr, and Iyengar (1993) and Paletz (1999) provide overviews of media effects. Lippman (1922) offered a early analysis of the impact of news on public opinion.

19. Price and Zaller (1993) point out the importance of determining who "gets the news," e.g., who is exposed to news, pays attention, comprehends, and remembers it. They conclude that (p. 133) "in survey research applications that require estimates of individual differences in the reception of potentially influential political communications, a measure of general prior knowledge—not a measure of news media use—is likely to be the most effective indicator."

20. Zaller (1992) analyzes how individuals' political predispositions affect their reaction to new information.

21. To see how researchers attempt to separate out the impact of news about the economy on public opinion from the impact of other factors such as real world economic conditions, see Iyengar and Kinder 1987, Nadeau, Niemi, Fan, and Amato 1999, Shah, Watts, Domke, Fan, and Fibison 1999, and Duch, Palmer, and Anderson 2000.

22. For lab experiments involving the political content of television, see Iyengar and Kinder 1987, Iyengar 1991, and Ansolabehere and Iyengar 1995. Lupia (2001a) uses data from an online lab study to analyze use of Internet political information in the 2000 elections.

23. Bartels begins his 1993 article "Messages Received: The Political Impact of Media Exposure" with this sobering assessment (p. 267), "The state of research on media effects is one of the most notable embarrassments of modern social science." He demonstrates that (p. 275) "attention to the effects of measurement error significantly increases the apparent impact of media exposure on opinion change in a presidential campaign setting." Zaller (1996) shows how attention to measurement effects and modeling of information flows can reveal large media effects.

24. For analyses of how citizens make decisions, see Sniderman, Brody, and Tetlock 1991, Lupia, McCubbins, and Popkin 2000, and Kuklinski, Quirk, Jerit, and Rich 2001. Brown (1996), Schudson (1998), and Keyssar (2000) examine how the image of the informed citizen changed over time. Just, Neuman, and Crigler (1992) lay out an economic theory of how individuals learn about news that emphasizes how learning costs may vary across issues and across media. Graber (2001) investigates how television conveys information about politics. Krause and Granato (1998) and Althaus (1998) explore the policy implications of the variation in knowledge across citizens. Nie, Junn, and Stehlik-Barry (1996) analyze the impact of education on citizenship. Zaller (1999b) offers several cautions about informed citizens, including (p. 2):

> Highly informed citizens have many good democratic virtues, but they also tend to be rigid, moralistic, and partisan. It is not obvious that democracy would work better if more voters were like the most informed voters in the current system. Poorly informed voters are not so disengaged from national politics as many believe. Indeed, at least as regards presidential elections, poorly informed voters are more systematically responsive to the content of political campaigns than their better-informed counterparts. More than others, they reward incumbents who preside over strong national economies and punish those who do not. Poorly informed voters [are] also more responsive to the ideological locations of the candidates.... It is not obvious that democracy would work better if fewer voters were animated by the concerns of the least informed citizens.

25. Graham (2002) analyzes the degree that information provision programs can enhance democracy. Raney (2002) reports on reorganization efforts within the executive branch to facilitate information use by the public.

26. One argument for the support of public broadcasting is that the news provided will be more likely than commercial programs to focus on topics that carry positive externalities, such as news of government and politics. Public broadcasting generates its own set of criticisms about story content, source selection, and funder influence. See Croteau and Hoynes 1994, Hoynes 1994, Ledbetter 1997, Baker and Dessart 1998, and Starr 2000.

27. Warner (2002) details the controversy over the funding of an environmental reporter at WHYY, a Philadelphia public radio station, by a nonprofit that received money from the Pennsylvania Department of Environmental Protection. Miner (2002) describes problems arising from the policy governing underwriting statements at WBEZ, a Chicago public radio station.

28. Roberts and Kunkel (2002) and Shister (2002) discuss the impact of corporate ownership on media content and possible remedies to encourage higher quality in journalism markets. Bergen (2002) reports on the survival of independent, family-owned newspapers.

29. Blogs operate as interactive newsletters, where authors can post their opinions on

the Web, invite comment from interested readers, and link to other sites to offer analysis of how events are being covered and interpreted. These forums allow individuals to criticize the media, and have recently started appearing as sources in mainstream media publications. See Tawa 2002.

30. See Sunstein 2000 for analysis of policy instruments to influence public interest programming, including discussion of pay-or-play provisions.

31. For analysis of the impact of the FCC's ownership policies, see Chester 2002, Levy, Ford-Livene, and Levine 2002, Pritchard 2002, Roberts, Frenette, and Stearns 2002, Spavins 2002, and Waldfogel 2002. Dean Baker (2002) critiques many of the studies generated during the FCC's ownership policy debate.

32. The FCC's website (www.fcc.gov), for example, contains information on the children's educational programs offered by local television stations. Hamilton (1998) discusses the use of information provision (program ratings and the V-chip) as a tool to limit the exposure of children to violent television programming.

33. Baker (2002b) effectively demonstrates how antitrust policies and regulations aimed at the structure of ownership have been interpreted in debates over media concentration. For evidence on the impact of media concentration, see Bagdikian 1997, Herman and McChesney 1997, Compaine and Gomery 2000, and McChesney 2000.

34. Baker (2002a) examines in detail the policy tools available to influence the provision of information with positive externalities in politics. The dispute between Time Warner and Fox News illustrates how antitrust concerns can affect the provision of news. When Time Warner merged with Turner Broadcasting in 1996, the Federal Trade Commission required the Time Warner cable systems to carry an all-news cable channel that was not CNN; this was because of fears that Time Warner would favor CNN (which it would own) and block the provision of other all-news channels on its cable systems. In New York City, Time Warner agreed to carry MSNBC and initially chose not to carry Fox News. Fox News sued Time Warner for antitrust violations. The city of New York chose to use two of its cable channels to show Bloomberg TV's business channel and the Fox News channel, though this action was later halted by a court injunction. Eventually Time Warner agreed to carry Fox News for a reported fee of $10 per subscriber (see Entertainment Law Reporter 1998).

35. Netanel (1996) discusses the relation between copyright and the functioning of democracy. For an examination of attempts to restrict the set of data and ideas within the public domain, see the papers prepared for the Duke Conference on the Public Domain (2001), especially Boyle (2001). Cohen (2000) examines the law and economics of intellectual property.

36. Ellickson (2001) describes the market for social norms. Niemi and Junn (1998) discuss evidence on how civic education can increase political knowledge.

37. Knutzen (1996) discusses Bill Nye's science program for children. Schmitt (1999) and Jordan (2000) analyze the implementation of the FCC's three-hour rule on children's educational programming. Minow and Lamay (1995), and Kunkel (1998) examine the public interest issues surrounding children's educational programming.

38. See Rosenkranz (1999) and Redish (2001) for discussion of the impact of campaign finance laws on political speech. Kurtz (2002, p. A7) notes that a study of the 2002 midterm elections found that "the average local newscast carried just 39 seconds of campaign coverage but more than a minute of political ads."

39. In May 2002 the California Supreme Court held that statements by Nike officials

about the company's labor practices in Asia were commercial speech that could be regulated in a manner similar to product claims. This meant activists could sue the company for these statements under California laws protecting consumers from deceptive advertising. For a description of the case, see Parloff 2002.

40. Walker (2002) describes the website run by Google (news.google.com) that selects news stories from four thousand websites by computer algorithm.

41. The *Mother Jones* Investigate Fund solicits contributions to support the liberal magazine's investigative reporting. See www.motherjones.com.

42. For analyses of how information affects decisions of parents in education markets, see Teske, Schneider, Mintrom, and Best 1993, 1995, and Schneider, Teske, Marschall, and Roch 1998. Craft (1998) analyzes how the social return to investment in information can be estimated for one type of information, weather reports. Jones, Marshall, and Bergman (1996) analyze the results of an information campaign aimed at increasing childhood immunizations.

43. This hypothetical was inspired by the assignment posed by Larry Bartels to his Woodrow Wilson School Policy Task Force in Spring 2002; the class was asked how they would advise a foundation to spend $500 million "to promote the production and consumption of high-quality information about public affairs and public policy." Edmonds (2001) details how the Henry J. Kaiser Family Foundation spends funds to influence the provision of information about health care policy. McChesney (1993) details the history of nonprofits' involvement in the early definition of broadcast regulation.

44. Shuit 1994.

45. See Goldmark 2001, and Bollier 2001.

46. See Kovach and Rosenstiel 2001 and the website, www.journalism.org. Rosen (1999) describes the reform movement called civic journalism, whose proponents argue that the media should provide news coverage that better engages citizens in public affairs. Friedland and Nichols (2002) assess the implementation of civic journalism programs. Gardner, Csikszentmihalyi, and Damon (2001) interviewed journalists about how they view their work and the potential conflicts between market incentives and professional norms of reporting.

47. Grossman and Minow (2001) outline this proposal. See also www.digitalpromise. org and Bowie 2000.

48. Arnold (1990) describes how a long chain of events may make it difficult for voters to connect real world outcomes with policy decisions.

49. Edmonds 2001.

50. The Kaiser Family Foundation Survey (1997) analysis concluded (p. 2) "it is possible that 5–6 million people learned about emergency contraception for the first time from the show." The follow-up survey lead the foundation's report to conclude that "without repetition, increased awareness from a single, brief exposure to a health message does not appear to be retained by viewers."

51. Testifying before a House subcommittee about the program, drug office director General Barry R. McCaffrey noted: "An on-strategy story line that is the main plot of a half-hour show can be valued at three 30-second ads. . . . If there is an end tag with an 800 number or more information at the end of a half-hour show, it is valued at an additional 15-second ad. A main story line in an hourlong prime-time show is valued at five 30-second ads, while such a story in a one-hour daytime show is valued at four 30-second ads" (see Lacey and Carter 2000, p. A1).

52. For histories of FCC regulation, see Cole and Oettinger 1978, Simmons 1978, Krasnow, Longley, and Terry 1982, Baughman 1985, Donahue 1989, and Ray 1990.

53. The availability of minute-by-minute Nielsen ratings for network news programs (see Downie and Kaiser 2002, p. 135) makes it easy for managers to monitor how viewers react to the content chosen by reporters and producers. McGowan (2001) describes how the Gannett company used content samples to evaluate editors at its local papers.

54. Grossman and Minow 2001, p. 6. For a critique of the operation of public television, see Hoynes 1994.

55. Hafner 2001, p. G8.

Bibliography

Adamic, Lada A., and Bernardo A. Huberman. 1999. "The Nature of Markets in the World Wide Web." Working paper, Xerox Palo Alto Research Center, Palo Alto, Calif.

Adams, Edward E. 1996. "Secret Combinations and Collusive Agreements: The Scripps Newspaper Empire and the Early Roots of Joint Operating Agreements." *Journalism and Mass Communication Quarterly*, 73(1): 195–205.

Adatto, Kiku. 1993. *Picture Perfect: The Art and Artifice of Public Image Making*. New York: Basic Books.

Ahrens, Frank. 2001. "The Great Deregulator: Five Months Into His Tenure as FCC Chairman, Michael Powell is Coming Through Loud and Clear." *Washington Post*, June 18, C1.

Aigrain, Philipe. "Attention, Media, Value and Economics." *First Monday*, 2(9). Sept. 1, 1997, at http://firstmonday.org/issues2_9/aigrain/index.html.

Akerlof, George A. 1970. "The Market for 'Lemons': Quality Uncertainty and the Market Mechanism." *Quarterly Journal of Economics*, 84: 488–500.

Aldrich, John H., John L. Sullivan, and Eugene Borgida. 1989. "Foreign Affairs and Issue Voting: Do Presidential Candidates 'Waltz before a Blind Audience?'" *American Political Science Review*, 83(1): 123–41.

Althaus, Scott L.1998. "Information Effects in Collective Preferences." *American Political Science Review*, 92(3): 545–58.

Alvarez, R. Michael. 1997. *Information and Elections*. Ann Arbor: University of Michigan Press.

American Conservative Union. 2002. "ACU Releases 2001 Rating of Congress." (February 22, 2002), at http://www.conservative.org/release/pr01282002.htm.

Americans for Democratic Action. 2002. "ADA 2001 Voting Record: United States Senate Vote Descriptions." (February 22, 2002), at http://adaction.org/senatevotedescrips2001.html.

Anand, Bharat N. and Ron Shachar. 2000. "Brands, Information, and Loyalty." Working paper, Harvard Business School, Boston, Mass.

Anderson, Richard D., Jr. 1998. "The Place of the Media in Popular Democracy." *Critical Review*, 12(4): 481–500.

Anderson, Simon P., and Stephen Coate. 2000. "Market Provision of Public Goods: The Case of Broadcasting." Working paper, National Bureau of Economic Research, Cambridge, Mass.

Ansolabehere, Stephen, Roy Behr and Shanto Iyengar. 1993. *The Media Game: American Politics in the Television Age*. New York: Macmillan.

Ansolabehere, Stephen, and Shanto Iyengar. 1995. *Going Negative: How Attack Ads Shrink and Polarize the Electorate*. New York: Free Press.

Arnold, R. Douglas. 1990. *The Logic of Congressional Action*. New Haven, Conn: Yale University Press.

Artwick, Claudette Guzan, and Margaret T. Gordon. 1998. "Portrayal of U.S. Cities by Daily Newspapers." *Newspaper Research Journal*, 19(1): 54–63.

Aucoin, Don. 1998. "Rather on the Rebound: With a Ratings Boost and new Contract, Fixture Hopes to Be the Fix at CBS." *Boston Globe*, January 7, p. D1.

Aufderheide, Patricia. 1999. *Communications Policy and the Public Interest.* New York: Guilford Press.

Auletta, Ken. 1992. *Three Blind Mice: How the TV Networks Lost Their Way.* New York: Vintage.

———. 2001a. "Synergy City." In *Leaving Readers Behind: The Corporate Age of Newspapering,* Gene Roberts, Thomas Kunkel, and Charles Layton, eds. Fayetteville: University of Arkansas Press.

———. 2001b. "Battle Stations: How Long Will the Networks Stick With the News?" *The New Yorker,* December 10, p. 60.

Avery, Christopher, and Peter Zemsky. 1998. "Multidimensional Uncertainty and Herd Behavior in Financial Markets." *American Economic Review,* 88(4): 724–48.

Bae, Hyuhn-Suhck. 1999. "Product Differentiation in Cable Programming: The Case in the Cable National All-News Networks." *Journal of Media Economics,* 12(4): 265–77.

Bagdikian, Ben H. 1997. *The Media Monopoly.* Boston: Beacon Press.

Baker, C. Edwin. 1978. "Scope of the First Amendment Freedom of Speech." *UCLA Law Review,* 25:964.

———. 1994a. *Advertising and a Democratic Press.* Princeton, N. J.: Princeton University Press.

———. 1994b. "Ownership of Newspapers: The View from Positivist Social Science." Joan Shorenstein Barone Center Research Paper R-12. John F. Kennedy School of Government, Harvard University, Cambridge, Mass.

———. 1997. "Giving the Audience What It Wants." *Ohio State Law Journal,* 58(2): 311–417.

———. 1998. "The Media That Citizens Need." *University of Pennsylvania Law Review,* 147(2): 317–408.

———. 2000. "An Economic Critique of Free Trade in Media Products." *North Carolina Law Review,* 78: 1357.

———. 2002a. *Media, Markets, and Democracy.* Cambridge: Cambridge University Press.

———. 2002b. "Media Concentration: Giving Up On Democracy." *Florida Law Review,* 54: 839–919.

Baker, Dean. 2002. "Democracy Unhinged: More Media Concentration Means Less Public Discourse." AFL-CIO Department for Professional Employees, Washington, D.C.

Baker, William F., and George Dessart. 1998. *Down the Tube: An Inside Account of the Failure of American Television.* New York: Basic Books.

Baldasty, Gerald J. 1992. *The Commercialization of News in the Nineteenth Century.* Madison: University of Wisconsin Press.

———. 1999. *E. W. Scripps and the Business of Newspapers.* Urbana: University of Illinois Press.

Balkin, J. M. 1995. "Book Review: Populism and Progressivism as Constitutional Categories. *Democracy and the Problem of Free Speech,* by Cass R. Sunstein." *Yale Law Journal.* 104: 1935.

Banerjee, Abhijit V. 1993. "The Economics of Rumours." *Review of Economic Studies,* 60(2): 309–27.

Barabasi, Albert-Laszlos and Reka Albert. 1999. "Emergence of Scaling in Random Networks." *Science,* 286: 509–12.

Barlow, John Perry. 1994. "The Economy of Ideas: A Framework for Patents and Copy-rights in the Digital Age; Everything You Know About Intellectual Property is Wrong." *Wired.* August 29, 2001, at http://www.wired.com/wired/archive/2.03/economy.ideas_pr.html.

Barringer, Felicity. 2001. "Growing Audience Is Turning to Established News Media On-line." *New York Times,* August 27, p. C1.

Bartels, Larry M. 1988. *Presidential Primaries and the Dynamics of Public Choice.* Prince-ton, N.J.: Princeton University Press.

———. 1993. "Messages Received: The Political Impact of Media Exposure." *American Political Science Review,* 87(2): 267–85.

———. 1996a. "Politicians and the Press: Who Leads, Who Follows?" Working paper, Woodrow Wilson School of Public and International Affairs, Princeton University, Princeton, N.J.

———. 1996b. "Uninformed Votes: Information Effects in Presidential Elections." *American Journal of Political Science,* 40(1): 194–230.

Bartels, Larry M., and Wendy M. Rahn. 2000. "Political Attitudes in the Post-Network Era." Paper prepared for the Annual Meeting of the American Political Science Asso-ciation, Washington, D.C., September.

Bartels, Larry M., and Lynn Vavreck, eds. 2000. *Campaign Reform: Insights and Evidence.* Ann Arbor: University of Michigan Press.

Bates, Stephen. 1995. *Realigning Journalism with Democracy: The Hutchins Commission, Its Times, and Ours.* Washington, D.C.: The Annenberg Washington Program in Communications Policy Studies of Northwestern University.

Baughman, James L. 1985. *Television's Guardians: The FCC and the Politics of Program-ming 1958–1967.* Knoxville: University of Tennessee Press.

Baum, Matthew A. 2003. *Soft News Goes to War: Public Opinion and American Foreign Policy in the New Media Age.* Princeton, N.J.: Princeton University Press.

Baum, Matthew A., and Samuel Kernell. 1999. "Has Cable Ended the Golden Age of Presidential Television?" *American Political Science Review,* 93(1): 99–114.

Beam, Randal A. 1998. "What It Means to be a Market-Oriented Newspaper." *Newspaper Research Journal,* 19(3): 2–20.

Beauprez, Jennifer. 2001. "Dirty Secret: Porn Pays; Ailing Mainstream Web Sites Tempted by Online Sex Sales' Profitable Lesson." *Denver Post,* April 22, p. K1.

Beebe, Jack H. 1977. "Institutional Structure and Program Choices in Television Mar-kets." *Quarterly Journal of Economics,* 91: 15–37.

Beniger, James R. 1986. *The Control Revolution: Technological and Economic Origins of the Information Society.* Cambridge, Mass.: Harvard University Press.

Bennett, W. Lance. 1996. *News: The Politics of Illusion.* 3rd ed. New York: Longman.

Bennett, W. Lance, and Robert M. Entman, eds. 2001. *Mediated Politics: Communication in the Future of Democracy.* New York: Cambridge University Press.

Bennett, W. Lance, and David L. Paletz, eds. 1994. *Taken by Storm: The Media, Public Opinion, and U.S. Foreign Policy in the Gulf War.* Chicago: University of Chicago Press.

Bergen, Kathy. 2002. "Survival Top Story for Independent Newspapers." *Chicago Tri-bune,* Sept. 12, p. A1.

Berger, Joseph. 1984. "Networks Give Ruling Little Impact." *New York Times,* June 28, p. C18.

Berke, Richard L. 1990. "Networks Quietly Abandon Competition and United to Survey Voters" *New York Times*, November 7, p. B1.

Bernstein, James M., Stephen Lacy, Catherine Cassara, and Tuen-yu Lau. 1990. "Geographic Coverage by Local Television News." *Journalism Quarterly*, 67(4): 663–71.

Bernstein, Sharon. 1990. "Who's in First? It's the War of the Network Anchors." *Los Angeles Times*, August 31, p. F1.

Berry, Steven T., and Joel Waldfogel. 1999a. "Free Entry and Social Inefficiency in Radio Broadcasting." *RAND Journal Of Economics*, 30(3): 397–420.

———. 1999b. "Public Radio in the United States: Does it Correct Market Failure or Cannibalize Commercial Stations?" *Journal of Public Economics*, 71: 189–211.

———. 1999c. "Mergers, Station Entry, and Programming Variety in Radio Broadcasting." Working paper 7080, National Bureau of Economic Research, Cambridge, Mass.

Besley, Timothy, and Robin Burgess. 2001. "The Political Economy of Government Responsiveness: Theory and Evidence from India." Working paper, London School of Economics, London.

Besley, Timothy, Robin Burgess, and Andrea Prat. 2002. "Mass Media and Political Accountability." Working paper, London School of Economics, London.

Besley, Timothy, and Andrea Prat. 2001. "Handcuffs for the Grabbing Hand? Media Capture and Government Accountability." Working paper, London School of Economics, London.

Bhushan, Ravi, David P. Brown, and Antonio S. Mello. 1997. "Do Noise Traders 'Create Their Own Space?'" *Journal of Financial and Quantitative Analysis*, 32(1): 25–45.

Bianco, Robert. 1993. "Captain of the Ship: Peter Jennings Sits Secure at the Top of the Ratings Heap." *Pittsburgh Post-Gazette*, November 4, p. D1.

Biddle, Frederic M. 1996. "TV Networks, Affiliates Play a Promotional Tie-In Game." *Boston Globe*, Nov. 25, p.1.

Bikhchandani, Sushil, David Hirshleifer, and Ivo Welch. 1992. "A Theory of Fads, Fashion, Custom, and Cultural Change as Informational Cascades." *Journal of Political Economy*, 100(5): 992–1026.

———. 1998. "Learning from the Behavior of Others: Conformity, Fads, and Informational Cascades." *Journal of Economic Perspectives*, 12(3): 151–70.

Blanchard, Margaret A. 1987. "The Associated Press Antitrust Suit; A Philosophical Clash Over Ownership of First Amendment Rights." *Business History Review*, 61: 43–86.

Bleyer, Willard Grosvenor, ed. 1918. *The Profession of Journalism*. Boston: Atlantic Monthly Press.

———. 1927. *Main Currents in the History of American Journalism*. Boston: Houghton Mifflin Company.

Blondheim, Menahem. 1994. *News Over the Wires: The Telegraph and the Flow of Public Information in America, 1844–1897*. Cambridge, Mass.: Harvard University Press.

Boemer, Marilyn Lawrence. 1987. "Correlating Lead-In Show Ratings with Local Television News Ratings." *Journal of Broadcasting and Electronic Media*, 31(1): 89–94.

Bollier, David. 1997. *The Networked Society: How Technologies Are Transforming Markets, Organizations, and Social Relationships*. Washington D.C.: Aspen Institute.

———. 1999. *Can Serious Journalism Survive in the New Media Marketplace? A Report of the Second Annual Cato Conference on Journalism and Society*. Washington, D.C.: Aspen Institute.

Borghans, Lex, and Loek Groot. 1998. "Superstardom and Monopolistic Power: Why Media Stars Earn More Than Their Marginal Contribution to Welfare." *Journal of Institutional and Theoretical Economics*, 154: 546–71.

Bourdieu, Pierre. 1998. *On Television.* New York: New Press.

Bovitz, Gregory L., James N. Druckman, and Arthur Lupia. 2002. "When Can a News Organization Lead Public Opinion? Ideology versus Market Forces in Decisions to Make News." *Public Choice*, 113(1–2): 127–55.

Bowie, Nolan A. 2000. "An E-Public Sphere for the Digital Age: What Needs to Be Done to Enhance Democratic Values and Engage Greater Civic Participation In the United States." Benton Foundation.

Boyer, Peter. 1988a. *Who Killed CBS: The Undoing of America's Number One News Network.* New York: Random House.

———. 1988b. "The Shift of Rather: Channel 2's Object is Better Ratings" *New York Times*, August 6, p. 50.

Boyle, James. 1996. *Shamans, Software, and Spleens: Law and the Construction of the Information Society.* Cambridge, Mass.: Harvard University Press.

———. 2001. "The Second Enclosure Movement and the Construction of the Public Domain." Duke Conference on the Public Domain.

Branscomb, Anne Wells. 1994. *Who Owns Information? From Privacy to Public Access.* New York: Basic Books.

Brennan, Timothy J. 1983. "Economic Efficiency and Broadcast Content Regulation." *Federal Communications Law Journal*, 35: 117.

Brill's Content. 1999. "1999 Salary Report: Who Gets Paid What." *Brill's Content*, 2(4): 84–95.

Broder, David S. 1987. *Behind the Front Page.* New York: Simon & Schuster.

Brooker-Gross, Susan R. 1983. "19th Century News Definitions and Wire-Service Usage." *Journalism Quarterly*, 60(1): 24–27.

Brown, Dan. 2001. "'Weakest Link' Hairdo Costs TV Anchor; Former Chicago Channel 5 Reporter." *Chicago Sun-Times*, May 8, p. 3.

Brown, Richard D. 1996. *The Strength of a People: The Idea of an Informed Citizenry in America, 1650–1870.* Chapel Hill: University of North Carolina Press.

Bruinius, Harry. 2001. "And Now, a Word from Our Sponsor: 'Gasp!'" *Christian Science Monitor*, February 5, p. 1.

Burnham, David. 1984. "FCC Eases Rules for Broadcast TV." *New York Times*, June 28, p. C18.

Burns, Eric. 1993. *Broadcast Blues: Dispatches from the Twenty-Year War between a Television Reporter and His Medium.* New York: Harper Collins Publishers.

Busterna, John C. 1991. "Price Discrimination as Evidence of Newspaper Chain Market Power." *Journalism Quarterly*, 68(1): 5–14.

Caplan, Bryan. 2000. "What Makes People Think Like Economists? Evidence on Economic Cognition from the *Survey of Americans and Economists on the Economy.*" Working paper, George Mason University, Fairfax, Va.

———. 2002. "How Do Voters Form Positive Economic Beliefs? Evidence on Economic Cognition from the *Survey of Americans and Economists on the Economy.*" Working paper, George Mason University, Fairfax, Va.

Cappella, Joseph N., and Kathleen Hall Jamieson. 1997. *Spiral of Cynicism: The Press and the Public Good.* New York: Oxford University Press.

Carlton, Dennis W., and Jeffrey M. Perloff. 1990. *Modern Industrial Organization*. Glenview, Ill.: Scott, Foresman/Little, Brown Higher Education.

Carmody, John. 1977. "ABC: No Move for Walters." *Washington Post*, February 4, p. B1.

Carter, Bill. 1991. "NBC 'Nightly News' to Move to 6:30 from 7." *New York Times*, June 13, p. C18.

Carter, Bill, and Allison Fass. 2000. "CBS Finally Lures Coveted Young Viewers with 'Survivor.'" *New York Times*, June 19, p. C1.

Caves, Richard E., and Peter J. Williamson. 1985. "What Is Product Differentiation, Really?" *The Journal of Industrial Economics*, 34(2): 113–32.

Center for Media and Public Affairs. 2000. "Journalists Monopolize TV Election News." May 16, 2001, at http://www.cmpa.com/presstel/electpr10.html.

Center for Responsive Politics. 2000. "Presidential Fund-Raising by State, Metro Area, and ZIP Code." Feb. 23, 2000, at http://www.opensecrets.org/2000elect/geog_look.htm.

Chae, Suchan, and Daniel Flores. 1998. "Broadcasting Versus Narrowcasting." *Information Economics and Policy*, 10(1): 41–57.

Chan-Olmsted, Sylvia M. 1997. "Theorizing Multichannel Media Economics: An Exploration of a Group-Industry Strategic Competition Model." *Journal of Media Economics*. 10(1): 39–49.

Chaudhri, Vivek. 1998. "Pricing and Efficiency of a Circulation Industry: The Case of Newspapers." *Information Economics and Policy*, 10: 59–76.

Chester, Jeff. 2002. "Strict Scrutiny: Why Journalist Should Be Concerned about New Federal and Industry Media Deregulation Proposals." *Harvard International Journal of Press/Politics*, 7(2): 105–15.

Chipty, Tasneem, and Christopher M. Snyder. 1999. "The Role of Firm Size in Bilateral Bargaining: A Study of the Cable Television Industry." *Review of Economics and Statistics*, 81(2): 326–40.

Chwe, Michael Suk-Young. 2001. *Rational Ritual: Culture, Coordination, and Common Knowledge*. Princeton, N.J.: Princeton University Press.

Clarke, Prue. 2001. "Frantic Search for Winning TV News Formula as Viewers Turn off in Droves." *Financial Times*, August 14, p. 5.

Clubb, Jerome M., William H. Flanigan, and Nancy H. Zingale. 1986. *Electoral Data for Counties in the United States: Presidential and Congressional Races, 1840–1972*. Ann Arbor, Mich: Inter-university Consortium for Political and Social Research.

Coase, R. H. 1974. "The Market for Goods and the Market for Ideas." *The American Economic Review*, 64(2): 384–91.

Cohen, Julie E. 2000. "Copyright and the Perfect Curve." *Vanderbilt Law Review*, 53: 1799.

Colander, David C., and A. W. Coats. 1989. *The Spread of Economic Ideas*. Cambridge: Cambridge University Press.

Cole, Barry, and Mal Oettinger. 1978. *Reluctant Regulators: The FCC and the Broadcast Audience*. Reading, Mass.:Addison-Wesley Publishing.

Columbia Journalism Review. 1999. "'Under No Circumstances Should Staff Members . . .'" *Columbia Journalism Review*. January/February, p. 45.

Commission on Freedom of the Press. 1947. *A Free and Responsible Press: A General Report on Mass Communication*. Chicago: University of Chicago Press.

Committee of Concerned Journalists. 1998. *Changing Definitions of News*. Washington, D.C.: Committee of Concerned Journalists.

————. 2000. "ePolitics: A Study of the 2000 Presidential Campaign on the Internet." Washington, D.C.: Committee of Concerned Journalists.

Compaine, Benjamin M., and Douglas Gomery. 2000. *Who Owns the Media? Competition and Concentration in the Mass Media Industry*. Mahwah, N.J.: Lawrence Erlbaum.

Comstock, George, and Erica Scharrer. 1999. *Television: What's on, Who's Watching, and What It Means*. San Diego: Academic Press.

Consumers Union, Consumer Federation of America, Media Access Project, Center for Digital Democracy, and The Civil Rights Forum. 2002. Reply Comments Before the Federal Communications Commission in the Matter of Cross-Ownership of Broadcast Stations and Newspaper and Newspaper/Radio Cross-Ownership Waiver Policy. MM Docket Nos. 01-235 and 96-197.

Cook, Philip S., Douglas Gomery, and Lawrence W. Lichty. 1992. *The Future of News: Television-Newspapers-Wire Services-Newsmagazines*. Washington D.C.: Woodrow Wilson Center Press; Baltimore: Johns Hopkins University Press.

Cook, Timothy E. 1998. *Governing with the News: The News Media as a Political Institution*. Chicago: University of Chicago Press.

Corn-Revere, Robert, ed. 1997. *Regulating the Electronic Media*. Washington, D.C.: The Media Institute.

Corry, John. 1993. *My Times: Adventures in the News Trade*. New York: G. P. Putnam's Sons.

Coulson, David C., and Anne Hansen. 1995. "The *Louisville Courier-Journal*'s News Content after Purchase by Gannett." *Journalism and Mass Communication Quarterly*, 72(1): 205–15.

Cowen, Tyler. 1998. *In Praise of Commercial Culture*. Cambridge, Mass.: Harvard University Press.

————. 2000. *What Price Fame?*. Cambridge, Mass.: Harvard University Press.

Cox, James C, and Alvin I. Goldman. 1994. "Accuracy in Journalism: An Economic Approach." In *Socializing Epistemology: The Social Dimensions of Knowledge*, Frederick F. Schmitt, ed., pp. 189–215. Lanham, Maryland: Rowman and Littlefield.

Craft, Erik D. 1998. "The Value of Weather Information Services for Nineteenth-Century Great Lakes Shipping." *American Economic Review*, 88(5): 1059–76.

Cranberg, Gilbert, Randall Bezanson, and John Soloski. 2001. *Taking Stock: Journalism and the Publicly Traded Newspaper Company*. Ames: Iowa State University Press.

Crawford, Gregory S. 1997a. "The Causes and Consequences of Growth in the Cable Television Industry." Working paper, Department of Economics, Duke University, Durham, N.C.

————. 1997b. "New Products, New Programs, and Prices: Measuring Consumer Benefits to Changes in Cable Television Choices, 1989–1995." Working paper, Department of Economics, Duke University, Durham, N.C.

Croteau, David. 1994. *By Invitation Only: How the Media Limit Political Debate*. Monroe, Maine: Common Courage.

D'Alessio, Dave, and Mike Allen. 2000. "Media Bias in Presidential Elections: A Meta-Analysis." *Journal of Communication*, 50(4): 133–56.

Daley, David. 1999. "What Makes Journalists Experts on Everything?" *Star Tribune* (Minneapolis, Minn.), July 14, 10E.

Dalton, Russell J., Paul A. Beck, and Robert Huckfeldt. 1998. "Partisan Cues and the Media: Information Flows in the 1992 Presidential Election." *American Political Science Review*, 92(1): 111–26.

Dalton, Russell J., Paul A. Beck, Robert Huckfeldt, and William Koetzle. 1998. "A Test of Media-Centered Agenda Setting: Newspaper Content and Public Interests in a Presidential Election." *Political Communication*, 15: 463–81.

Davis, Peter. 1997. "Spatial Competition in Retail Markets: Movie Theaters." Working paper, Yale University, New Haven, Conn.

Dearing, James W., and Everett M. Rogers. 1992. *Communication Concepts 6: Agenda-Setting.* Thousand Oaks, Calif.: Sage.

Dee, Jonathan. 2002. "The Myth of '18 to 34.'" *New York Times Magazine*, Oct.13, 58–61.

Delli Carpini, Michael X., and Scott Keeter. 1996. *What Americans Know about Politics and Why It Matters.* New Haven: Yale University Press.

DeLong, J. Bradford, and Michael Froomkin. 2000. "Speculative Microeconomics for Tomorrow's Economy." *First Monday*, 5(2).

DeLong, J. Bradford, Andrei Shleifer, Lawrence H. Summers, and Robert J. Waldmann. 1990. "Noise Trader Risk in Financial Markets." *Journal of Political Economy*, 98(4): 703–38.

Demers, David. 1996. *The Menace of the Corporate Newspaper: Fact or Fiction?* Ames: Iowa State University Press

———. 1999. "Corporate Newspaper Bashing: Is It Justified?" *Newspaper Research Journal*, 20(1): 83–97.

De Moraes, Lisa. 1999a. "The Smooch That Drew a Crowd." *Washington Post*, November 4, p. C1

Demsetz, Harold. 1989. *Efficiency, Competition, and Policy: The Organization of Economic Activity*, vol. 2. Oxford: Basil Blackwell.

Demsetz, Harold and Kenneth Lehn. 1985. "The Structure of Corporate Ownership: Causes and Consequences." *The Journal of Political Economy*, 93(6): 1155–77.

———. 1999b. "Back to the Movies: Grodin's Tirade, Er, Talk Show Tanks." *Washington Post*, November 11, p. C7.

De Vany, Arthur, and W. David Walls. 1996. "Bose-Einstein Dynamics and Adaptive Contracting in the Motion Picture Industry." *The Economic Journal*, 106: 1493–1514.

Diamond, Edwin. 1991. *The Media Show: The Changing Face of the News, 1985–1990.* Cambridge: MIT Press.

———. 1993. *Behind the Times: Inside the New* New York Times. New York: Villard Books.

Djankov, Simeon, Caralee McLiesh, Tatiana Nenova, and Andrei Shleifer. 2001. "Who Owns the Media." Harvard Institute of Economic Research Discussion Paper 1919. Cambridge, Mass.: Harvard University.

Domke, David, Mark D. Watts, Dhavan V. Shah, and David P. Fan. 1999. "The Politics of Conservative Elites and the 'Liberal Media' Argument." *Journal of Communication*, 49(4): 35–58.

Donahue, Hugh C. 1989. *The Battle to Control Broadcast News: Who Owns the First Amendment?* Cambridge, Mass.: Massachusetts Institute of Technology Press.

Donaldson, Sam. 1987. *Hold on, Mr. President.* New York: Fawcett Crest.

Dow, James, and Gary Gorton. 1997. "Noise Trading, Delegated Portfolio Management, and Economic Welfare." *Journal of Political Economy*, 105(5): 1024–50.

Downey, Kevin. 2001. "Reality TV: Wrinkle Cream for Networks." *Media Life*, Sept. 10. (Oct. 22, 2001), at http://www.medialifemagazine.com/pages/templates/scripts/prfr.asp.

Downie, Leonard, and Robert G. Kaiser. 2002. *The News about the News: American Journalism in Peril.* New York: Knopf.

Downs, Anthony. 1957. *An Economic Theory of Democracy.* New York: Harper Books.

Drinkard, Jim. 2001. "The Two Major Parties May Be Losing Grip on Voters." *USA Today,* August 31, p.4A

Druckman, James N. 2001a. "On the Limits of Framing Effects: Who Can Frame?" *Journal of Politics,* 6394): 1041–66.

———. 2001b. "Using Credible Advice to Overcome Framing Effects." *Journal of Law, Economics, and Organization,* 17(1): 62–82.

DuBoff, Richard B.1980. "Business Demand and the Development of the Telegraph in the United States, 1844–1860." *Business History Review,* 54(4): 459–79.

———. 1983. "The Telegraph and the Structure of Markets in the United States, 1845–1890." *Research in Economic History,* 8: 253–77.

———. 1984a. "The Rise of Communications Regulation: The Telegraph Industry, 1844–1880."*Journal of Communication,* 34(3): 52–66.

———. 1984b. "The Telegraph in Nineteenth-Century America: Technology and Monopoly." *Comparative Studies in Society and History,* 26(4): 571–86.

Duch, Raymond M., Harvey D. Palmer, and Christopher J. Anderson. 2000. "Heterogeneity in Perceptions of National Economic Conditions." *American Journal of Political Science,* 44(4): 635–52.

Duke Conference on the Public Domain. 2001. Duke University School of Law Center for the Public Domain.

Dyson, Esther. 1998. *Release 2.1: A Design for Living in the Digital Age.* New York: Broadway Books.

Editor and Publisher Company. 1999. *Editor and Publisher International Year Book,* 79th ed. New York: Editor and Publisher.

Edmonds, Rick. 2001. "A Kaiser Prescription for Healthcare News."*Poynter Report,* May 21. (May 24, 2001), at http:/www.poynter.org/centerpiece/foundations/kaiser.htm.

Edwards, George C., and B. Dan Wood. 1999. "Who Influences Whom? The President, Congress, and the Media." *American Political Science Review,* 93(2): 327–61.

Ellickson, Robert C. 2001. "The Market for Social Norms." *American Law and Economics Review,* 3(1): 1–49.

Elster, Jon. 1998. *Deliberative Democracy.* Cambridge: Cambridge University Press.

Emmons, William M. III, and Robin A. Prager. 1997. "The Effects of Market Structure and Ownership on Prices and Service Offerings in the U.S. Cable Television Industry." *RAND Journal of Economics,* 28(4): 732–50.

Endersby, James W., and Ekaterina Ognianova. 1997. "A Spatial Model of Ideology and Political Communication." *Press/Politics,* 2(1): 23–39.

Endrst, James. 1997. "Foreign News on TV? In U.S., Out of Sight Is Out of Mind" *Hartford Courant,* March 30, p. A1

Entertainment Law Reporter. 1998. "Time Warner Cable Systems Agree to Carry Fox News." *Entertainment Law Reporter,* April.

Entman, Robert M. 1989. *Democracy Without Citizens: The Media and the Decay of American Politics.* New York: Oxford University Press.

———. 1993. "Putting the First Amendment in Its Place: Enhancing American Democracy through the Press." *University of Chicago Legal Forum,* p. 61.

Entman, Robert M., and Andrew Rojecki. 2000. *The Black Image in the White Mind: Media and Race in America.* Chicago: University of Chicago Press.

Entman, Robert M., and Steven S. Wildman. 1992. "Reconciling Economic and Non-Economic Perspectives on Media Policy: Transcending the 'Marketplace of Ideas.'" *Journal of Communication,* 42(1): 5–19.

Epstein, Edward Jay. 1973. *News from Nowhere: Television and the News.* New York: Random House.

Epstein, Lee, and Jeffrey A. Segal. 2000. "Measuring Issue Salience." *American Journal of Political Science,* 44(1): 66–83.

Eskridge, William N. 1988. "Politics Without Romance: Implications of Public Choice Theory for Statutory Interpretation." *Virginia Law Review,* 74: 275.

Essary, J. Frederick. 1927. *Covering Washington: Government Reflected to the Public in the Press, 1822–1926.* Boston: Houghton Mifflin Company.

Eveland, William P., and Dietram A. Scheufele. 2000. "Connecting News Media Use with Gaps in Knowledge and Participation." *Political Communication,* 17: 215–37.

Fallows, James M. 1996. *Breaking the News: How the Media Undermine American Democracy.* New York: Pantheon Books.

Farnsworth, Stephen J., and S. Robert Lichter. 2002. *The Nightly News Nightmare: Network Television's Coverage of U.S. Presidential Elections, 1988–2000.* Lanham, M.D.: Rowman and Littlefield.

Federal Communications Commission. 2001. Roundtable Discussion on Media Ownership Policies.

Ferejohn, John A., and James H. Kuklinski. 1990. *Information and Democratic Processes.* Urbana: University of Illinois Press.

Fiorina, Morris P. 1990. "Information and Rationality in Elections." In *Information and Democratic Processes,* John A. Ferejohn and James H. Kuklinski, eds., pp. 329–44. Urbana: University of Illinois Press.

Fish, Stanley. 1994. *There's No Such Thing as Free Speech.* New York: Oxford University Press.

Fishman, Mark. 1988. *Manufacturing the News.* Austin: University of Texas Press.

Flickinger, Joe Arden. 1993. *'Info-tainment' and the Question of Legitimacy: A Case Study of CBS News in the 1980s.* Ph.D. dissertation, University of Oregon.

Fournier, Gary M. 1985. "Nonprice Competition and the Dissipation of Rents from Television Regulation." *Southern Economic Journal,* 51: 754–65.

———. 1986. "The Determinants of Economic Rents in Television Broadcasting." *The Antitrust Bulletin,* 31(4): 1045–66.

Fowler, Mark S. and Daniel L. Brenner. 1982. "A Marketplace Approach to Broadcast Regulation." *University of Texas Law Review,* 60: 207–57.

Fox, Richard L., and Robert W. Van Sickel. 2001. *Tabloid Justice: Criminal Justice in an Age of Media Frenzy.* Boulder, Colo: Lynne Rienner.

Frankel, Max. 1999. *Media Madness: The Revolution So Far.* Washington, D.C.: Aspen Institute.

Frederick, Lane. 2000. *Obscene Profits: The Entrepreneurs of Pornography in the Cyber Age.* New York: Routledge.

Friedland, Lewis A., and Sandy Nichols. 2002. "Measuring Civic Journalism's Progress: A Report across a Decade of Activity." Washington, D.C.: The Pew Center for Civic Journalism.

Friedman, Jeffrey. 1998. "Public Ignorance and Democratic Theory." *Critical Review*, 12(4): 397–411.

Froot, Kenneth A., David S. Scharfstein, and Jeremy C. Stein. 1992. "Herd on the Street: Informational Inefficiencies in a Market with Short-Term Speculation." *Journal of Finance*, 47(4): 1461–84.

Gans, Herbert J. 1980. *Deciding What's News: A Study of CBS Evening News, NBC Nightly News, Newsweek, and Time.* New York: Vintage Books.

Garbade, Kenneth D., and William L. Silber. 1978. "Technology, Communications and the Performance of Financial Markets: 1840–1975." *The Journal of Finance*, 33(3): 819–32.

Gardner, Howard, Mihaly Csikszentmihalyi, and William Damon. 2001. *Good Work: When Excellence and Ethics Meet.* New York: Basic Books.

Gay, Verne. 1989. "'World News' Expected to Beat 'CBS Evening News' for '89" *Newsday*, December 15, p. 5.

Geller, Henry. 1998. "Public Interest Regulation in the Digital TV Era." In *A Communications Cornucopia: Markle Foundation Essays on Information Policy*, Roger G. Noll and Monroe E. Price, eds., pp. 543–72. Washington, D.C.: Brookings Institution Press.

Genesove, David. 1999. "The Adoption of Offset Presses in the Daily Newspaper Industry in the United States." Working Paper 7076, National Bureau of Economic Research, Cambridge, Mass.

George, Lisa. 2001. "What's Fit to Print: The Effect of Ownership Concentration on Product Variety in Daily Newspaper Markets." Working paper, Michigan State University, East Lansing, Mich.

George, Lisa and Joel Waldfogel. 2000. "Who Benefits Whom in Daily Newspaper Markets?" Working Paper 7944, National Bureau of Economic Research, Cambridge, Mass.

———. 2001. "Does the *New York Times* Spread Ignorance and Apathy?" Working paper, Michigan State University, East Lansing, Mich.

Gerard, Jeremy. 1989. "ABC Surpasses CBS in Evening News Ratings" *New York Times*, November 29, p. C22.

Germond, Jack W. 1999. *Fat Man in a Middle Seat: Forty Years of Covering Politics.* New York: Random House

Gitlin, Todd. 2001. *Media Unlimited: How the Torrent of Images and Sounds Overwhelms Our Lives.* New York: Metropolitan.

Goettler, Ronald. 1999. "Advertising Rates, Audience Composition, and Competition in the Network Television Industry." Working paper, Graduate School of Industrial Administration, Carnegie Mellon University, Pittsburgh, Pa.

Goettler, Ronald and Ron Shachar. 1999. "Estimating Product Characteristics and Spatial Competition in the Network Television Industry." Working paper, Graduate School of Industrial Administration, Carnegie Mellon University, Pittsburgh, Pa.

———. 2000. "Spatial Competition in the Network Television Industry." Working paper, Graduate School of Industrial Administration, Carnegie Mellon University, Pittsburgh, Pa.

Goldberg, Bernard. 2002. *Bias: A CBS Insider Exposes How the Media Distort the News.* Lanham, MD: Regnery.

Goldberg, Robert. 1990. *Anchors: Brokaw, Jennings, Rather and the Evening News.* Secaucus, N.J.: Carol.

Goldberg, Robert, and Gerald Jay Goldberg. 1995. *Citizen Turner: The Wild Rise of an American Tycoon.* New York: Harcourt Brace & Co.

Goldhaber, Michael H. 1997. "The Attention Economy and the Net." *First Monday,* 2(4). April 7, 1997, at http://firstmonday.org/issues2_4/goldhaber/index.html.

Goldman, Kevin. 1988. "Network vs. Net Gain: CBS Will Resist Airing Dan Rather at 6:30, but the Bottom Line May Prevail" *Newsday,* February 15, p. 3.

Goldmark, Peter C. 2001. *Old Values, New World: Harnessing the Legacy of Independent Journalism for the Future.* Washington, D.C.: Aspen Institute.

Goldstein, Tom, ed. 1989. *Killing the Messenger: 100 Years of Media Criticism.* New York: Columbia University Press.

Gould, James A., and Willis H. Truitt, eds. 1973. *Political Ideologies.* New York: Macmillan.

Graber, Doris A, ed. 2000. *Media Power in Politics.* Washington, D.C.: Congressional Quarterly.

———. 2001. *Processing Politics: Learning from Television in the Internet Age.* Chicago: University of Chicago Press.

Graber, Doris A., Denis McQuail, and Pippa Norris, eds. 1998. *The Politics of News: The News of Politics.* Washington, D.C.: Congressional Quarterly.

Graham, John R. 1999. "Herding among Investment Newsletters: Theory and Evidence." *Journal of Finance,* 59(1): 237–68.

Graham, Mary. 2002. *Democracy by Disclosure: The Rise of Technopopulism.* Washington, D.C.: Brookings Institution.

Green, Donald P., and Ian Shapiro. 1994. *Pathologies of Rational Choice Theory: A Critique of Applications in Political Science.* New Haven, Conn.: Yale University Press.

Greene, Jason, and Scott Smart. 1999. "Liquidity Provision and Noise Trading: Evidence from the 'Investment Dartboard' Column." *Journal of Finance,* 54(5): 1885–99.

Greenhouse, Linda. 2001. "Copyrights: Freelancers Win in Copyright Case." *New York Times,* June 26, p.A1.

Groeling, Tim, and Samuel Kernell. 1998. "Is Network News Coverage of the President Biased?" *Journal of Politics,* 60(4): 1063–87.

Grossman, Lawrence K. 1995. *The Electronic Republic: Reshaping Democracy in the Information Age.* New York: Penguin Books.

Grossman, Lawrence K, and Newton N. Minow. 2001. *A Digital Gift to the Nation: Fulfilling the Promise of the Digital and Internet Age.* New York: Century Foundation.

Gunter, Barrie. 1987. *Poor Reception: Misunderstanding and Forgetting Broadcast News.* Hillsdale, N.J.: Lawrence Erlbaum Associates.

Gunther, Marc. 1994. *The House That Roone Built: The Inside Story of ABC News.* New York: Little, Brown, and Co.

Hackett, Robert A. 1984. "Decline of a Paradigm? Bias and Objectivity in News Media Studies." Critical Studies in Mass Communication, 1(3): 229–59.

Hafner, Katie. 2001. "A New Way of Verifying Old and Familiar Sayings." *New York Times,* Feb. 1, p. G8,

Hall, Jane. 1991. "All Smiles Now on 'CBS Evening News.' *Los Angeles Times,* April 18, p. F1.

———. 1992. "'CBS Evening News' Hot on Heels of Leader ABC." *Los Angeles Times,* May 28, p. F1.

———. 1993. "Chung-Rather Team Losing the Ratings Battle." *Los Angeles Times,* October 6, p. F1.

———. 1997. "NBC Gives Dominant ABC the Evening News Challenge." *Los Angeles Times*, February 5, p. F1.

Hamill, Pete. 1998. *News Is a Verb*. New York: Ballantine Publishing Group.

Hamilton, James T. 1996. "Private Interests in 'Public Interest' Programming: An Economic Assessment of Broadcaster Incentives." *Duke Law Journal*, 45: 1177–92.

———. 1997. "Taxes, Torts and the Toxics Release Inventory: Congressional Voting on Instruments to Control Pollution." *Economic Inquiry*, 35: 745–62.

———. 1998. *Channeling Violence: The Economic Market for Violent Television Programming*. Princeton, N.J.: Princeton University Press.

Hamilton, John Maxwell, and George A. Krimsky. 1996. *Hold the Press: The Inside Story on Newspapers*. Baton Rouge: Lousiana State University Press.

Hamlen, William A., Jr. 1991. "Superstardom in Popular Music: Empirical Evidence." *Review of Economics and Statistics*, 73(4): 729–33.

Haneman, W. Michael. 1994. "Valuing the Environment Through Contingent Valuation." *Journal of Economic Perspectives*, 8(4): 19–43.

Harmon, Mark D. 1989. "Market Size and Local Television Judgment." *Journal of Media Economics*, 2(1): 15–29.

Harper, Christopher. 1997. "The Daily Me." *American Journalism Review*, 19(3): 40–43.

Hart, Roderick P. 1994. *Seducing America: How Television Charms the Modern Voter*. New York: Oxford University Press.

———. 1997. *DICTION 4.0: The Text Analysis Program User's Manual*. Thousand Oaks, Calif.: Sage Publications.

———. 2000. *Campaign Talk: Why Elections Are Good for Us*. Princeton, N.J.: Princeton University Press.

Hausman, Jerry. 1997. "Taxation by Telecommunications Regulation." Working paper, National Bureau of Economic Research.

Hausman, Jerry A., and Gregory K. Leonard. 1997. "Superstars in the National Basketball Association: Economic Value and Policy." *Journal of Labor Economics*, 15(4): 586–24.

Hausman, Jerry A., and J. Gregory Sidak. 1999. "A Consumer-Welfare Approach to the Mandatory Unbundling of Telecommunications Networks." *Yale Law Journal*, 109: 417.

Hazel, Dicken Garcia. 1989. *Journalistic Standards in Nineteenth Century America*. Madison: The University of Wisconsin Press.

Hazlett, Thomas W. 1997. "Prices and Outputs Under Cable TV Reregulation." *Journal of Regulatory Economics*, 12: 173–95.

———. 2001. "The U.S. Digital TV Transition: Time to Toss the Negroponte Switch." Working paper, Social Science Research Network.

Hazlett, Thomas W., and Matthew L. Spitzer. 1997. *Public Policy toward Cable Television: The Economics of Rate Controls*. Cambridge, Mass.: MIT Press; Washington, D.C.: AEI Press.

Hazlett, Thomas W., and David W. Sosa. 1997. "Was the Fairness Doctrine a 'Chilling Effect'? Evidence from the Post-Deregulation Radio Market." *Journal of Legal Studies*, 26: 279.

Heath, Thomas. 2001. "WUSA, WNBA's Plan: To Market, to Market; Timing, New Audiences Key to Success." *Washington Post*, April 1, p. D1.

Helmore, Edward. 2000. "News Going Nowhere?" *The Observer*, August 20, p. 7.

Herman, Edward S., and Robert W. McChesney. 1997. *The Global Media: The New Missionaries of Corporate Capitalism.* Washington D.C.: Cassell.

Hinich, Melvin J., and Michael C. Munger. 1994. *Ideology and the Theory of Political Choice.* Ann Arbor: University of Michigan Press.

Hoffman, Tom. 1998. "Rationality Reconceived: The Mass Electorate and Democratic Theory." *Critical Review,* 12(4): 459–80.

Hotelling, Harold. 1929. "Stability in Competition." *Economic Journal,* 34: 41–57.

Hower, Ralph M. 1949. *The History of an Advertising Agency.* Cambridge, Mass.: Harvard University Press.

Hoyer, Svennik, Stig Hadenius, and Lennart Weibull. 1975. *The Politics and Economics of the Press: A Developmental Perspective.* Beverly Hills, Calif.: Sage Publications.

Hoynes, William. 1994. *Public Television for Sale: Media, the Market, and the Public Sphere.* Boulder, Colo.: Westview Press.

Hudson, Frederic. 1873. *Journalism in the United States, from 1690–1872.* New York: Harper & Brothers.

Hundt, Reed E. 1996. "The Public's Airwaves: What Does the Public Interest Require of Television Broadcasters?" *Duke Law Journal,* 45: 1089.

———. 2000. *You Say You Want a Revolution: A Story of Information Age Politics.* New Haven: Yale University Press.

Huntington, Samuel P. 1953. "Conservatism as an Ideology." *American Political Science Review,* 51(2): 454–73.

Institute for Politics, Democracy, and the Internet. 2002. "The Virtual Trail: Political Journalism on the Internet." Washington, D.C.: The Graduate School of Political Management, George Washington University.

Inter-university Consortium for Political and Social Research. 1992. *Historical, Demographic, Economic, and Social Data: The United States, 1790–1970.* Ann Arbor, Mich.: Inter-university Consortium for Political and Social Research.

Ippolito, Pauline M., and Alan D. Mathios. 1995. "Information and Advertising: The Case of Fat Consumption in the United States." *American Economic Review,* 85(2): 91–95.

Irwin, Neil. 2000. "Political Web Sites Look Past Election; Firms Strive to Inaugurate Profitable Models." *Washington Post,* December 7, p. E4.

Ise, Sabrina J., and Jeffrey M. Perloff. 1997. "Effects of FCC Regulations on Television Profits." *Information Economics and Policy,* 9: 37–49.

Iyengar, Shanto. 1991. *Is Anyone Responsible? How Television Frames Political Issues.* Chicago: University of Chicago Press.

Iyengar, Shanto, and Donald R. Kinder. 1987. *News That Matters: Television and American Opinion.* Chicago: University of Chicago Press.

Jackson, Terry. 2001. "TV Anchors Find News Isn't Always the Focus." (June 12, 2001), at http://tv.miami.com/tvmiami/criticdocs/105121.html

Jacoby, William G. 1991. "Ideological Identification and Issue Attitudes." *American Journal of Political Science,* 35(1): 178–205.

Jamieson, Kathleen Hall. 1992. *Dirty Politics.* New York: Oxford University Press.

———. 2000. *Everything You Think You Know about Politics . . . and Why You Are Wrong.* New York: Basic Books.

Jamieson, Kathleen Hall, and Paul Waldman. 2003. *The Press Effect: Politicians, Journalists, and the Stories That Shape the Political World.* New York: Oxford University Press.

Janeway, Michael. 1999. *Republic of Denial: Press, Politics, and Public Life.* New Haven: Yale University Press.

Jennings, M. Kent. 1996. "Political Knowledge over Time and across Generations." *Public Opinion Quarterly*, 60: 228–52.

Jensen, Michael C. 1979. "Toward a Theory of the Press." In *Economics and Social Institutions*, Karl Brunner, ed., pp. 267–87. Boston: Martinus Nijoff.

Jones, Alex S. 1986. "The Anchors: Who They Are, What They Do, the Tests They Face." *New York Times*, July 27, sec. 6, p. 12.

Jones, Russell W., Carolyn Marshall, and Thomas P. Bergman. 1996. "Can a Marketing Campaign Be Used to Achieve Public Policy Goals?" *Journal of Public Policy and Marketing*, 15(1): 98–107.

Jordan, Amy B. 2000. "Is the Three-Hour Rule Living up to Its Potential? An Analysis of Educational Television for Children in the 1999/2000 Broadcast Season." Annenberg Public Policy Center of the University of Pennsylvania, Philadelphia.

Just, Marion R., W. Russell Neuman, and Ann Crigler. 1992. "An Economic Theory of Learning from News." Joan Shorenstein Barone Center Research Paper R-6. Cambridge, Mass.: Harvard University John F. Kennedy School of Government.

Justman, Moshe. 1994. "The Effect of Local Demand on Industry Location." *Review of Economics and Statistics*, 76(4): 742–53.

Kahn, Kim F., and Patrick J. Kenney. 2002. "The Slant of the News: How Editorial Endorsements Influence Campaign Coverage and Citizens' Views of Candidates." *American Political Science Review*. 96(2): 381–94.

Kaiser Family Foundation. 1997. "Survey of ER Viewers."

Kalb, Marvin. 1998. "The Rise of the 'New News': A Case Study of Two Root Causes of the Modern Scandal Coverage." Joan Shorenstein Barone Center Discussion Paper D-34. John F. Kennedy School of Government, Harvard University, Cambridge, Mass.

———. 2001. *One Scandalous Story: Clinton, Lewinsky, and Thirteen Days That Tarnished American Journalism*. New York: Free Press.

Kandel, Eugene, and Ben-Zion Zilberfarb. 1999. "Differential Interpretation of Information in Inflation Forecasts." *Review of Economics and Statistics*, 81(2): 217–26.

Kaplan, Richard L. 1993. "The Economics and Politics of Nineteenth-Century Newspapers." *American Journalism*, 10(1): 84–101.

———. 1995. "The Economics of Popular Journalism in the Gilded Age." *Journalism History*, 21(2): 65–79.

Kennedy, Robert E. 1999. "Strategy Fads and Competitive Convergence." Working paper, Harvard Business School, Boston, Mass.

Keogh, James. 1972. *President Nixon and the Press*. New York: Funk & Wagnalls.

Kerbel, Matthew Robert. 1994. *Edited for Television: CNN, ABC, and the 1992 Presidential Campaign*. Boulder, Colo.: Westview Press.

———. 2000. *If It Bleeds, It Leads: An Anatomy of Television News*. Boulder Colo.: Westview Press.

Kerber, Ross. 2001. "Voter.com Closed Its Doors after Discovering the Most Basic Lesson in Politics and Business: People Have to Buy What You're Selling." *Boston Globe*, February 19, p. D1.

Keyssar, Alexander. 2000. *The Right to Vote: The Contested History of Democracy in the United States*. New York: Basic Books.

Kiewiet, D. Roderick, and Mathew D. McCubbins. 1991. *The Logic of Delegation: Congressional Parties and the Appropriations Process*. Chicago: University of Chicago Press.

Kimball, Penn. 1994. *Downsizing the News: Network Cutbacks in the Nation's Capital*. Washington D.C.: Woodrow Wilson Center Press; Baltimore: Johns Hopkins University Press.

Knights, Peter. 1968. "'Competition' in the U.S. Daily Newspaper Industry, 1865–68." *Journalism Quarterly*, 45: 473–80.

Knutzen, Erik. 1996. "The Nye Guy." *Toronto Star*, July 20, p.65

Kovach, Bill., and Tom Rosenstiel. 1999. *Warp Speed: America in the Age of Mixed Media.* New York: Century Foundation Press.

———. 2001. *The Elements of Journalism: What Newspeople Should Know and the Public Should Expect.* New York: Crown Publishers.

Krajicek, David J. 1998. *Scooped! Media Miss Real Story on Crime While Chasing Sex, Sleaze, and Celebrities.* New York: Columbia University Press.

Krasnow, Erwin, and Jack N. Goodman. 1998. "The 'Public Interest' Standard: The Search for the Holy Grail." *Federal Communications Law Journal*, 50: 605.

Krasnow, Erwin, Lawrence D. Longley, and Herbert A. Terry. 1982. *The Politics of Broadcast Regulation.* New York: St. Martin's Press.

Krattenmaker, Thomas, and Lucas A. Powe, Jr. 1994. *Regulating Broadcast Programming.* Cambridge, Mass: MIT Press.

Krause, George A., and Jim Granato. 1998. "Fooling Some of the Public Some of the Time? A Test for Weak Rationality with Heterogeneous Information Levels." *Public Opinion Quarterly*, 62(2): 135–51.

Krotoszynski, Ronald J., Jr., and Richard M. Blaiklock. 2000. "Enhancing the Spectrum: Media Power, Democracy, and the Marketplace of Ideas." *University of Illinois Law Review*, 2000(3): 813.

Kuczynski, Alex. 2000. "On CBS News, Some of What You See Isn't There." *New York Times*, January 12, p. A1.

Kuklinski, James H., Paul J. Quirk, Jennifer Jerit, David Schwieder, and Robert F. Rich. 2000. "Misinformation and the Currency of Democratic Citizenship." *Journal of Politics*, 62(3): 790–816.

Kuklinski, James H., Paul J. Quirk, Jennifer Jerit, and Robert F. Rich. 2001. "The Political Environment and Citizen Competence." *American Journal of Political Science*, 45(2): 410–24.

Kunkel, D. 1998. "The Implementation Gap: Policy Battles about Defining Children's Educational Programming." *Annals of the American Academy of Political and Social Science*, 557: 39–53.

Kuran, Timur. 1995. *Private Truths, Public Lies: The Social Consequences of Preference Falsification.* Cambridge, Mass: Harvard University Press.

Kurtz, Howard. 1991. "The Lite Stuff of Network News: Tight Budgets, Viewer Defections Leading to Blander Coverage." *Washington Post*, September 19, p. D1.

———. 1993. *Media Circus: The Trouble with America's Newspapers.* New York: Times Books.

———. 2000. *The Fortune Tellers: Inside Wall Street's Game of Money, Media, and Manipulation.* New York: Free Press.

———. 2002. "Local TV News and the Elections: Ads Infinitum, but Few Stories." *Washington Post*, Nov. 2, A7.

Lacey, Marc, and Bill Carter. 2000. "In Trade-off with TV Networks, Drug Office Is Reviewing Scripts." *New York Times*, January 14, p.A1.

Lacy, Stephen. 1989. "A Model of Demand for News: Impact of Competition on Newspaper Content." *Journalism Quarterly*, 66: 40–48.

———. 1992. "The Financial Commitment Approach to News Media Competition." *Journal of Media Economics*, 5(2): 5–21.

Lacy, Stephen, Tony Atwater, and Xinmin Qin. 1989. "Competition and the Allocation of Resources for Local Television News." *Journal of Media Economics*, 2: 3–13.

Lacy, Stephen, and James M. Bernstein. 1992. "The Impact of Competition and Market Size on the Assembly Cost of Local Television News." *Mass Comm Review*, 19(1): 41–48.

Lacy, Stephen, and Frederick Fico. 1991. "The Link between Newspaper Content Quality and Circulation." *Newspaper Research Journal*, 12(2): 46–57.

Ladha, Krishna. 1992. "The Condorcet Jury Theorem, Free Speech, and Correlated Votes." *American Journal of Political Science*, 36(3): 617–34.

Lamberton, Donald M., ed.. 1996. *The Economics of Communication and Information*. Cheltenham, UK: Edward Elgar.

Ledbetter, James. 1997. *Made Possible By—: The Death of Public Broadcasting in the United States*. New York: Verso.

Lee, Alfred McClung. 1937. *The Daily Newspaper in America: The Evolution of a Social Instrument*. New York: The Macmillan Company.

Lehrer, James. 1992. *A Bus of My Own*. New York: G. P. Putnam's Sons.

Lessig, Lawrence. 2001. *The Future of Ideas: The Fate of the Commons in a Connected World*. New York: Random House.

Levi, Lili. 2000. "Reporting the Official Truth: The Revival of the FCC's News Distortion Policy." *Washington University Law Quarterly*, 78: 1005–1156.

Levin, Harvey J. 1980. *Fact and Fancy in Television Regulation: An Economic Study of Policy Alternatives*. New York: Russell Sage Foundation.

Levit, Kenneth J. 1993. "Campaign Finance Reform and the Return of *Buckley v. Valeo*." *Yale Law Journal*, 103(2): 469–503.

Levy, Jonathan, Marcelino Ford-Livene, and Anne Levine. 2002. "Broadcast Television: Survivor in a Sea of Competition." Working paper, Office of Plans and Policy, Federal Communications Commission.

Lewis, Michael. 1999. *The New New Thing: A Silicon Valley Story*. New York: W. W. Norton.

Lichter, Robert and Richard Noyes. 1995. *Good Intentions Make Bad News: Why Americans Hate Campaign Journalism*. Lanham, Md.: Rowman & Littlefield Publishers, Inc.

Lippmann, Walter. 1922. *Public Opinion*. New York: Harcourt Brace.

Litman, Barry. 1988. "Microeconomic Foundations." In *Press Concentration and Monopoly: New Perspectives on Newspaper Ownership and Operation*, Robert G. Picard, James P. Winter, Maxwell E. McCombs, and Stephen Lacy, eds. Norwood, N.J.: Ablex Publishing Corporation.

Littlewood, Thomas B. 2000. *Calling Elections: The History of Horse-Race Journalism*. Notre Dame: University of Notre Dame Press.

Lohmann, Suzanne. 1998. "An Information Rationale for the Power of Special Interests." *American Political Science Review*, 92(4): 809–27.

Loomis, David, and Philip Meyer. 2000. "Opinion Without Polls: Finding a Link between Corporate Culture and Public Journalism." *International Journal of Public Opinion Research*, 12(3): 276–84.

Lott, John R. 1999. "Public Schooling, Indoctrination, and Totalitarianism." *Journal of Political Economy*, 107(6): 127–57.

Lowery, David, W. E. Lyons, and Ruth Highland Dehong. 1995. "The Empirical Evidence for Citizen Information and a Local Market for Public Goods." *American Political Science Review*, 89(3): 705–7.

Lupia, Arthur. 1994. "Shortcuts versus Encyclopedias: Information and Voting Behavior in California Insurance Reform Elections." *American Political Science Review*, 88(1): 63–76.

——. 2001a. "Evaluation: The Web White and Blue Network 2000." Working paper, University of California, San Diego.

——. 2001b. "What We Should Know: Can Ordinary Citizens Make Extraordinary Choices?" Paper prepared for WCFIA Conference on Individual Opinion Formation and Societal Choice.

——. 2001c. "Institutions as Informational Crutches? Using Rational Choice Theory to Improve Civic Competence." Working paper, University of Michigan, Ann Arbor.

Lupia, Arthur, and Mathew D. McCubbins. 1998. *The Democratic Dilemma: Can Citizens Learn What They Need to Know?* Cambridge: Cambridge University Press.

MacNeil, Robert. 1997. *Market Journalism: New Highs, New Lows*. Washington, D.C.: Aspen Institute.

Mankiw, N. Gregory and Michael D. Whinston. 1986. "Free Entry and Social Inefficiency." *Rand Journal of Economics*, 17(1): 48–58.

Marks, Alexandra. 1996. "New Media Alliances Test Press Objectivity." *Christian Science Monitor*, July 2, p.1.

Mason, Dave. 2001. "Going Up the Hill of Post-College Life." *Newsday*, January 10, p. B27.

Matusow, Barbara. 1983. *The Evening Stars: The Making of the Network News Anchor*. Boston: Houghton Mifflin.

Mayer, Jane. 2000. "Bad News; What's Behind the Recent Gaffes at ABC?" *The New Yorker*, August 14, p. 30

McCabe, Peter. 1987. *Bad News at Black Rock: The Sell-out of CBS News*. New York: Arbor House.

McChesney, Robert W. 1993. *Telecommunications, Mass Media, and Democracy: The Battle for Control of U.S. Broadcasting, 1928–1935*. New York: Oxford University Press.

——. 2000. *Rich Media, Poor Democracy: Communication Politics in Dubious Times*. New York: New Press.

McGowan, William. 2001. *Coloring the News: How Crusading for Diversity Has Corrupted American Journalism*. San Francisco, Calif: Encounter.

McLennan, Andrew. 1998. "Consequences of the Condorcet Jury Theorem for Beneficial Information Aggregation by Rational Agents." *The American Political Science Review*, 92(2): 413–18.

McLuhan, Marshall. 1964. *Understanding Media: The Extensions of Man*. New York: Signet.

McManus, John H. 1994. *Market-Driven Journalism: Let the Citizen Beware*. Thousand Oaks, Calif.: Sage Publications.

McMillan, John. 1994. "Selling Spectrum Rights." *Journal of Economic Perspectives*, 8(3): 145–62.

Media Dynamics. 2000. *TV Dimensions*. New York: Media Dynamics.

——. 2001. *TV Dimensions*. New York: Media Dynamics.

Mediamark Research Inc. 1998. *Mediamark Research, Spring 1998*. Volumes P1–P20. New York: Mediamark Research.

Meiklejohn, Alexander. 1948. *Free Speech and Its Relation to Self-Government*. New York: Harper.

Mickiewicz, Ellen. 1997. *Changing Channels: Television and the Struggle for Power in Russia.* New York: Oxford University Press.

Mifflin, Lawrie, and Stuart Elliott. 1999. "Lewinsky Proves to Be Popular with Both Viewers and Sponsors" *New York Times,* March 5, p. A14.

Miller, Greg. 1999. "Judge Rejects 'Fair Use' of News Protection." *Los Angeles Times,* November 9, p. C1.

Miller, Joanne M., and Jon A. Krosnick. 2000. "News Media Impact on the Ingredients of Presidential Evaluations: Politically Knowledgeable Citizens Are Guided by a Trusted Source." *American Journal of Political Science,* 44(2): 295–309.

Miller, Mark C. 2002. "What's Wrong with This Picture?" *The Nation,* Jan. 7, p. 18–22.

Milyo, Jeffrey, and Joel Waldfogel. 1999. "The Effect of Price Advertising on Prices: Evidence in the Wake of 44 Liquormart." *American Economic Review,* 89(5): 1081–96.

Mindich, David T. Z. 1998. *Just the Facts: How "Objectivity" Came to Define American Journalism.* New York: New York University Press.

Miner, Michael. 2002. "Money and Morals: WBEZ Draws the Line." *Chicago Reader* Jan. 8, 2003, at http://www.cireader.com/hottype/2002/021025_1.html

Mink, Eric. 2000. "No Network Is an Island? Tell That to CBS: Smash 'Survivor' Is Carrying Ratings Torch for Network." *New York Daily News,* July 12, p. 38.

Minow, Newton N., and Craig L. LaMay. 1995. *Abandoned in the Wasteland: Children, Television, and the First Amendment.* New York: Hill and Wang.

Morgan Stanley Dean Witter. 2001. "Internet Direct Marketing and Advertising Services." New York: Morgan Stanley Dean Witter.

Mott, Frank Luther. 1950. *American Journalism: A History of Newspapers in the United States through 260 Years: 1690 to 1950.* New York: Macmillan.

Mueller, Dennis C. 1979. *Public Choice.* Cambridge: Cambridge University Press.

Mullainathan, Sendhil. 2000. "Thinking through Categories." Working paper, Massachusetts Institute of Technology and the National Bureau of Economic Research, Cambridge, Mass.

Mullainathan, Sendhil, and Andrei Shleifer. 2002. "Media Bias." Working paper, National Bureau of Economic Research, Cambridge, Mass.

Mutz, Diana C. 1995. "Effects of Horse-Race Coverage on Campaign Coffers: Strategic Contributing in Presidential Primaries." *Journal of Politics,* 57(4): 1015–42.

———. 1998. *Impersonal Influence: How Perceptions of Mass Collectives Affect Political Attitudes.* New York: Cambridge University Press

Mutz, Diana C., and Paul S. Martin. 2001. "Facilitating Communication across Lines of Political Difference: The Role of Mass Media." *American Political Science Review,* 95(1): 97–114.

Mutz, Diana C., and Joe Soss. 1997. "Reading Public Opinion: The Influence of News Coverage on Perceptions of Public Sentiment." *Public Opinion Quarterly,* 61(3): 431–51.

Nadeau, Richard, Richard G. Niemi, David P. Fan, and Timothy Amato. 1999. "Elite Economic Forecasts, Economic News, Mass Economic Judgments, and Presidential Approval." *Journal of Politics,* 61(1): 109–35.

Napoli, Philip M. 2001. "Market Conditions and Public Affairs Programming: Implications for Digital Television Policy." *Harvard International Journal of Press/Politics,* 6(2): 15–29.

National Television Violence Study. 1998. *National Television Violence Study.* Volume 3. Thousand Oaks, Calif.: Sage Publications.

Neiva, Elizabeth MacIver. 1996. "Chain Building: The Consolidation of the American Newspaper Industry, 1953–1980." *Business History Review,* 70(1): 1–42.

Nelson, Phillip. 1970. "Information and Consumer Behavior." *Journal of Political Economy,* 78: 311–29.

———. 1974. "Advertising as Information." *Journal of Political Economy,* 82(4): 729–54.

Nerone, John C. 1987. "The Mythology of the Penny Press." *Critical Studies in Mass Communication,* 4: 376–404.

Netanel, Neil W. 1996. "Copyright and a Democratic Civil Society." *Yale Law Journal,* 106: 283.

Netz, Janet S. and Beck Taylor. 1998. "Maximum or Minimum Differentiation? An Empirical Investigation into the Location of Firms." Working paper, Purdue University, West Lafayette, Ind.

Neuman, W. Russell. 1986. *The Paradox of Mass Politics: Knowledge and Opinion in the American Electorate.* Cambridge, Mass.: Harvard University Press.

———. 1993. *The Future of the Mass Audience.* Cambridge: Cambridge University Press.

Neuman, W. Russell, Marion Just, and Ann Crigler. 1992. *Common Knowledge: News and the Construction of Political Meaning.* Chicago: University of Chicago Press.

Nie, Norman H., Jane Junn, and Kenneth Stehlik-Barry. 1996. *Education and Democratic Citizenship in America.* Chicago: University of Chicago Press.

Nielsen Media Research. *1988 Report on Television.* New York: Nielsen Media Research.

———. 1999. *Nielsen Station Index: Test Market Profiles 1999.* New York: Nielsen Media Research.

———. 2000a. *Nielsen Television Index: Household and Persons Cost per Thousand Report, November 1999.* New York: Nielsen Media Research.

———. 2000b. *Nielsen Television Index: National Audience Demographics, November 1999.* Volume 2. New York: Nielsen Media Research.

———. 2000c. *Nielsen Station Index: Viewers in Profile, November 1999.* New York: Nielsen Media Research.

Niemi, Richard G., and Jane Junn. 1998. *Civic Education: What Makes Students Learn.* New Haven, Conn.: Yale University Press.

Niven, David. 1999. "Partisan Bias in the Media? A New Test." *Social Science Quarterly,* 80(4): 847–57.

Noam, Eli M. 1987. "A Public and Private-Choice Model of Broadcasting." *Public Choice,* 55: 163–87.

———. 1991. *Television in Europe.* New York: Oxford University Press.

Noe, Thomas, and Geoffrey Parker. 2000. "Winner Take All: Competition, Strategy, and the Structure of Returns in the Internet Economy." Working paper, Tulane University, New Orleans, La.

Noll, Roger G. 1993. "Downsian Thresholds and the Theory of Political Advertising." In *Information, Participation, and Choice: An Economic Theory of Democracy in Perspective,* Bernard Grofman, ed., pp. 37–55. Ann Arbor: University of Michigan Press.

———. 2002. "Resolving Policy Chaos in High Speed Internet Access." Stanford Law School Working Paper.

Noll, Roger G., Merton J. Peck, and John J. McGowan. 1973. *Economic Aspects of Television Regulation.* Washington, D.C.: Brookings Institution Press.

Noll, Roger G., and Monroe E. Price. 1998. *A Communications Cornucopia: Markle Foundation Essays on Information Policy.* Washington D.C.: Brookings Institution Press.

Nord, David Paul. 1986. "Working-Class Readers: Family, Community, and Reading in Late Nineteenth-Century America." *Communication Research,* 13(2): 156–81.

————. 1988. "A Republican Literature: A Study of Magazine Reading and Readers in Late Eighteenth-Century New York." *American Quarterly,* 40(1): 42–64.

Norris, Pippa. 2000. *A Virtuous Circle: Political Communications in Postindustrial Societies.* Cambridge: Cambridge University Press

North, Simon Newton Dexter. 1884. *History and Present Condition of the Newspaper and Periodical Press of the United States.* Washington, D.C.: Government Printing Office.

Norton, Seth W., and Will Norton, Jr. 1986. "Economies of Scale and the New Technology of Daily Newspapers: A Survivor Analysis." *Quarterly Review of Economics and Business,* 26(2): 66–83.

N. W. Ayer & Son. 1880. *N. W. Ayer & Son's American Newspaper Annual.* Philadelphia: N. W. Ayer & Son.

————. 1890. *N. W. Ayer & Son's American Newspaper Annual.* Philadelphia: N. W. Ayer & Son.

————. 1900. *N. W. Ayer & Son's American Newspaper Annual.* Philadelphia: N. W. Ayer & Son.

Oberholzer-Gee, Felix, and Joel Waldfogel. 2001. "Electoral Acceleration: The Effect of Minority Population on Minority Voter Turnout." Working paper, National Bureau of Economic Research, Cambridge, Mass.

Owen, Bruce M. 1975. *Economics and Freedom of Expression, Media Structure and the First Amendment.* Cambridge, Mass.: Ballinger Publishing.

————. 1999. *The Internet Challenge to Television.* Cambridge, Mass.: Harvard University Press.

Owen, Bruce M., Jack H. Beebe, and W. G. Manning, Jr. 1974. *Television Economics.* Lexington Mass.: Lexington Books.

Owen, Bruce M., and Steven S. Wildman. 1992. *Video Economics.* Cambridge, Mass.: Harvard University Press.

Owen, Rob, and Barbara Vancheri. 2001. "TV Stations Go All out to Attract Viewers When Playing the Promotional Ratings Game." *Pittsburgh Post-Gazette,* Feb. 22, p. D1.

Page, Benjamin I., and Robert Y. Shapiro. 1992. *The Rational Public: Fifty Years of Trends in Americans' Policy Preferences.* Chicago: University of Chicago Press.

Paletz, David L. 1999. *The Media in American Politics: Contents and Consequences.* New York: Longman.

Papandrea, Franco. 1997. "Modeling Television Programming Choices." *Information Economics and Policy,* 9: 203–18.

Parker, Kimberly, and Claudia Deane. 1997. "Ten Years of the Pew News Interest Index: A Report for Presentation at the 1997 Meeting of the American Association for Public Opinion Research." Washington, D.C.: Pew Research Center for the People and the Press.

Parker, Richard. 1997. "Journalism and Economics: The Tangled Webs of Profession, Narrative, and Responsibility in a Modern Democracy." Joan Shorenstein Barone Center Discussion Paper D-25. John F. Kennedy School of Government, Harvard University, Cambridge, Mass.

Parloff, Roger. 2002. "Can We Talk? A Shocking First Amendment Ruling against Nike Radically Reduces the Rights of Corporations to Speak Their Minds. Will the Supreme Court Let It Stand?" *Fortune*, September, p. 102.

Patterson, Thomas E. 1993. *Out of Order.* New York: A. Knopf.

———. 2000. *Doing Well and Doing Good: How Soft News and Critical Journalism Are Shrinking the News Audience and Weakening Democracy—and What News Outlets Can Do about It.* Joan Shorenstein Center Soft News Project Report. John F. Kennedy School of Government, Harvard University, Cambridge, Mass.

Petrocik, John R. 1996. "Issue Ownership in Presidential Elections, with a 1980 Case Study." *American Journal of Political Science*, 40(3): 825–50.

Pew Research Center for the People and the Press. 1999. *Retro-Politics: The Political Typology, Version 3.0.* Washington, D.C.: Pew Research Center for the People and the Press.

———. 2000a. *Audiences Fragmented and Skeptical: The Tough Job of Communicating with Voters.* Washington, D.C.: Pew Research Center for the People and the Press.

———. 2000b. *Investors Now Go Online for Quotes, Advice: Internet Sapping Broadcast News Audience.* Washington, D.C.: Pew Research Center for the People and the Press.

———. 2000c. *Youth Vote Influenced by Online Information: Internet Election News Audience Seeks Convenience, Familiar Names.* Washington, D.C.: Pew Research Center for the People and the Press

———. 2002. "Public's News Habits Little Changed by September 11." Washington, D.C.: Pew Research Center for the People and the Press.

Picard, Robert G. 1997. "Modeling the Problem: De Novo Entry into Daily Newspaper Markets." *Newspaper Research Journal*, 18(3): 94–108.

———. 1998. "Measuring and Interpreting Productivity of Journalists." *Newspaper Research Journal*, 19(4): 71–84.

Picard, Robert G., James P. Winter, Maxwell E. McCombs, and Stephen Lacy. 1988. *Press Concentration and Monopoly: New Perspectives on Newspaper Ownership and Operation.* Norwood, N.J.: Ablex Publishing Corporation.

Piller, Charles. 2000. "Web Sites Fail to Click: Online Media Attract Millions of 'Eyeballs,' but Few Sites Have Figured out How to Turn a Profit." *Los Angeles Times*, August 18, p. A1.

Png, I.P.L. and David Reitman. 1995. "Why Are Some Products Branded and Others Not?" *Journal of Law and Economics*, 38(1): 207–24.

Popkin, Samuel L. 1994. *The Reasoning Voter: Communication and Persuasion in Presidential Campaigns.* Chicago: University of Chicago Press.

Portney, Paul R. 1994. "The Contingent Valuation Debate: Why Economists Should Care." *Journal of Economic Perspectives*, 8(4): 3–17.

Posner, Eric A. 1998. "Symbols, Signals, and Social Norms in Politics and the Law." *Journal of Legal Studies*, 27: 765–98.

Posner, Richard. 1986. "Free Speech in an Economic Perspective." *Suffolk University Law Review*, 20(1): 1–54.

———. 2001. *Public Intellectuals: A Study of Decline.* Cambridge, Mass: Harvard University Press.

Postman, Neil. 1985. *Amusing Ourselves to Death: Public Discourse in the Age of Show Business.* New York: Penguin Books.

Postman, Neil, and Steve Powers. 1992. *How to Watch TV News.* New York: Penguin Books.

Powers, Angela. 1993. "Competition, Conduct, and Ratings in Local Television News: Applying the Industrial Organization Model." *Journal of Media Economics,* 6(2): 37–44.

Powers, Ron. 1977. *The Newscasters.* New York: St. Martin's Press.

Presbrey, Frank. 1929. *History and Development of Advertising.* Garden City, N.Y.: Doubleday.

Price, Linda L., Lawrence F. Feick, and Robin A. Higie. 1987. "Information Sensitive Consumers and Market Information." *The Journal of Consumer Affairs,* 21(2): 328–41.

Price, Monroe E. 1994. "The Market for Loyalties: Electronic Media and the Global Competition for Allegiances." *Yale Law Journal,* 104: 667.

Price, Vincent, and John Zaller. 1993. "Who Gets the News? Alternative Measures of News Reception and Their Implications for Research." *Public Opinion Quarterly,* 55(2): 133–64.

Prior, Markus. 2001a. "The Costs of Free Choice: How Increasing Media Options Widen the Gap in Political Knowledge and Participation." Working paper, Department of Communication, Stanford University, Stanford, Calif.

————. 2001b. "Avoiding Politics: The Relation of Entertainment Preference and Partisan Feelings." Paper prepared for 97th Annual Meeting of the American Political Science Association, Aug. 30–Sept. 2.

————. 2002. "The Incumbent in the Living Room: The Rise of Television and the Incumbency Advantage in U.S. House Elections." Working paper, Stanford University, Stanford, Calif.

————. 2003. "Any Good News in Soft News? The Impact of Soft News Preference on Political Knowledge." Working paper, Princeton University, Princeton, N.J.

Pritchard, David. 2002. "Viewpoint Diversity in Cross-Owned Newspapers and Television Stations: A Study of News Coverage of the 2000 Presidential Campaign." Working paper, Media Ownership Working Group, Federal Communications Commission.

Project for Excellence in Journalism. 2001. "Local TV News Project." Nov. 15, 2001, at http://www.journalism.org/publ_research/local-tv.2001_public_toc.html.

Rabin, Matthew, and Joel L. Schrag. 1999. "First Impressions Matter: A Model of Confirmatory Bias." *Quarterly Journal of Economics,* 114(1): 37–82.

Radio and Television News Directors Foundation. 1996. *Dollars and Demographics: The Evolving Market for News.* Washington, D.C.: Radio and Television News Directors Foundation.

Rahn, Wendy M. 1993. "The Role of Partisan Stereotypes in Information Processing about Political Candidates." *American Journal of Political Science,* 37(2): 472–96.

Rainey, R. Randall. 1993. "The Public's Interest in Public Affairs Discourse, Democratic Governance, and Fairness in Broadcasting: A Critical Review of the Public Interest Duties of the Electronic Media." *Georgetown Law Journal,* 82: 269–372.

Raney, Rebecca Fairley. 2002. "New Economy: In the Next Year, the Federal Government Will Move to Give the Public Easier Online Access to Data and Services." *New York Times,* Dec. 23, C4.

Ray, William B. 1990. *The Ups and Downs of Radio-TV Regulation.* Ames: Iowa State University Press.

Redish, Martin H. 2001. *Money Talks: Speech, Economic Power, and the Values of Democracy*. New York: New York University Press.

Reeves, Richard. 1998. *What the People Know: Freedom and the Press*. Cambridge, Mass.: Harvard University Press.

Roberts, Gene, and Thomas Kunkel, eds. 2002. *Breach of Faith: A Crisis of Coverage in the Age of Corporate Newspapering*. Fayetteville: University of Arkansas Press.

Roberts, Gene, Thomas Kunkel, and Charles Layton, eds. 2001. *Leaving Readers Behind: The Age of Corporate Newspapering*. Little Rock: University of Arkansas Press.

Roberts, Scott, Jane Frenette, and Dione Stearns. 2002. "A Comparison of Media Outlets and Owners for Ten Selected Markets: 1960, 1980, 2000." Working paper, Media Ownership Working Group, Federal Communications Commission.

Roemer, John E. 1994. "The Strategic Role of Party Ideology When Voters Are Uncertain about How the Economy Works." *American Political Science Review*, 88(2): 327–35.

Rogers, Everett M., and James W. Dearing. 1988. "Agenda Setting Research: Where Has It Been, Where Is It Going?" In *Communication Yearbook*, James A. Anderson, ed., 11: 555–94. Beverly Hills: Sage Publications.

Rogers, Robert P., and John R. Woodbury. 1996. "Market Structure, Program Diversity, and Radio Audience Size." *Contemporary Economic Policy*, 14: 81–91.

Rosen, Jay. 1999. *What Are Journalists For?* New Haven: Yale University Press.

Rosen, Sherwin. 1981. "The Economics of Superstars." *American Economic Review*, 71(5): 845–58.

Rosenkranz, E. Joshua, ed. 1999. *If Buckley Fell: A First Amendment Blueprint for Regulating Money in Politics*. New York: Century Foundation.

Rosenstiel, Tom. 1985. "'Infotainment': Latest News at Networks—Cutting Cost." *Los Angeles Times*, November 22, p.1

———. 1993. *Strange Bedfellows: How Television and the Presidential Candidates Changed American Politics*. New York: Hyperion.

———. 1994. "Role of TV News in Shaping Foreign Policy under Increasing Scrutiny." *Los Angeles Times*, July 25, p. A14.

Rosenstiel, Tom, Carl Gottlieb, and Lee Ann Brady. 1998. "Local TV: What Works, What Flops, and Why." *Project for Excellence in Journalism*. Feb.29, 2000, at http://www.jounalism.org/1998/html/whatworks.html.

———. 1999. "Quality Brings Higher Ratings, but Enterprise Is Disappearing." *Columbia Journalism Review*, November/December: 80–87.

———. 2000. "Time of Peril for TV News." *Columbia Journalism Review*, November/December: 84–92.

Rosse, James N. 1967. "Daily Newspapers, Monopolistic Competition, and Economies of Scale." *The American Economic Review*, 57(2): 522–33.

———. 1970. "Estimating Cost Function Parameters without Using Cost Data: Illustrated Methodology." *Econometrica*, 38(2): 256–75.

———. 1978. "The Evolution of One Newspaper Cities." Working paper, Department of Economics, Stanford University, Stanford, Calif.

Rosse, James N., Bruce M. Owen, and James Dertouzos. 1975. "Trends in the Daily Newspaper Industry, 1923–1973." Working paper, Department of Economics, Stanford University, Stanford, Calif.

Rouner, Donna, Michael D. Slater, and Judith M. Buddenbaum. 1999. "How Perceptions of News Bias in News Sources Relate to Beliefs about Media Bias." *Newspaper Research Journal*, 20(2): 41–51.

Rowell, George Presbury. 1870. *Geo. P. Rowell and Co.'s American Newspaper Directory.* New York: Geo. P. Rowell & Co.

Rust, Ronald T. 1986. *Advertising Media Models: A Practical Guide.* Lexington, Mass.: Lexington Books.

Rutenbeck, Jeffrey B. 1990a. "Editorial Perception of Newspaper Independence and the Presidential Campaign of 1872." *Journalism History*, 17: 13–22.

———. 1990b. "The Rise of Independent Newspapers in the 1870s: A Transformation in American Journalism." Ph.D. dissertation University of Washington.

———. 1991. "Toward a History of the Ideologies of Partisanship and Independence in American Journalism." *Journal of Communication Inquiry*, 15(2): 126–39.

———. 1995. "Newspaper Trends in the 1870s: Proliferation, Popularization, and Political Independence." *Journalism and Mass Communication Quarterly*, 72(2): 361–75.

Sabato, Larry J. 1991. *Feeding Frenzy: How Attack Journalism Has Transformed American Politics.* New York: The Free Press.

Sabato, Larry, J., Mark Stencel, and S. Robert Lichter. 2000. *Peepshow: Media and Politics in an Age of Scandal.* Lanham, Md.: Rowman and Littlefield.

Salant, Richard. 1988. "In the Eye of the Storm: Network News—Prospects for Its Future, If Any." *Los Angeles Times*, May 20, p. 6-1.

Schauer, Frederick. 1982. *Free Speech: A Philosophical Enquiry.* Cambridge: Cambridge University Press.

Scheuer, Jeffrey. 1999. *The Sound Bite Society: Television and the American Mind.* New York: Four Walls Eight Windows.

Schiller, Dan. 1981. *Objectivity and the News: The Public and the Rise of Commercial Journalism.* Philadelphia: University of Pennsylvania Press.

Schmitt, Kelly L. 1999. "The Three-Hour Rule: Is It Living up to Expectations?" Annenberg Public Policy Center of the University of Pennsylvania.

Schneider, Mark, Paul Teske, Melissa Marschall, and Christine Roch. 1998. "Shopping for Schools: In the Land of the Blind, The One-Eyed Parent May Be Enough." *American Journal of Political Science*, 42(3): 769–93.

Schudson, Michael. 1978. *Discovering the News: A Social History of American Newspapers.* New York: Basic Books.

———.1996. *New Technology, Old Values . . . and a New Definition of News.* Washington, D.C.: Radio and Television News Directors Foundation.

———. 1998. *The Good Citizen: A History of American Civic Life.* New York: Free Press.

Schwartz, John. 2000. "Seamy and Steamy: A Group of Savvy Entrepreneurs Is Exploiting the Latest Technology to Pioneer the Web's Full Commercial Potential; They're Smut Merchants." *Washington Post*, May 17, p. G6

Schwer, R. Keith, and Rennae Daneshvary. 1995. "Willingness to Pay for Public Television and the Advent of 'Look-Alike' Cable Television Channels: A Case Study." *Journal of Media Economics*, 8(3): 95–109.

Scott, David K., and Robert H. Gobetz. 1992. "Hard News/Soft News Content of the National Broadcast Networks, 1972–1987." *Journalism Quarterly*, 69(2): 406–12.

Scripps Treasure Coast Publishing. 2001. "Newspaper Delivers the Best Prospects." Nov. 16, 2001, at http://tcpublishingco.com/special/specpubdemos.html.

Seelye, Katharine Q. 2002. "White House Seeks a Change in Rules on Air Pollution." *New York Times*, June 14, p.1.

Sen, Amartya. 1970. "The Impossibility of a Paretian Liberal." *Journal of Political Economy*, 78(1): 152–57.

———. 1976. "Poverty: An Ordinal Approach to Measurement." *Econometrica*, 44(2): 219–31.

Shachar, Ron and Bharat N. Anand. 1996. "All This and More, in the Next Episode of . . ." Yale School of Management Working Paper Series H-1. New Haven, CT: Yale School of Management.

———. 1998. "The Effectiveness and Targeting of Television Advertising." *Journal of Economics and Management Strategy*, 7(3): 363–96.

Shachar, Ron, and John W. Emerson. 1996. "How Old Should Seinfeld Be?" Yale School of Management Working Papers Series H-4. New Haven, Conn.: Yale School of Management.

Shachtman, Tom. 1995. *The Inarticulate Society: Eloquence and Culture in America*. New York: Free Press.

Shah, Dhavan V., Mark D. Watts, David Domke, David P. Fan, and Michael Fibison. 1999. "News Coverage, Economic Cues, and the Public's Presidential Preferences, 1984–1996." *Journal of Politics*, 61(4): 914–43.

Shales, Tom. 1983. "NBC Drops Mudd as 'Nightly News' Anchor." *Washington Post*, July 27, p. A1.

Shapiro, Carl, and Hal R. Varian. 1999. *Information Rules: A Strategic Guide to the Network Economy*. Boston: Harvard Business School Press.

Sharbutt, Jay. 1987. "The State of the Network News Business." *Los Angeles Times*, December 28, p. 6-1.

Shaw, Colin. 1999. *Deciding What We Watch: Taste, Decency, and Media Ethics in the UK and the USA*. New York: Oxford University Press.

Shaw, David. 1986a. "Better Than Ever? TV News: Demise Is Exaggerated." *Los Angeles Times*, December 28, p. 1

———. 1986b. "Pressure to Show Profits: Future of Network News—Is the Signal Weakening?" *Los Angeles Times*, December 29, p. 1.

Shaw, Donald L. 1967. "News Bias and the Telegraph: A Study of Historical Change." *Journalism Quarterly*, 44(1): 3–12.

———. 1981. "At the Crossroads: Change and Continuity in American Press News 1820–1860." *Journalism History*, 8(2): 38–50.

Shiller, Robert J. 2000. *Irrational Exuberance*. Princeton, N.J.: Princeton University Press.

Shiller, Robert J., and John Pound. 1989. "Survey Evidence of Diffusion of Interest and Information among Investors." *Journal of Economic Behavior and Organization*, 12: 47–66.

Shister, Gail. 2001. "Jennings Gaining on Brokaw in the Race for Viewers." *Philadelphia Inquirer*, November 15.

Shister, Neil. 2002. "Journalism and Commercial Success: Expanding Business Case for Quality News and Information." Washington, D.C.: The Aspen Institute.

Shmanske, Stephen. 1986. "New as a Public Good: Cooperative Ownership, Price Commitments, and the Success of the Associated Press." *Business History Review*, 60: 55–80.

Shuit, Douglas P. 1994. "Nonprofit Groups' Media Blitz on Health Care Reform to Focus on Californians." *Los Angeles Times*, July 22, p. A14.

Simmons, Steven J. 1978. *The Fairness Doctrine and the Media.* Berkeley, Calif: University of California Press.

Simon, Herbert A. 1978. "Rationality as Process and as Product of Thought." *The American Economic Review*, 68(2): 1–16.

Slotnick, Elliot E., and Jennifer A. Segal. 1998. *Television News and the Supreme Court: All the News That's Fit to Air?* Cambridge: Cambridge University Press.

Slovin, Myron B., Marie E. Sushka, and John A. Polonchek. 1992. "Informational Externalities of Seasoned Equity Issues." *Journal of Financial Economics*, 32: 87–101.

Smith, Culver Gaygood. 1977. *The Press, Politics and Patronage: The American Government's Use of Newspapers, 1789–1875.* Athens, Ga.: The University of Georgia Press.

Smith, Michael D., Joseph Bailey, and Erik Brynjolfsson. 2000. "Understanding Digital Markets: Review and Assessment." In *Understanding the Digital Economy: Data, Tools, and Research*, Erik Brynjolfsson and Brian Kahin, eds. Cambridge, Mass.: MIT Press.

Smith, Sally Bedell. 1983. "The Great Chase in Network News." *New York Times*, November 28, p. C21.

Smith, Terence. 2001. "Evening News Evolution." *NewsHour with Jim Lehrer.* July 3, 2001, at http://www.pbs.org/newshour/media/evening_news/index.html.

Smolla, Rodney A. 1992. *Free Speech in an Open Society.* New York: Knopf.

Smulyan, Susan. 1994. *Selling Radio: The Commercialization of American Broadcasting, 1920–1934.* Washington D.C.: Smithsonian Institution Press.

Snider, J. H., and Benjamin I. Page. 1997. "The Political Power of TV of Broadcasters: Covert Bias and Anticipated Reactions." Working paper, Northwestern University, Evanston, Ill.

Sniderman, Paul M., Richard A. Brody, and Philip E. Tetlock. 1991. *Reasoning and Choice: Explorations in Political Psychology.* New York: Cambridge University Press.

Somin, Ilya. 1998. "Voter Ignorance and the Democratic Ideal." *Critical Review*, 12(4): 413–58.

Spavins, Thomas. 2002. "The Measurement of Local Television News and Public Affairs Programs." Working paper, Media Ownership Working Group, Federal Communications Commission.

Spence, A. Michael. 1975. "Monopoly, Quality, and Regulation." *Bell Journal of Economics*, 6(2): 417–29.

———. 1976. "Product Selection, Fixed Costs, and Monopolistic Competition." *The Review of Economic Studies*, 43(2): 217–35.

Spence, A. Michael, and Bruce M. Owen. 1977. "Television Programming, Monopolistic Competition and Welfare." *Quarterly Journal of Economics*, 91: 103–26.

Spitzer, Matthew L. 1991. "Justifying Minority Preferences in Broadcasting." *Southern California Law Review*, 64: 293–361.

———. 1997. "An Introduction to the Law and Economics of the V-Chip." *Cardozo Arts and Entertainment Law Journal*, 15: 429–501.

———. 1998. "Speech Markets and Economic Markets." In *The New Palgrave Dictionary of Economics and the Law*, Peter Newman, ed. New York: Stockton Press.

Spot Quotations and Data. 1999. *Media Market Guide: Fall 1999.* Tarrytown, N.Y.: Spot Quotations and Data.

Squires, James D. 1994. *Read All about It! The Corporate Takeover of America's Newspapers.* New York: Times Books.

Starr, Jerold M. 2000. *Air Wars: The Fight to Reclaim Public Broadcasting.* Boston: Beacon.

Steele, Catherine A., and Kevin G. Barnhurst. 1996. "The Journalism of Opinion: Network News Coverage of U.S. Presidential Campaigns, 1968–1988." *Critical Studies in Mass Communication,* 13(3): 187–209.

Steiner, Peter O. 1952. "Program Patterns and Preferences, and the Workability of Competition in Radio Broadcasting." *Quarterly Journal of Economics,* 66: 194–223.

Stensaas, Harlan S. 1987. "Development of the Objectivity Ethic in U.S. Daily Newspapers." *Journal of Mass Media Ethics,* 2: 50–60.

Stigler, George J. 1961. "The Economics of Information." *The Journal of Political Economy,* 69(3): 213–25.

Strate, John M., Coit Cook Ford III, and Thomas B. Jankowski. 1994. "Women's Use of the Print Media to Follow Politics." *Social Science Quarterly,* 75(1): 166–86.

Stromberg, David. 2001. "Radio's Impact on Public Spending." Working paper, Stockholm University.

Sullivan, Kathleen M. 1995. "Free Speech and Unfree Markets." *UCLA Law Review,* 42: 949.

Summers, Mark W. 1994. *The Press Gang: Newspapers and Politics (1865–1878).* Chapel Hill: University of North Carolina Press.

Sunstein, Cass R. 1990. *After the Rights Revolution: Reconceiving the Regulatory State.* Cambridge, Mass: Harvard University Press.

———. 1993. *Democracy and the Problem of Free Speech.* New York: Free Press.

———. 2000. "Television and the Public Interest." *California Law Review,* 88(2): 499–564.

———. 2001a. *Republic.com.* Princeton, N.J.: Princeton University Press.

———. 2001b. *Echo Chambers: Bush v. Gore, Impeachment, and Beyond.* Princeton, N.J.: Princeton University Press.

Sutter, Daniel. 2001. "Can the Media Be So Liberal? The Economics of Media Bias." *Cato Journal,* 20(3): 431–51.

———. 2002a. "Advertising and Political Bias in the Media: The Market for Criticism of the Market Economy." *American Journal of Economics and Sociology,* 61(3): 725–45.

———. 2002b. "An Indirect Test of the Liberal Media Thesis Using Newsmagazine Circulation." Working paper, University of Oklahoma, Norman, Okla.

———. 2002c. "The 'Liberal' Media: Bias or Customer Preferences?" Working paper, University of Oklahoma, Norman, Okla.

Task Force on Campaign Reform. 1998. *Campaign Reform: Insights and Evidence, Report of the Task Force on Campaign Reform.* Princeton, N.J.: Woodrow Wilson School of Public and International Affairs.

Tawa, Renee. 2002. "Crashing the Blog Party." *Los Angeles Times,* September 12, A1.

Tech Law Journal. 2000. "Judge Releases Order in Free Republic Copyright Infringement Case." *Tech Law Journal,* August 7. August 29, 2001, at http://www.techlawjournal.com/ intelpro/20000807.asp.

Television Bureau of Advertising. 2000. "Television Facts." January 6, 2000, at http://www.tvb.org/tvfacts/docs/body.html.

———. 2001. "Network Television Cost and CPM Trends." July 3, 2001, at http://www.tvb.org/tvfacts/trends/media/1c.html.

Teske, Paul, Mark Schneider, Michael Mintrom, and Samuel Best. 1993. "Establishing the Micro Foundations of a Macro Theory: Information, Movers, and the Competitive Local Market for Public Goods." *American Political Science Review*, 87(3): 702–13.

———. 1995. "The Empirical Evidence for Citizen Information and a Local Market for Public Goods." *American Political Science Review*, 89(3): 707–709.

Thompson, R. S. 1988. "Product Differentiation in the Newspaper Industry: An Hedonic Price Approach." *Applied Economics*, 20: 367–76.

Tifft, Susan E. and Alex Jones. 1999. *The Trust: The Private and Powerful Family behind the New York Times*. Boston: Little Brown.

Tugend, Alina. 2002. "Cigarette Makers Take Anti-Smoking Ads Personally." *New York Times*, Oct. 27, C4.

Turegano, Preston. 2001. "Station Identification: 'WB5 News at Ten' and 'Fox6' Carve out a Niche for Themselves." *San Diego Union-Tribune*, April 29, p. F1.

Udell, Jon G. 1978. *The Economics of the American Newspaper*. New York: Hastings House.

Underwood, Doug. 1993. *When MBAs Rule the Newsroom: How the Marketers and Managers Are Reshaping Today's Media*. New York: Columbia University Press.

United States Bureau of the Census. 1997. *Historical Statistics of the United States, Colonial Times to 1970*. New York: Cambridge University Press.

United States Congress Joint Committee on Printing. 1870. *Congressional Directory*. Washington, D.C.: Government Printing Office.

———. 1880. *Congressional Directory*. Washington, D.C.: Government Printing Office.

———. 1890. *Congressional Directory*. Washington, D.C.: Government Printing Office.

———. 1900. *Congressional Directory*. Washington, D.C.: Government Printing Office.

United States Department of Commerce. 2000. "Regional Accounts Data: Local Area Personal Income." July 19, 2000, at http://www.bea.doc.gov/bea/regional/reis/action.cfm.

United States Department of Health and Human Services and Centers for Disease Control and Prevention. 1999. *HIV/AIDS Surveillance Report*. Atlanta, Ga.: Centers for Disease Control and Prevention.

United States Department of Justice. 1999a. *Uniform Crime Reports: January–June 1999*. Washington, D.C.: U.S. Department of Justice.

———. 1999b. *Sourcebook of Criminal Justice Statistics 1998*. Washington, D.C.: U.S. Department of Justice.

United States Department of Justice and the Federal Trade Commission. 1997. *Horizontal Merger Guidelines*. Washington, D.C.: U.S. Department of Justice.

United States Department of Labor. 2000. *Occupational Employment Statistics: 1998 Metropolitan Area Occupational Employment and Wage Estimates*. Washington, D.C.: Bureau of Labor Statistics.

United States Environmental Protection Agency. 2000. *EPA AIRS Graphics*. March 20, 2000, at http://www.epa.gov/agweb.

Utley, Garrick. 2000. *You Should Have Been Here Yesterday: A Life in Television News*. New York: Public Affairs.

Wakin, Daniel. 2001. "Report Calls Networks' Election Night Coverage a Disaster." *New York Times*, February 3, p. A10.

Warren Publishing. 1999. *Television and Cable Factbook: Stations 1999*. Vol. 67. Washington, D.C.: Warren Publishing.

Waldfogel, Joel. 1999. "Preference Externalities: An Empirical Study of Who Benefits Whom in Differentiated Product Markets." Working Paper 7391, National Bureau of Economic Research, Cambridge, Mass.

———. 2002. "Consumer Substitution among Media." Working paper, Media Ownership Working Group, Federal Communications Commission.

Walker, Leslie. 2002. "Google News, Untouched by Human Hands." *Washington Post*, Sept. 26, p. E1.

Warner, Bob. 2002. "News Ethics in Question with DEP Funding." Dec. 10, 2002, at http://www.philly.com

Waterman, David. 1992a. "Diversity and Quality of Information Products in a Monopolistically Competitive Industry." *Information Economics and Policy*, 4: 291–303.

———. 1992b. "'Narrowcasting' and 'Broadcasting' on Nonbroadcast Media: A Program Choice Model." *Communications Research*, 19(1): 3–28.

———. 1996. "Local Monopsony and Free Riders." *Information Economics and Policy*, 8: 337–55.

Waterman, David, and August Grant. 1991. "Cable Television as an Aftermarket." *Journal of Broadcasting and Electronic Media*, 35(2): 179–88.

Waterman, David, and Andrew A. Weiss. 1996. "The Effects of Vertical Integration between Cable Television Systems and Pay Cable Networks." *Journal of Econometrics*, 72: 357–95.

———. 1997. *Vertical Integration in Cable Television*. Cambridge, Mass.: MIT Press; Washington, D.C.: AEI Press.

Watt, James H., Mary Mazza, and Leslie Snyder. 1993. "Agenda-Setting Effects of Television News Coverage and the Effects Decay Curve." *Communication Research*, 20(3): 408–35.

Watts, Mark D., David Domke, Dhavan V. Shah, and David P. Fan. 1999. "Elite Cues and Media Bias in Presidential Campaigns: Explaining Public Perceptions of a Liberal Press." *Communication Research*, 26(2): 144–75.

Watson, Elmo Scott. 1936. *A History of Newspaper Syndicates in the United States, 1865–1935*. Chicago, Ill.

Webster, James G. and Patricia F. Phalen. 1997. *The Mass Audience: Rediscovering the Dominant Model*. Mahwah, N.J.: Lawrence Erlbaum Associates, Publishers.

Werts, Diane. 2001. "TV Press Tour 2001: At Midseason, a Tale of Two Networks; UPN Pumps up the Violence While the WB Unleashes Star Power." *Newsday*, January 8, p. B2.

Whitehouse, Beth. 2000. "Guys 2000: Work Hard, Play Hard Is Their Motto; Just about Anyone with Something to Sell Is Trying to Reach Them." *Newsday*, June 20, p. B6.

Wildman, Steven S. 1998. "Toward a Better Integration of Media Economics and Media Competition Policy." In *A Communications Cornucopia: Markle Foundation Essays on Information Policy*, Roger G. Noll and Monroe E. Price, eds., pp. 573–93. Washington, D.C.: Brookings Institution Press.

Wildman, Steven S., and N. Y. Lee. 1989. "Program Choice in Broadband Environment." Paper presented at Integrated Broadband Networks Conference, Columbia University.

Wildman, Steven S., and Bruce M. Owen. 1985. "Program Competition, Diversity, and Multichannel Bundling in the New Video Industry." In *Video Media Competition: Regulation, Economics, and Technology*, E. M. Noam, ed., pp. 244–73. New York: Columbia University Press.

Wildman, Steven S., and Karla Salmon Robinson. 1995. "Network Programming and Off-Network Syndication Profits: Strategic Links and Implications for Television Policy." *Journal of Media Economics*, 8(2): 27–48.

Wolinsky, Howard. 1997. "Court Backs Motorola, STATS in NBA Lawsuit." *Chicago Sun-Times*, January 31, p.41

Wood, B. Dan. 1988. "Principals, Bureaucrats, and Responsiveness in Clean Air Enforcements." *American Political Science Review*, 82(1): 213–34.

Zaller, John R. 1992. *The Nature and Origins of Mass Opinion.* New York: Cambridge University Press.

———. 1996. "The Myth of Massive Media Impact Revived: New Support for a Discredited Idea." In Diana C. Mutz, Paul M. Sniderman, and Richard A. Brody, eds., *Political Persuasion and Attitude Change.* Ann Arbor: University of Michigan Press.

———. 1997. "A Theory of Media Politics: How the Interests of Politicians, Journalists and Voters Shape Coverage of Presidential Campaigns." Working paper, UCLA, Los Angeles, Calif.

———. 1999a. "Market Competition and News Quality." Working paper, UCLA, Los Angeles, Calif.

———. 1999b. "Perversities in the Ideal of the Informed Citizenry." Working paper, UCLA, Los Angeles, Calif.

———. 2000. "The Statistical Power of Election Studies to Detect Media Exposure Effects in Presidential Campaigns." Working paper, UCLA, Los Angeles, Calif.

Zurawik, David. 1999. "Hits and Must-Misses." *Baltimore Sun*, November 6, p. 1E

Index

Rahn